Holt McDo
Earth Science

Interactive Reader
and Study Guide

Priscilla

ISBN-13: 978-0-55-403341-9

ISBN-10: 0-55-403341-0

  8 9 10 0982 15 14

4500496907

Contents

CHAPTER 1 | Introduction to Earth Science

SECTION 1
What Is Earth Science?

KEY IDEAS

As you read this section, keep these questions in mind:

- What are two cultures that contributed to modern science?
- What are the four main branches of Earth science?
- How do Earth scientists help us understand the world?

How Did Ancient People Study Earth?

People have wondered about natural events on Earth for thousands of years. They felt earthquakes shake the ground, saw volcanoes erupt, and watched eclipses darken the sky.

Some people created myths or stories to explain how these events happened. Others carefully watched and studied these events. They tried to learn what caused the events. Each time someone discovered a possible cause, it helped people develop explanations for other events.

The table below shows some historical observations that were important to the study of Earth.

Approximate Date	Development
780 BCE	People in China began to keep records about earthquakes.
200 BCE	Ancient Greeks gathered and recorded information about rocks and minerals.
300–900 CE	Ancient Maya watched the moon and recorded information about eclipses.
1600s	The microscope was invented.
1700s	The telescope was invented.

For a long time, people could use only their unaided eyes to study Earth and space. After the telescope and microscope were invented, people could observe objects and events more clearly. For example, Galileo used a telescope to see Jupiter's moons.

Today, scientists continue to study the natural world. **Earth science** is the study of Earth and the universe around it. Earth scientists use observations and experiments to find the causes of events in nature. ☑

READING TOOLBOX

Organize As you read this section, make a spider map that identifies the major branches of Earth science. Add details about each branch, such as what it focuses on and how knowledge from that branch can be helpful to society.

☑ **READING CHECK**

1. Define What is Earth science?

Is the study of Earth and the universe arou...

SECTION 1 **What Is Earth Science?** *continued*

What Are the Main Branches of Earth Science?

Most Earth scientists focus their work on one of these four main branches:

- Geology – the study of rocks and soil
- Oceanography – the study of Earth's oceans
- Meteorology – the study of Earth's atmosphere
- Astronomy – the study of the universe beyond Earth ☑

GEOLOGY

Geology is the study of the rocks and soil on Earth. Geologists may

- search for natural resources near Earth's surface
- study forces within Earth to predict when earthquakes will happen or volcanoes will erupt
- study fossils to learn about Earth's history

OCEANOGRAPHY

Oceanography is the study of Earth's oceans. Some oceanographers study waves, tides, or ocean currents. Others explore the floor of the ocean. These scientists might find useful minerals, or they might discover clues about the history of Earth.

METEOROLOGY

Meteorology is the study of Earth's atmosphere. Meteorologists study the atmosphere to understand weather patterns. Many meteorologists measure wind speed, temperature, and rainfall. They use those measurements to create maps. Other meteorologists use the maps to predict future weather.

Some meteorologists study climate. *Climate* is the weather patterns in one place over a long span of time.

ASTRONOMY

Astronomy is the study of the universe beyond Earth. It is one of the oldest branches of Earth science. Today, astronomers use technology to learn about the universe. For example, spacesuits are a technology that allows astronauts to explore space. Telescopes are a technology that lets humans see and study other galaxies.

☑ **READING CHECK**

2. List What are the four main branches of Earth science?

Geology,
Oceanography,
Meteorology,
Astronomy

Talk About It

Connect Choose the branch of Earth science you think is most interesting. With a partner, discuss what interests you about this branch of Earth science.

Critical Thinking

3. Infer In which branch of Earth science would a scientist most likely study how a mountain chain formed?

Meteorology

SECTION 1 What Is Earth Science? *continued*

What Is Environmental Science?

Some Earth scientists study the ways that humans interact with their environment. This field is called *environmental science*. Environmental scientists use information from many sciences, including biology, Earth science, and social sciences. Environmental scientists try to understand how human actions affect the environment. They also try to solve problems that human actions cause. ☑

Why Is Earth Science Important?

Understanding how forces on Earth and in the atmosphere work can save people's lives. For example, geologists may alert people to leave an area if a volcano is about to erupt. Meteorologists may predict the path of a dangerous storm. Their predictions can help people prepare properly.

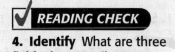

READING CHECK

4. Identify What are three fields that contribute to environmental science?

Biology,
Earth Science
Social sciences

These meteorologists are risking their lives to study tornadoes. The information they collect may help other scientists predict when and where other tornadoes might happen.

Talk About It

In a small group, talk about events that you have heard about or read about that are related to Earth science. For example, you might discuss a recent earthquake or tornado. Talk about when and where the event happened and about any damage the event caused.

Earth scientists can also help us understand our place in the universe. Astronomers study other galaxies to try to understand how the universe formed. Geologists study rock layers to discover clues about Earth's history.

Earth scientists work to find and gather the resources people need. People use resources from Earth every day. The fuel in a jet, the metal in electric wires, and the ink on this page are made from Earth's resources. Earth scientists also look for ways to use resources wisely.

Section 1 Review

SECTION VOCABULARY

astronomy the scientific study of the universe **Earth science** the scientific study of Earth and the universe around it **geology** the scientific study of the origin, history, and structure of Earth and the processes that shape Earth	**meteorology** the scientific study of Earth's atmosphere, especially in relation to weather and climate **oceanography** the scientific study of the ocean, including the properties and movements of ocean water, the characteristics of the ocean floor, and the organisms that live in the ocean

1. Summarize Fill in the missing information in the table below.

Branch of Earth Science	Focus of Study	Areas of Study
Geology	rock and soil	1. search for natural resources near Earth's surface 2. study Earth's forces to predict earthquakes or volcanoes 3. study fossils
Oceanography	Earth's Ocean	1. study waves, tides, or ocean currents 2. find minerals
Meteorology	Earth's Atmosphere	1. measure wind speed, temperature, and rainfall 2. use maps to predict future weather 3. study climate
Astronomy	study of the universe	study the sun, moon, planets, and the rest of the universe

2. Discuss Name one ancient culture that studied Earth. How were the activities of this culture similar to the activities of Earth scientists today?

_____

_____

3. Identify Relationships What is the relationship between Earth science and environmental science?

The relationship between Earth science & environmental science. Earth science deal with the formation of earth and environmental deal with environment

4. Explain How has technology affected the work of astronomers?

Technology affected the work of astronomers is that helps astronauts in their lives

CHAPTER 1 Introduction to Earth Science

SECTION 2 Science as a Process

As you read this section, keep these questions in mind:

- How is science different from other fields of study?
- What are scientific methods?
- How does scientific knowledge change?
- How does science affect society?

How Is Science Different from Other Fields of Study?

Art, architecture, philosophy, and science are all examples of fields of study. However, science has different goals than other fields of study. For example, a philosopher may ask questions such as "Why do we exist?" or "What is the place of humans in the universe?" Scientists do not seek to answer questions such as these. Instead, the goal of scientists is to explain natural events.

Scientists look for answers about how the natural world works by making observations and by doing experiments. As they study the natural world, scientists assume two things:

- It is possible to understand nature.
- Nature is predictable. ☑

Scientists must first assume that people can understand nature. That is, scientists assume that with the right tools and correct methods, they can find the answers they are looking for. There are many natural events that scientists do not yet understand. Scientists assume that they will someday be able to understand these events.

Scientists also assume that nature is predictable. In general, scientists observe patterns in nature. From the way a pattern repeats, scientists can predict that an event will happen in a similar way in the future. For example, suppose a scientist observes that certain weather conditions happen before a tornado forms. The scientist may predict that when these same weather conditions happen again, another tornado will form.

READING TOOLBOX

Organize As you read, make an outline of this section. Use the headings from the section in your outline.

READING CHECK

1. Explain What are two assumptions that all scientists make?

It is possible to understand nature. Nature is predictable

SECTION 2 **Science as a Process** *continued*

What Are Scientific Methods?

Over time, scientists have developed methods, or a set of ways, to study the natural world. The methods scientists use are organized and logical. However, these *scientific methods* are not a set of rules that scientists must follow in an exact order. Instead, scientific methods are guidelines that scientists follow to help them solve scientific problems. The flowchart below shows one way that a scientist may use scientific methods.

LOOKING CLOSER
2. Infer Why is there an arrow pointing from "Drawing conclusions" to "Asking questions"?

_____

_____

_____

_____

_____

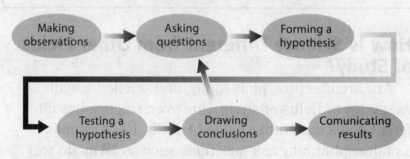

OBSERVING AND ASKING QUESTIONS

Scientific methods generally begin with observation. **Observation** is the process of using the five senses to collect information about the world. When you compare the colors and texture of two different rocks or listen to waves crashing on a beach, you are making observations.

Observations that scientists make often lead them to ask questions. For example, a scientist might observe that the weather is often cooler after a thunderstorm. He may then ask the question, "Why is the weather cooler after a thunderstorm?"

FORMING A HYPOTHESIS

Once scientists have asked a question and made a few observations, they might then form a hypothesis. A **hypothesis** is a possible way to explain or solve a problem. Scientists base their hypotheses on observations or on known facts about similar events. ☑

For example, a scientist might know that when hot air and cool air mix, they can form clouds and rain. She could make the hypothesis that thunderstorms happen when cool air moves into an area and mixes with hot air. The mixing air causes the thunderstorm. The weather is cooler after the storm because the cool air has moved into the area.

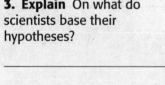
3. Explain On what do scientists base their hypotheses?

_____

_____

_____

SECTION 2 Science as a Process *continued*

TESTING THE HYPOTHESIS

After scientists form a hypothesis, they look for ways to test it in an investigation. In some investigations, the scientist will make more observations and see if they fit the hypothesis. For example, a scientist may use tools to study the movements of cool and warm air. He could use the measurements he takes to learn whether cool air moves into an area after a thunderstorm.

In other investigations, a scientist will do an experiment to test a hypothesis. An *experiment* is a set of procedures that a scientist carries out. Every experiment has conditions or factors that can change. These factors are called *variables*. There are two types of variables. **Independent variables** are factors that the scientist changes. **Dependent variables** are factors that change as a result of the independent variables. ☑

For example, suppose a scientist did an experiment to learn how water affects a plant's growth. The independent variable is the amount of water the plants get. The dependent variable is how much the plants grow. In this experiment, the scientist would change only the amount of water each plant gets. She would keep all other conditions, such as amount of sunlight, temperature, and type of plant, the same.

This astronaut, Shannon Lucid, is observing wheat plants growing in space. Experiments like this one will help scientists learn how plants grow in space where the pull of Earth's gravity is weaker.

✓ **READING CHECK**

4. Discuss What are two ways scientists can test a hypothesis?

_____

_____

_____

_____

LOOKING CLOSER

5. Apply Ideas What might be the dependent variable in Shannon Lucid's experiment?

_____

_____

_____

DRAWING CONCLUSIONS

Scientists must decide if their observations support the hypothesis, or show that the hypothesis was correct. In many cases, the results of an experiment are unexpected. If the results do not support the hypothesis, the scientists must throw out the hypothesis or change it. Unexpected results are important to science. They can cause scientists to ask new questions.

How Do Scientists Use Models?

In Earth science, it is often impossible to use an experiment to test a hypothesis. Instead, scientists make additional observations to gather evidence. Then they test the hypothesis by thinking about how well the hypothesis explains the evidence that they gathered.

Scientists also may use models to test hypotheses they cannot test using an experiment. A *model* is a description or a representation of an object, an idea, a system, or an event. Some models describe objects, such as atoms. Others describe processes, such as the water cycle. Scientists often use models to study things that are too big, too small, too fast, too slow, or too dangerous to study directly. ☑

TYPES OF MODELS

The table below describes five types of models that scientists use.

Type of Model	Definition	Examples
Physical	three-dimensional models	globe
Graphical	two-dimensional models (pictures)	map, chart
Conceptual	description of an idea	flowchart
Mathematical	mathematical equation that describes the way a system or process works	2 + 2 = 4 (used to represent two items joined to two other items)
Computer	a type of mathematical model that uses a computer to do calculations and display results	computer model of Mount Everest

✓ **READING CHECK**

6. Explain What is the main reason scientists use models?

_____

_____

_____

_____

LOOKING CLOSER

7. Evaluate Methods What are two advantages this physical model has over the actual mountain?

_____

_____

_____

_____

_____

This scientist is working with a physical model of Mount Everest. The model has the same shape and relative position of the features that the real mountain has.

SECTION 2 **Science as a Process** *continued*

How Do Scientists Make Accurate Measurements?

Scientists gather information during investigations. Measurement is a very important method for gathering information in most scientific investigations.

SI UNITS

Scientists need to be able to compare and analyze each other's results. Therefore, scientists around the world use a common system of measurement. The system is called the International System of Units, or SI. Meters and kilograms are examples of SI units. ☑

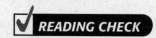

✓ READING CHECK

8. Explain Why is the International System of Units important?

_____

_____

_____

_____

ACCURACY AND PRECISION

Accuracy and precision are two ways to describe measurements. *Accuracy* describes how close a measurement is to the true value. *Precision* describes how exact a measurement is. For example, stating the length of a string as 1 m is less precise than stating that the length of the string is 1.05 m.

A measurement can be accurate but not precise. A measurement can also be precise but not accurate. Scientists want to have measurements that are both accurate and precise. The figure below shows the difference between accuracy and precision.

Good overall accuracy but poor precision

Poor accuracy but good precision

Good accuracy and good precision

No measurement can be completely precise. There are two ways to express error: as a percentage error or as a confidence interval.

LOOKING CLOSER
9. Infer If there were another picture labeled "Poor accuracy and poor precision," what would it look like?

_____

_____

_____

_____

SECTION 2 **Science as a Process** *continued*

10. Calculate You have made a meterstick out of cardboard, but you're not sure how accurate it is. You measure your stick against a real meterstick. You find that your meterstick is only 90 cm long. What is your percentage error?

Talk About It

Calculate As a class, make a list of shoe sizes. Discuss what confidence interval you could use to discuss shoe sizes.

READING CHECK

11. Define What happens during peer review?

_____

_____

_____

_____

PERCENTAGE ERROR

A *percentage error* is one way of expressing how far a measured value is from the true value. You can use the following equation to find the percentage error of a measurement.

$$\text{percentage error} = \left[\frac{(\text{actual value} - \text{measured value})}{\text{actual value}}\right] \times 100$$

CONFIDENCE INTERVAL

A *confidence interval* describes the range of values for a sample of measurements. For example, suppose a scientist wants to express the values for the length of ears of corn in a field. The average length of all the ears of corn in the field is 23 cm. Of all the ears, 90% of them are within 3 cm of this average length. The scientist may report the average length of all the ears of corn in the field as "23 ± 3 cm with 90% confidence."

How Does Scientific Knowledge Grow?

When scientists discover something new, they share their ideas with other scientists. The other scientists review and test the ideas before accepting the new ideas.

SHARING RESULTS

Scientists typically share their results as papers in scientific journals. They also share ideas at meetings with other scientists. Many journals are now published online so that scientists can share their ideas more quickly and easily.

PEER REVIEW

Before scientists publish their work, they show it to other scientists who are experts on the topic. Those experts review the work. The reviewers may suggest changes to the investigation. They may also point out errors in thinking that scientists did not see. This process is called **peer review**.

If reviewers think that the ideas are incorrect or that the investigation was invalid, or flawed, the journal will not publish the paper. The peer review process helps make sure only well-supported ideas are published. ☑

SECTION 2 **Science as a Process** *continued*

DEVELOPING A THEORY

After a scientist publishes his ideas and results, other scientists typically test the hypothesis and build on the results. The process of repeated testing may continue for years. In time, the hypothesis may be proved incorrect, be changed, or be accepted by most scientists.

When a hypothesis has been tested many times and becomes accepted, the hypothesis may help form a theory. A **theory** is an explanation that is supported by all existing observations and study results. However, if repeated results from later tests do not support the theory, scientists may need to change it. ☑

THE IMPORTANCE OF INTERDISCIPLINARY SCIENCE

Scientists from many different fields of science share their ideas. Sharing ideas between fields is important because discoveries in different fields may add support to one idea. When an idea is supported by evidence from more than one field, the idea is more likely to be accurate.

The figure below shows one hypothesis that is based on evidence from several fields of science.

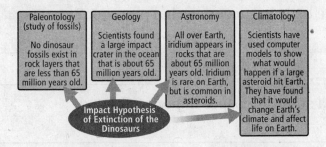

Discoveries and ideas from different fields of science have helped scientists develop a hypothesis about how dinosaurs became extinct.

Scientific knowledge helps people understand the natural world. It also helps people develop new technologies, such as tools, materials, and processes.

Many technologies are helpful, but some new technologies can cause problems. For example, plastic is a technology that is useful in many products. However, plastics can cause pollution and harm wildlife. An understanding of science is important for all citizens. Thinking scientifically can help people make wise decisions about products they buy, where they live, and even how they vote.

✔ READING CHECK

12. Identify Relationships What is the relationship between a hypothesis and a theory?

_____

_____

_____

_____

LOOKING CLOSER
13. Draw Conclusions Suppose scientists find evidence of dinosaur fossils that are only 30 million years old. What effect would this new evidence have on the hypothesis that the figure describes?

_____

_____

_____

_____

_____

_____

_____

Section 2 Review

SECTION VOCABULARY

dependent variable in an experiment, the factor that changes as a result of manipulation of one or more other factors (the independent variables)	**observation** the process of obtaining information by using the senses; the information obtained by using the senses
hypothesis a testable idea or explanation that leads to scientific investigation	**peer review** the process in which experts in a given field examine the results and conclusions of a scientist's study before that study is accepted for publication
independent variable in an experiment, the factor that is deliberately manipulated	**theory** a system of ideas that explains many related observations and is supported by a large body of evidence acquired through scientific investigation

1. Identify Relationships What is the relationship between a dependent variable and an independent variable?

_____

_____

_____

2. List What are the six main processes that are part of scientific methods?

_____

_____

_____

3. Compare What is the difference between accuracy and precision?

_____

_____

_____

4. Explain Why is peer review of a scientific paper important?

_____

_____

_____

5. Apply Ideas Give one example of a technology that can be both helpful and harmful. Think of a different example from the one given in the text.

_____

_____

_____

_____

SECTION 1 Earth: A Unique Planet

KEY IDEAS

As you read this section, keep these questions in mind:

• What are the size and shape of Earth?

• What are Earth's compositional and structural layers?

• What is a possible source for Earth's magnetic field?

• What does Newton's law of gravitation state?

What Shape Is Earth?

Earth formed about 4.6 billion years ago. It is the only planet in our solar system that scientists think has liquid water on its surface. Earth is the only planet we know of that supports life.

If you looked at Earth from space, it would look like a perfect sphere, or ball. However, Earth is not perfectly round. It is an *oblate spheroid*, or flattened sphere. The diagram below shows what an oblate spheroid looks like. ☑

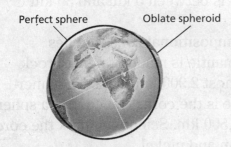

Perfect sphere   Oblate spheroid

Earth's shape is exaggerated in this picture. In real life, you would not be able to see the difference between Earth and a perfect sphere.

What Is Inside Earth?

Scientists can study Earth's interior directly by drilling. However, scientists can drill only a few kilometers into Earth's surface. To learn about the rest of Earth's interior, scientists must use indirect methods. ☑

One way scientists learn about Earth's interior is by studying seismic waves. *Seismic waves* are vibrations that travel through Earth. Earthquakes cause most seismic waves. Seismic waves move differently in different substances. Therefore, by studying these waves, scientists can learn what Earth's interior is made of. Scientists divide Earth's interior into three compositional zones and five structural zones.

READING TOOLBOX

Re-Read After you read the section, write out answers to the Key Ideas questions. If you cannot answer the questions, re-read the text under the appropriate heading.

Critical Thinking

1. Apply Concepts Which would take longer, a trip around Earth's equator or a trip around Earth from pole to pole? Why? (Assume you travel at the same speed for both trips.)

_____

_____

_____

_____

☑ READING CHECK

2. Explain Why must scientists use indirect methods to study Earth's interior?

_____

_____

_____

Talk About It

Discuss In a small group, talk about ways you have learned about something when you could not observe it directly. For example, many people try to learn what is in a gift box by shaking it. Talk about how these methods are related to how scientists learn about Earth's interior.

LOOKING CLOSER

3. Identify Relationships Which three structural zones overlap with the mantle?

_____

_____

_____

Math Skills

4. Calculate Earth's layers have the following thicknesses: crust, 35 km; mantle, 2,900 km; outer core, 2,250 km; inner core, 1,228 km. A seismic wave moves at the following speeds through each layer: crust, 8 km/s; mantle, 12 km/s; outer core, 9.5 km/s; inner core, 10.5 km/s. How long would a seismic wave take to travel from Earth's surface to its center?

_____

_____

✓ READING CHECK

5. Compare How are the inner core and outer core different?

_____

_____

_____

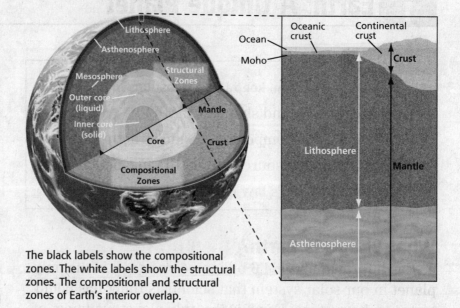

The black labels show the compositional zones. The white labels show the structural zones. The compositional and structural zones of Earth's interior overlap.

COMPOSITIONAL ZONES

Compositional zones are made up of different materials. The thin, solid, outermost compositional zone is the **crust**. Crust beneath oceans is called *oceanic crust*. Crust that makes up continents is called *continental crust*. In general, continental crust is much thicker than oceanic crust. The crust is between 5 km and 35 km thick.

The **mantle** is the compositional zone that lies beneath the crust. The mantle is made of denser rock than the crust and is almost 2,900 km thick. The innermost compositional zone is the core. The **core** is a sphere with a radius of about 3,500 km. Scientists think the core is made up mainly of iron and nickel.

STRUCTURAL ZONES

Structural zones have different properties. The **lithosphere** is made up of the crust and the top part of the mantle. The lithosphere is relatively cool and brittle. The **asthenosphere** is made of hot, solid mantle rock. The rock of the asthenosphere is also under a great deal of pressure. The heat and pressure allow the solid rock to flow. The **mesosphere** is a layer of solid mantle rock beneath the asthenosphere.

The core is divided into the outer core and inner core. The *outer core* is made of liquid iron and nickel. Scientists think the *inner core* is a made of solid iron and nickel. ✓

SECTION 1 Earth: A Unique Planet *continued*

What Is the Source of Earth's Magnetic Field?

Earth acts as a giant magnet. Like all magnets, it has two magnetic poles. Earth's magnetic field extends beyond Earth's atmosphere, and it affects a region of space called the *magnetosphere*.

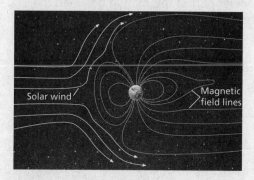

Solar wind

Magnetic field lines

The magnetic field lines around Earth show the shape of Earth's magnetosphere. The solar wind affects the shape of the magnetosphere.

Most scientists think that the liquid iron in Earth's outer core is the source of Earth's magnetic field. They think that motions within the core produce electric currents that produce the magnetic field. ☑

What Is Newton's Law of Gravitation?

Gravity is a force that pulls matter together. In the 1600s, Isaac Newton explained how gravity affects objects in his *law of universal gravitation*. This law states that the force of gravity between two objects depends on the masses of the objects and the distance between them.

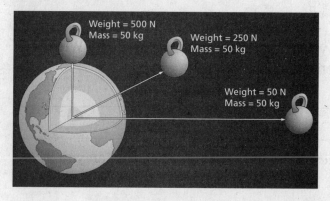

Weight = 500 N
Mass = 50 kg

Weight = 250 N
Mass = 50 kg

Weight = 50 N
Mass = 50 kg

The force of gravity decreases as an object moves farther from Earth's center.

Earth's gravity pulls objects toward Earth's center. Weight is a measure of the strength of this pull. The newton (N) is the SI unit of weight. The mass of an object does not change with location, but the weight of an object can change.

READING CHECK

6. Identify What do most scientists think is the source of Earth's magnetic field?

_____

_____

LOOKING CLOSER

7. Describe How does the distance between two objects affect the gravitational force between them?

_____

_____

_____

Name _____ Class _____ Date _____

Section 1 Review

SECTION VOCABULARY

asthenosphere the solid, plastic layer of the mantle beneath the lithosphere; made of mantle rock that flows very slowly, which allows tectonic plates to move on top of it

crust the thin and solid outermost layer of the Earth above the mantle

core the central part of the Earth below the mantle

lithosphere the solid, outer layer of Earth that consists of the crust and the rigid upper part of the mantle

mantle in Earth science, the layer between Earth's crust and core

mesosphere literally the "middle sphere"; the strong, lower part of the mantle between the asthenosphere and the outer core

1. Organize Complete the concept map below to show the relationship between Earth's compositional zones and structural zones.

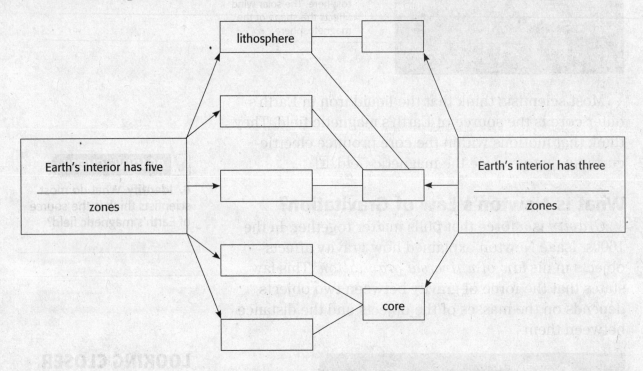

2. Apply Concepts A compass needle is a very small magnet that can move. Why can you use a compass to determine direction on Earth?

_____

_____

3. Analyze Ideas Why would you weigh less on a high mountain peak than you would at sea level?

_____

_____

_____

CHAPTER 2 **Earth as a System**

SECTION
2 Energy in the Earth System

KEY IDEAS

As you read this section, keep these questions in mind:

• What is the difference between an open system and a closed system?

• What are the characteristics of Earth's four spheres?

• What are the two main sources of energy in the Earth system?

• What are four cycles of matter on Earth?

What Is a System?

Earth scientists often say that Earth is a system. A **system** is a group of related objects or processes that work together to form a whole. Systems can be as small as an atom or as large as the whole universe.

The Earth system is made up of many smaller systems. Each smaller system is made up of even smaller systems. For example, one part of the Earth system is the ocean system. One part of the ocean system is coral reefs. Coral reefs are systems made up of even smaller systems, such as rocks and living things.

The parts of a system interact, or affect one another. Systems can also interact with other systems. Systems can interact by exchanging matter or energy. *Matter* is anything that has mass and takes up space. *Energy* is the ability to do work. Heat, light, and vibrations are examples of energy.

OPEN SYSTEMS

There are two main kinds of systems on Earth: open systems and closed systems. An *open system* is a system that exchanges both matter and energy with the surroundings. The jar shown below is an open system.

This jar of tea is an open system. Both matter and energy can enter and leave the system.

READING TOOLBOX

Outline Use the boldface headings to make an outline of the section. As you read, fill in the outline with the important ideas from the section.

Talk About It

Apply Concepts Think of five examples of systems you see every day. Share your ideas with a partner. Explain why you think each example is a system.

LOOKING CLOSER

1. Explain Why is the jar of tea in the picture considered an open system?

_____

_____

SECTION 2 **Energy in the Earth System** *continued*

Critical Thinking

2. Compare How is a closed system different from an open system?

_____

_____

_____

_____

_____

CLOSED SYSTEMS

A closed system is a system that exchanges energy but not matter with the surroundings. The sealed jar in the figure below is an example of a closed system. Energy can move into and out of the jar. Because the jar is sealed, no matter can enter or leave the system.

This jar of tea is a closed system. Energy can enter and leave, but matter cannot.

Earth is almost a closed system. Energy enters the Earth system in the form of sunlight. Energy leaves the system in the form of heat. Only tiny amounts of matter enter and leave the system. Therefore, scientists often model Earth as a closed system.

What Are Earth's Four Spheres?

The Earth system is made up of four "spheres." These spheres are not large round objects. They are the different areas where all of Earth's matter is found. The four spheres are the atmosphere, the hydrosphere, the geosphere, and the biosphere. ☑

✔ READING CHECK

3. Identify What are Earth's four spheres?

_____

_____

_____

_____

THE ATMOSPHERE

The **atmosphere** is the layer of gases that surrounds Earth. The air we breathe is part of the atmosphere. The atmosphere also protects Earth from much of the sun's harmful radiation. About 78% of Earth's atmosphere is nitrogen gas. About 21% is oxygen gas. The rest is made up of other gases, such as argon and carbon dioxide.

Critical Thinking

4. Infer What percentage of Earth's water is salty?

_____

THE HYDROSPHERE

All the water on Earth makes up the **hydrosphere**. Almost all the water in the hydrosphere is salty. Only 3% is fresh water. Fresh water is found in streams, lakes, and rivers. It is also frozen in glaciers and the polar ice sheets and is found underground in soil and bedrock.

SECTION 2 **Energy in the Earth System** *continued*

THE GEOSPHERE

The **geosphere** is all the rock and soil on the continents and on the ocean floor. The geosphere also includes the solid and liquid rock and metal inside Earth. Some natural processes, such as volcanic eruptions, bring matter from Earth's interior to its surface. Other natural processes move surface matter into Earth's interior.

THE BIOSPHERE

The **biosphere** is made up of all Earth's living things. Organic matter from dead organisms is also part of the biosphere. Once this organic matter has decomposed, it becomes part of the other three spheres. The biosphere extends from within Earth's crust to a few kilometers above Earth's surface.

This photo shows examples of all four of Earth's spheres.

Talk About It

Learn Word Roots Use a dictionary to look up the meanings of the word roots *hydro-, geo-,* and *bio-.* With a partner, discuss how these word roots are related to the meanings of the words *hydrosphere, geosphere,* and *biosphere.*

LOOKING CLOSER

5. Apply Concepts Label the parts of the photograph that represent the atmosphere, hydrosphere, geosphere, and biosphere.

EXCHANGE OF MATTER AND ENERGY

You can think of Earth's four spheres as huge storehouses. They store matter and energy. The matter and energy can move from one sphere to another, or within a sphere. However, matter and energy can only change forms. They cannot be created out of nothing or completely destroyed.

Certain processes move matter and energy from place to place in predictable ways. These processes include chemical reactions, radioactive decay, and the growth and decay of living things.

What Are the Sources of Energy in the Earth System?

Energy enters the Earth system in the form of sunlight. Energy also leaves the Earth system as heat. The amount of energy that enters the Earth system is the same as the amount of energy that leaves it. In other words, the energy that enters and leaves the system is balanced. ☑

The diagram below shows what happens to the light energy that enters the Earth system. It also shows how energy is transferred, or passed, through Earth's systems.

6. Explain What do scientists mean when they say that the energy that enters and leaves the Earth system is balanced?

_____

_____

_____

LOOKING CLOSER

7. Calculate What percentage of solar radiation is absorbed by the atmosphere, land, and water?

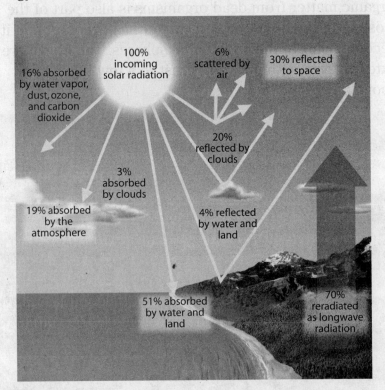

100% incoming solar radiation

16% absorbed by water vapor, dust, ozone, and carbon dioxide

6% scattered by air

30% reflected to space

20% reflected by clouds

3% absorbed by clouds

19% absorbed by the atmosphere

4% reflected by water and land

51% absorbed by water and land

70% reradiated as longwave radiation

EXTERNAL SOURCES OF ENERGY ON EARTH

For living things to carry out their life processes, energy must enter the Earth system constantly. The sun is the most important external, or outside, source of energy. Most living things ultimately get their energy from sunlight. Sunlight also heats Earth's atmosphere, land, and oceans. This heating produces winds and ocean currents that move matter through the Earth system.

Gravitational energy from the moon and sun is another external source of energy. The pull of the sun and moon on the oceans helps create tides that cause currents and help ocean water mix.

SECTION 2 **Energy in the Earth System** *continued*

INTERNAL SOURCES OF ENERGY ON EARTH

Not all of the energy in the Earth system comes from the sun. Earth also has some sources of energy that are *internal,* or come from inside. One important internal energy source is radioactive decay. The energy from radioactive decay inside Earth warms the rock below the surface.

The heating of the rock inside Earth affects Earth's surface. When rock in the mesosphere and asthenosphere gets warmer, it rises toward the surface. Cooler rock that is near the surface sinks. The rock moves in a circular pattern, like water in a pan on a stove. This type of motion is called *convection.* Convection transfers heat from within Earth to Earth's surface. This heat affects many processes on Earth, such as volcanic eruptions. ☑

How Does Matter Move on Earth?

Like energy, matter moves between the parts of the Earth system. A place where matter or energy is stored is called a *reservoir.* For example, the oceans, atmosphere, and living things are some of the reservoirs for water. The group of processes that move matter between reservoirs is called a *cycle.* Four important matter cycles on Earth are the nitrogen cycle, the carbon cycle, the phosphorus cycle, and the water cycle.

THE NITROGEN CYCLE

Living things use nitrogen to build proteins and other important chemicals. The diagram below shows the processes that are part of the nitrogen cycle.

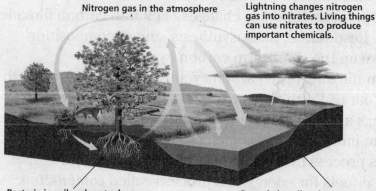

Nitrogen gas in the atmosphere

Lightning changes nitrogen gas into nitrates. Living things can use nitrates to produce important chemicals.

Bacteria in soil and roots change nitrogen gas into ammonia. Plants can use ammonia, but they cannot use nitrogen gas.

Bacteria in soil and water change nitrates and ammonia into nitrogen gas. The gas goes back into the atmosphere.

✔ **READING CHECK**

8. Describe What causes convection in the asthenosphere and mesosphere?

_____

_____

LOOKING CLOSER

9. Identify What kinds of living things change nitrogen gas into ammonia?

_____

_____

SECTION 2 **Energy in the Earth System** *continued*

THE CARBON CYCLE

Almost all the chemicals that make up living things are based on carbon. Like nitrogen, carbon cycles through the Earth system. The diagram below shows the parts of the carbon cycle.

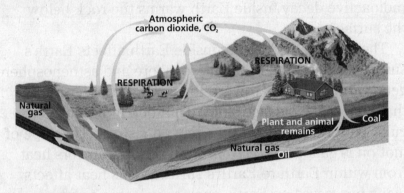

LOOKING CLOSER

10. Identify What are two processes that add carbon dioxide to the atmosphere?

_____

_____

Critical Thinking

11. Describe Which two reservoirs are part of the short-term carbon cycle?

_____

_____

Scientists often break the carbon cycle into two parts: the short-term carbon cycle and the long-term carbon cycle. In one part of the short-term carbon cycle, plants take carbon dioxide from the atmosphere. They change the carbon dioxide into sugars and other chemicals in the process of *photosynthesis*. The plants use these chemicals to build and repair their cells.

Animals that eat the plants break down the chemicals in the plants. They use some of the chemicals for energy. In the process of *respiration*, they break the chemicals down to release the energy stored in them. Respiration produces carbon dioxide gas, which moves back into the atmosphere. Plants also carry out respiration, in addition to photosynthesis.

When living things die, bacteria break down their bodies. This process is called *decomposition*. Most of the carbon in their bodies changes back into carbon dioxide gas. Respiration, photosynthesis, and decomposition make up the short-term carbon cycle.

In the long-term carbon cycle, carbon moves through all four of Earth's spheres. The remains of some living things are buried underground. Heat and pressure change them into *fossil fuels*, such as coal, oil, and natural gas. This process takes millions of years. People burn fossil fuels for energy in a process called *combustion*. Combustion produces carbon dioxide gas.

THE PHOSPHORUS CYCLE

Phosphorus is another element that living things use to build important chemicals. Unlike carbon and nitrogen, phosphorus generally does not exist as a gas. Therefore, it is not found in the atmosphere. Most of the phosphorus on Earth is stored in rocks. Water and wind can break down the rocks and release the phosphorus. It can then flow into water and soil. ☑

Plants get phosphorus from the soil. Animals get phosphorus by eating plants or other animals. The phosphorus in living things returns to the soil when the living things die and decompose.

12. Identify Where is most of the phosphorus on Earth stored?

_____

_____

THE WATER CYCLE

Water is always moving between the atmosphere, land, oceans, and living things. This movement of water is called the water cycle. In the water cycle, water changes state, from solid to liquid to gas and back again. The table below describes some of the processes in the water cycle.

Process	Description	Example
Evaporation	Water changes from a liquid to a gas.	Water evaporates from the oceans and moves into the atmosphere.
Condensation	Water changes from a gas to a liquid.	Water vapor in the atmosphere condenses into tiny droplets. The droplets form clouds.
Precipitation	Water falls from the atmosphere to the surface.	Water in clouds falls to the ground as rain, snow, or hail.
Transpiration	Plant leaves release water into the air.	Trees give off water through their leaves.

LOOKING CLOSER

13. Apply Concepts Which two processes in the water cycle move water from Earth's surface into the atmosphere?

_____

_____

HOW PEOPLE AFFECT MATTER CYCLES

Human actions can affect Earth processes. For example, when people burn fossil fuels for energy, they affect the carbon cycle. Burning the fossil fuels makes carbon move from the geosphere into the atmosphere. This movement happens much more quickly than it would naturally.

People can also affect other matter cycles. Many people use chemicals called *fertilizers* to help their lawns and gardens grow. Fertilizers have nitrogen and phosphorus in them. Therefore, using fertilizers can change the way nitrogen and phosphorus move through the Earth system.

Section 2 Review

SECTION VOCABULARY

atmosphere a mixture of gases that surrounds a planet, moon, or other celestial body	**hydrosphere** the portion of the Earth that is water
biosphere the part of Earth where life exists; includes all the living organisms on Earth	**system** a set of particles or interacting components considered to be a distinct physical entity for the purpose of study
geosphere the mostly solid, rocky part of the Earth; extends from the center of the core to the surface of the crust	

1. Identify Relationships Describe ways that you interact with each of Earth's four spheres every day. Give one example for each sphere.

_____

_____

_____

_____

2. Apply Concepts Is the human body a closed system or an open system? Use examples to support your answer.

_____

_____

_____

_____

3. Describe How do external sources of energy make matter move through the Earth system?

_____

_____

4. Identify Describe two ways nitrogen gas is changed into forms that living things can use.

_____

_____

5. Compare What is one way the phosphorus cycle is different from the carbon, nitrogen, and water cycles?

_____

_____

_____

CHAPTER 2 | Earth as a System
SECTION 3 | Ecology

KEY IDEAS

As you read this section, keep these questions in mind:

• How is energy transferred through an ecosystem?

• What three factors control the balance of an ecosystem?

• What is one way ecosystems respond to change?

What Is an Ecosystem?

Organisms on Earth live in many different environments. All the organisms in an area and the nonliving parts of the environment make up an **ecosystem**. An ecosystem may be as large as an ocean or as small as a drop of water. A healthy ecosystem is a self-supporting system.

The study of the relationships between living things and the nonliving environment is called *ecology*. Scientists who work in the field of ecology also study how communities of organisms change over time. ☑

How Does Energy Move in an Ecosystem?

The sun is the main source of energy for most ecosystems on Earth. Remember that in photosynthesis, plants use energy from sunlight to produce food from carbon dioxide and water. When an animal eats a plant, the energy that is stored in the plant's parts passes to the animal. When one organism eats another, energy is transferred, or passed, through the ecosystem.

FOOD CHAINS AND FOOD WEBS

A *food chain*, like the one below, is a model that shows the order in which one organism eats another. The arrow points from the organism that is eaten to the organism that eats it.

algae ⟶ krill ⟶ cod

Most organisms, however, eat more than one kind of food. Many organisms are eaten by more than one other kind of organism. A **food web** represents the feeding relationships in an ecosystem better than a food chain does.

READING TOOLBOX

Organize After you read this section, create a concept map using the following terms from the section: *ecology, ecosystem, producer, decomposer, carrying capacity,* and *food web.*

✓ READING CHECK

1. Identify What do ecologists study?

_____

_____

_____

_____

LOOKING CLOSER

2. Identify Based on the food chain, which kind of organism eats krill?

_____

SECTION 3 **Ecology** *continued*

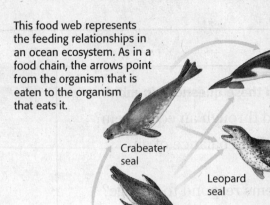

This food web represents the feeding relationships in an ocean ecosystem. As in a food chain, the arrows point from the organism that is eaten to the organism that eats it.

Killer whale

Elephant seal

Crabeater seal

Leopard seal

Squid

Adélie penguin

Cod

Small animals and one-celled organisms

Herring

Krill

Algae

LOOKING CLOSER

3. Interpret Diagrams
Name four organisms the leopard seal eats.

_____

_____

_____

Critical Thinking

4. Apply Concepts Look at the food web for an ocean ecosystem shown above. Which organisms in the ecosystem are producers?

_____

Talk About It

Apply Concepts Choose an ecosystem you are familiar with. With a partner, talk about the different organisms that are part of the ecosystem. Classify each kind of organism as a producer, a consumer, or a decomposer.

What Factors Control the Balance in Ecosystems?

FEEDING INTERACTIONS

Most ecosystems contain a variety of plants, animals, and other organisms, such as bacteria and fungi. Organisms such as plants that make their own food are called *producers*. Organisms that eat other organisms are called *consumers*. Some consumers eat producers. Some consumers eat other consumers.

Members of a special group of consumers called *decomposers* get energy by breaking down the body tissues of dead organisms. Bacteria and fungi are common decomposers. Producers, consumers, and decomposers are all important parts of a healthy ecosystem.

CARRYING CAPACITY

Organisms in an ecosystem use matter and energy to live, grow, and reproduce. However, the amounts of matter and energy in an ecosystem are limited. Because organisms have to share these resources, not all the organisms will have enough to survive. Some will die. The largest population an ecosystem can support is called the ecosystem's **carrying capacity**.

SECTION 3 **Ecology** *continued*

ENERGY PYRAMIDS

Unlike matter, energy cannot be recycled in an ecosystem. Every time one organism eats another, some energy is "lost." Because of this energy loss, an ecosystem typically has many more producers than consumers. An ecosystem typically has only a small number of organisms at the highest steps in a food chain. An energy pyramid represents the relative numbers of organisms at each step in a food chain.

RESPONSES TO CHANGE

Changes in any one part of an ecosystem may affect the ecosystem in ways that scientists cannot predict. However, in general, ecosystems react to small changes in a way that restores a balance.

A forest fire is an example of a disturbance of an ecosystem. A fire can cause a great deal of damage, as shown in the figure below. In time, however, grasses and other small plants can start to grow again in the area. Then, shrubs and small animals will return. Eventually, larger trees and animals will return to the area.

How Do Humans Affect Ecosystems?

Human activities can reduce the carrying capacities of ecosystems for themselves and for other organisms. Activities such as farming, building, and manufacturing disrupt the balance in ecosystems by removing habitats and food sources for many organisms. However, by using resources such as land, clean water, and fossil fuels wisely, humans can be good stewards of Earth. Good stewards protect Earth's resources and help keep ecosystems in balance.

Critical Thinking

5. Apply Concepts Which group of organisms in an ecosystem would be larger—grasses or wolves? Explain your answer.

_____

_____

_____

_____

LOOKING CLOSER

6. Analyze The elk shown in the figure will probably die or have to leave the ecosystem. Explain this result of the forest fire in terms of carrying capacity.

_____

_____

_____

_____

_____

_____

Section 3 Review

SECTION VOCABULARY

carrying capacity the largest population that an environment can support at any given time	**food web** a diagram that shows the feeding relationships among organisms in an ecosystem
ecosystem a community of organisms and their abiotic environment	

1. Compare Identify one way a food chain and a food web are similar and one way they are different.

_____

_____

_____

2. Classify In a grassland ecosystem, vultures and hyenas are feeding on the body of a dead elephant. How would you classify the vultures and hyenas? Explain your answer.

_____

_____

_____

3. Summarize Describe how energy moves from the sun through the organisms in an ecosystem.

_____

_____

_____

4. Predict Suppose people pave an area of forest to create a parking lot. How will this activity affect the carrying capacity of the forest?

_____

_____

_____

5. Describe How is the balance restored to an ecosystem after a disturbance such as a fire or a hurricane?

_____

_____

_____

_____

_____

CHAPTER 3 | Models of the Earth

SECTION 1 | # Finding Locations on Earth

As you read this section, keep these questions in mind:

• What is the difference between longitude and latitude?

• How can longitude and latitude be used to locate places on Earth's surface?

• How can a magnetic compass be used to find directions on Earth's surface?

What Is Latitude?

On a globe, the equator is the line halfway between the North Pole and the South Pole. It divides Earth into two *hemispheres*, or halves—the Northern Hemisphere and the Southern Hemisphere.

Parallels are imaginary lines on Earth's surface that are parallel to the equator. Each parallel has a specific latitude. **Latitude** is the distance north or south of the equator. Latitude is measured in degrees. The equator represents 0° latitude. The North Pole is 90°N latitude, and the South Pole is 90°S latitude. North latitudes are in the Northern Hemisphere, and south latitudes are in the Southern Hemisphere.

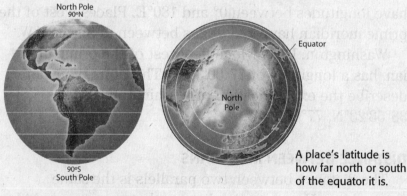

North Pole
90°N

Equator

North
Pole

90°S
South Pole

A place's latitude is how far north or south of the equator it is.

READING TOOLBOX

Organize After you read this section, create a concept map using the terms *latitude, longitude, parallel, meridian, degrees, equator,* and *prime meridian.*

LOOKING CLOSER

1. Estimate Which parallel in the figure do you think is closest to where you live?

_____

_____

Talk About It

Apply Concepts Use the library or Internet to find the latitude of a city or town you are interested in. Share what you learn with a partner. Together, talk about what you can know about a city if you know its latitude.

MINUTES AND SECONDS

Each degree of latitude equals 111 km. A degree is made up of 60 equal parts, which are called *minutes* (symbol: '). Each minute is divided into 60 equal parts, which are called *seconds* (symbol: "). For example, you can describe the latitude of the center of Washington, D.C., as 38°53'23"N.

SECTION 1 Finding Locations on Earth *continued*

What Is Longitude?

The latitude of a particular place indicates only its position north or south of the equator. That information isn't enough for you to know exactly where a place is. You also need to know how far east or west of a given location it is.

A **meridian** is an imaginary line that links the North Pole and the South Pole. Meridians are similar to the lines on a basketball. They are farthest apart at the equator, and they meet at the poles. ☑

The *prime meridian* is the line that all meridians are compared to. It runs through Greenwich, England. **Longitude** is the distance east or west of the prime meridian. The prime meridian has a longitude of 0°.

✔ **READING CHECK**

2. Define What is a meridian?

_____

_____

LOOKING CLOSER

3. Identify Label the prime meridian in the figure.

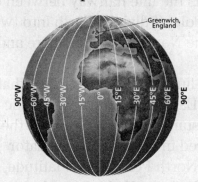

Meridians are imaginary lines that touch the North and South Poles. Notice how the lines get closer together as they near the poles.

DEGREES OF LONGITUDE

Like latitude, longitude is measured in degrees, minutes, and seconds. Places east of the prime meridian have longitudes between 0° and 180°E. Places west of the prime meridian have longitudes between 0° and 180°W.

Washington, D.C., which lies west of the prime meridian, has a longitude of 77°00'33"W. Therefore, you can describe the exact location of Washington, D.C., as 38°53'23"N, 77°00'33"W.

Critical Thinking

4. Apply Look at the latitude and longitude of Washington, D.C. Use that information to describe where the city is compared to the equator and the prime meridian.

_____

_____

_____

_____

_____

_____

DISTANCE BETWEEN MERIDIANS

The distance between two parallels is the same everywhere. However, the distance between two meridians depends on where you measure it. At the equator, one degree of longitude equals about 111 km. However, meridians meet at the poles. Therefore, the distance between meridians decreases if you measure it closer to the poles. For example, at a latitude of 80°N, 1° of longitude equals only about 20 km.

What Are Great Circles?

A great circle is any circle that divides the globe into two halves. Any two meridians that are directly across the globe from each other form a great circle. The equator is the only parallel that is a great circle.

On a flat surface, a straight line is the shortest way to get from one place to another. On a sphere, the shortest path between two places is along part of a great circle. Planes and ships often travel along great circles.

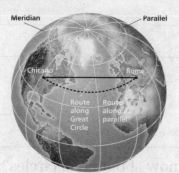

When a plane travels from Chicago to Rome, it travels along a great circle. It would take longer if the plane traveled along a parallel.

How Does a Compass Work?

The North and South Poles are known as geographic poles. However, Earth also has two geomagnetic poles, which are near the geographic poles. Earth is like a giant magnet. The needle on a compass points to the geomagnetic pole that is near the geographic North Pole. The compass uses Earth's magnetism to show direction.

The geographic North Pole and the geomagnetic north pole are not in the same place. Therefore, when you use a compass, you have to correct for this difference. True north is the direction of the geographic North Pole. The angle between true north and the direction a compass needle points is called *magnetic declination*.

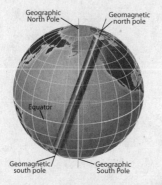

Earth's geomagnetic poles are not in exactly the same place as Earth's geographic poles.

Talk About It

Infer With a partner, talk about how many great circles there are. Use a prop, such as a fist or a piece of paper crumpled into a ball, in your discussion.

LOOKING CLOSER

5. Draw Extend the two routes on the map to show more of the parallel and the great circle.

LOOKING CLOSER

6. Label Add the following two labels to the globe: "true north" and "direction a compass needle points."

Name _____ Class _____ Date _____

Section 1 Review

SECTION VOCABULARY

latitude the distance north or south from the equator; expressed in degrees	**meridian** any semicircle that runs north and south around Earth from the geographic North Pole to the geographic South Pole; a line of longitude
longitude the angular distance east or west from the prime meridian; expressed in degrees	**parallel** any circle that runs east and west around Earth and that is parallel to the equator; a line of latitude

1. Compare What is the difference between a meridian and a parallel?

_____

_____

2. Define What is the prime meridian?

_____

_____

3. Explain Why is it important for an airplane pilot to know about great circles?

_____

_____

4. Explain Why doesn't the needle on a compass point directly to the North Pole?

_____

_____

5. Infer Explain why the equator is a great circle.

_____

_____

6. Apply Concepts Label the meridians and parallels on the globe shown below.

SECTION 2 | Mapping Earth's Surface

KEY IDEAS

As you read this section, keep these questions in mind:

• What are two ways scientists get data for making maps?

• What are the characteristics and uses of three types of map projections?

• How can you use keys, legends, and scales to read maps?

How Do Mapmakers Collect Information?

Cartography is the science of making maps. Scientists who create maps are called *cartographers*. Cartographers gather information from many sources. Two common ways they gather information are field surveys and remote sensing.

FIELD SURVEYS

During a field survey, cartographers walk or drive through an area and make measurements. Then, they plot those measurements on a map. However, cartographers cannot take measurements at every place. Therefore, they use the information they gather to estimate information about the rest of the area. ☑

This cartographer is using a machine to measure a distance for his map.

REMOTE SENSING

Much of the information used to make maps today comes from remote sensing. Remote sensing is a way to gather information about an object without actually touching the object. In **remote sensing**, cartographers use equipment on satellites or airplanes to create images of Earth's surface. ☑

READING TOOLBOX

Outline As you read this section, create an outline of the section. Use the headings in the section in your outline.

✓ READING CHECK

1. Explain Why do cartographers often have to estimate measurements?

_____

_____

_____

✓ READING CHECK

2. Define What is remote sensing?

_____

_____

_____

_____

_____

What Are Map Projections?

A globe is the most accurate model of Earth. However, a globe cannot show very much detail. Therefore, scientists often use maps to study Earth's surface.

Maps are flat, but they represent Earth's curved surface. There are different ways to change Earth's curved surface into a flat map. These different ways of showing Earth on a map are called **map projections**. Moving information from a curved to a flat surface causes errors in shapes, sizes, and distances. These errors are called *distortions*. All map projections have some distortions. ☑

To understand how map projections are made, think of a clear globe with a light inside it. If you wrap a piece of paper around the globe, the continents will make shadows on the paper. If you wrap the paper in different ways, the shadows will look different. Each way of wrapping the paper produces a different map projection.

✓ **READING CHECK**

3. Explain Why do map projections have distortions?

_____

_____

_____

_____

_____

_____

CYLINDRICAL PROJECTIONS

Suppose you wrap a piece of paper around a globe in the shape of a cylinder. The map projection you would make is called a *cylindrical projection*. In a cylindrical projection, latitude and longitude lines are straight.

A cylindrical projection has two main distortions. First, the space between longitude lines is equal everywhere, instead of being wider at the equator. Second, latitude lines are farther apart in the far north and south, instead of being evenly spaced everywhere. The distortions in a cylindrical projection make areas near the poles look wider and longer than they really are.

LOOKING CLOSER

4. Describe Which areas on this map are most distorted?

_____

_____

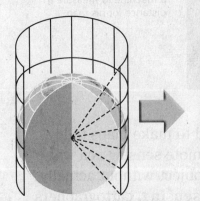 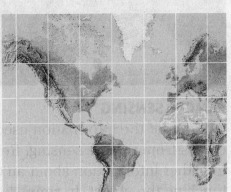

On a cylindrical projection, the areas near the equator are least distorted.

SECTION 2 **Mapping Earth's Surface** *continued*

CONIC PROJECTIONS

You can make a *conic projection* by wrapping the paper in a cone around Earth. The cone touches the globe along one parallel. Areas on this line of latitude are not distorted. Areas far from this latitude look distorted.

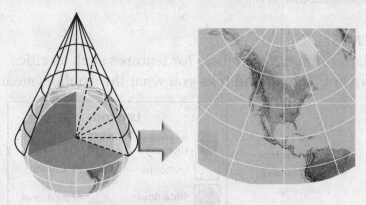

This conic projection is less distorted near the equator. It is more distorted near the North Pole.

You can also wrap several cones around the globe, with each cone touching a different parallel. This produces a *polyconic projection*. A polyconic projection has less distortion than a conic projection.

AZIMUTHAL PROJECTIONS

You could make an *azimuthal projection* by placing a piece of paper flat against the globe. The paper would touch the globe at only one point. That point is the North or South Pole in most azimuthal projections. The distortion near this point is very small, but it increases as you move away from the point.

As you know, a great circle is the shortest distance between any two points on the globe. On an azimuthal projection, a great circle looks like a straight line. Therefore, people use azimuthal projections to plot routes for planes and ships.

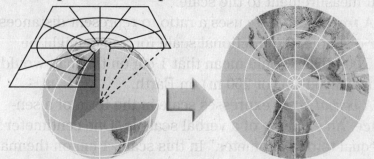

This azimuthal projection is less distorted near the North Pole. It is more distorted near the equator.

LOOKING CLOSER
5. Describe Where would a conic projection of the Southern Hemisphere be most distorted?

_____

_____

Critical Thinking
6. Infer Why might a cartographer create a polyconic projection instead of a conic projection?

_____

_____

_____

LOOKING CLOSER
7. Identify Where does this azimuthal projection touch the globe?

_____

SECTION 2 **Mapping Earth's Surface** *continued*

How Can Symbols Help You Read a Map?

The information on a map is in the form of symbols. To read a map well, you must understand the symbols on the map. You also need to be able to find directions and calculate distances.

LEGENDS

Maps often have symbols for features such as cities and rivers. The **legend** tells you what the symbols mean.

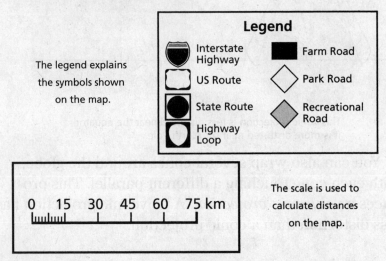

The legend explains the symbols shown on the map.

Legend

Interstate Highway
US Route
State Route
Highway Loop
Farm Road
Park Road
Recreational Road

0   15   30   45   60   75 km

The scale is used to calculate distances on the map.

SCALES

Maps represent real places on Earth. It is important for people to know how the distances on a map are related to distances in real life. The map's **scale** shows this relationship. A map scale can be expressed as a graphic scale, a fractional scale, or a verbal scale.

The figure above shows a *graphic scale*. Each part of a graphic scale represents one unit of measurement, such as a kilometer or a mile. To find the actual distance between two points, you need to measure the distance between the points on a map. Then, you can compare that measurement to the scale.

A *fractional scale* uses a ratio to represent distances. For example, the fractional scale for a map might be 1:25,000. That would mean that 1 cm on the map would equal 25,000 cm (or 250 m) on Earth.

A *verbal scale* expresses scale in the form of a sentence. An example of a verbal scale is "One centimeter is equal to one kilometer." In this scale, 1 cm on the map equals 1 km on Earth.

Critical Thinking

8. Calculate A map has a fractional scale of 1:10,000. The distance between two buildings is 3 cm on the map. What is the actual distance between the two buildings?

_____

_____

_____

SECTION 2 Mapping Earth's Surface *continued*

DIRECTIONS

When you read a map, it is important to understand how the map shows direction. Most maps are drawn with north at the top, but some maps are not. If a map has latitude and longitude lines, you can use them to understand how the map shows direction. Other maps include an arrow pointing north or a compass rose, such as the one below. ☑

A compass rose shows which direction the North Pole is.

✔ **READING CHECK**

10. List What are three ways a map can show direction?

_____
_____
_____

ISOGRAMS

An **isogram** is a line that connects many points with the same value (*iso-* means "equal"). All points along an isogram have the same value for whatever property is being shown. For example, some isograms connect points that have the same temperature. Those lines are called *isotherms* (*therm* means "heat").

Isograms can be used to show other types of information, too. For example, some isograms connect points that have the same atmospheric pressure. These isograms are called *isobars*. Other isograms can show which areas have the same levels of rainfall, gravity, density, or height.

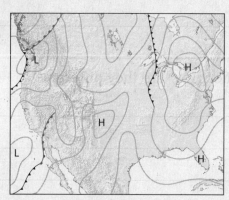

The isobars on this weather map connect points that have the same atmospheric pressure.

LOOKING CLOSER

11. Identify Label one of the isograms on the map. What does the isogram show?

_____
_____
_____
_____

Section 2 Review

SECTION VOCABULARY

isogram a line on a map that represents a constant or equal value of a given quantity	**remote sensing** the process of gathering and analyzing information about an object without physically being in touch with the object
legend a list of map symbols and their meanings	
map projection a flat map that represents a spherical surface	**scale** the relationship between the distance shown on a map and the actual distance

1. Describe Complete the table below to describe the three main types of map projections.

Map Projection	How It Can Be Made	Areas of Least Distortion	Areas of Greatest Distortion
			Areas near the poles are most distorted.
	Place a piece of paper so that it touches the globe at only one point.		
		area near the parallel that the cone touches	Areas far from the parallel the cone touches are most distorted.

2. Infer What is one advantage of remote sensing over field surveying?

_____

_____

_____

3. Explain How can a legend help you read a map?

_____

_____

4. Apply Concepts The scale on a map is given as the following: "One centimeter equals 10 meters." What kind of scale is this? If two areas are 40 m apart in real life, how far apart will they be on the map?

_____

_____

5. Compare How are isotherms and isobars the same? How are they different?

_____

_____

_____

CHAPTER 3 Models of the Earth
SECTION 3 Types of Maps

KEY IDEAS

As you read this section, keep these questions in mind:

- How are elevation and topography shown on a map?
- What are three types of information shown in geologic maps?
- What are two uses of soil maps?

What Is a Topographic Map?

There are many different kinds of maps. Each kind of map shows different information. One common kind of map is a *topographic map*. A topographic map is a map that shows the surface features, or **topography**, of an area. Topographic maps show three main things:

- natural features, such as rivers and lakes
- features made by people, such as bridges
- **elevation**, or the height of an object above sea level

Look at the two figures below. The figure on the left shows a picture of an island. The figure on the right shows a topographic map of the same island.

The topographic map on the right shows the features and elevation of the picture on the left. An X marks the highest point on the map.

The picture of the island shows the island's shape. A regular map of the island could use a scale to show its size. The topographic map shows the island's topography, in addition to its shape and size. In this way, a topographic map gives more detail than a picture or a regular map. ☑

READING TOOLBOX

Ask Questions Read this section silently. As you read, write down questions that you have about this section. Discuss your questions in a small group.

LOOKING CLOSER

1. Apply Concepts About how long is this island from the southwest corner to the northeast corner?

READING CHECK

2. Compare How is a topographic map different from a regular map?

_____

_____

SECTION 3 **Types of Maps** continued

Type of Model	What It Shows		
	Shape	Size	Elevation
Picture	X		
Regular map	X	X	
Topographic map	X	X	X

Critical Thinking

3. Infer Why is a contour line a type of isogram?

_____

_____

_____

_____

LOOKING CLOSER

4. Identify Circle an area on the map that has a steep slope. Put a square around an area that has a gentle slope.

Critical Thinking

5. Apply Concepts A point on a map is halfway between the 50 m contour line and the 60 m contour line. What is the elevation of the point?

_____

CONTOUR LINES

Topographic maps use contour lines to show elevation. A **contour line** is an isogram that connects points with the same elevation. Contour lines that are far apart show a gradual change in elevation. Contour lines that are close to each other show a steeper slope.

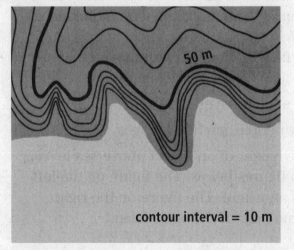

The distance between contour lines shows how steep or gentle a slope is.

A *contour interval* is the difference in elevation between two contour lines. For example, the map above has a contour interval of 10 m. Therefore, the difference in elevation between two contour lines is 10 m.

Some contour lines are drawn darker than others. These darker lines are called *index contours*. They make the map easier to read. In the map above, every fifth contour line is an index contour.

You can estimate the elevation of a point on a map by looking at the two contour lines near it. The elevation of that point is between the elevations of the two contour lines. For example, a point halfway between the 100 m and 110 m contour lines has an elevation of about 105 m.

Some points on a topographic map are marked with an ×. A number is written next to the ×. That number is the exact elevation of that point.

SECTION 3	**Types of Maps** *continued*

RELIEF ON TOPOGRAPHIC MAPS

Relief is the difference between the highest elevation and the lowest elevation on a topographic map. On some maps, the relief can be as large as 100 m. On other maps, it may be as small as 1 m.

OTHER SYMBOLS ON TOPOGRAPHIC MAPS

Most topographic maps use colors and symbols to represent objects. For example, a map might have symbols to show roads, railroads, and buildings. These symbols are generally black. Bodies of water are generally blue, and forests are generally green. Major highways are red. ☑

The shapes of contour lines can give you information about the landforms on a map. For example, a contour line may be shaped like a small, closed circle. That contour line represents either a hill or a very low area. A contour line shaped like a V represents a valley. If there is a river in the valley, the V will point upstream. It points in the direction opposite that of the river's flow.

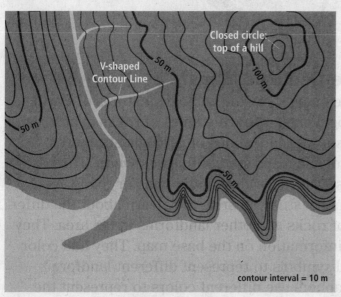

The shapes of contour lines give information about landforms.

Labels on figure: Closed circle: top of a hill; V-shaped Contour Line; 50 m; 100 m; 50 m; 50 m; contour interval = 10 m

READING CHECK

6. Identify What color is generally used to show water on a topographic map?

_____

LOOKING CLOSER

7. Apply Concepts What is the elevation of the top of the mountain in the top right corner of the map?

_____

What Is a Soil Map?

Earth scientists use soil maps to show the properties of the soil in an area. People can use soil maps to understand how to use land most efficiently. They can also use the maps to identify ways to conserve soil.

SOIL SURVEYS

To create a soil map, cartographers do a soil survey of the area. During the soil survey, they record information about the types of soils in the area. They collect samples of soil from many different places in the area. The figure below shows an example of a soil map.

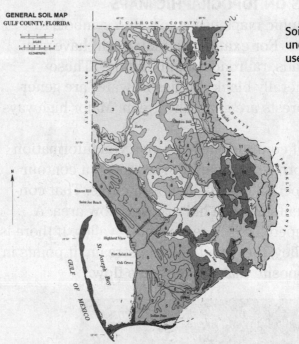

GENERAL SOIL MAP
GULF COUNTY, FLORIDA

Soil maps help scientists understand how to best use the land in an area.

Talk About It

Investigate Use the Internet or library to find a soil map for your county or for another area. Find out which areas on the map are best for growing different kinds of plants, such as corn, wheat, or pine trees. Share what you learn with a partner or a small group.

What Are Geologic Maps?

Geologic maps show the geologic features of Earth. Most geologic maps show the types of rocks in an area. They also show the locations of geologic structures.

Most geologic maps start with a *base map*. The base map shows features such as mountains or roads. As Earth scientists study an area, they learn about the different kinds of rocks and other landforms in the area. They mark that information on the base map. They add color and special symbols to represent different landforms.

Cartographers use different colors to represent the geologic units on a geologic map. A *geologic unit* is a layer of rock that is all the same age and type. Units that are similar ages generally have similar colors. ☑

Cartographers label each geologic unit with a set of letters. The set contains one capital letter and one or more lowercase letters. The capital letter stands for the rock's age. The lowercase letters stand for the type of rock.

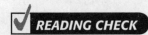

READING CHECK

8. Describe How do geologic maps show different geologic units?

_____

_____

SECTION 3 **Types of Maps** *continued*

CONTACT LINES

Geologic maps also contain symbols called *contact lines.* A contact line is a place where two geologic units meet. There are two main kinds of contact lines: depositional contacts and faults. Depositional contacts show where one rock layer formed above another. Faults are cracks where rocks move past each other.

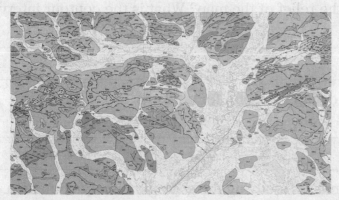

Each color on this map shows a different type and age of rock. Scientists can use this geologic map to see which types of rocks are in this area.

LOOKING CLOSER

9. Identify The geologic units on this map are separated by black lines. What are the black lines called?

_____

_____

What Are Some Other Types of Maps?

Topographic maps, geologic maps, and soil maps are not the only kinds of maps Earth scientists use. Earth scientists may use maps to show the movements of wind and water. They may use maps to show where earthquakes and volcanoes are likely to happen.

Different scientists use maps in different ways. For example, meteorologists use some maps to predict weather events. These maps may show the amount of precipitation that falls on different areas. They may also show the location of high and low atmospheric pressure. Meteorologists use these maps to predict weather and to warn people about weather emergencies. ☑

Some maps show where and how groundwater flows. Structures and systems such as power plants, garbage dumps, and new communities can pollute groundwater. Geologists can use groundwater maps to find the best places to build such structures. Other maps help geologists to study changes in Earth's surface over time. Geologists may use these maps to study changes in topography, in the amounts of available natural resources, and in climate.

✓ **READING CHECK**

10. Explain Why is it important for meteorologists to share the information on their maps with the public?

_____

_____

_____

_____

Section 3 Review

SECTION VOCABULARY

contour line a line that connects points of equal elevation on a map	**relief** the difference between the highest and lowest elevations in a given area
elevation the height of an object above sea level	**topography** the size and shape of the land surface features of a region, including its relief

1. Explain A small topographic map contains the following contour lines (in meters): 40, 50, 60, 70, 80, 90. What is the relief of the map? What is the contour interval?

_____

_____

2. Infer How could a topographic map be useful for a hiker?

_____

_____

3. Apply Concepts An Earth scientist is studying the geologic history of an area. She wants to know when different rock layers in the area formed. Which kind of map should she use? Explain your answer.

_____

_____

4. Identify What are two ways people use soil maps?

_____

_____

5. Compare Complete the table below to compare topographic maps, geologic maps, and soil maps.

Type of Map	What Colors Represent on the Map	What Lines Represent on the Map
Topographic map	black = roads and buildings; blue = water; green = forest; red = major highways	
	different geologic units	
		places where different kinds of soil touch

6. Identify Give two examples of how people can use maps to help the environment.

_____

_____

_____

CHAPTER 4 Earth Chemistry

SECTION 1 Matter

As you read this section, keep these questions in mind:

- How are chemical properties and physical properties of matter different?

- What is the basic structure of an atom?

- What are atomic number, mass number, and atomic mass?

- What is an isotope?

- How are elements arranged in the periodic table?

What Are the Properties of Matter?

All objects are made of matter. **Matter** is anything that takes up space and has mass. Mass is the amount of matter in an object.

Matter has two types of properties, or characteristics: physical properties and chemical properties. You can observe *physical properties* without changing the composition of a substance. Color, hardness, boiling point, and density are physical properties.

You can observe *chemical properties* when a substance reacts with other substances. For example, one chemical property of iron is that it can react with oxygen to form rust. ☑

What Is an Element?

Every substance is made of one or more elements. An **element** is a substance that cannot be separated into simpler substances by chemical reactions. There are about 111 known elements. The graph below shows the elements that are most common in Earth's crust.

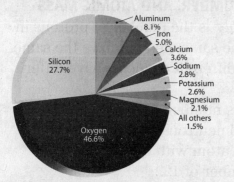

Eight elements make up 98% of the mass of Earth's crust.

READING TOOLBOX

Clarify Concepts Take turns reading this section aloud with a partner. Pause to discuss confusing or unfamiliar ideas.

✓ READING CHECK

1. Describe What has to happen for you to be able to observe a chemical property?

_____

_____

_____

LOOKING CLOSER

2. Identify Which element makes up the largest percentage of Earth's crust?

_____

SECTION 1 **Matter** *continued*

Talk About It

Use Prefixes Use a dictionary to look up the meaning of the prefix *sub-*. With a partner, talk about why protons, neutrons, and electrons are called *subatomic particles*.

✓ **READING CHECK**

3. List What are the three kinds of subatomic particles in an atom?

_____

_____

LOOKING CLOSER
4. Describe Which subatomic particles are found in the nucleus?

_____

_____

What Is an Atom?

All matter is made up of atoms. An **atom** is the smallest unit of an element that has the chemical properties of that element. A single atom is very small. One million atoms stacked up would be as thick as a piece of paper.

THE STRUCTURE OF AN ATOM

Atoms are made of even smaller parts called *subatomic particles*. The three kinds of subatomic particles are protons, electrons, and neutrons. **Protons** have a positive charge. **Electrons** have a negative charge. **Neutrons** have no charge. ✓

Protons and neutrons form the *nucleus* of an atom. The nucleus is at the center of an atom. The nucleus contains only protons and neutrons, so it has a positive charge.

Electrons are found outside the nucleus. Electrons move so quickly that there is no way to know where an electron is at any given time. The *electron cloud* is the area around the nucleus where electrons are most likely to be. The electrons stay around the nucleus because they are negatively charged. The positive charge of the nucleus attracts the electrons.

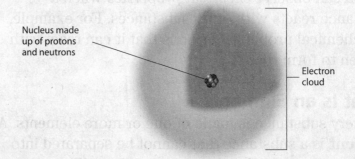

Nucleus made up of protons and neutrons

Electron cloud

The nucleus makes up only a tiny fraction of an atom's volume. If the nucleus were the size of a gumdrop, the whole atom would be the size of a football stadium.

ATOMIC NUMBER, MASS NUMBER, AND ATOMIC MASS

An atom's *atomic number* is the number of protons in its nucleus. All atoms of the same element have the same atomic number. Atoms of different elements have different atomic numbers.

An atom also has a mass number. The *mass number* is the number of protons and neutrons in the nucleus of the atom. For example, an atom with 6 protons and 6 neutrons has a mass number of 12.

SECTION 1 **Matter** *continued*

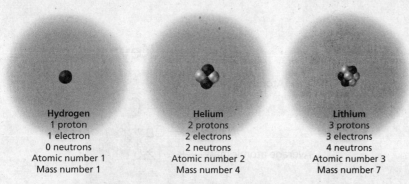

Hydrogen
1 proton
1 electron
0 neutrons
Atomic number 1
Mass number 1

Helium
2 protons
2 electrons
2 neutrons
Atomic number 2
Mass number 4

Lithium
3 protons
3 electrons
4 neutrons
Atomic number 3
Mass number 7

Mass number is not the same as atomic mass. *Atomic mass* is the actual mass of an atom. Scientists describe atomic mass using the *unified atomic mass unit* (u). Protons and neutrons have an atomic mass that is close to 1 u. Electrons have much less mass than protons and neutrons. Therefore, you can ignore the masses of the electrons in an atom when you calculate atomic mass. ☑

ISOTOPES AND AVERAGE ATOMIC MASS

All atoms of an element have the same number of protons. However, atoms of an element may have different numbers of neutrons. Atoms with the same number of protons but different numbers of neutrons are called **isotopes**. Isotopes have the same atomic number but different mass numbers and atomic masses.

Most elements have more than one isotope. An element's *average atomic mass* is the weighted average of the atomic masses of all the isotopes of the element.

How Is the Periodic Table Organized?

Scientists use the periodic table to organize the elements. Elements in the periodic table are arranged in columns called *groups*. The atoms of elements in each group have the same number of valence electrons. Some electrons in an atom are farther from the nucleus than others. *Valence electrons* are the outer electrons in an atom's electron cloud.

Valence electrons determine an atom's chemical properties. Therefore, elements in the same group have similar chemical properties. In chemical reactions, elements in Groups 1 and 2 tend to lose electrons easily. Elements in Groups 15–17 tend to gain electrons easily. Elements in Groups 3–14 can lose or gain electrons. Elements in Group 18 do not gain or lose electrons easily. ☑

Critical Thinking

5. Apply Concepts Why are the atomic number and mass number of hydrogen equal?

_____
_____
_____
_____

✔ **READING CHECK**

6. Explain Why can you ignore the masses of electrons when you calculate atomic mass?

_____
_____
_____

✔ **READING CHECK**

7. Compare How are elements in the same group similar?

_____
_____
_____
_____

SECTION 1 **Matter** *continued*

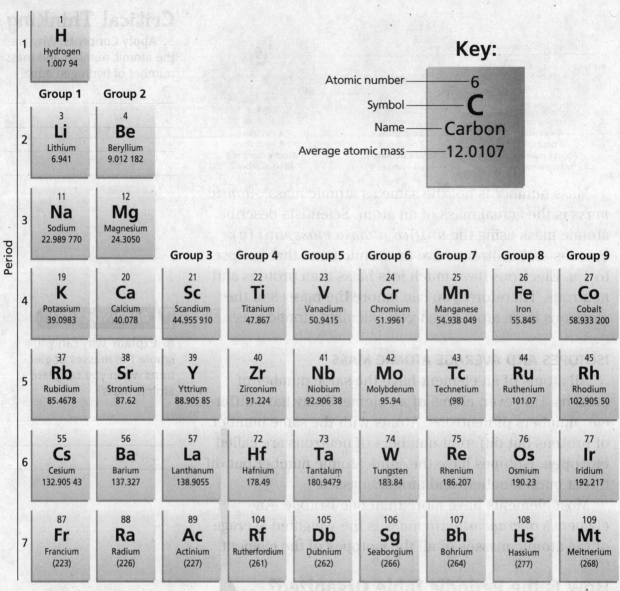

Key:

Atomic number —— 6
Symbol —— **C**
Name —— Carbon
Average atomic mass —— 12.0107

* The systematic names and symbols for elements greater than 111 will be used until the approval of trivial names by IUPAC.

SECTION 1 **Matter** *continued*

Metals
Nonmetals
Semiconductors
(also known as metalloids)
Noble gases

Group 18

2	
He	
Helium	
4.002 602	

Group 13 **Group 14** **Group 15** **Group 16** **Group 17**

5	6	7	8	9	10
B	**C**	**N**	**O**	**F**	**Ne**
Boron	Carbon	Nitrogen	Oxygen	Fluorine	Neon
10.811	12.0107	14.0067	15.9994	18.998 4032	20.1797

13	14	15	16	17	18
Al	**Si**	**P**	**S**	**Cl**	**Ar**
Aluminum	Silicon	Phosphorus	Sulfur	Chlorine	Argon
26.981 538	28.0855	30.973 761	32.065	35.453	39.948

Group 10 **Group 11** **Group 12**

28	29	30	31	32	33	34	35	36
Ni	**Cu**	**Zn**	**Ga**	**Ge**	**As**	**Se**	**Br**	**Kr**
Nickel	Copper	Zinc	Gallium	Germanium	Arsenic	Selenium	Bromine	Krypton
58.6934	63.546	65.409	69.723	72.64	74.921 60	78.96	79.904	83.798

46	47	48	49	50	51	52	53	54
Pd	**Ag**	**Cd**	**In**	**Sn**	**Sb**	**Te**	**I**	**Xe**
Palladium	Silver	Cadmium	Indium	Tin	Antimony	Tellurium	Iodine	Xenon
106.42	107.8682	112.411	114.818	118.710	121.760	127.60	126.904 47	131.293

78	79	80	81	82	83	84	85	86
Pt	**Au**	**Hg**	**Tl**	**Pb**	**Bi**	**Po**	**At**	**Rn**
Platinum	Gold	Mercury	Thallium	Lead	Bismuth	Polonium	Astatine	Radon
195.078	196.966 55	200.59	204.3833	207.2	208.980 38	(209)	(210)	(222)

110	111	112	113	114	115	116		118
Ds	**Rg**	**Uub***	**Uut***	**Uuq***	**Uup***	**Uuh***		**Uuo***
Darmstadtium	Roentgenium	Ununbium	Ununtrium	Ununquadium	Ununpentium	Ununhexium		Ununoctium
(281)	(272)	(285)	(284)	(289)	(288)	(292)		(294)

The discoveries of elements with atomic numbers 112 through 116 and 118 have been reported but not fully confirmed.

63	64	65	66	67	68	69	70	71
Eu	**Gd**	**Tb**	**Dy**	**Ho**	**Er**	**Tm**	**Yb**	**Lu**
Europium	Gadolinium	Terbium	Dysprosium	Holmium	Erbium	Thulium	Ytterbium	Lutetium
151.964	157.25	158.925 34	162.500	164.930 32	167.259	168.934 21	173.04	174.967

95	96	97	98	99	100	101	102	103
Am	**Cm**	**Bk**	**Cf**	**Es**	**Fm**	**Md**	**No**	**Lr**
Americium	Curium	Berkelium	Californium	Einsteinium	Fermium	Mendelevium	Nobelium	Lawrencium
(243)	(247)	(247)	(251)	(252)	(257)	(258)	(259)	(262)

The atomic masses listed in this table reflect the precision of current measurements. (Each value listed in parentheses is the mass number of that radioactive element's most stable or most common isotope.)

Name _____ Class _____ Date _____

Section 1 Review

SECTION VOCABULARY

atom the smallest unit of an element that maintains the chemical properties of that element	**matter** anything that has mass and takes up space
electron a subatomic particle that has a negative charge	**neutron** a subatomic particle that has no charge and that is located in the nucleus of an atom
element a substance that cannot be separated or broken down into simpler substances by chemical means	**proton** a subatomic particle that has a positive charge and that is located in the nucleus of an atom; the number of protons of the nucleus is the atomic number, which determines the identity of an element
isotope one of two or more atoms that have the same number of protons (atomic number) but different numbers of neutrons (atomic mass)	

1. Describe Complete the chart below to describe the properties of the subatomic particles.

	Proton		**Neutron**
Charge			
Location		outside the nucleus	in the nucleus

2. Compare What is the difference between a chemical property and a physical property?

_____

_____

3. Apply Concepts An atom has 14 protons and 15 neutrons. What is its mass number? What element is it an atom of? Explain your answer. You can use the periodic table to help you answer.

_____

_____

4. Explain Why do isotopes of an element have the same atomic number but different mass numbers?

_____

_____

5. Infer Sodium and potassium are in the same group on the periodic table. Name two other ways sodium and potassium are similar.

_____

_____

CHAPTER 4 **Earth Chemistry**

SECTION 2 # Combinations of Atoms

As you read this section, keep these questions in mind:
- What are compounds and molecules?
- What are chemical formulas?
- What are two types of chemical bonds?
- What is the difference between compounds and mixtures?

What Are Compounds?

Different elements can combine to form compounds. A **compound** is a substance that forms when atoms of two or more elements join together. A compound has different properties than the elements that form it.

MOLECULES

The atoms in a compound are joined together in groups called **molecules**. A molecule is the smallest unit of a compound that has the chemical properties of that compound. ☑

Most molecules are made of atoms of more than one kind of element. However, some molecules are made of atoms of the same element. For example, the element oxygen naturally exists as molecules of two oxygen atoms. Molecules that are made up of only two atoms are called *diatomic molecules*.

What Are Chemical Formulas?

A *chemical formula* is a group of letters and numbers that describes a compound. The letters are symbols from the periodic table. They represent the elements in the compound. The numbers show how many atoms of an element are in a molecule of the compound. For example, the chemical formula for water is H_2O. The table below shows how to interpret this chemical formula.

Formula	Symbol	Element	Interpretation
H_2O	H	hydrogen	There are two hydrogen atoms in each water molecule.
	O	oxygen	There is one oxygen atom in each water molecule.

READING TOOLBOX

Compare As you read this section, use a double-door fold to compare the terms *compound* and *mixture*.

✓ READING CHECK

1. Identify What is a molecule?

_____

_____

LOOKING CLOSER

2. Identify Which two elements combine to form water?

_____

_____

What Are Chemical Equations?

A chemical reaction happens when atoms combine in new ways to form new substances. The substances that react are called *reactants*. The new substances that form are called *products*. The diagram below shows the chemical reaction between methane and oxygen.

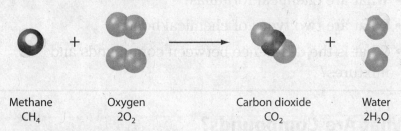

Methane	Oxygen	Carbon dioxide	Water
CH_4	$2O_2$	CO_2	$2H_2O$

Methane and oxygen react to form carbon dioxide and water.

Scientists use *chemical equations* to represent chemical reactions. In a chemical equation, the chemical formulas for the reactants appear on the left side of an arrow. The chemical formulas for the products appear on the right side of the arrow. The chemical reaction below represents the reaction between methane and oxygen.

$$CH_4 + 2O_2 \rightarrow CO_2 + 2H_2O$$

BALANCED EQUATIONS

Look again at the chemical equation for the reaction of methane and oxygen. The chemical formulas for oxygen (O_2) and water (H_2O) have the number 2 in front of them. These numbers are called *coefficients*. They show that two molecules of oxygen react with each molecule of methane. They also show that the reaction forms two molecules of water.

Scientists use coefficients to balance chemical equations. A chemical reaction is balanced when the number of each kind of atom is the same on both sides of the arrow. The number of atoms of an element must be the same in the reactants and the products. For example, if there are four oxygen atoms in the reactants, there must be four oxygen atoms in the products. To calculate the number of atoms present, multiply the coefficient by the subscript.

You can use only coefficients to balance a chemical equation. You cannot change the chemical formulas of the reactants or products.

What Are Chemical Bonds?

A *chemical bond* is a force that holds the atoms in a molecule together. There are two main ways atoms can form chemical bonds. Atoms can form bonds by

- transferring electrons from one atom to another
- sharing electrons ☑

Scientists study the properties of elements to predict how atoms will bond. Atoms of some kinds of elements lose or gain electrons easily. Atoms of other elements are more likely to bond by sharing electrons. Elements bond in ways that make their atoms more stable. Most atoms are stable when they have eight valence electrons.

What Happens When Atoms Transfer Electrons?

An atom has the same number of protons and electrons. Each proton has a charge of 1+. Each electron has a charge of 1−. Therefore, the positive and negative charges in an atom exactly balance out. The atom is *neutral*. It has no charge. If a neutral atom gains or loses electrons, it is no longer neutral. If the atom loses an electron, it becomes positively charged. If it gains an electron, it becomes negatively charged.

IONS AND IONIC BONDS

An **ion** is a particle that has a positive or negative charge. Ions form when atoms or molecules gain or lose electrons. For example, a neutral chlorine atom has 7 valence electrons. If the atom accepts an electron, it will have 8 valence electrons and become chemically stable. The extra electron will also give the atom a negative charge. The neutral chlorine atom becomes an ion.

An **ionic bond** is the attraction between ions with opposite charges. A compound that forms from ionic bonds is an *ionic compound*. Sodium chloride, or table salt, is an ionic compound. The compound can form when a sodium atom loses one electron. The sodium atom becomes a sodium ion with a 1+ charge. The chlorine atom gains the electron and becomes a chloride ion with a 1− charge. The oppositely charged ions attract one another. This attraction is an ionic bond. ☑

✔ READING CHECK

5. Identify What are the two main ways atoms can bond?

_____

_____

_____

Critical Thinking

6. Apply Concepts Does an ion with a positive charge have more protons or electrons?

_____

_____

✔ READING CHECK

7. Explain Why do the ions in an ionic bond stay together?

_____

_____

_____

_____

SECTION 2 **Combinations of Atoms** *continued*

LOOKING CLOSER
8. Identify Which ion in the diagram has a positive charge?

_____

_____

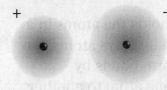

+ −

Sodium   Chloride

Sodium chloride (NaCl) forms when sodium ions (Na⁺) and chloride ions (Cl⁻) form ionic bonds.

What Happens When Atoms Share Electrons?

Some atoms do not transfer electrons easily. These atoms may bond by sharing electrons. When atoms share electrons, the electrons move around the nuclei of all of the atoms, instead of just one of them. The attraction between the positive nuclei and the negative electrons holds the atoms together.

A bond that forms when atoms share electrons is called a **covalent bond**. A compound formed from covalent bonds is a *covalent compound*. Water is a covalent compound. In a water molecule, two hydrogen atoms share valence electrons with an oxygen atom. This sharing of electrons gives each atom a more stable number of electrons. ☑

Some covalent bonds form between atoms of the same element. For example, remember that oxygen naturally exists as diatomic molecules. The two oxygen atoms in an oxygen molecule are joined by a covalent bond.

READING CHECK
9. Define What is a covalent bond?

_____

_____

_____

LOOKING CLOSER
10. Describe How does the covalent bond in an oxygen molecule form?

_____

_____

_____

Oxygen   Oxygen

A covalent bond joins two oxygen atoms in a molecule of oxygen (O_2).

POLAR COVALENT BONDS

In a *polar covalent bond*, the atoms in the bond do not share their electrons equally. The electrons spend more time around one of the atoms. The bonds in water molecules are polar covalent bonds. The oxygen atoms attract electrons more than the hydrogen atoms do.

The electrons spend more time around the oxygen atom than around the hydrogen atoms. Therefore, the oxygen atom has a slight negative charge. The hydrogen atoms have slight positive charges.

SECTION 2 **Combinations of Atoms** *continued*

What Is a Mixture?

Elements and compounds can combine to form mixtures. A **mixture** is a combination of two or more substances that are not joined by chemical bonds. A mixture is different from a compound. Remember that the properties of substances change when they react to form compounds. When substances form a mixture, their properties do not change. ☑

Unlike the parts of a compound, the parts of a mixture can be separated by physical means. For example, you can separate a mixture of sand and iron shavings using a magnet. Compounds cannot be separated into elements by physical means.

HETEROGENEOUS MIXTURES

There are two main types of mixtures: heterogeneous mixtures and homogeneous mixtures. The parts of a *heterogeneous mixture* are not evenly mixed together. Different parts of the mixture have different amounts of each substance. A mixture of mud and water is an example of a heterogeneous mixture.

HOMOGENEOUS MIXTURES

In a *homogeneous mixture*, the parts of the mixture are evenly mixed. Every part of the mixture has the same properties and composition. A homogeneous mixture of two or more substances is a **solution**.

Sea water is a solution. In sea water, ionic compounds such as sodium chloride are mixed evenly with water molecules. All parts of a sample of sea water have the same composition.

Gases and solids can also form solutions. Air is an example of a solution of gases. An *alloy* is a solution of two or more metals. Steel is an alloy made of iron, carbon, and many other elements. The table below shows some other examples of heterogeneous and homogeneous mixtures.

Heterogeneous Mixtures	Homogeneous Mixtures
salad	tea
granite and many other rocks	nail polish
soil	paint
vegetable soup	lemonade

✓ **READING CHECK**

11. Compare How is a compound different from a mixture?

_____

_____

_____

Critical Thinking

12. Apply Concepts You stir salt into a bowl of water. Is this a compound or a mixture?

_____

_____

Talk About It

Discuss Make a list of the foods you ate yesterday. Share your list with a partner. Together, figure out which of the foods were homogeneous mixtures and which were heterogeneous mixtures.

LOOKING CLOSER

13. Identify What is one other example of a heterogeneous mixture?

_____

_____

Name _____ Class _____ Date _____

Section 2 Review

SECTION VOCABULARY

compound a substance made up of atoms of two or more different elements joined by chemical bonds	**mixture** a combination of two or more substances that are not chemically combined
covalent bond a bond formed when atoms share one or more pairs of electrons	**molecule** a group of atoms that are held together by chemical forces
ion an atom or molecule that has gained or lost one or more electrons and has a negative or positive charge	**solution** a homogeneous mixture throughout which two or more substances are uniformly dispersed
ionic bond the attractive force between oppositely charged ions, which form when electrons are transferred from one atom or molecule to another	

1. Organize Complete the concept map with the terms *compounds, mixtures, covalent bonds, ionic bonds, heterogeneous,* and *homogeneous.*

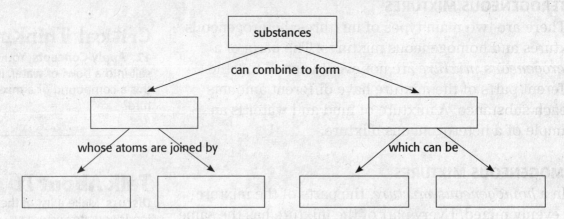

2. Analyze This chemical equation represents a chemical reaction:

$$2H_2 + O_2 \rightarrow 2H_2O$$

Identify the reactants and products of this reaction. Explain whether the equation is balanced or not.

_____

_____

_____

3. Identify Give one example of a homogeneous solution and one example of a heterogeneous solution. Use examples that are not given in this section.

_____

_____

SECTION 1 | # What Is a Mineral?

KEY IDEAS

As you read this section, keep these questions in mind:

• What is a mineral?

• What are the two main groups of minerals?

• What are the six types of silicate crystal structures?

• What are three nonsilicate crystal structures?

What Is a Mineral?

A gold nugget, a grain of road salt, and a ruby may seem very different, but they have one thing in common: they are all minerals. A **mineral** has these properties:

• It forms naturally.

• It is not made by living things.

• It is solid.

• Its atoms and molecules are arranged in a pattern.

• It is made up of certain elements combined in specific ratios.

• It has specific physical properties.

All minerals form naturally. In other words, people do not make them. Therefore, steel is not a mineral, because people make it. ☑

Organic matter is matter that is found in living things, or that is made by living things. *Inorganic matter* is matter that is not made by living things. All minerals are inorganic. For example, coal is not a mineral, because it forms from the remains of plants.

The atoms and molecules in a solid mineral are arranged in a pattern. This arrangement causes the mineral to form crystals. A **crystal** is a solid with a regular arrangement of atoms or molecules. Crystals generally have geometric shapes, such as cubes.

Every sample of a mineral is made up of the same elements. For example, every sample of the mineral quartz is made up mainly of the elements silicon and oxygen. Those elements are combined in a ratio of 1:2 (SiO_2). Scientists describe this property of minerals by saying that minerals have a *consistent chemical composition*.

READING TOOLBOX

Make Connections As you read, make flash cards for the highlighted terms in this section. Add any other terms you think are important. After you read, work with a partner to practice using each term correctly in a sentence.

✓ READING CHECK

1. Explain Why is steel not a mineral?

_____

_____

Critical Thinking

2. Apply Concepts Glass is made up of silicon and oxygen atoms in a 1:2 ratio. The SiO_2 molecules in glass are arranged in a random way. Is glass a mineral? Explain your answer.

_____

_____

_____

Talk About It

What Are the Two Main Kinds of Minerals?

There are thousands of different minerals. However, only about 20 minerals are common on Earth. These 20 common minerals are called *rock-forming minerals* because they make up most rocks on Earth.

Scientists divide minerals into two main groups based on their chemical compositions. The two groups are silicate minerals and nonsilicate minerals.

SILICATE MINERALS

Most minerals on Earth are silicate minerals. A **silicate mineral** contains combinations of silicon (Si) and oxygen (O) atoms. Quartz, feldspars, micas, and olivine are examples of silicate minerals. ☑

Quartz is made up of silicon and oxygen. All other silicate minerals also contain other elements. For example, feldspars contain sodium, calcium, or potassium in addition to silicon and oxygen. Olivine contains magnesium, iron, silicon, and oxygen.

☑ **READING CHECK**

3. List What two elements do all silicate minerals contain?

_____

_____

NONSILICATE MINERALS

Only about 4% of Earth's crust is made of nonsilicate minerals. A **nonsilicate mineral** does not contain combinations of silicon and oxygen. It may contain silicon or oxygen, but they are not bonded together.

There are six main groups of nonsilicate minerals. The table below describes these six groups.

LOOKING CLOSER

4. Compare Which element is found in all sulfate minerals, but not in sulfide minerals?

_____

_____

Type of Nonsilicate Mineral	Description	Examples
Carbonates	contain a carbonate group (CO_3)	dolomite, $CaMg(CO_3)_2$; calcite, $CaCO_3$
Halides	contain chlorine or fluorine combined with sodium, potassium, or calcium	fluorite, CaF_2; halite, NaCl
Native elements	made of atoms of a single element	silver, Ag; copper, Cu
Oxides	contain oxygen and an element other than silicon	corundum, Al_2O_3; hematite, Fe_2O_3
Sulfates	contain a sulfate group (SO_4)	anhydrite, $CaSO_4$
Sulfides	contain sulfur combined with another element (a metal)	galena, PbS; pyrite, FeS_2

What Types of Crystals Do Minerals Form?

The atoms and molecules in different minerals are arranged in different patterns. The arrangement of the atoms and molecules affects the shape of the crystals the mineral forms.

One way scientists identify minerals is by studying their crystal shapes. The atoms and molecules in a mineral are always arranged the same way. Therefore, a mineral always forms the same crystal shape. ☑

CRYSTALLINE STRUCTURE OF SILICATE MINERALS

There are many different kinds of silicate minerals. They form many different kinds of crystals. However, the crystals of all silicate minerals have similar building blocks.

The building blocks of silicate minerals are made of atoms of silicon and oxygen. Each building block contains one silicon atom and four oxygen atoms. The oxygen atoms form a pyramid. The silicon atom is in the center of the pyramid. This structure is called a **silicon-oxygen tetrahedron**.

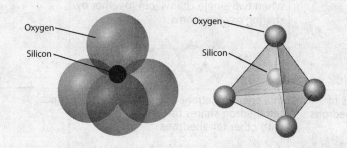

Oxygen
Silicon
Oxygen
Silicon

These drawings show two different models of a silicon-oxygen tetrahedron.

Silicon-oxygen tetrahedrons are arranged in different ways in different silicate minerals. There are two factors that affect how the tetrahedrons are arranged. First, the tetrahedrons may form bonds with atoms of other elements, such as potassium or magnesium. Those bonds change the way the tetrahedrons are arranged.

Second, the tetrahedrons may share oxygen atoms. When tetrahedrons share oxygen atoms, they can form chains, rings, and networks, or webs. The table on the next page shows how tetrahedrons can share atoms.

READING CHECK

5. Explain Why does a mineral always form crystals with the same shape?

_____

_____

_____

_____

_____

Talk About It

Make Connections Use a dictionary to look up the meaning of the word *tetrahedron*. With a partner, discuss why the building blocks of silicate minerals are called *silicon-oxygen tetrahedrons*.

SECTION 1 **What Is a Mineral?** *continued*

Arrangement of Silicon-Oxygen Tetrahedrons	Description	Examples
Isolated tetrahedrons	The tetrahedrons in these minerals are not linked to other silicon or oxygen atoms. They may be linked to atoms of other elements. Silicon-oxygen tetrahedron	olivine
Rings of tetrahedrons	The tetrahedrons in these minerals share oxygen atoms. They form rings with three, four, or six sides. Atoms of other elements can also bond to the rings.	beryl, tourmaline
Single chain of tetrahedrons	The tetrahedrons in these minerals share oxygen atoms to form long chains. Each tetrahedron shares two oxygen atoms with other tetrahedrons.	pyroxene
Double chain of tetrahedrons	These minerals have double chains of tetrahedrons. The double chains form when two single chains join together by sharing oxygen atoms.	amphibole
Sheets of tetrahedrons	In a sheet of tetrahedrons, each tetrahedron shares three oxygen atoms with other tetrahedrons.	mica
Framework of tetrahedrons	Every tetrahedron in these minerals shares four oxygen atoms with other tetrahedrons. The tetrahedrons form a framework, or web.	quartz

LOOKING CLOSER

6. Identify How are the silicon-oxygen tetrahedrons in beryl arranged?

_____

_____

7. Apply Concepts How many oxygen atoms does each silicon-oxygen tetrahedron in pyroxene share?

_____

_____

8. Compare Which mineral listed in the table contains silicon-oxygen tetrahedrons that share the most oxygen atoms with other tetrahedrons?

_____

_____

SECTION 1 **What Is a Mineral?** *continued*

GROUPS OF SILICATE MINERALS

There are six main groups of silicate minerals. The minerals in each group have the same arrangement of silicon-oxygen tetrahedrons. The names of the groups are related to the arrangement of the tetrahedrons.

Name of Group	Arrangement of Tetrahedrons
Single-tetrahedron silicates	isolated tetrahedrons
Ring silicates	rings of tetrahedrons
Single-chain silicates	single chains of tetrahedrons
Double-chain silicates	double chains of tetrahedrons
Sheet silicates	sheets of tetrahedrons
Framework silicates	frameworks of tetrahedrons

LOOKING CLOSER
9. List What are the six main groups of silicate minerals?

_____

_____

_____

_____

_____

_____

CRYSTAL STRUCTURES OF NONSILICATE MINERALS

Remember that there are many different kinds of nonsilicate minerals. Each nonsilicate mineral contains different atoms and molecules. The atoms and molecules in nonsilicate minerals can be arranged in many different ways. Therefore, nonsilicate minerals can have a variety of crystal shapes. The three most common crystal structures for nonsilicate minerals are cubes, hexagonal (six-sided) prisms, and irregular shapes.

Some nonsilicate minerals have similar arrangements of atoms and molecules. These minerals also have similar crystal structures. For example, many halide and sulfide minerals form cubes, because their atoms and molecules are arranged in similar ways.

LOOKING CLOSER
10. Explain Why do galena and halite form crystals with similar shapes?

_____

_____

_____

Galena, a sulfide mineral

Halite, a halide mineral

Halite and galena both form cubic crystals. They form crystals with similar shapes because the atoms in the minerals are arranged in a similar way.

The arrangement of atoms and molecules in a crystal affects the mineral's properties. For example, many native elements are very dense. They are dense because the atoms in them are packed very close together.

Section 1 Review

SECTION VOCABULARY

crystal a solid whose atoms, ions, or molecules are arranged in a regular, repeating pattern	**silicate mineral** a mineral that contains a combination of silicon and oxygen and that may also contain one or more metals
mineral a natural, usually inorganic solid that has a characteristic chemical composition, an orderly internal structure, and a characteristic set of physical properties	**silicon-oxygen tetrahedron** the basic unit of the structure of silicate minerals; a silicon ion chemically bonded to and surrounded by four oxygen ions
nonsilicate mineral a mineral that does not contain compounds of silicon and oxygen	

1. **Compare** What is the difference between silicate minerals and nonsilicate minerals?

_____

_____

2. **Identify** What are the three most common nonsilicate crystal structures?

_____

3. **Apply Concepts** Give one example of a mineral. Describe at least three characteristics that show that it is a mineral.

_____

_____

4. **Infer** An Earth scientist discovers a new mineral. The mineral is made up of gold and sulfur atoms bonded together. Which group of nonsilicate mineral does this mineral belong in?

_____

5. **Compare** Quartz is a framework silicate. Pyroxene is a single-chain silicate. Describe how these two minerals are different and how they are similar.

_____

_____

_____

6. **Explain** Corundum (Al_2O_3) and hematite (Fe_2O_3) both contain oxygen, but they are not considered to be silicate minerals. Why is this?

_____

_____

Name ______________________ Class ______________ Date ______________

CHAPTER 5 Minerals of Earth's Crust

SECTION 2

Identifying Minerals

KEY IDEAS

As you read this section, keep these questions in mind:

- What are seven physical properties scientists use to identify minerals?
- What are five special properties some minerals have?

How Do Scientists Identify Minerals?

Earth scientists who study minerals are called **mineralogists**. Mineralogists identify and classify minerals. The main way a mineralogist identifies a mineral is by studying its properties. The seven main physical properties that mineralogists can use to identify minerals are shown below.

Property	Description
Color	what color the mineral has in white light
Streak	the color of a mineral when it is a powder
Luster	how the mineral reflects light
Cleavage and fracture	how the mineral breaks
Hardness	how difficult it is to scratch the mineral
Crystal shape	what kind of crystal the mineral forms
Density	the mass of a given volume of a mineral

READING TOOLBOX

Summarize As you read this section, make two-column notes to summarize the mineral properties described in the section. Write the name of the property in the first column. Write a description of the property in the second column. If you wish, use drawings to help you remember the different properties.

COLOR

A mineral's color is one of the easiest properties to observe. However, the color of a mineral sample is generally not enough to identify the mineral. Different minerals can have the same color. For example, many different minerals are clear or white. In addition, different samples of the same mineral can have different colors. For example, quartz can be clear, purple, pink, or even black. ☑

READING CHECK

1. Explain Why is color usually not enough to identify a mineral?

____

____

____

____

STREAK

If you grind a mineral into a fine powder, its color may seem to change. The color of a mineral in powdered form is known as the mineral's **streak**. You can see the color of a mineral's streak by rubbing the mineral against a tool called a *streak plate*. No matter what color they are, all samples of a given mineral have the same streak.

SECTION 2 **Identifying Minerals** *continued*

Talk About It

Research Use the Internet or library to find pictures of minerals with different lusters. Describe the luster of each mineral in your own words. Share your descriptions with a partner.

READING CHECK

2. Describe What do minerals with a metallic luster look like?

_____

_____

Critical Thinking

3. Explain Why do people who cut minerals for jewelry need to know about a mineral's cleavage or fracture?

_____

_____

_____

_____

_____

_____

_____

_____

LUSTER

Some minerals, such as pyrite, look shiny when light shines on them. Others, such as talc, look dull. These minerals look different because they reflect light differently. The way a mineral reflects light is called its **luster**.

Some minerals look like polished metal. These minerals have a *metallic luster*. Galena, gold, and pyrite are examples of minerals with a metallic luster. Minerals that do not look like polished metal have a *nonmetallic luster*. Talc, quartz, and calcite are examples of minerals with a nonmetallic luster. ☑

Minerals with a nonmetallic luster may look greasy, like talc does. They may look bright and glassy, like quartz does. They may look pearly, like mica does. They may even look dull, as if they do not reflect light at all.

CLEAVAGE AND FRACTURE

If you hit a diamond in the right way, it will break along a smooth, flat surface. People who cut minerals to make jewelry must know how different minerals break. Minerals such as diamond that break along smooth, flat surfaces show the property of **cleavage**. Mica is another example of a mineral that shows cleavage. Mica breaks easily into thin, flat sheets.

Some minerals, such as quartz, do not break along flat surfaces. Instead, they break unevenly. A mineral that breaks unevenly shows the property of **fracture**.

Minerals that show fracture may form different shapes when they break. If the mineral breaks to form a rough surface, it has an *uneven* or *irregular* fracture. If the mineral looks like broken wood, it has a *splintery* or *fibrous* fracture. If the mineral forms a curved surface, it has a *conchoidal* fracture.

Quartz shows conchoidal fracture. It breaks along a curved surface.

SECTION 2 **Identifying Minerals** *continued*

HARDNESS AND THE MOHS SCALE

You may have heard that diamonds are the hardest substance on Earth. This does not mean that diamonds are hard to break. When mineralogists talk about a mineral's *hardness*, they are talking about how difficult it is to scratch the mineral. Diamonds are the hardest minerals because no other mineral can scratch them. ☑

Mineralogists use a scale called the **Mohs hardness scale** to describe the hardness of a mineral. The Mohs scale is a list of 10 minerals. Each mineral is harder than the minerals below it on the scale. Therefore, each mineral will scratch all the minerals below it on the scale.

You can use the Mohs scale to find the hardness of a mineral not on the scale. To do this, scratch the unknown mineral with each of the minerals on the scale. The mineral's hardness is higher than the hardest mineral it will scratch. It is lower than the softest mineral it will not scratch.

For example, galena will scratch gypsum, but it will not scratch calcite. Gypsum's hardness is 2. Calcite's hardness is 3. Therefore, galena's hardness is between 2 and 3.

The table below shows the Mohs hardness scale. It also describes some common tests you can do to identify the hardness of a mineral.

Mineral	Hardness	Common Test
Talc	1	easily scratched by a fingernail
Gypsum	2	can barely be scratched by a fingernail
Calcite	3	can barely be scratched by a copper penny
Fluorite	4	easily scratched by glass or steel
Apatite	5	can barely be scratched by glass or steel
Feldspar	6	scratches glass, but does not scratch steel
Quartz	7	easily scratches glass and steel
Topaz	8	scratches quartz
Corundum	9	scratches topaz
Diamond	10	scratches everything

CRYSTAL SHAPE

Remember that a mineral always forms crystals of the same shape. There are six main crystal *systems*, or shapes. The table on the next page shows the crystal systems.

READING CHECK

4. Define What do mineralogists mean when they talk about the hardness of a mineral?

_____

_____

LOOKING CLOSER
5. Apply Concepts A particular mineral will scratch apatite, but not feldspar. What is the hardness of the mineral?

_____

SECTION 2 **Identifying Minerals** *continued*

Talk About It

Make Connections Use a dictionary to look up the meaning of the prefix *iso-*. With a partner, discuss why cubic crystals are sometimes also called isometric crystals.

Crystal System	Description
Isometric (also called cubic)	The crystals have three axes. All three axes are the same length. They form 90° angles where they meet. 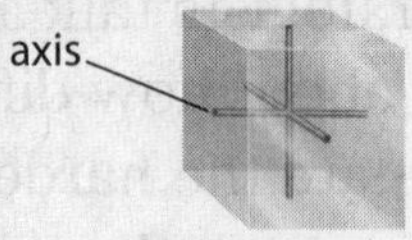
Orthorhombic	The crystals have three axes. All the axes are different lengths. They form 90° angles where they meet. 
Tetragonal	The crystals have three axes. Two of the axes are the same length. The third axis is longer or shorter than the other two. The axes form 90° angles where they meet. 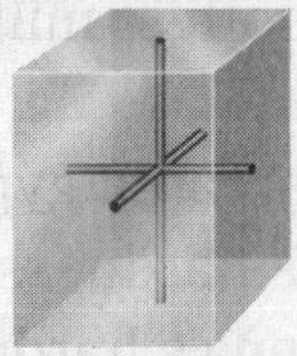
Hexagonal	The crystals have four axes. Three of the axes are the same length. They form 120° angles where they meet. The fourth axis is longer or shorter than the other three. 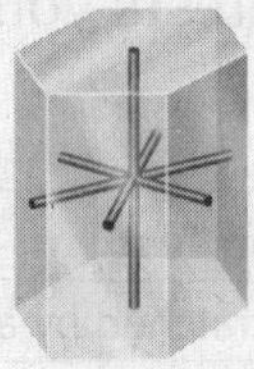
Monoclinic	The crystals have three axes. All three are different lengths. Two of the axes form 90° angles where they meet. 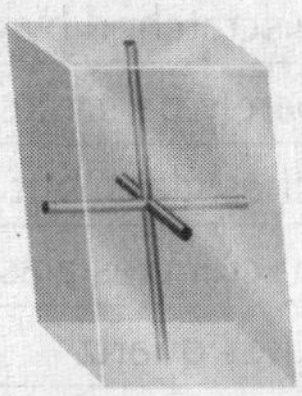
Triclinic	The crystals have three axes. All three are different lengths. None of the axes form 90° angles where they meet. 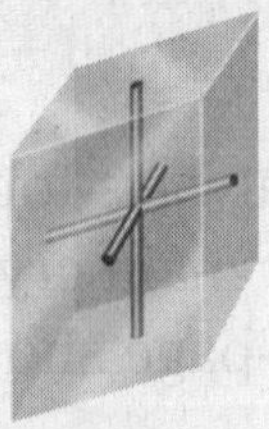

LOOKING CLOSER

6. Compare What is the main difference between cubic crystals and orthorhombic crystals?

_____

_____

_____

7. Compare What is the main difference between monoclinic crystals and triclinic crystals?

_____

_____

_____

_____

DENSITY

A mineral's **density** is the ratio of the mineral's mass to its volume. You can calculate density using the formula below. The most common units of density are grams per cubic centimeter (g/cm³). Water has a density of about 1 g/cm³.

$$\text{density} = \frac{\text{mass}}{\text{volume}}, \text{ or } D = \frac{m}{V}$$

The density of a specific mineral is always the same. Most minerals on Earth have densities between 2 g/cm³ and 3 g/cm³. Minerals that contain heavy metals, such as lead or gold, may have much higher densities.

What Other Properties Can Minerals Have?

Some minerals have special properties. Mineralogists can use these properties to identify the minerals more easily. The table below describes five examples of special properties.

Property	Description
Fluorescence or phosphorescence	Minerals that glow under ultraviolet light have the property of *fluorescence.* Some samples of calcite show the property of fluorescence. If a mineral keeps glowing after the light is shut off, it has the property of *phosphorescence.*
Chatoyancy or asterism	Some minerals look silky when light reflects off of them. These minerals have the property of *chatoyancy.* Asterism is a similar property. When light shines on a mineral with *asterism,* a six-sided star shape appears on the mineral.
Double refraction	When light passes through some minerals, it is split into two rays. If you look at a picture or line through one of these minerals, it will seem to be doubled. This property is called *double refraction.* Calcite is an example of a mineral that shows double refraction.
Magnetism	Some minerals will stick to magnets. Other minerals can act like magnets. These minerals have the property of *magnetism.* Lodestone is an example of a magnetic mineral.
Radioactivity	The atoms of some elements, such as uranium, are unstable. Over time, they break down into atoms of other elements. When they break down, they give off energy, such as X rays. Minerals that contain these elements also give off radiation. A mineral that gives off radiation has the property of *radioactivity.* Pitchblende is an example of a mineral that shows radioactivity.

Math *Skills*

8. Calculate A mineral sample has a mass (*m*) of 85 g and a volume (*V*) of 34 cm³. What is its density?

_____

_____

_____

_____

Talk About It

Discuss Talk with a partner about other words you have heard that include the root *aster.* Make a prediction of what you think that root means. Use a dictionary to test your prediction.

LOOKING CLOSER

9. Compare How is fluorescence different from phosphorescence?

_____

_____

_____

_____

Section 2 Review

SECTION VOCABULARY

cleavage the tendency of a mineral to split along specific planes of weakness to form smooth, flat surfaces	**fracture** the manner in which a mineral breaks along either curved or irregular surfaces
density the ratio of the mass of a substance to the volume of the substance; commonly expressed as grams per cubic centimeter for solids and liquids and as grams per liter for gases	**luster** the way in which a mineral reflects light
	mineralogist a person who examines, analyzes, and classifies minerals
	Mohs hardness scale the standard scale against which the hardness of minerals is rated
	streak the color of a mineral in powdered form

1. Compare Complete the Venn diagram below to compare cleavage and fracture.

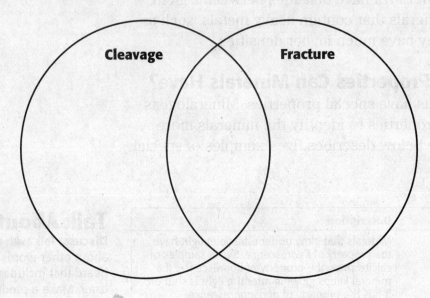

2. Apply Concepts Gold has a hardness between 2 and 3. Describe what would happen if you scratched a piece of gold with a piece of talc, a piece of calcite, and a piece of quartz.

_____

_____

3. Explain Why is streak generally a more useful property than color in identifying a mineral?

_____

_____

4. Infer A scientist places a sample of a mineral on top of a drawing. When he looks through the mineral at the drawing, each line in the drawing is doubled. What property does the mineral show?

_____

CHAPTER 6 | Rocks

SECTION 1 | Rocks and the Rock Cycle

KEY IDEAS

As you read this section, keep these questions in mind:

• What are the three main kinds of rock, and how does each kind form?

• What are the main steps in the rock cycle?

• What is Bowen's reaction series?

• What determines how stable a rock is on Earth's surface?

What Are the Three Main Kinds of Rock?

Rock is the material that makes up the solid parts of Earth. Most rocks are made up of one or more minerals. Some rocks are made up of organic matter. A few kinds of rock are made up of inorganic matter that is not a mineral, such as glass.

Geologists classify, or group, rocks based on how they form. There are three main types of rock: igneous rock, sedimentary rock, and metamorphic rock. The table below describes how each kind of rock forms. ☑

Kind of Rock	How It Forms	Examples
Igneous	Igneous rock forms when melted rock cools and hardens.	granite, obsidian, basalt
Sedimentary	Sedimentary rock forms when pieces of rocks and organic matter are buried and pressed together.	sandstone, shale, limestone
Metamorphic	Metamorphic rock forms when heat and pressure change the chemical composition of a rock without melting it.	gneiss, slate, quartzite

What Is the Rock Cycle?

Rocks can change from one form to another. For example, wind and water can break rocks into pieces called *sediment*. The sediment can be carried away and laid down at the bottom of a lake. Over time, the sediment can be buried and compressed. It can become sedimentary rock. A sedimentary rock can be buried and heated until it melts. When the melted rock cools, an igneous rock forms.

The processes that change rock from one form to another make up the **rock cycle**.

READING TOOLBOX

Clarify As you read this section, underline words or phrases you do not understand. Work with a partner to figure out what they mean. Then, write a short summary of the section in your own words.

☑ READING CHECK

1. List What are the three main kinds of rock?

_____

_____

_____

Critical Thinking

2. Apply Concepts Suppose a sedimentary rock was broken down into sediment. The sediment was laid down at the bottom of a river. Over time, the sediment was buried and pressed together. What type of rock would the sedimentary rock become?

_____

_____

SECTION 1 **Rocks and the Rock Cycle** *continued*

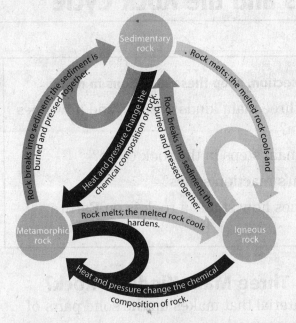

Several different processes are part of the rock cycle.

LOOKING CLOSER

3. Draw On the figure, draw three paths through the rock cycle that lead from one of the rock types to metamorphic rock. If you wish, you may draw each path in a different color.

What Happens When Melted Rock Cools?

Igneous rocks form when melted rock cools and hardens. Melted rock below Earth's surface is called *magma*. Magma that rises to Earth's surface is called *lava*.

When rock melts to form magma, the minerals in the rock melt. The different elements in the minerals mix together. As the magma cools, the elements can come together to form new minerals.

Different minerals form at different temperatures. As each mineral forms, it removes elements from the magma. As the magma cools, different minerals form because different elements are available. ☑

In the early 1900s, a Canadian geologist named N. L. Bowen was studying how minerals form from cooling magma. He showed that minerals tend to form in a certain order as magma cools. Some minerals, such as olivine, form early. Other minerals, such as quartz, form later in the process. The order in which minerals form from cooling magma is called **Bowen's reaction series**.

Bowen's reaction series shows that minerals can form in one of two main ways. In the first way, the composition of the minerals changes slowly over time. Many feldspars form this way. In the second way, the kind of mineral that forms changes suddenly over time. Olivine, pyroxene, and amphibole generally form this way.

READING CHECK

4. Explain Why do different minerals form as magma cools?

_____

_____

_____

SECTION 1 **Rocks and the Rock Cycle** *continued*

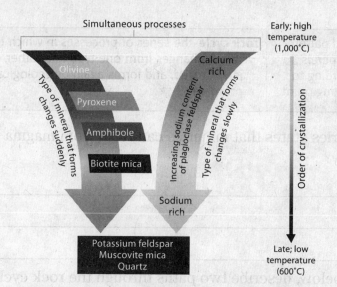

LOOKING CLOSER
5. Identify Name two minerals that form at high temperatures.

_____

_____

What Affects How Strong Rocks Are?

Some rocks, such as granite, are very strong. They do not break down very easily. Other rocks, such as limestone and sandstone, are softer. They break down quickly. How quickly a rock breaks down depends on two things: the minerals in the rock and the structure of the rock.

Some minerals are very stable on Earth's surface. In other words, they do not break down very easily. They do not react with water or air to form softer substances. Rocks that are made up mainly of such minerals tend to be hard. Most stable minerals, such as quartz, form at low temperatures. They are some of the last minerals to form in Bowen's reaction series. ☑

Other minerals are not very stable. They react easily with water or air. Rocks that are made up mainly of such minerals tend to be soft and break down easily. Most unstable minerals, such as olivine, form at high temperatures. They are some of the first minerals to form in Bowen's reaction series.

The structure of a rock also affects how easily it breaks down. Rocks that have cracks or layers are generally soft. The rock is weakest along the cracks or between the layers. It can easily break in those areas.

✔ **READING CHECK**

6. Describe Which of the minerals in Bowen's reaction series tend to be most stable on Earth's surface?

_____

_____

Section 1 Review

SECTION VOCABULARY

Bowen's reaction series the simplified pattern that illustrates the order in which minerals crystallize from cooling magma according to their chemical composition and melting point	**rock cycle** the series of processes in which rock forms, changes from one type to another, is destroyed, and forms again by geological processes

1. **Describe** Bowen's reaction series states that minerals can form from magma in two main ways. What are they?

   _____

   _____

   _____

2. **Apply Concepts** In the space below, describe two paths through the rock cycle that an igneous rock could follow to become a metamorphic rock. Your answer can be a labeled diagram or a written description.

3. **Compare** How is the way an igneous rock forms different from the way a metamorphic rock forms?

   _____

   _____

4. **Infer** Granite is an igneous rock made up of large crystals of quartz, feldspar, and mica. Basalt is an igneous rock made up of large crystals of olivine, pyroxene, and amphibole. Basalt often forms in a way that produces large cracks in the rock. Which of these rocks is probably most stable at Earth's surface? Explain your answer.

   _____

   _____

   _____

   _____

   _____

CHAPTER 6 | Rocks

SECTION 2 | Igneous Rock

KEY IDEAS

As you read this section, keep these questions in mind:

- What three factors affect whether rock melts?
- How does the cooling rate of magma or lava affect the texture of igneous rocks?
- What are the possible textures and compositions of igneous rock?
- What structures can igneous rock form?

How Does Magma Form?

Remember that **igneous rock** forms when melted rock (magma or lava) cools and hardens. Magma forms when rock is heated. The heat makes the minerals in the rock melt. However, not all rocks melt at the same temperature. There are three main factors that affect whether a rock will melt at a certain temperature. Those factors are

- the chemical composition of the rock
- the pressure on the rock
- whether there are any fluids in the rock ☑

Imagine mixing sugar crystals and ice together in a pan on a hot stove. The ice would melt at a much lower temperature than the sugar would. Just as ice and sugar melt at different temperatures, different minerals melt at different temperatures. The chemical composition of a mineral affects the temperature at which it melts. Therefore, the minerals that make up a rock affect how hot the rock has to become before it will melt.

The pressure on a rock also affects whether it will melt. In general, the lower the pressure on a rock is, the lower the temperature the rock will melt at. Therefore, lowering the pressure on a hot rock can make it melt. ☑

A third factor that affects whether a rock melts is whether there are any fluids in the rock. Fluids cause a rock to melt at a lower temperature. Therefore, adding fluid to a rock can make the rock melt. Also, rocks that contain fluids tend to melt at lower temperatures than rocks that do not contain fluids.

READING TOOLBOX

Identify Main Ideas As you read this section, underline the main idea in each paragraph. When you finish reading, write a summary of the section using the underlined ideas.

✓ READING CHECK

1. List What are the three factors that affect whether a rock will melt at a certain temperature?

_____

_____

_____

✓ READING CHECK

2. Describe What may happen to a hot rock if the pressure on it decreases?

_____

_____

SECTION 2 **Igneous Rock** *continued*

PARTIAL MELTING

Different minerals melt at different temperatures. As the rock heats up, the minerals with the lowest melting temperatures will melt first. The higher the temperature becomes, the more minerals will melt. As each mineral in the rock melts, the elements in it enter the magma. As a result, the composition of the magma changes. The process in which different minerals in a rock melt at different temperatures is called *partial melting*.

LOOKING CLOSER

3. Explain What causes the composition of the magma to change?

_____

_____

_____

Mineral   **Magma**

A solid rock is made up of several different minerals. In this picture, each mineral is a different color.

When the rock begins to heat up, some of the minerals melt.

As the temperature rises, more minerals melt. As the minerals melt, the composition of the magma changes.

FRACTIONAL CRYSTALLIZATION

Remember that Bowen's reaction series describes the order in which minerals form from magma. As magma cools, different minerals crystallize. The minerals that were the last to melt generally crystallize first. The minerals that melted first crystallize last. The formation of different minerals as magma cools is called *fractional crystallization*.

When magma cools, it does not always form the same minerals that originally melted to form the magma. The elements in the magma can combine in new ways to form new minerals.

Critical Thinking

4. Infer A scientist is studying the rock that formed when a magma chamber cooled completely. Where in the rock will the scientist probably find minerals that form early in Bowen's reaction series?

_____

_____

_____

Most magma is found underground in large holes called *magma chambers*. The crystals that form at the beginning of fractional crystallization can sink to the bottom of the magma chamber. They can also stick to the sides or top of the magma chamber.

Crystals take time to grow. The slower the magma in the chamber cools, the larger the crystals that grow from it are. Because the composition of the magma changes as it cools, the composition of the crystal might change as it grows. A crystal that forms this way will have a different composition on its outside than on its inside.

What Affects the Texture of an Igneous Rock?

Many igneous rocks contain mineral crystals. The *texture* of an igneous rock is a description of the size of the crystals in it. The main factor that affects the texture of an igneous rock is how quickly it forms. ☑

Remember that melted rock below Earth's surface is called *magma*, and melted rock above Earth's surface is called *lava*. Igneous rock can form from either magma or lava. If an igneous rock forms from magma, which cools underground, it is an **intrusive igneous rock**. If an igneous rock forms from lava, which cools on Earth's surface, it is an **extrusive igneous rock**.

Intrusive and extrusive igneous rocks generally look very different. Because magma cools slowly, large crystals can form. Therefore, intrusive igneous rocks generally contain large mineral crystals. Igneous rocks that contain large crystals have a *coarse-grained texture*. Granite and gabbro are examples of coarse-grained igneous rocks. ☑

In contrast, lava generally cools very quickly. Only small crystals can form. Therefore, extrusive igneous rocks generally contain only very small mineral crystals. Igneous rocks that contain small crystals have a *fine-grained texture*. Rhyolite and basalt are examples of fine-grained igneous rocks.

Extrusive igneous rocks may also have porphyritic, glassy, or vesicular textures. The table below describes each of these kinds of textures.

Texture	Description	How It Forms	Example
Porphyritic	some large mineral crystals mixed with many small crystals	Magma begins to cool slowly, and some large crystals form. The magma erupts and finishes cooling quickly, producing small crystals.	some kinds of granite and basalt
Glassy	looks like glass; contains no crystals	Lava cools so quickly that crystals cannot form.	obsidian
Vesicular	fine-grained or glassy rock with tiny holes in it	Gas in lava bubbles out as it cools, like the bubbles in a soda. As the lava hardens, the bubbles are frozen in place.	pumice

READING CHECK

5. **Identify** What is the main factor that affects the texture of an igneous rock?

_____

_____

READING CHECK

6. **Explain** Why do intrusive igneous rocks generally contain large mineral crystals?

_____

_____

_____

Critical Thinking

7. **Apply Concepts** Do the minerals that form the large crystals in porphyritic rocks probably form at high temperatures or low temperatures?

_____

What Compositions Can Igneous Rock Have?

Different igneous rocks contain different minerals. The chemical composition of the magma or lava affects the minerals that form. Scientists have defined three main groups of igneous rock compositions: felsic, mafic, and intermediate. ☑

The main difference between the three types of rock is the amount of silica they contain. *Silica* refers to the ratio of silicon-oxygen tetrahedrons to other elements in a mineral. Minerals that are high in silica have large ratios of silicon-oxygen tetrahedrons to other elements. Minerals that are low in silica have low ratios of silicon-oxygen tetrahedrons to other elements.

Felsic igneous rocks contain large amounts of silica. **Mafic** igneous rocks contain smaller amounts of silica. They also contain large amounts of iron and magnesium. Intermediate igneous rocks contain less silica than felsic rocks, but more silica than mafic rocks. The table below summarizes the three main igneous rock compositions.

✓ **READING CHECK**

8. Identify What are the three groups of igneous rock compositions?

_____

_____

_____

Talk About It

Make Connections With a partner, discuss the meaning of the word *intermediate*. If you wish, look it up in a dictionary. Together, talk about why some igneous rocks are said to have an intermediate composition.

Composition	Description	Common Minerals	Examples
Felsic	high in silica; generally light-colored	quartz, some kinds of feldspar and mica	granite, rhyolite, obsidian, pumice
Mafic	low in silica; high in iron and magnesium; generally dark-colored	olivine, some kinds of feldspar, amphibole	basalt, gabbro
Intermediate	higher in silica than mafic rocks; lower in silica than felsic rocks; may be light-colored or dark-colored	some kinds of feldspar and mica, pyroxene, amphibole	andesite, diorite

LOOKING CLOSER

9. Compare Which type of rock has the largest amount of silica: diorite, gabbro, or granite?

_____

_____

What Structures Can Intrusive Rock Form?

Remember that intrusive igneous rocks form when magma cools underground. Magma can move through cracks and gaps in rock underground. Therefore, intrusive igneous rocks can be found in many different places. A body of intrusive igneous rock is called an *intrusion*. Batholiths, stocks, laccoliths, sills, dikes, and volcanic necks are examples of intrusions.

SECTION 2 **Igneous Rock** *continued*

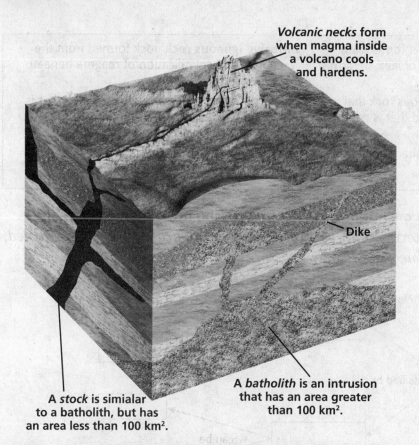

Volcanic necks form when magma inside a volcano cools and hardens.

Dike

A *stock* is simialar to a batholith, but has an area less than 100 km².

A *batholith* is an intrusion that has an area greater than 100 km².

Use Logic The word root *lith* comes from a Greek word that means "rock." With a partner, discuss the words you have learned so far that include the root *lith*. Talk about why that word root is appropriate for each of the words.

LOOKING CLOSER

10. Describe What is the main difference between a stock and a batholith?

_____

_____

What Structures Can Extrusive Rock Form?

A body of extrusive igneous rock is called an *extrusion*. The most common kind of extrusion is a *lava flow*. A lava flow forms when lava moves out of a volcano, cools, and hardens. The lava flow forms flat masses of rock. ☑

In some areas, a volcano has erupted many times. The lava flows have built up to form a *lava plateau*. A lava plateau is made up of many thick layers of extrusive igneous rock.

Some volcanoes do not give off large amounts of lava. Instead, they mainly give off volcanic ash and dust. The ash and dust can build up to form a type of rock called *tuff*. Because ash and dust are light, wind can carry them long distances. They can form thick layers of tuff that cover very large areas. These layers of tuff are called *tuff deposits*.

✓ **READING CHECK**

11. Describe How does a lava flow form?

_____

_____

_____

Section 2 Review

SECTION VOCABULARY

extrusive igneous rock rock that forms from the cooling and solidification of lava at Earth's surface	**intrusive igneous rock** rock formed from the cooling and solidification of magma beneath Earth's surface
felsic describes magma or igneous rock that is rich in feldspars and silica and that is generally light in color	**mafic** describes magma or igneous rock that is rich in magnesium and iron and that is generally dark in color
igneous rock rock that forms when magma cools and solidifies	

1. **Describe** Complete the concept map below to describe how scientists classify igneous rocks. Use the terms *composition, texture, fine grained, coarse grained, mafic, felsic,* and *intermediate.*

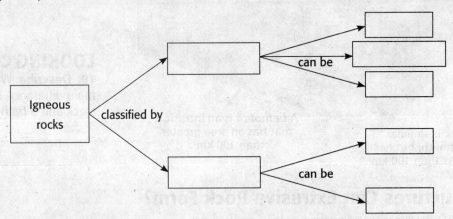

2. **Apply Concepts** Which will probably melt at the lower temperature, a rock that contains fluids and is under low pressure or a rock that does not contain fluids and is under high pressure? Explain your answer.

_____

_____

3. **Compare** Describe two differences between intrusive igneous rocks and extrusive igneous rocks.

_____

_____

4. **Infer** If there were a laccolith below the ground in an area, what might the area look like? Explain your answer.

_____

_____

_____

CHAPTER 6 | Rocks

SECTION 3

Sedimentary Rock

As you read this section, keep these questions in mind:

• How do compaction and cementation happen?

• How do chemical and organic sedimentary rocks form?

• How does clastic sedimentary rock form?

• What are seven features that sedimentary rock can have?

What Are Compaction and Cementation?

Recall that *sedimentary rock* is made up of fragments of other rocks, minerals, and organic matter. These fragments are called *sediment*. Most sedimentary rock forms when sediment is laid down, or deposited, by water, wind, or ice. Over time, two processes can change the sediment into sedimentary rock: compaction and cementation.

After a layer of sediment is laid down, more sediment may bury it. The weight of the top layers of sediment presses down on the bottom layers. The pressure squeezes water and air out of the spaces between the sediment particles. The particles get closer together. The sediment becomes smaller, or more compact. Therefore, this process is called **compaction**. ☑

Sometimes, water moves through sediment. The water may have minerals, such as calcite and quartz, dissolved in it. As the water moves through the sediment, those minerals may crystallize between the sediment particles. The minerals "glue," or *cement*, the sediment particles together. Therefore, this process is called **cementation**.

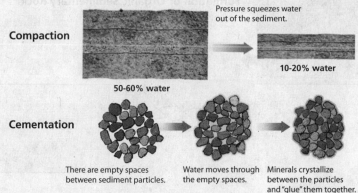

Compaction

Pressure squeezes water out of the sediment.

50-60% water

10-20% water

Cementation

There are empty spaces between sediment particles.

Water moves through the empty spaces.

Minerals crystallize between the particles and "glue" them together.

Summarize Cause and Effect As you read this section, mark examples of cause and effect or a chain of events. Then, make chain-of-events charts to summarize each example.

1. Describe What happens during compaction?

_____

_____

_____

LOOKING CLOSER

2. Compare How is compaction different from cementation?

_____

_____

_____

_____

SECTION 3 **Sedimentary Rock** *continued*

What Are the Different Kinds of Sedimentary Rock?

Scientists put sedimentary rocks into three different groups: chemical sedimentary rocks, organic sedimentary rocks, and clastic sedimentary rocks. The rocks in the different groups form in different ways.

CHEMICAL SEDIMENTARY ROCK

The water in natural water bodies, such as lakes and oceans, contains many dissolved minerals. As the water evaporates, the minerals are left behind. As the minerals crystallize, they form a type of sedimentary rock called **chemical sedimentary rock**. ☑

ORGANIC SEDIMENTARY ROCK

Remember that organic matter is matter that comes from living things. Some kinds of sedimentary rock are made from organic matter. These sedimentary rocks are called **organic sedimentary rocks**.

Coal is one example of an organic sedimentary rock. Coal forms from the remains of plants that live in swamps. When the plants die, their remains fall to the bottom of the swamp. Over time, they are buried. Pressure changes the plant remains into coal, which is made up mostly of the element carbon.

Some kinds of limestone are also organic sedimentary rocks. These kinds of limestone form from the shells of animals that live in the oceans. The animals use the compound calcium carbonate to make their shells. When the animals die, their shells sink to the bottom of the ocean. Over time, the shells are pressed together. They form the rock limestone.

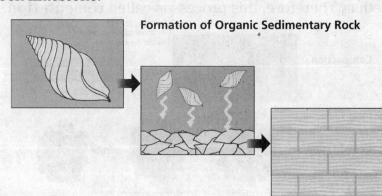

Formation of Organic Sedimentary Rock

READING CHECK

3. Explain What causes chemical sedimentary rocks to form?

_____

_____

Critical Thinking

4. Apply Concepts Some kinds of limestone form when calcium carbonate crystallizes from shallow ocean water. Are these limestones chemical sedimentary rocks or organic sedimentary rocks?

_____

Talk About It

Describe Discuss this figure with a partner. Take turns describing to each other what is happening in each part of the figure.

CLASTIC SEDIMENTARY ROCK

The most common kind of sedimentary rock is clastic sedimentary rock. **Clastic sedimentary rock** is made up of pieces of rocks that have been carried from their source and deposited. The rock pieces in a clastic sedimentary rock may be pieces of igneous, metamorphic, or other sedimentary rocks. ☑

Scientists classify clastic sedimentary rock based on the sizes of the rock pieces in the rock. If most of the rock pieces are more than 2 mm in diameter, the rock is a *conglomerate*. If the rock pieces have sharp angles, the rock is a *breccia*. If most of the rock pieces are the size of sand grains, the rock is a *sandstone*. If most of the rock pieces are very small, the rock is a *shale*.

No matter what size the particles in the rock are, all clastic sedimentary rocks form the same way. First, water, wind, or ice deposit the sediment in layers. As the layers build up, the sediment at the bottom is compacted. Over time, the sediment may be cemented together to form clastic sedimentary rock.

What Are Some Characteristics of Sediment?

The sediment in clastic sedimentary rocks can have different characteristics. The characteristics of the sediment can tell scientists about how the sediment formed and how it was laid down. Two important characteristics of sediment are sorting and angularity.

SORTING

Some sediment is made up of particles that are all about the same size. Other sediment contains particles of many different sizes. The range of particles sizes in a sediment determines how well sorted the sediment is.

READING CHECK

5. Identify Where do the sediments that form clastic sedimentary rock come from?

_____

_____

Math Skills

6. Calculate The rate at which sediment collects, or accumulates, is called the *sedimentation rate*. Suppose the sedimentation rate for an area is 1.5 mm per year. How many years will it take for 10 cm of sediment to accumulate?

_____

_____

LOOKING CLOSER

7. Compare What is the main difference between well-sorted sediment and poorly sorted sediment?

_____

_____

_____

_____

| Very well sorted | Well sorted | Moderately sorted | Poorly sorted | Very poorly sorted |

SECTION 3 **Sedimentary Rock** *continued*

WHAT SORTING INDICATES

Water and wind can carry sediment over long distances. However, the speed of the water or wind affects the size of the sediment they can carry. Fast-moving water can carry very large sediment pieces. Slow-moving water can carry only small sediment pieces.

When fast-moving water slows suddenly, it may drop a lot of sediment all at once. The sediment pieces it drops will have a range of sizes. In other words, water that slows suddenly can drop poorly sorted sediment. ☑

However, if the water slows gradually, it will drop the sediment over a larger distance. In other words, water that slows gradually can drop well-sorted sediment. Therefore, the sorting in a sediment can tell a scientist how the sediment was deposited.

ANGULARITY

Some sediment pieces are smooth and rounded. Others are rough and have sharp angles. A sediment's *angularity* describes how smooth or rough the sediment particles are.

As wind or water carry sediment over Earth's surface, the sediment particles hit one another. They may also hit other objects, such as larger rocks. When the particles hit other objects, they can break apart. They may also become worn down and smooth. The longer the particle is carried along, the smoother and rounder it becomes. Therefore, the angularity of a sediment can tell a scientist how far the sediment has traveled. ☑

What Structures Can Sedimentary Rock Form?

The areas where sediment is laid down are called *depositional environments*. Beaches, lakes, deltas, and oceans are examples of depositional environments. Sediment laid down in different depositional environments will form different features. Those features include

- stratification
- cross-beds and graded beds
- ripple marks
- mud cracks
- fossils and concretions

READING CHECK

8. Identify What type of water can drop poorly sorted sediment?

_____

_____

READING CHECK

9. Explain What causes a sediment particle to become smoother and rounder over time?

_____

_____

SECTION 3 **Sedimentary Rock** *continued*

STRATIFICATION

Most sediment is laid down in layers. Sedimentary rock that forms from layers of sediment generally also has layers. Layering in sedimentary rock is called *stratification*. ☑

CROSS-BEDS AND GRADED BEDS

The layers in a sedimentary rock are called *beds*. Most beds are parallel to one another. However, in some rocks, the beds form angles with one another. Beds that are at different angles are called *cross-beds*.

This photo shows sedimentary rock with cross-beds.

Most beds are made up of sediment particles that are all about the same size. However, some beds contain particles of different sizes. The particles in the bed are sorted from top to bottom. A bed made up of particles of different sizes that are sorted from top to bottom is a *graded bed*.

RIPPLE MARKS AND MUD CRACKS

When water flows over sediment, it may move some of the sediment to form ripples. *Ripples* are wavy lines in sediment. Sedimentary rocks that form from sediment that has ripples may show *ripple marks*.

Sedimentary rocks may also show mud cracks. *Mud cracks* form when wet mud dries. As mud dries, it shrinks and cracks. The cracks may then fill with sediment and form sedimentary rock. ☑

FOSSILS AND CONCRETIONS

A *fossil* is a sign that a living thing once existed. The hard parts of organisms can become fossils. Footprints and other marks can also become fossils. Most fossils are found in sedimentary rock.

Some sedimentary rocks contain lumps of rock that are different from the rest of the rock. These lumps are called *concretions*. They form when minerals crystallize out of water that flows through the rock.

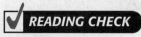

READING CHECK

10. Describe What is stratification?

_____

_____

Talk About It

Discuss Use a dictionary to look up the word root *strat*. With a partner, discuss why this word root is found in the word that describes layering in sedimentary rocks.

READING CHECK

11. Explain What causes mud to crack as it dries?

_____

_____

Section 3 Review

SECTION VOCABULARY

cementation the process in which minerals precipitate into pore spaces between sediment grains and bind sediments together to form rock	**compaction** the process in which the volume and porosity of a sediment is decreased by the weight of overlying sediments as a result of burial beneath other sediments
chemical sedimentary rock sedimentary rock that forms when minerals precipitate from a solution or settle from a suspension	**organic sedimentary rock** sedimentary rock that forms from the remains of plants or animals
clastic sedimentary rock sedimentary rock that forms when fragments of preexisting rocks are compacted or cemented together	

1. **Classify** A scientist is studying a sedimentary rock that did not form through compaction and cementation. What kind of sedimentary rock is the scientist studying? Explain your answer.

_____

_____

2. **Identify** List the seven features that sedimentary rocks can have.

_____

_____

3. **Infer** A clastic sedimentary rock is made up of smooth, round sediment pieces that are all about the same size. What can you infer about how the sediment that formed the rock was transported and deposited? Explain your answer.

_____

_____

_____

4. **Synthesize Concepts** Which structure are you more likely to find in an organic sedimentary rock, mud cracks or fossils? Explain your answer.

_____

_____

_____

_____

CHAPTER 6 Rocks

SECTION 4

Metamorphic Rock

KEY IDEAS

As you read this section, keep these questions in mind:

• What happens during metamorphism?

• How are regional metamorphism and contact metamorphism different?

• What are foliated and nonfoliated metamorphic rocks?

What Is Metamorphism?

Heat, pressure, and hot fluids can change the chemical composition of rock. They can cause minerals to react with one another and form new minerals. They can cause mineral crystals to change size or shape. They can even cause mineral molecules to move through the rock. Molecules of similar minerals move together and form bands, or stripes, of mineral crystals.

Metamorphism is the process in which heat, pressure, or hot fluids change the chemical composition of rock. Rock that has been affected by metamorphism is called *metamorphic rock*. All metamorphic rock forms from sedimentary, igneous, or other metamorphic rock. ☑

What Are the Two Types of Metamorphism?

Two main types of metamorphism happen in Earth's crust. One type is contact metamorphism. Another type is regional metamorphism.

CONTACT METAMORPHISM

Contact metamorphism can happen when magma moves through cracks underground. The magma heats the rock nearby. The heat can cause metamorphism.

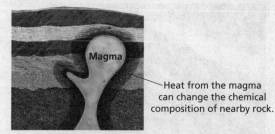

Magma

Heat from the magma can change the chemical composition of nearby rock.

Contact Metamorphism

READING TOOLBOX

Ask Questions Read this section silently. In your notebook, write down questions that you have about the section. Work with a partner or a small group to figure out the answers to your questions.

☑ **READING CHECK**

1. Define What is metamorphism?

_____

_____

_____

_____

Critical Thinking

2. Apply Concepts The rock that is nearest the magma may melt. Would this melted rock become metamorphic rock? Explain your answer.

_____

_____

_____

REGIONAL METAMORPHISM

Earth's lithosphere is broken up into large pieces called *tectonic plates*. The tectonic plates are constantly moving. In some places, two plates collide, or come together. When the plates collide, they produce a lot of heat and pressure. The heat and pressure can cause metamorphism. This process is known as **regional metamorphism**. ☑

Regional metamorphism affects rocks in a much larger area than contact metamorphism does. However, regional metamorphism produces so much heat that it can cause some rock to melt. The magma can cause some contact metamorphism. Therefore, rocks formed by contact metamorphism are often found in areas that also contain rocks formed by regional metamorphism.

How Do Scientists Classify Metamorphic Rocks?

The main way that scientists classify metamorphic rocks is by the textures of the rocks. There are two main types of metamorphic rock: foliated metamorphic rock and nonfoliated metamorphic rock. ☑

FOLIATED METAMORPHIC ROCK

Most kinds of metamorphic rocks have layers or bands. These bands form when pressure and temperature cause mineral molecules in the rock to move. Molecules of similar minerals move together and form larger crystals. This type of rock texture is known as **foliation**. Metamorphic rocks that show foliation are called *foliated metamorphic rocks*.

In many cases, light-colored minerals and dark-colored minerals separate to form different bands. Therefore, many foliated metamorphic rocks have light and dark bands, as shown in the photo below.

NONFOLIATED METAMORPHIC ROCK

Some kinds of metamorphic rock do not show foliation. Metamorphic rocks that do not show foliation are called **nonfoliated** metamorphic rocks. Most nonfoliated metamorphic rocks form from rocks that were made mainly of only one mineral. Metamorphism causes the mineral crystals in the original rock to grow larger. ☑

Nonfoliated metamorphic rocks can also form from rocks that contain mainly square or rounded mineral crystals. All the sides of those crystals are about the same length. Therefore, pressure from only one side does not cause the crystals to move or shift. Because the minerals do not move, they cannot form bands.

The table below gives some examples of foliated and nonfoliated metamorphic rocks.

6. Describe How does metamorphism affect a rock that is made up of only one mineral?

_____

_____

_____

Rock Name	Description	Description
Slate	foliated rock with very small mineral crystals that form thin, flat sheets	Pressure acts on the sedimentary rock shale. The minerals in the shale are compressed into thin layers.
Schist	foliated rock with relatively thick layers; contains large amounts of mica	Large amounts of heat and pressure act on slate. The heat and pressure cause minerals to react and form layers of mica and other minerals.
Gneiss	foliated rock with very thick, dark and light layers	Very high heat and pressure act on schist. Light-colored minerals separate from dark-colored minerals to form bands.
Quartzite	nonfoliated rock made up mainly of the mineral quartz; very hard and strong	Heat and pressure cause quartz in sandstone to *recrystallize*, or grow new crystals.
Marble	nonfoliated rock made up mainly of calcium carbonate; relatively hard, but breaks down easily in acid rain	Heat and pressure cause calcite in limestone to recrystallize.

The texture and composition of a metamorphic rock give clues to how it formed. Therefore, scientists can use information from metamorphic rocks to learn about the geologic history of an area.

LOOKING CLOSER
7. Identify Which of the foliated metamorphic rocks forms under the highest heat and pressure?

_____

Section 4 Review

SECTION VOCABULARY

contact metamorphism a change in the texture, structure, or chemical composition of a rock due to contact with magma	**nonfoliated** the metamorphic rock texture in which mineral grains are not arranged in planes or bands
foliation the metamorphic rock texture in which mineral grains are arranged in planes or bands	**regional metamorphism** a change in the texture, structure, or chemical composition of a rock due to changes in temperature and pressure over a large area, generally as a result of tectonic forces
metamorphism the process in which one type of rock changes into metamorphic rock because of chemical processes or changes in temperature and pressure	

1. **Compare** Complete the Venn diagram below to compare regional metamorphism and contact metamorphism.

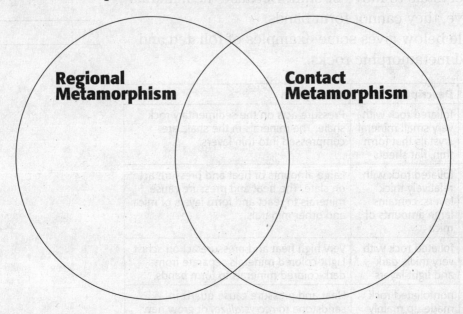

2. **Identify** What are three ways a rock can change during metamorphism?

_____

_____

_____

3. **Infer** The Himalaya Mountains are found where two tectonic plates collide. Does most of the metamorphic rock in that area probably occur in small patches or in wide regions? Explain your answer.

_____

_____

_____

_____

_____

SECTION
1 **Mineral Resources**

As you read this section, keep these questions in mind:
- What are ores, and where do they form?
- Why are mineral resources important?
- What are four ways humans get mineral resources?

What Resources Are in Earth's Crust?

Earth's crust contains many minerals that humans can use. Some minerals are metals, such as gold and silver. Others are nonmetals, such as sulfur and quartz.

ORES

Minerals can be native elements or compounds. *Native elements* are minerals that are made of only one element. Gold, silver, diamond, and sulfur are examples of native elements. *Compounds* are minerals that are made of two or more elements. Quartz, gypsum, and halite (salt) are examples of minerals that are compounds. ☑

Most rocks contain only one or two minerals or elements that are useful to people. People must break up the rocks or minerals to get the useful materials out. This process takes time and energy.

Some rocks and minerals contain large amounts of useful materials. A rock or mineral that contains a lot of useful minerals or elements is called an **ore**. Ores can form in different ways. The table below describes different ways ores can form.

Process	Description	Examples
Cooling magma	As magma cools, crystals of different minerals form.	ores of nickel, chromium, and lead
Evaporation	When a body of water evaporates, minerals that were dissolved in the water crystallize.	halite (rock salt), gypsum
Contact metamorphism	Magma heats nearby rock. The heat makes minerals in the rock react to form new minerals.	ores of lead, copper, and zinc
Hydrothermal veins	Hot fluids move through small cracks in solid rock. Minerals from the rock dissolve into the fluid. Later, the minerals crystallize and form narrow veins in the rock.	gold, tin, lead, copper

Ask Questions Read this section silently. On a piece of paper, write down questions you have about this section. Discuss your questions with a partner or small group. Together, try to figure out the answers to your questions.

1. Identify What are the two main kinds of minerals?

_____

_____

LOOKING CLOSER
2. Describe What causes new minerals to form in contact metamorphism?

_____

_____

SECTION 1 **Mineral Resources** *continued*

ORE DEPOSITS

When cooling magma forms ores, the ores sink to the bottom of the magma chamber. When evaporation forms ores, the ores sink to the ocean floor. In both of these cases, the ores are clustered in one place. An *ore deposit* is a collection of ores that are all in one place.

Ore deposits can form in other ways, too. For example, many thick hydrothermal veins may form in one place. When that happens, they form an ore deposit called a **lode**. ☑

Moving water can also form ore deposits. When rocks break down, water can wash away tiny pieces of heavy minerals, such as gold. When the water slows down, it can no longer carry the heavy minerals. The minerals drop to the bottom of the water. They may get trapped in the curve of a river or in deep places on the bottom of a stream. As the heavy minerals build up, they form an ore deposit called a **placer deposit**.

> ☑ **READING CHECK**
>
> **3. Define** What is a lode?
>
> _____
>
> _____
>
> _____
>
> _____

LOOKING CLOSER

4. Describe What are two places where placer deposits commonly form?

_____

_____

_____

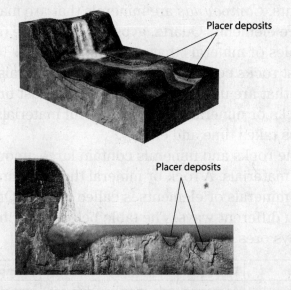

Placer deposits

Placer deposits

Some placer deposits form in places where rivers bend. Others form in deep areas in streams. The deposits form when pieces of heavy minerals get trapped as water slows down.

What Do People Use Minerals For?

People use different minerals for different purposes. Some minerals are valuable because they are beautiful and rare. For example, people use gold, silver, and gemstones in jewelry. **Gemstones** are nonmetallic minerals that can be cut or polished until they shine. The table on the next page shows some uses of different minerals.

SECTION 1 **Mineral Resources** *continued*

Substance	Examples of Uses
Gold	electronics, dental work, jewelry
Diamond (a form of carbon)	drill bits, jewelry
Graphite (a form of carbon)	pencils, paint, batteries
Calcite	building materials, cement
Halite (also called rock salt)	foods, food preservation
Kaolinite (a type of clay)	ceramics, paper, cement, bricks
Quartz (found in sand)	glass, computer chips
Sulfur	gunpowder, medicine, rubber

How Do Miners Collect Minerals?

Mining companies are always looking for new ore deposits. These companies search for places that contain a lot of ores in one area. There are several ways that the companies can identify the best mining areas:

- They study local geology.
- They collect and test rock samples.
- They use airplanes with special equipment to find patterns in magnetism, gravity, and rock color.

SUBSURFACE MINING AND SURFACE MINING

Many mineral deposits are far beneath Earth's surface. Miners work in underground mines to collect these minerals. This type of mining is called *subsurface mining*.

Some mineral deposits are close to Earth's surface. They may be covered with a layer of soil or rock. Miners take off this top layer so that they can collect the minerals. This type of mining is called *surface mining*. ☑

PLACER MINING

Miners can use large ships to mine placer deposits. They attach large buckets to a ship. The buckets scoop up solid material from the bottom of a lake or ocean. Then miners separate the minerals from the other materials.

UNDERSEA MINING

The ocean floor also contains mineral deposits. However, it is difficult for miners to gather minerals from beneath the ocean. Undersea mining is also more expensive than other types of mining.

LOOKING CLOSER
5. Identify Which two minerals are used to make cement?

_____

_____

Critical Thinking

6. Explain Why is it important for mining companies to identify places with large ore deposits?

_____

_____

_____

_____

_____

_____

✓ READING CHECK

7. Describe What types of mineral deposits can be mined by surface mining?

_____

_____

Section 1 Review

SECTION VOCABULARY

gemstone a mineral, rock, or organic material that can be used as jewelry or an ornament when it is cut and polished	**ore** a natural material whose concentration of economically valuable minerals is high enough for the material to be mined profitably
lode a mineral deposit within a rock formation	**placer deposit** a deposit that contains a valuable mineral that has been concentrated by mechanical action

1. Explain What are ores, and why are they important?

_____

_____

2. Contrast What is the difference between a native element and a compound?

_____

_____

3. Describe How do hydrothermal veins form?

_____

_____

_____

4. List What are four ways that ore deposits can form?

_____

_____

_____

_____

5. Explain Where do the minerals in placer deposits come from?

_____

_____

6. Compare Complete the table below with descriptions of the four types of mining.

Type of Mining	Description
Subsurface mining	
Surface mining	
Placer mining	
Undersea mining	

CHAPTER 7 | Resources and Energy
SECTION
2 | # Nonrenewable Energy

As you read this section, keep these questions in mind:
• How do petroleum and natural gas form?
• Why is coal considered a fossil fuel?
• How are fossil fuels used today?
• How does nuclear fission generate electricity?

What Are Fossil Fuels?

A **fossil fuel** is an energy resource made of hydrocarbons. *Hydrocarbons* are compounds of the elements carbon and hydrogen. Hydrocarbons contain a lot of stored energy. The energy comes from plants and animals that lived millions of years ago.

When fossil fuels burn, they release the energy as heat and light. People use fossil fuels to heat their homes, power their vehicles, and produce electricity. In fact, most of the energy we use today comes from fossil fuels. Petroleum, coal, and natural gas are the three types of fossil fuels. ☑

How Do Petroleum and Natural Gas Form?

Petroleum and natural gas form in similar ways. The main difference between petroleum and natural gas is their states. Petroleum is a liquid. Natural gas is a gas. Both are made up of hydrocarbons.

Petroleum and natural gas take hundreds of millions of years to form. The chart below shows how they form.

Tiny sea creatures die. Their bodies sink to the ocean floor. Sediment buries them.

↓

The sediment around the bodies slowly becomes rock.

↓

Over millions of years, heat and pressure chemically change the bodies. The carbon and hydrogen in them change into hydrocarbons. Some of the hydrocarbons are liquids, and they become petroleum. Other hydrocarbons are gases, and they become natural gas.

READING TOOLBOX

Summarize As you read this section, create a three-panel flip chart to compare the three types of fossil fuels.

☑ READING CHECK

1. Identify What are the three types of fossil fuels?

_____

_____

_____

LOOKING CLOSER
2. Explain What causes the remains of sea creatures to change into fossil fuels?

_____

OIL TRAPS

Most of the petroleum and natural gas on Earth are found together. Petroleum and natural gas are most commonly found in permeable rock layers. *Permeable rock* is rock that has spaces in it. Liquids and gases can move through these spaces. The petroleum and natural gas move through the permeable rock until they meet a layer of impermeable rock. The petroleum and natural gas cannot flow through the impermeable rock. ☑

The petroleum and natural gas become trapped beneath the impermeable rock. The area where they are trapped is called an *oil trap*. Because natural gas is less dense than petroleum, the natural gas rises to the top of the oil trap. Petroleum is less dense than water, so the petroleum rises above any water in the oil trap. When people drill into the oil trap, the petroleum and natural gas flow out.

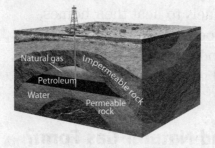
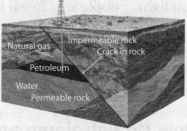
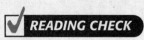

Oil traps can form in different ways.

READING CHECK

3. Describe What keeps petroleum and natural gas from reaching Earth's surface?

_____

_____

Critical Thinking

4. Predict What might happen if a person drilled a well too deep into an oil trap?

_____

_____

How Does Coal Form?

Coal is a solid fossil fuel that is made of partly decayed plant material. It is the most commonly burned fossil fuel in the world. Coal forms through a process called *carbonization.* ☑

Carbonization happens when plants die and fall into swamp water. Bacteria in the water begin to break down the plants. Because there is no oxygen in the water, the plants do not break down completely. Instead, the compounds in the plant change into new compounds that are rich in carbon. The pictures on the next page show what happens during carbonization.

READING CHECK

5. Define What is coal made from?

_____

_____

SECTION 2 **Nonrenewable Energy** *continued*

Peat

Stage 1: Peat
Dead swamp plants that have not decayed can turn into *peat*. Peat is crumbly and brown, and it is mostly made up of plant material and water. Peat is not coal, but it can turn into coal. It is about 60% carbon.

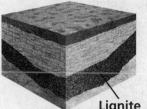

Lignite

Stage 2: Lignite
If sediment buries the peat, pressure and temperature increase. The peat slowly turns into a type of coal called *lignite*. Lignite is harder than peat. Lignite is also called *brown coal*. It is about 70% carbon.

Bituminous coal

Stage 3: Bituminous Coal
If more sediment is added, pressure and temperature continue to increase. This forces more water and gas out of the lignite. Lignite slowly changes to *bituminous coal*. Bituminous coal is also called *soft coal*. It is about 80% carbon.

Anthracite

Stage 4: Anthracite
Movements of the lithosphere may put additional heat and pressure on bituminous coal. This forces more water and gas out of the bituminous coal, which slowly changes to *anthracite*. Anthracite is the hardest form of coal. It is about 90% carbon.

LOOKING CLOSER
6. Identify Which type of coal has the most carbon in it?

_____

_____

Critical Thinking
7. Draw Conclusions Why do you think the process shown in the pictures is called *carbonization*?

_____

_____

_____

_____

_____

_____

What Is Nuclear Fission?

Most of the energy we use today comes from burning fossil fuels. However, fossil fuels produce pollution when they burn. Therefore, many people are interested in *alternative energy sources*, or other ways of producing energy. The most common alternative energy source is nuclear fission.

Remember that the nucleus of an atom contains protons and neutrons. Some atomic nuclei are unstable. If a neutron hits an unstable nucleus, the nucleus can break apart into smaller nuclei. This process is called **nuclear fission**. ☑

Nuclear fission releases energy. It also releases more neutrons. Those neutrons can hit other nuclei and cause more fission. If the process is not controlled, it can cause an explosion. However, if the process is controlled, the energy it releases can be used to make electricity.

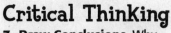

READING CHECK
8. Define What happens during nuclear fission?

_____

_____

SECTION 2 **Nonrenewable Energy** *continued*

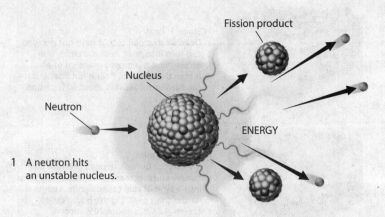

1 A neutron hits an unstable nucleus.

Neutron

Nucleus

Fission product

ENERGY

2 The neutron makes the nucleus break apart.
It forms smaller nuclei and neutrons.
It also releases a great deal of energy.
The neutrons can hit other unstable nuclei
and cause the reaction to keep going.

LOOKING CLOSER

9. Describe What causes the nuclear reaction to keep going once it has started?

_____

_____

_____

_____

NUCLEAR REACTORS

Nuclear power plants use *nuclear reactors* to produce energy. In a nuclear reactor, the fission reaction is controlled. The reactor has special *control rods* in it that absorb extra neutrons. They keep the reaction from getting out of control. The picture below shows how a nuclear reactor produces electricity. ☑

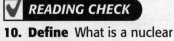

READING CHECK

10. Define What is a nuclear reactor?

_____

_____

_____

1 Fission in the fuel rods produces
heat. The water around the fuel
rods gets very hot.

3 The steam flows across a turbine.
The steam makes the turbine spin.
The spinning turbine turns a generator,
which makes electricity.

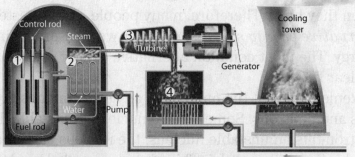

Control rod

Steam

Turbine

Generator

Cooling tower

Water

Pump

Fuel rod

LOOKING CLOSER

11. Describe What happens to the water around the fuel rods after it is heated?

_____

_____

_____

2 Pipes carry the hot water into
another container of water.
The hot water in the pipes
makes the water in the
container boil. This process
prevents harmful radiation
from getting out of the reactor.

4 As the steam cools, it turns back into water.
The extra heat from the water is released from
the cooling tower.

SECTION 2 **Nonrenewable Energy** *continued*

ADVANTAGES AND DISADVANTAGES OF NUCLEAR FISSION POWER

One advantage of using nuclear fission to produce electricity is that nuclear fission does not cause air pollution. Also, mining the fuel used in nuclear reactors does not harm the environment as much as mining fossil fuels does. A third advantage is that only a small amount of nuclear fuel can produce a large amount of electricity.

However, the products of nuclear fission are very *toxic*, or harmful. They produce radiation that can harm living things. The radiation lasts for thousands of years, so storing the products of nuclear fission can be difficult.

Another disadvantage of nuclear fission is that it uses nonrenewable resources. **Nonrenewable resources** cannot be easily replaced once they are used. The fuel for nuclear reactors, uranium, is a nonrenewable resource. Fossil fuels are also nonrenewable resources.

What Is Nuclear Fusion?

During **nuclear fusion**, the nuclei of two hydrogen atoms combine. They form a larger helium nucleus. Like nuclear fission, nuclear fusion releases a lot of energy.

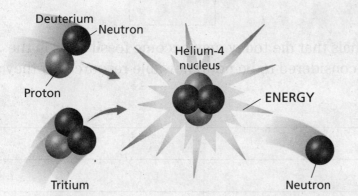

Deuterium — Neutron — Proton — Tritium — Helium-4 nucleus — ENERGY — Neutron

Nuclear fusion power could have many advantages. It could produce a lot of electricity using only water as fuel. Because water is the fuel for the reaction, the supply of fuel would be almost never ending. Scientists think the products of nuclear fusion would not be harmful to the environment. However, nuclear fusion normally happens only at very high temperatures. So far, scientists have not been able to carry out nuclear fusion on Earth.

Talk About It
Evaluate Many people think that countries should try to use more nuclear power. Do you agree? Summarize your opinion in writing. Then, discuss your opinion with a partner or small group.

LOOKING CLOSER
12. Identify How many protons and how many neutrons are there in the helium-4 nucleus?

_____

_____

Section 2 Review

SECTION VOCABULARY

fossil fuel a nonrenewable energy resource formed from the remains of organisms that lived long ago	**nuclear fission** the process by which the nucleus of a heavy atom splits into two or more fragments; the process releases neutrons and energy
nonrenewable resource a resource that forms at a rate that is much slower than the rate at which the resource is consumed	**nuclear fusion** the process by which nuclei of small atoms combine to form a new, more massive nucleus; the process releases energy

1. Describe Complete the concept map below to describe how nuclear fission can be used to produce electricity.

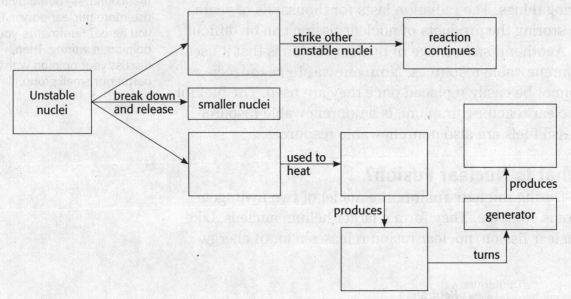

2. Explain The plants and animals that die today may become fossil fuels in the future. Why are fossil fuels considered to be nonrenewable resources, if they are still forming?

_____

_____

_____

3. Compare How are the three types of fossil fuels similar? How are they different?

_____

_____

_____

_____

4. Describe What are three ways people use fossil fuels today?

_____

CHAPTER 7	Resources and Energy

SECTION 3

Renewable Energy

As you read this section, keep these questions in mind:

- How can geothermal energy be used as a substitute for fossil fuels?
- What are two ways of collecting energy from the sun?
- What are four forms of renewable alternative energy?

Why Are Renewable Resources So Important?

Experts predict that we will probably use up Earth's fossil fuels in the next 200 years. Nuclear fission power could replace some fossil fuels. However, nuclear fission power produces harmful wastes, and many people think it is unsafe. Therefore, many nations are searching for energy sources that come from renewable resources. **Renewable resources** can be replaced as quickly as they are used.

How Can People Use Geothermal Energy?

Geothermal energy is energy from within Earth. The rock below Earth's surface is very hot in many places. The water in the hot rock also becomes very hot. The hot water and the steam it forms can be used to produce electricity and to heat buildings. ☑

Engineers have worked to find ways that we can use geothermal energy. They can drill wells to reach the hot water. People can then use the water or the steam as a source of heat. In addition, engineers can use the hot water to turn generators. A *generator* is a device that uses motion to produce electricity.

People around the world already use geothermal energy. The list below gives some examples of how people use geothermal energy:

- San Francisco gets some of its electricity from a geothermal power plant.
- In Iceland, the heat in 85% of the homes comes from geothermal energy.
- Italy and Japan have built geothermal power plants.

READING TOOLBOX

Connect As you read this section, create a concept map about renewable resources. Make sure to include the vocabulary words in your concept map.

READING CHECK

1. Define What is geothermal energy?

_____

_____

_____

Talk About It

Infer With a partner, talk about some of the reasons that only some places in the world use geothermal energy.

How Can People Use Solar Energy?

The sun also provides renewable energy. Energy from the sun is called **solar energy**. The solar energy that Earth receives every 15 minutes equals the amount of energy that humans use in a year. However, engineers have not been able to figure out how to capture most of that energy. ☑

There are two types of systems that convert the sun's rays into heat energy: passive systems and active systems. If a house has windows that face the sun, sunlight will warm the house. This is called a *passive system*.

In an *active system*, people create a device to collect sunlight. For example, they may put a special glass box on the roof of a house. Water flows through pipes in the box. Sunlight heats the water in the pipes, which produces heat and hot water for the house. On cloudy days, when sunlight cannot heat the water, the system uses energy stored from other days. ☑

Another type of active solar system involves using *photovoltaic cells*. Photovoltaic cells change sunlight into electricity. Many people use them to provide some electricity for their homes. However, engineers have not yet developed photovoltaic cells that can produce enough electricity to power a city.

How Can People Use Hydroelectric Energy?

People have used moving water to do work for many years. Today, people can use moving water to produce electricity. Energy produced by moving water is called **hydroelectric energy**. The figure below shows how running water can be used to produce electricity.

✓ **READING CHECK**

2. Explain Why do we not get all of our energy from the sun?

_____

_____

✓ **READING CHECK**

3. Describe What would an active solar system do on a cloudy day, when solar energy is not available?

_____

_____

_____

Talk About It

Decode Words Use a dictionary to look up the word roots *photo* and *volt*. Talk with a partner about how you can use these word roots to help you remember what photovoltaic cells do.

LOOKING CLOSER

4. Identify What happens to the water after it turns the turbine?

_____

_____

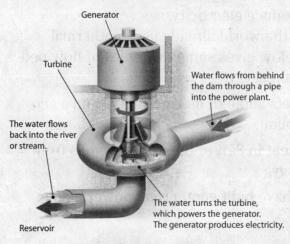

Generator

Turbine

Water flows from behind the dam through a pipe into the power plant.

The water flows back into the river or stream.

The water turns the turbine, which powers the generator. The generator produces electricity.

Reservoir

Hydroelectric power plants use water to turn turbines. The turbines power generators, which generate electricity.

SECTION 3 **Renewable Energy** *continued*

ENERGY FROM TIDES

Tides in the oceans can also be used to produce electricity. *Tides* are increases and decreases in sea level during certain times of day. People have developed special dams that trap ocean water at high tide. The dams release the water at low tide. As the water flows out of the dam, it turns a generator, which produces electricity.

How Can People Get Energy from Plants?

For thousands of years, people have burned wood, leaves, and even animal dung to cook and to heat their homes. Today, people are learning how to use these kinds of biomass to produce electricity. **Biomass** is organic matter that can be a source of energy. ☑

People can burn biomass directly to produce heat and to cook. Biomass can also be used in other ways. When organic matter breaks down, it produces gases, such as methane. It can also produce liquids, such as ethanol, a kind of alcohol. These gases and liquids can be burned to produce electricity.

How Can People Use Energy from Wind?

Wind is moving air. It contains energy. People can use *wind turbines*, or windmills, to collect some of that energy. A wind turbine spins when the wind blows. The spinning turbine turns a generator. The generator produces electricity.

The figure below shows a wind farm. Wind farms may have hundreds of huge wind turbines. They can produce energy for an entire community. People can also use smaller wind turbines to produce energy for just one home.

READING CHECK

5. Identify Give three examples of biomass.

_____

_____

Critical Thinking

6. Infer On a very windy day, what would happen to the generator connected to this wind farm?

_____

_____

_____

These turbines are connected to a generator. The faster the turbines spin, the more electricity the generator produces.

Section 3 Review

SECTION VOCABULARY

biomass plant material, manure, or any other organic matter that is used as an energy source	**renewable resource** a natural resource that can be replaced at the same rate at which the resource is consumed
geothermal energy the energy produced by heat within Earth	**solar energy** the energy received by Earth from the sun in the form of radiation
hydroelectric energy electrical energy produced by the flow of water	

1. Explain Why are renewable resources important?

_____

_____

_____

2. Identify Describe two examples of systems people can use to collect solar energy.

_____

_____

_____

3. Describe Identify one common use of fossil fuels, and describe how geothermal energy could replace that use of fossil fuels.

_____

_____

_____

4. Infer Solar energy, wind energy, geothermal energy, and hydroelectric energy produce almost no pollution. What is one disadvantage that all of these forms of energy have? Use examples to support your answer.

_____

_____

_____

_____

5. Describe What are three ways biomass can be used for energy?

_____

_____

_____

_____

CHAPTER 7 | Resources and Energy

SECTION
4 **Resources and Conservation**

KEY IDEAS

As you read this section, keep these questions in mind:

• How can the environmental effects of mining be reduced?

• Why is it important to use fossil fuels wisely?

• How does conservation protect natural resources?

How Does Mining Affect the Environment?

Mining is the process in which people remove useful materials from below Earth's surface. Mining can harm or destroy ecosystems. The table below describes some of the ways that mining can harm the environment.

Type of Harm	Description
Air and noise pollution	Machines that are used for mining produce harmful gases, which can pollute the air. The machines can also make loud noises, which can disturb people and harm other animals.
Water pollution	Rain can wash harmful chemicals from mines into rivers and oceans. The chemicals can harm fish, plants, and animals in the water.
Erosion	Miners loosen the soil. Loosening the soil causes the soil to wash away easily. The soil can end up in rivers and ponds. Soil in rivers and ponds can harm fish and other water animals.
Soil degradation	Harmful chemicals from mines can pollute soil. Most plants cannot grow in polluted soil.
Sinkholes	Land above a subsurface mine can collapse into the mine. This creates a large hole in the ground called a *sinkhole*. Sinkholes can damage roads and homes. Sinkholes are difficult to repair.
Fires	Fires that start in coal mines are hard to put out. Therefore, miners often leave them to burn out on their own. This burning process can take hundreds of years.

How Can People Make Mining Better for the Environment?

Many governments and other groups are working to make mining safer for the environment. They have created laws and policies to try to fix the problems that mines cause.

READING TOOLBOX

Summarize Read this section silently. In pairs, take turns summarizing the material. Stop to discuss ideas and words that seem confusing or unfamiliar.

LOOKING CLOSER
1. Explain What are two ways that mining can harm fish?

_____

_____

SECTION 4 **Resources and Conservation** *continued*

LAWS ABOUT MINING

In the United States, the government has created laws that affect the mining industry. These laws help prevent miners from polluting the air, water, and soil. Some of these laws are

- the Clean Water Act
- the Safe Drinking Water Act
- the Comprehensive Environmental Response, Compensation, and Liability Act
- the Endangered Species Act

MINE RECLAMATION

Many mining companies are careful to protect mined land from harm. They may inspect the mines often to make sure that they are not causing harm to the environment.

In the United States, mining companies must return mined land to its original condition. This process is called *reclamation*. Reclamation can reduce the effects of mining on ecosystems. ☑

Why Is It Important to Use Fossil Fuels Wisely?

It is important for people to use fossil fuels wisely. Remember that fossil fuels are nonrenewable resources. If people use too many fossil fuels, the fossil fuels will run out. Burning fossil fuels can also cause air pollution. The diagram below gives one example of how burning fossil fuels can harm the environment.

People burn coal in power plants to produce electricity.

↓

As the coal burns, it produces the gas sulfur dioxide (SO_2). The SO_2 rises into the atmosphere.

↓

In the atmosphere, the SO_2 mixes with water. It forms acid rain. The acid rain falls to Earth's surface.

↓

The acid rain harms trees and other plants. It can also pollute lakes and rivers and harm the living things in them.

Talk About It

Infer With a partner, discuss the four laws in the bulleted list. What do you think the laws are about? How would they affect the mining industry? If you wish, use the Internet or the library to find out more about one of the laws. Discuss your findings with your partner.

☑ **READING CHECK**

2. Define What is reclamation?

_____

_____

_____

LOOKING CLOSER

3. Explain What must happen for acid rain to form?

_____

_____

_____

SECTION 4 **Resources and Conservation** *continued*

How Can People Conserve Resources?

People are using up more of Earth's mineral resources every year. Scientists predict that people will use up all of Earth's coal in 200 years. Many scientists also think that people have already used up half of Earth's oil.

Because fossil fuels such as coal and oil are nonrenewable, it is important to conserve them. **Conservation** is the practice of using natural resources wisely, and using less of them. Conserving natural resources helps them last longer. Conservation also reduces harm to the environment.

One way to conserve nonrenewable resources is to use renewable resources instead. For example, solar energy is renewable. People can use solar energy instead of fossil fuels for heat. However, in some situations, renewable resources cannot replace nonrenewable resources. The two best ways to conserve nonrenewable resources are to recycle them and to use less of them. ☑

RECYCLING

Recycling is the process of using things more than once. Recycling does use energy, but it uses less energy than mining and manufacturing new products. For example, it takes less energy to make paper from old paper than from trees.

USING FEWER RESOURCES

Recycling helps to conserve mineral resources. The best ways to conserve fossil fuels and other resources, such as fresh water, is to use less of them. Because most of our energy comes from fossil fuels, reducing energy use conserves fossil fuels. The table below describes some ways to reduce the use of energy and fresh water.

Resource	Ways to Reduce the Use of the Resource
Energy (fossil fuels)	• Use more insulation in buildings, so less heat and air conditioning are needed. • Turn off lights and other electronic devices when you are not using them. • Walk or ride a bike instead of driving.
Fresh water	• Use water-efficient faucets, toilets, and shower heads. • Take shorter showers. • Run the dishwasher and clothes washer only when they are full.

Critical Thinking

4. Predict Scientists think that the oil we have already used was the easiest oil to find. In the future, it will be harder and harder to get enough oil. What do you think will happen to the price of oil in the future?

_____

_____

☑ **READING CHECK**

5. Explain Why can't we replace all nonrenewable resources with renewable resources?

_____

_____

_____

_____

Talk About It

Apply What are some things you can do to conserve nonrenewable resources? Discuss your ideas with the class.

Section 4 Review

SECTION VOCABULARY

conservation the preservation and wise use of natural resources	**recycling** the process of recovering valuable or useful materials from waste or scrap; the process of reusing some items

1. Evaluate Is it more important to conserve renewable resources or nonrenewable resources? Why?

_____

_____

2. Explain How can mining create a sinkhole?

_____

_____

3. Explain How does recycling conserve energy?

_____

_____

4. Identify List two ways that the United States is trying to make mining less harmful to the environment.

_____

_____

_____

5. Explain Give two reasons why it is important to conserve fossil fuels.

_____

_____

6. List What are two ways that people can conserve fresh water?

_____

_____

7. Explain How does using less energy help conserve fossil fuels?

_____

_____

_____

CHAPTER 8 | The Rock Record
SECTION 1 | Determining Relative Age

KEY IDEAS

As you read this section, keep these questions in mind:

- What is the principle of uniformitarianism?

- How does the law of superposition help scientists to determine the relative age of rocks?

- How do the three types of unconformities compare?

- How does the law of crosscutting relationships help scientists to determine the relative age of rocks?

What Is Uniformitarianism?

At one time, many people thought Earth was only a few thousand years old. However, scientific evidence now shows that Earth is much older. Scientists think Earth is about 4.6 billion years old.

The idea that Earth is billions of years old started in the 1700s with a Scottish physician and farmer named James Hutton. The diagram below describes how Hutton found evidence that Earth is very old.

READING TOOLBOX

Color Code Choose four colored pencils, one color for each Key Ideas question. As you read, use the color you chose for each question to underline the answer in the text. You might want to use the pencils to add notes in the margin that apply to the Key Ideas.

Hutton saw that his farmland changed slightly each year.

↓

He observed that the processes that changed his land worked slowly.

↓

He guessed that those same processes could produce large changes in Earth's surface over long periods of time.

↓

He guessed that Earth is very old. It has changed slowly over time by the same processes that are changing it today.

Hutton thought that people could learn about Earth's past by studying the present. His principle of **uniformitarianism** states that geologic processes happened the same way in the past as they do today. Volcanic eruptions, erosion, and earthquakes are examples of geologic processes.

Later scientists added to Hutton's principle of uniformitarianism. They found evidence that the processes of the past and present are the same. They also learned that the rates of those processes can vary over time. ☑

READING CHECK

1. Identify How did later scientists adjust Hutton's law of uniformitarianism?

_____

_____

_____

_____

What Is Relative Age?

If you look at a group of brothers and sisters, you might not know the exact age of each person. However, you might use clues such as height to help you figure out which child is youngest. Scientists use a similar method to learn about Earth's past.

If scientists determine the order in which *strata*, or rock layers, formed, they can determine the relative age of rocks. *To date* is another way of saying "to determine the age of." **Relative age** is the age of an object or event compared to another object or event. The relative age of a rock can tell you that one rock layer is older than another. However, it cannot tell you the rock's age in years. ☑

Although igneous and metamorphic rock may form layers, scientists generally use the layers in sedimentary rocks to determine relative ages. The figure below shows a landform made up of layers of sedimentary rock.

LOOKING CLOSER

3. Predict Where do you think the oldest rock layers in the rock formations are found?

_____

_____

The layers of sedimentary rock that make up these rock formations in Utah were deposited over millions of years.

Remember that sedimentary rocks form as new sediments are deposited on old layers of sediment. As more sediments are added, the layers become compressed, or squeezed. The compressed sediments become stuck together in sedimentary rock layers called *beds*. The boundary between two beds is called a *bedding plane*.

What Is the Law of Superposition?

Scientists use the **law of superposition** to determine the relative ages of layers of sedimentary rocks. This law states that a layer of rock is older than the layers above it. It also states that a layer of rock is younger than the layers below it. Scientists can use the law of superposition only if the rock layers have not been disrupted or deformed. ☑

SECTION 1 **Determining Relative Age** *continued*

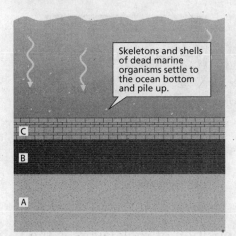

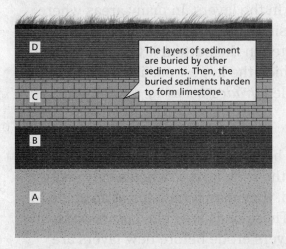

Scientists can apply the law of superposition to determine the relative ages of the rock layers.

Talk About It

Extend Concepts With a partner, talk about ways you have found the relative ages of two or more people, objects, or events. For example, you might determine the relative ages of two trees by comparing the thicknesses of their trunks.

LOOKING CLOSER

5. Apply Concepts According to the law of superposition, is layer B older or younger than layer C?

_____

_____

Examine the figures above. According to the law of superposition, layer A was the first layer that was deposited. Thus, it is the oldest layer. Layer D was the last layer deposited. Thus, it is the youngest layer.

What Is the Principle of Original Horizontality?

Sedimentary rock generally forms in horizontal layers. The *principle of original horizontality* states that if sedimentary rocks are undisturbed, the horizontal layers will remain. If scientists find rock layers that are not horizontal, they can assume that movements of Earth's crust have tilted or deformed the layers.

In many cases, the movement of tectonic plates pushes older rock layers on top of younger layers. In such cases, scientists cannot easily apply the law of superposition. Scientists must first use other clues to figure out the original positions of the layers. Then, they can use the law of superposition to find the relative ages of the rock layers.

Critical Thinking

6. Identify Relationships In what way is the law of original horizontality important to the law of superposition?

_____

_____

_____

_____

_____

_____

_____

SECTION 1 **Determining Relative Age** *continued*

Graded Bedding Heavy particles settle to the bottom of a river or lake faster than smaller particles do. This pattern of settling produces graded bedding.

Cross-Beds As sand piles up, it forms slanting layers.

Critical Thinking

7. Draw Conclusions Suppose you find layers of rock in which the top layers have larger particles than the lower layers. What is one conclusion you might make?

_____

_____

_____

8. Describe What does an unconformity indicate?

_____

_____

_____

_____

_____

GRADED BEDDING

One clue to the original position of rock layers is the size of the particles in the layers. In many areas where sediments are deposited, the largest, heaviest sediment particles are deposited in the bottom layer. The arrangement of layers in which the largest particles are found in bottom layers is called *graded bedding*.

CROSS-BEDS

The shape of the bedding plane is another clue to the original position of the rock layers. When sandy sediments are deposited, they may form beds at an angle to the bedding plane. These beds are called *cross-beds*. The tops of these layers erode before new layers are deposited.

RIPPLE MARKS

Wind or moving water can cause small waves called *ripple marks* to form on the surface of sand. When the sand becomes sandstone, the ripple marks may be preserved. If sedimentary rock layers are undisturbed, the crests, or tops, of the ripple marks point upward. By looking at the direction the ripple crests point, scientists can figure out the original positions of disturbed layers.

What Is an Unconformity?

In many cases, rock layers have been disturbed from their original positions or changed in some way. Disturbing rock layers can create an **unconformity**, or a break in the geologic record. An unconformity shows that deposition stopped for a period of time or that erosion happened before deposition continued. The table on the next page describes three types of unconformities. ☑

SECTION 1 **Determining Relative Age** *continued*

Types of Unconformities

Type of Unconformity	Example
Nonconformity Sediments are deposited on top of layers of igneous or metamorphic rock. The boundary between the layers represents a time gap and is called a *nonconformity*.	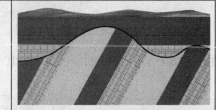
Angular unconformity A new horizontal sediment layer is deposited on top of sediment layers that were folded or tilted and then eroded. The bedding planes of the new layers are not parallel to the bedding planes of the older layers.	
Disconformity Layers of new sediment are deposited on horizontal layers of old sediment that has eroded. The boundary between the eroded layers and new sediment layers represents a time gap. The boundary is called a *disconformity*.	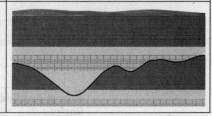

LOOKING CLOSER
9. Compare How is a nonconformity different from a disconformity?

_____
_____
_____
_____
_____
_____

What Are Crosscutting Relationships?

Horizontal rock layers may be disturbed by features such as faults or intrusions. A *fault* is a break or crack in Earth's crust along which rocks shift their position. An *intrusion* is igneous rock that forms when magma flows between layers of solid rock and then cools and hardens. When faults or intrusions have disturbed rock layers, scientists may have a hard time determining relative age.

In such cases, scientists may apply the law of crosscutting relationships. The **law of crosscutting relationships** states that a fault or intrusion is always younger than the rock it cuts through.

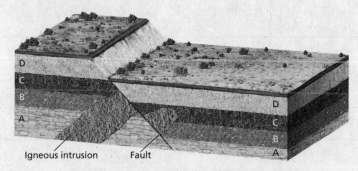

Scientists use the law of crosscutting relationships to determine the relative ages of rocks and the faults and intrusions within them.

LOOKING CLOSER
10. Analyze Which is younger—the fault or the intrusion? Explain your answer.

_____
_____
_____
_____
_____
_____

Section 1 Review

SECTION VOCABULARY

law of crosscutting relationships the principle that a fault or body of rock is younger than any other body of rock that it cuts through **law of superposition** the principle that a sedimentary rock layer is older than the layers above it and younger than the layers below it if the layers are not disturbed	**relative age** the age of an object in relation to the ages of other objects **unconformity** a break in the geologic record created when rock layers are eroded or when sediment is not deposited for a long period of time **uniformitarianism** a principle that geologic processes that occurred in the past can be explained by current geologic processes

1. Define In your own words, state the principle of uniformitarianism.

_____

_____

2. Identify Relationships Complete the table below to describe how each concept or feature relates to determining the relative age of rock layers.

Concept or Feature	How It Applies to Determining Relative Ages of Rocks
Law of superposition	
	Scientists know sedimentary rocks form in horizontal layers and stay in horizontal layers unless disturbed. If they find layers that are not horizontal, they must figure out the original position of the layers. Then they can determine relative ages.
Law of crosscutting relationships	
Ripple marks	

3. Compare How is an angular unconformity different from a disconformity?

_____

_____

_____

CHAPTER 8 | The Rock Record

SECTION 2 | # Determining Absolute Age

As you read this section, keep these questions in mind:

• Why can't scientists use rates of erosion and deposition as the only ways of determining absolute age?

• How do varves form?

• How can scientists use radioactive decay to determine the absolute age of rocks?

What Is Absolute Age?

Remember that relative dating indicates only that one rock is older or younger than another. To learn more about Earth's history, scientists often need to learn a rock's **absolute age**, or age in years. Scientists use a variety of methods to measure absolute age. Some methods require scientists to observe and measure geologic processes over time. Other methods involve the chemical composition of materials in rocks. ☑

RATES OF EROSION

Studying rates of erosion is one way scientists estimate the absolute age of rocks. For example, scientists may measure the rate at which a stream *erodes*, or wears away, its stream bed. They can use that measurement to estimate the absolute age of the stream.

Scientists cannot use rates of erosion in all cases. This method is useful only for geologic features that formed within the past 10,000 to 20,000 years. For features such as the Grand Canyon that formed over millions of years, the method is less useful. Rates of erosion vary greatly over millions of years. Therefore, estimates based on recent erosion rates are not dependable.

The rocky ledge that forms Niagara Falls has been eroding at a rate of 1.3 m per year for almost 9,900 years.

READING TOOLBOX

Summarize Make a key-term fold to identify the methods that scientists can use to determine absolute age. Include at least two facts about each method.

✓ READING CHECK

1. Compare How does absolute age differ from relative age?

_____

_____

_____

_____

LOOKING CLOSER

2. Calculate How many kilometers has the ledge been eroded in the last 9,900 years?

_____

SECTION 2 **Determining Absolute Age** *continued*

Critical Thinking

3. Estimate On average, how long would it take for 10 m of sediments to accumulate?

_____

_____

RATES OF DEPOSITION

Rivers can carry sediment, and then deposit it. Calculating rates of deposition is another way scientists can estimate absolute age. Scientists can estimate the average rate of deposition of common sedimentary rocks. These common rocks include limestone, shale, and sandstone. Scientists have found that, in general, about 30 cm of sedimentary rock are deposited over a period of 1,000 years.

However, a given sediment layer might not have been deposited at the average rate. For example, a flood may deposit many meters of sediment in just one day. Therefore, this method for determining absolute age is not always accurate.

VARVE COUNT

You may know that you can estimate a tree's age by counting the growth rings in the tree's trunk. Scientists use a similar method to estimate the age of certain sedimentary rocks. Some sedimentary rocks show layers called **varves**. In general, varves are annual, or yearly, layers. They have a light band of coarse particles and a dark band of fine particles. ☑

✔ **READING CHECK**

4. Identify About how long does it take for one varve to form?

_____

_____

Scientists can count varves to determine the absolute age of a sedimentary rock.

✔ **READING CHECK**

5. Describe What does one varve look like?

_____

_____

_____

_____

Most varves form in glacial lakes. During summer, snow and ice melt quickly. The water carries large amounts of sediment into the lake. Most of the coarser (larger) sediment particles settle quickly to the bottom and form a layer. When winter comes, the lake starts to freeze. Finer clay particles that stayed mixed in the water settle slowly on top of the layer of coarse particles.

A coarse summer layer and a fine winter layer make up one varve. By counting the varves, scientists can estimate the age of the sediments in years. ☑

SECTION 2 **Determining Absolute Age** *continued*

What Is Radiometric Dating?

Remember that all atoms of an element have the same number of protons. Atoms of the same element may, however, have different numbers of neutrons. Atoms of the same element with different numbers of neutrons are called *isotopes*. *Radioactive isotopes* have nuclei that emit, or give off, particles and energy at a constant rate. This process is called *radioactive decay*. The figure below shows two forms of radioactive decay.

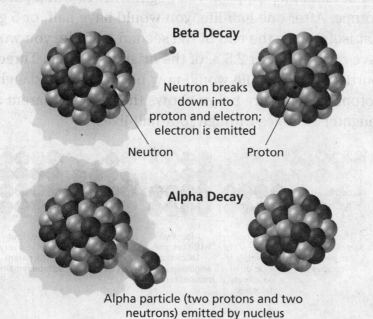

Beta Decay

Neutron breaks down into proton and electron; electron is emitted

Neutron   Proton

Alpha Decay

Alpha particle (two protons and two neutrons) emitted by nucleus

Beta decay and alpha decay are two forms of radioactive decay. In both forms of decay, an atom emits particles and energy.

Scientists can use the rates of decay of radioactive isotopes to measure absolute age. This method of finding absolute age is called **radiometric dating**.

As a radioactive isotope decays, it may change to a different isotope of the same element. It may even change to an isotope of a different element. Scientists can measure the concentrations of the original radioactive isotope and the newly formed isotopes in a sample. The original radioactive isotopes are called *parent isotopes*. The newly formed isotopes are called *daughter isotopes*.

Scientists determine the ratio of parent and daughter isotopes in a sample of rock. Using this ratio and the known decay rate, scientists can determine the absolute age of the rock.

Talk About It

Analyze Word Parts With a partner, use a dictionary to find the meanings of the prefix *iso-* and the root *metric*. Talk about how these word parts can help you remember the meanings of terms such as *isotope* and *radiometric*.

Critical Thinking

6. Identify On what process does radiometric dating rely?

_____

_____

SECTION 2 **Determining Absolute Age** *continued*

Critical Thinking

7. Extend Concepts Suppose you had a sample containing 20 g of a parent isotope. After how many half-lives would less than 2 g of the parent isotope remain?

_____

HALF-LIFE

Radioactive decay happens at a constant rate. Temperature, pressure, and other environmental conditions do not change the decay rate. Scientists have found that the time needed for a certain radioactive isotope to decay is always the same. Scientists typically talk about the half-life of a radioactive isotope. **Half-life** is the time it takes for half the mass of a parent isotope to decay into daughter isotopes.

For example, suppose you begin with 10 g of a parent isotope. After one half-life, you would have half, or 5 g, of that isotope. At the end of the second half-life, you would have one-fourth, or 2.5 g, of the original isotope. Three-fourths of the sample would now be made up of daughter isotopes. The figure below shows the ratios of parent and daughter isotopes through four half-lives.

| The original sample contains all parent isotopes. | After one half-life, 1/2 of the sample is made up of daughter isotopes. | After two half-lives, only 1/4 of the original parent isotopes remain. | After three half-lives, only 1/8 of the parent isotopes remain. | After four half-lives, very little parent isotope remains. |

LOOKING CLOSER

8. Identify After four half-lives, what fraction of the original parent isotopes remain?

_____

RADIOACTIVE ISOTOPES

Scientists can choose from a variety of radioactive isotopes for radiometric dating. The method they use depends mainly on how long ago the rock probably formed. If too little time has passed since the rock formed, the amount of daughter isotope will be too small. Scientists will be unable to determine age accurately. If too much time has passed since a rock formed, the amount of parent isotope will be too small. ☑

For example, uranium-238 has a half-life of 4.5 billion years. Uranium-238 is most useful for dating rock samples that contain uranium and that are more than 10 million years old. For younger rocks, the sample would have too few daughter isotopes for scientists to find an accurate age.

✓ **READING CHECK**

9. Describe Relationships How does the half-life of an isotope affect the accuracy of the radiometric dating method?

_____

_____

_____

_____

SECTION 2 **Determining Absolute Age** *continued*

Radiometric Dating Methods

Method	Parent Isotope	Daughter Isotope	Half-Life (years)	Dating Range
Radiocarbon dating	carbon-14, ^{14}C	nitrogen-14, ^{14}N	5,730	organic matter, less than 70,000 years
Argon-argon dating	argon-39, ^{39}Ar	argon-40, ^{40}Ar	1.25 billion	10,000 to 4.6 billion years
Potassium-argon dating	potassium-40, ^{40}K	argon-40, ^{40}Ar	1.25 billion	50,000 to 4.6 billion years
Rubidium-strontium dating	rubidium-87, ^{87}Rb	strontium-87, ^{87}Sr	48.1 billion	10 million to 4.6 billion years
Uranium-lead dating	uranium-235, ^{235}U	lead-207, ^{207}Pb	704 billion	10 million to 4.6 billion years
Uranium-lead dating	uranium-238, ^{238}U	lead-206, ^{206}Pb	4.5 billion	10 million to 4.6 billion years
Thorium-lead dating	thorium-232, ^{232}Th	lead-208, ^{208}Pb	14.0 billion	more than 200 million years

LOOKING CLOSER

10. Apply Concepts Scientists find a rock that they think is about 250 million years old. Name three radiometric dating methods they could use to date the rock.

_____

_____

How Do Scientists Use Carbon Dating?

Scientists can date some younger sediments indirectly. They can date organic material, such as wood and bones, found in sediment layers. Scientists can use *carbon-14 dating* to find the age of organic material that is less than about 70,000 years old. Another term for carbon-14 dating is *radiocarbon dating*.

Carbon-14, ^{14}C, is a radioactive isotope. It is far less common than the carbon-12, ^{12}C, isotope. Both ^{14}C and ^{12}C combine with oxygen to form carbon dioxide (CO_2). Plants take CO_2 into their bodies during photosynthesis. The carbon becomes part of the bodies of the plants. When animals eat the plants or other animals, the carbon becomes part of their bodies.

After an organism dies, it stops taking in carbon. Like all radioactive isotopes, ^{14}C decays at a constant rate. The amount of ^{14}C in a sample decreases as the ^{14}C decays. Therefore, to find the age of a sample of organic material, scientists find the ratio of ^{14}C to ^{12}C. They compare the ratio with the ratio they know is found in a living organism. The higher the ratio is, the younger the sample is.

Talk About It

Connect to Prior Knowledge In a small group, talk about situations you have read or heard about in which scientists use radiocarbon dating. For example, scientists use radiocarbon dating to find the ages of mummies, such as those from Egypt.

Section 2 Review

SECTION VOCABULARY

absolute age the numeric age of an object or event, often stated in years before the present, as established by an absolute-dating process, such as radiometric dating	**radiometric dating** a method of determining the absolute age of an object by comparing the relative percentages of a radioactive (parent) isotope and a stable (daughter) isotope
half-life the time required for half of a sample of radioactive isotope to break down by radioactive decay to form a daughter isotope	**varve** a pair of sedimentary layers (one coarse, one fine) that is deposited in an annual cycle, commonly in glacial lakes, and that can be used to determine absolute age

1. **Define** In your own words, define *half-life*.

_____

_____

2. **Explain** Why can't scientists use only rates of erosion and deposition to determine the absolute ages of rocks?

_____

_____

_____

_____

3. **Describe** Where and how do varves form?

_____

_____

_____

4. **Compare** How are varves like tree rings?

_____

_____

5. **Apply Concepts** Suppose you have a shark's tooth that you think is about 15,000 years old. Would you use uranium-238 or carbon-14 to date the tooth? Explain your answer.

_____

_____

_____

CHAPTER 8 | The Rock Record

SECTION 3 The Fossil Record

KEY IDEAS

As you read this section, keep these questions in mind:

• What are four ways whole organisms can be preserved as fossils?

• What are examples of fossilized traces of organisms?

• How can scientists use index fossils to determine the age of rocks?

What Are Fossils?

Fossils are the body remains or traces of organisms that lived in the past. The study of fossils is called **paleontology**. Scientists can learn many things from fossils, including

• the ages of rock layers

• information about past climates

• how life on Earth has changed over time

Almost all fossils that scientists find are in sedimentary rock. Fossils are rare in igneous and metamorphic rock because those rocks form under conditions of high heat and pressure. Such conditions generally destroy existing fossils or material that could become fossils. ☑

The fossil record is made up of all fossils that scientists have found so far. The fossil record shows how organisms have changed over time. These changes give scientists information about Earth's past environments and how these environments have changed. For example, scientists have found fossils of marine plants and animals in areas far from present oceans. The fossils tell us that these areas were once covered by ocean.

How Can Fossils Form?

Normally, the bodies of dead plants and animals are eaten by animals or decomposed by bacteria. An organism can become a fossil only if it is preserved before it is eaten or decays. In most cases, the only parts of an organism that are preserved are hard parts. The table on the next page describes ways parts of an organism's body can *fossilize*, or become fossils. ☑

READING TOOLBOX

Outline Make an outline of this section. Use the heading questions to help you develop your outline. Be sure to include the vocabulary terms and answers to the Key Ideas questions.

✓ **READING CHECK**

1. Explain Why are fossils uncommon in igneous and metamorphic rock?

_____

_____

_____

_____

_____

✓ **READING CHECK**

2. Explain Most organisms never become fossils. Why?

_____

_____

_____

_____

SECTION 3 **The Fossil Record** *continued*

How Fossils Form

Method	Example
Mummification Most bacteria, which cause decay, cannot survive in very dry places. Thus, mummified remains are often found in dry places.	
Amber Hardened tree sap is called *amber*. Insects can be trapped in sap. When the sap hardens, the insect is preserved in the amber. In rare cases, scientists have been able to collect DNA from animals preserved in amber.	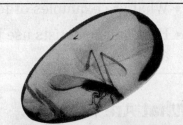
Tar Seeps In some places, petroleum oozes to Earth's surface, where it becomes a tar seep. Water often covers tar seeps. Animals that come to drink the water may fall in and become trapped by the tar. The tar preserves their bodies.	
Freezing Most bacteria cannot survive very low temperatures. Thus, organisms that are buried in frozen soil or ice do not decay.	
Petrification Minerals in groundwater may seep into the tissue of a dead organism buried in sediment. The minerals may replace the tissues. When minerals replace the tissues of a dead organism, the minerals can form a mineral copy of the organism. This is the most common way fossils form.	

LOOKING CLOSER

3. Compare How does petrification differ from the other methods listed in the table?

_____

_____

_____

_____

☑ **READING CHECK**

4. Define What is a trace fossil?

_____

_____

_____

What Are Trace Fossils?

Trace fossils are any evidence other than body parts that an organism once existed. Examples of trace fossils include tracks, footprints, and burrows. These traces can fossilize when sediments cover them and harden. Trace fossils can give scientists clues about how an animal looked and how it lived. ☑

SECTION 3 **The Fossil Record** *continued*

Types of Trace Fossils

Type of Trace Fossil	Example
Carbon Films When organic material decays partially, it leaves behind a thin carbon-rich layer, or *film*. The film shows the surface features of the organism.	
Molds and Casts Sediment may bury a shell. If the shell dissolves, it leaves a space in the sediment called a *mold*. If mud or sand fills a mold and hardens, a cast forms. A *cast* is a copy of the original organism.	
Coprolites Fossilized solid wastes from animals are called *coprolites*. Scientists can look at sections of a coprolite under a microscope to discover what an animal ate.	
Gastroliths Some dinosaurs swallowed stones to help grind their food. These smooth stones, which are called *gastroliths*, can survive as fossils.	

LOOKING CLOSER

5. Classify Many scientists consider molds and casts to be trace fossils. Why do you think this is so?

_____

_____

_____

What Are Index Fossils?

Index fossils are fossils found only in rock layers of a certain geologic age. To be an index fossil, a fossil must

• be present in rocks found over a large region

• have features that make it clearly different from other fossils

• be from an organism that lived during a short span of geologic time

• be found with many other fossils of the same organism

Because index fossils meet very specific requirements, scientists can use them to determine the age of rocks. For example, suppose scientists find the same index fossils in different parts of the world. They can conclude that the rock in these areas formed at about the same time. Recall that the original organisms of index fossils lived during short spans of time. Scientists can use this information to determine the absolute age of the rock.

Critical Thinking

6. Apply Concepts Scientists think horseshoe crabs have existed unchanged for hundreds of millions of years. Could a fossilized horseshoe crab be an index fossil? Explain.

_____

_____

_____

_____

Section 3 Review

SECTION VOCABULARY

fossil the trace or remains of an organism that lived long ago, most commonly preserved in sedimentary rock	**paleontology** the scientific study of fossils
	trace fossil a fossilized mark that formed in sedimentary rock by the movement of an animal on or within soft sediment
index fossil a fossil that is used to establish the age of rock layers because it is distinct, abundant, and widespread and existed for only a short span of geologic time	

1. Describe Identify and describe four processes in which whole organisms may be fossilized.

_____

_____

_____

_____

2. Identify List four types of fossils that scientists can use as indirect evidence that an organism existed.

_____

_____

3. Compare How are the processes of mummification and petrification similar? How are they different?

_____

_____

_____

4. Apply Concepts Suppose a rock layer in Mexico and a rock layer in Australia contain the same index fossil. What do you know about the absolute age of the layer in both places? Explain your answer.

_____

_____

_____

_____

CHAPTER 9 | **A View of Earth's Past**

SECTION 1 Geologic Time

As you read this section, keep these questions in mind:

• How did scientists work together to develop the geologic column?

• What are the major divisions of geologic time?

What Is a Geologic Column?

Earth's surface is always changing. The layers of rock in Earth's crust record these changes. Scientists study these rock layers to learn about Earth's history.

No one area on Earth has a complete record of Earth's history. Therefore, scientists from around the world share what they learn from the rock record. These scientists developed a standard order of rock layers called a **geologic column**. The oldest rocks are at the bottom of the column. The more recent rocks are at the top of the column. ☑

In a geologic column, different layers hold different types of rock and fossils. Fossils in the upper layers look like modern plants and animals. Many fossils in the lower, older layers are from extinct plants and animals.

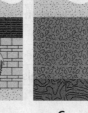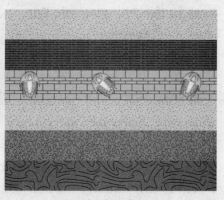

A   B   C

Scientists share information about rock layers A, B, and C to make a geologic column.

Geologic column

USING A GEOLOGIC COLUMN

Scientists can use geologic columns to estimate the ages of rock layers. Scientists compare a layer of rock with a similar layer in a geologic column. The layers they compare may be in the same position relative to other layers. They may have the same fossils. If the two rock layers match, they probably formed around the same time.

READING TOOLBOX

Summarize in Pairs Read this section quietly to yourself. Then, talk with a partner about what you read. Work together to figure out the parts that you did not understand.

✓ READING CHECK

1. Explain Why did scientists have to work together to develop the geologic column?

_____

_____

_____

LOOKING CLOSER

2. Identify Circle the oldest layer of rock in the geologic column.

SECTION 1 **Geologic Time** continued

What Are the Divisions of Geologic Time?

Scientists use what they have learned from rocks and fossils to create a geologic time scale. The geologic time scale identifies major events in Earth's past. It also summarizes changes in Earth's surface, climate, and organisms over time. Scientists use these changes to divide the geologic time scale into smaller units. Fossils from certain organisms characterize each unit of geologic time, as shown on the next page.

EONS

The largest unit of geologic time is an *eon*. Geologic time has four eons, as shown below. The first three eons are part of *Precambrian time*. Precambrian time lasted 4 billion years. It makes up most of Earth's history. After Precambrian time, the Phanerozoic Eon began.

Precambrian time
- Hadean Eon
- Archean Eon
- Proterozoic Eon
- Phanerozoic Eon

ERAS

Eons are divided into shorter units of time called **eras**. The Phanerozoic Eon has three eras.

Eras in the Phanerozoic Eon

Era	Length	Common Fossil Types
Paleozoic	291 million years	variety of sea and land organisms
Mesozoic	186 million years	early birds and reptiles
Cenozoic	65 million years (continuing)	mammals

PERIODS, EPOCHS, AND AGES

Eras are divided into shorter units of time called **periods**. Each period has specific types of fossils. Periods are usually named for the place where the fossils were first found. For example, the *Jurassic Period* is named for the Jura Mountains in Europe.

Sometimes periods are divided into shorter units called **epochs**. Scientists make this division only if there is enough information from the fossil record. Epochs can be divided into even shorter units called *ages*. Scientists need a detailed fossil record to mark ages.

Talk About It

Make Comparisons Just like human society, Earth has a history. With a partner, discuss how a geologic time scale is similar to a timeline found in history books.

LOOKING CLOSER

3. List Which three eons are part of Precambrian time?

_____

_____

_____

LOOKING CLOSER

4. Identify Which era are we living in right now?

_____

SECTION 1 **Geologic Time** *continued*

Era	Period	Epoch	Beginning of Interval (millions of years ago)	Characteristics from Fossils and Geologic Evidence
Cenozoic	Quaternary	Holocene	0.0115	The last glacial period ends; complex human societies develop.
		Pleistocene	1.8	Woolly mammoths, rhinos, and humans appear.
	Tertiary	Pliocene	5.3	Large carnivores, such as bears and lions, appear.
		Miocene	23.0	Grazing herds are abundant; raccoons and wolves appear.
		Oligocene	33.9	Deer, pigs, camels, cats, and dogs appear.
		Eocene	55.8	Horses, flying squirrels, bats, and whales appear.
		Paleocene	65.5	The age of mammals begins; the first primates appear.
Mesozoic	Cretaceous		146	Flowering plants and modern birds appear. Mass extinctions mark the end of the Mesozoic Era.
	Jurassic		200	Dinosaurs are the dominant animals; primitive birds and flying reptiles appear.
	Triassic		251	Dinosaurs and mammals appear; ammonites are common in the oceans; cycads and conifers are common plants.
Paleozoic	Permian		299	Pangaea comes together. Mass extinctions mark the end of the Permian Era.
	Carboniferous	Pennsylvanian Period	318	Giant insects are common; reptiles appear. Huge coal deposits begin to form.
		Mississippian Period	359	Amphibians are common on land; brachiopods are common in the oceans. Forests and swamps cover most of the land.
	Devonian		416	The age of fishes begins; amphibians appear; giant ferns and seed-bearing plants appear.
	Silurian		444	Eurypterids and land plants and animals appear.
	Ordovician		488	Echinoderms appear; brachiopods become more common; trilobites begin to decline.
	Cambrian		542	Trilobites and other shelled marine organisms are common. The atmosphere becomes rich in oxygen.
Precambrian time			4,600	Earth forms; continents begin to form; fossils are rare; bacteria are the most common organisms.

Section 1 Review

SECTION VOCABULARY

epoch a subdivision of geologic time that is longer than an age but shorter than a period	**geologic column** an ordered arrangement of rock layers that is based on the relative ages of the rocks and in which the oldest rocks are at the bottom
era a unit of geologic time that includes two or more periods	**period** a unit of geologic time that is longer than an epoch but shorter than an era

1. Organize List the following units of time from shortest to longest: *age, eon, epoch, era, period, year.*

_____

2. Infer Where on a geologic column would you most likely find fossils of extinct organisms? Explain your answer.

_____

_____

3. Explain How can scientists use a geologic column to determine a rock layer's age?

_____

_____

_____

4. Describe Choose one period from the geologic time scale and describe its major events.

_____

_____

_____

5. Infer The Tertiary Period is divided into five epochs. What can you infer about the fossil record of this period?

_____

_____

6. Predict Consequences Suppose a scientist found a mammal fossil from the Paleozoic Era. How would this change our understanding of Earth's history?

_____

_____

_____

CHAPTER 9 | A View of Earth's Past

SECTION
2 **Precambrian Time and the Paleozoic Era**

KEY IDEAS

As you read this section, keep these questions in mind:

• How is evolution related to geologic change?

• What are two characteristics of Precambrian rock?

• What were the major events of the Paleozoic Era?

What Is Evolution?

Earth's history is recorded in rock layers. The fossils from each layer show which species of organisms existed when the layer formed.

Scientists study and compare fossils from different times in Earth's history. By studying fossils, scientists have discovered evidence that species have changed over time. Scientists use the term *evolution* to describe this change. **Evolution** is the process in which new species develop from existing species. Scientists find evidence for evolution when they compare fossils to living organisms.

This huge species existed from 110 million to 90 million years ago.

The group that includes modern crocodiles has existed for 65 million years.

Modern crocodiles look very similar to their crocodilian ancestors.

EVOLUTION AND GEOLOGIC CHANGE

Geologic and climatic changes affect the ability of many organisms to survive. Scientists use evidence from rocks and fossils to find out how environmental changes affected organisms in the past.

The fossil record shows that some species survived environmental changes but that some species disappeared. Scientists study fossils to find out why some species changed over time and why some stayed almost the same. They also try to find out why species became extinct.

READING TOOLBOX

Outline As you read, make a chart showing major events that happened during Precambrian time and the Paleozoic Era.

LOOKING CLOSER
1. Analyze How do these two skulls support the theory of evolution?

_____

_____

_____

_____

SECTION 2 **Precambrian Time and the Paleozoic Era** *continued*

Why Do Scientists Know Relatively Little About Precambrian Time?

Most scientists agree that Earth formed about 4.6 billion years ago. Earth formed as part of a cloud of dust, or *nebula*. Over time, particles from the cloud formed Earth and other planets.

The formation of Earth was the beginning of **Precambrian time**. Precambrian time lasted about 4 billion years and makes up about 88% of Earth's history.

Scientists do not know much about what happened during Precambrian time. Geologic changes have deformed the rock layers from the time. The layers are not in their original order. Thus, the rock record is hard to interpret, or understand.

PRECAMBRIAN ROCKS

Earth has many areas of exposed, or uncovered, Precambrian rocks. These areas are called *shields*. Precambrian shields result from millions of years of geologic changes.

Precambrian rocks have very few fossils. Precambrian organisms did not have hard parts such as bones or shells that fossilize easily. Precambrian rocks are also very old. Volcanic eruptions, erosion, and movement of tectonic plates probably destroyed most Precambrian fossils. ☑

PRECAMBRIAN LIFE

Scientists have discovered a few Precambrian fossils. The most common fossils are cyanobacteria. These fossils are found in *stromatolites*, or reeflike deposits that form in water. Scientists have also discovered Precambrian fossils of marine worms and jellyfish.

Critical Thinking

2. Analyze Methods Why do scientists not divide Precambrian time into smaller units based on the fossil record?

_____

_____

_____

_____

✓ READING CHECK

3. Explain Give one reason Precambrian rocks do not have many fossils.

_____

_____

_____

Precambrian stromatolites show that shallow seas covered much of Earth during Precambrian time.

What Changes Happened in the Paleozoic Era?

The **Paleozoic Era** began 542 million years ago and ended 251 million years ago. When the Paleozoic Era began, many small continents were scattered over Earth. By the end of the Paleozoic Era, the smaller continents had moved and collided, or crashed into each other. This movement formed the supercontinent Pangaea. The collisions lifted large areas of land and formed mountain ranges. ☑

Paleozoic rocks have many fossils. These fossils show that the number of plant and animal species increased during the Paleozoic Era. Scientists have used the detailed fossil record to divide the Paleozoic Era into six periods: Cambrian, Ordovician, Silurian, Devonian, Carboniferous, and Permian.

READING CHECK

4. Explain How did Pangaea form?

_____

_____

_____

TIMELINE OF THE PALEOZOIC ERA

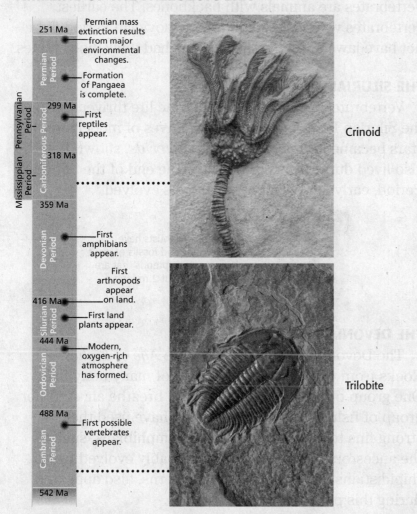

Crinoid

Trilobite

LOOKING CLOSER

5. Identify What was the earliest period in the Paleozoic Era?

_____

6. Identify During which period did the first land plants appear?

_____

7. Interpret Diagrams Which group of organisms evolved first—amphibians or reptiles?

_____

SECTION 2 **Precambrian Time and the Paleozoic Era** *continued*

THE CAMBRIAN PERIOD

Many marine, or sea, organisms appeared during the Cambrian Period. The warm, shallow waters on Earth were perfect for marine *invertebrates*, or animals without backbones. The most common Cambrian invertebrates were *trilobites*. Scientists use many kinds of trilobite fossils as index fossils.

Cambrian invertebrates also included *brachiopods*, a kind of animal with a shell. Many kinds of brachiopods lived during this period, but very few exist today. Worms, jellyfish, snails, and sponges also existed during the Cambrian Period. ☑

THE ORDOVICIAN PERIOD

During the Ordovician Period, brachiopods and other marine organisms, such as *graptolites*, became more common. At the same time, the number of trilobite species decreased. By this period, *vertebrates* had appeared. Vertebrates are animals with backbones. The earliest vertebrates were fish. Fish in the Ordovician Period did not have jaws or teeth. Their bodies had thick, bony plates.

THE SILURIAN PERIOD

Vertebrate and invertebrate marine life thrived during the Silurian Period. Corals and relatives of modern sea stars became more common. *Eurypterids*, shown below, also lived during this period. Near the end of the Silurian Period, early land plants and animals evolved.

Scientists have found fossils of giant eurypterids that are about 2 m long.

THE DEVONIAN PERIOD

The Devonian Period is called the *Age of Fishes*. Rocks from this period hold fossils of many bony fish. One group of fishes, *lungfish*, could breathe air. Another group of fishes, *rhipidistians*, may have used their strong fins to crawl on land. Early amphibians, such as the ancestors of modern frogs, probably evolved from rhipidistians. Land plants, such as ferns, also appeared during this period.

READING CHECK

8. List Identify three kinds of organisms that existed during the Cambrian Period.

_____

_____

_____

Critical Thinking

9. Infer Land animals evolved only after land plants evolved. Why do you think events happened in this order?

_____

_____

_____

_____

SECTION 2 **Precambrian Time and the Paleozoic Era** *continued*

THE CARBONIFEROUS PERIOD

During the Carboniferous Period, Earth's climate was generally warm. Humidity was often very high. Forests and swamps covered much of the land. Over many millions of years, these forests and swamps became coal deposits. These coal deposits exist today in places such as Pennsylvania and Ohio. In North America, scientists divide the Carboniferous Period into the Mississippian Period and the Pennsylvanian Period.

Mississippian Pennsylvanian
Period   Period

Carboniferous Period

318 Ma   299 Ma

First reptiles appear.

Amphibians and fish thrived during the Carboniferous Period. *Crinoids* were common ocean animals. Insects such as giant cockroaches and dragonflies were common land animals. Near the end of the period, early reptiles, which looked like large lizards, appeared.

THE PERMIAN PERIOD

The Permian Period is the last period in the Paleozoic Era. Many environmental changes happened during this period. By the start of the Permian Period, the continents had joined to form Pangaea. New mountain ranges formed, and areas of dry land developed. The warm, shallow seas became smaller.

The environmental changes caused a mass extinction of Paleozoic organisms. In a *mass extinction*, a very large number of species becomes extinct at about the same time. As the seas became smaller, there were fewer habitats for marine species. During the mass extinction at the end of the Permian Period, most marine invertebrates, such as trilobites, died out. ☑

However, fossils show that many reptiles and amphibians survived the changes. Animals from these groups dominated Earth for millions of years after the Paleozoic Era.

LOOKING CLOSER

10. Analyze Graphics About when did reptiles first appear on Earth?

_____

_____

READING CHECK

11. Identify What group of organisms was most affected by changing environments at the end of the Permian Period?

_____

_____

Section 2 Review

SECTION VOCABULARY

evolution the process of change by which new species develop from preexisting species over time **Paleozoic Era** the geologic era that followed Precambrian time and that lasted from 542 million years ago to 251 million years ago	**Precambrian time** the interval of time in the geologic time scale from Earth's formation to the beginning of the Paleozoic era, from 4.6 billion to 542 million years ago

1. Summarize Complete the table below to describe the major developments in the six periods of the Paleozoic Era.

Period	When Period Began (Ma)	Major Events and Biological Developments
Cambrian		
Ordovician	488	
Silurian		
Devonian		
Carboniferous		
Permian		

2. Identify What are two characteristics of Precambrian rock?

_____

_____

3. Analyze Relationships How do geologic changes affect evolution?

_____

_____

_____

CHAPTER 9 A View of Earth's Past

SECTION 3 The Mesozoic and Cenozoic Eras

As you read this section, keep these questions in mind:

• What were the periods of the Mesozoic and Cenozoic Eras?

• What were the major geologic and biological developments during the Mesozoic Era?

• What were the major geologic and biological developments during the Cenozoic Era?

What Changes Happened During the Mesozoic Era?

During a **mass extinction**, large numbers of species become extinct around the same time. At the end of the Permian Period, more than 70% of land organisms and 90% of marine organisms became extinct. The **Mesozoic Era** followed this mass extinction. The mass extinction left space and resources for the species that survived. During the Mesozoic Era, many new species evolved.

READING TOOLBOX

Graphic Organizer As you read, make a concept map using the following terms: *Mesozoic Era, Age of Reptiles, Jurassic Period, Triassic Period, Cretaceous Period, Cenozoic Era, Age of Mammals, Tertiary Period,* and *Quaternary Period.*

TIMELINE OF THE MESOZOIC ERA

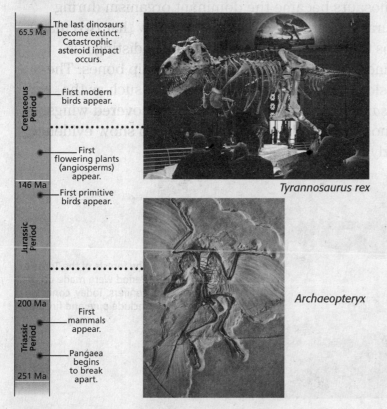

65.5 Ma — The last dinosaurs become extinct. Catastrophic asteroid impact occurs.

Cretaceous Period
— First modern birds appear.

— First flowering plants (angiosperms) appear.

146 Ma — First primitive birds appear.

Jurassic Period

200 Ma — First mammals appear.

Triassic Period

251 Ma — Pangaea begins to break apart.

Tyrannosaurus rex

Archaeopteryx

LOOKING CLOSER

1. Identify What is one geologic change that happened in the Mesozoic Era?

_____

_____

2. Interpret Graphics When did the first mammals appear?

_____

_____

SECTION 3 **The Mesozoic and Cenozoic Eras** *continued*

GEOLOGIC AND BIOLOGICAL DEVELOPMENTS

During the Mesozoic Era, Pangaea broke into smaller continents. Shallow seas and marshes covered much of the land. In general, the climate was warm and humid. The conditions were good for reptiles. Lizards, turtles, crocodiles, snakes, and many dinosaurs thrived during the Mesozoic Era. This era is often called the *Age of Reptiles.* ☑

The Mesozoic Era left a rich fossil record. Based on the fossil record, scientists divide the Mesozoic Era into three periods: Triassic, Jurassic, and Cretaceous.

☑ **READING CHECK**

3. Describe Describe the general climate during the Mesozoic Era.

_____

_____

THE TRIASSIC PERIOD

Many dinosaur species lived during the Triassic Period. Some dinosaurs were the size of squirrels. Others were nearly 30 m long. Most dinosaurs were about 2 m to 5 m long and moved quickly.

Reptiles called *ichthyosaurs* lived in the oceans during the Triassic Period. New marine invertebrates evolved, such as the *ammonite*. On land, small mammals appeared in the forests.

THE JURASSIC PERIOD

Dinosaurs became the dominant organism during the Jurassic Period. Fossil records show that two major groups of dinosaurs evolved. Scientists distinguish the dinosaurs in these groups by their hip bones. The Jurassic Period also had flying reptiles, such as the *pterosaur.* The pterosaur flew on skin-covered wings, like modern bats do. Jurassic rocks also show evidence of early birds, such as *Archaeopteryx.*

Talk About It

Make Comparisons Just how big was a 30-m-long dinosaur? Imagine 30 meter sticks lying end to end. With a partner, discuss everyday objects or buildings that are about the same size as a large dinosaur. Share your ideas with the class.

The forests of the Triassic Period were made up of conifers. Today, conifers include pine and fir trees.

The Two Major Groups of Dinosaurs

	Saurischians	Ornithischians
Meaning of the name	"lizard-hipped"	"bird-hipped"
Herbivores (plant eaters) or carnivores (meat eaters)?	herbivores and carnivores	herbivores
Example	*Apatosaurus*	*Stegosaurus*

THE CRETACEOUS PERIOD

Dinosaurs continued to dominate Earth during the Cretaceous Period. *Tyrannosaurus rex* was almost 6 m tall, which made it one of the largest carnivores from this time. Its sharp teeth were up to 15 cm long. The armored *ankylosaurs* and the horned *ceratopsians* were other dinosaurs of the Cretaceous Period.

Flowering plants, or *angiosperms*, evolved during this period. Angiosperms include magnolia and willow trees. Later, trees such as maples, oaks, and walnuts became common. Angiosperms are the dominant type of land plant today.

The Cretaceous Period ended in a mass extinction that included the dinosaurs. Some scientists think that changes such as volcanoes and continental shifts caused the extinction. However, many scientists use the impact hypothesis to explain the mass extinction.

According to the *impact hypothesis*, an asteroid crashed into Earth 65 million years ago. The crash threw dust into the air. The dust blocked the sun and caused Earth's climate to cool. Many species could not survive the cooler climate. Over time, the dust settled over Earth and formed a layer of sediment. This sediment was full of the element *iridium*. Iridium is common in asteroids, but uncommon in rocks on Earth. ☑

What Changes Happened During the Cenozoic Era?

The **Cenozoic Era** began 65 million years ago after the mass extinction at the end of the Mesozoic Era. Earth had many climate changes during the Cenozoic Era. At times, ice sheets covered almost one-third of Earth's land. New species that could survive in cool climates appeared. Mammals became the dominant organisms. Thus, the Cenozoic Era is called the *Age of Mammals*.

Critical Thinking

4. Synthesize Graphics and Text To which group of dinosaurs did *T. rex* belong? Explain your answer.

_____

_____

_____

_____

READING CHECK

5. Evaluate Hypotheses In what way does the presence of an iridium layer give evidence for an asteroid impact?

_____

_____

_____

_____

_____

SECTION 3 **The Mesozoic and Cenozoic Eras** *continued*

TIMELINE OF THE CENOZOIC ERA

LOOKING CLOSER

6. Calculate How long did the Tertiary Period last? How long has the Quaternary Period lasted?

_____

_____

7. Interpret Graphics Which two epochs make up the Quaternary Period?

_____

_____

8. Identify Name the era, the period, and the epoch we live in today.

_____

_____

_____

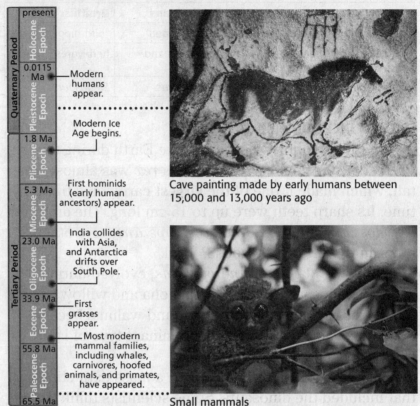

present	
Holocene Epoch	— Modern humans appear.
0.0115 Ma	
Pleistocene Epoch	— Modern Ice Age begins.
1.8 Ma	
Pliocene Epoch	First hominids (early human ancestors) appear.
5.3 Ma	
Miocene Epoch	India collides with Asia, and Antarctica drifts over South Pole.
23.0 Ma	
Oligocene Epoch	
33.9 Ma	— First grasses appear.
Eocene Epoch	— Most modern mammal families, including whales, carnivores, hoofed animals, and primates, have appeared.
55.8 Ma	
Paleocene Epoch	
65.5 Ma	

Cave painting made by early humans between 15,000 and 13,000 years ago

Small mammals

This timeline is not drawn to scale. In other words, the length of an epoch on the timeline is not related to how long the epoch actually lasted.

The Cenozoic Era is divided into two periods: the Tertiary and the Quaternary. These periods are divided into seven epochs: the Paleocene, Eocene, Oligocene, Miocene, Pliocene, Pleistocene, and Holocene.

During the Paleocene Epoch, many new mammal species evolved. The first primates also evolved during this time. The *tarsier* is a modern primate with ancestors from the Paleocene Epoch. ☑

During the Eocene Epoch, the first horses, whales, flying squirrels, and bats appeared. Small reptiles continued to thrive. At the end of the Eocene Epoch, Earth's climate cooled further.

During the Oligocene Epoch, continents collided and formed the Himalayas in Asia. Earth's climate became cooler and drier. Many early mammals became extinct. However, large species of deer, pigs, horses, camels, cats, and dogs survived. Marine invertebrates, such as clams and snails, continued to thrive. Grasses and hardwood trees flourished in this climate.

☑ **READING CHECK**

9. Identify During which epoch did the first primates evolve?

_____

_____

SECTION 3 The Mesozoic and Cenozoic Eras *continued*

THE MIOCENE EPOCH

The Miocene Epoch had changes in currents and sea levels. The largest known land mammals existed during this epoch. Miocene rocks contain fossils of horses, camels, deer, rhinoceroses, pigs, raccoons, wolves, and foxes. They also contain fossils of saber-toothed cats, which are now extinct.

THE PLIOCENE EPOCH

During the Pliocene Epoch, predators such as bears, dogs, and cats evolved into their modern forms. Modern horses also appeared.

Giant ground sloths lived during the late Pliocene in parts of North America and South America.

Near the end of the Pliocene, climate changes caused the ice sheets to grow. As more water froze, sea levels fell. A land bridge appeared between Eurasia and North America. Changes in Earth's crust formed a land bridge between North and South America. Organisms moved between the continents on these land bridges. ☑

THE PLEISTOCENE EPOCH

During the Pleistocene Epoch, ice sheets changed in size many times. Some animals, such as the woolly mammoth, had thick fur that helped them survive the cold climate. Other species survived by moving to warmer areas. Some species became extinct. Pleistocene rocks have fossils of early modern humans. Cave paintings suggest that early humans may have been hunters.

THE HOLOCENE EPOCH

The Holocene Epoch began about 11,500 years ago as the last glacial period ended. The Holocene continues today. As the ice sheets melted, sea levels rose. Coastlines took on their present shapes. In the early Holocene Epoch, modern humans began to farm and use tools made of bronze and iron.

Critical Thinking

10. Apply Concepts
Scientists have a harder time dividing the Mesozoic Era into epochs than dividing the Cenozoic Era. Why do you think this is true?

_____
_____
_____
_____
_____
_____

✓ READING CHECK

11. Explain How did climate changes affect Earth's surface in the Pliocene Epoch?

_____
_____
_____

Math Skills

12. Calculate About what percent of the Cenozoic Era does the Holocene Epoch represent?

_____

Section 3 Review

SECTION VOCABULARY

Cenozoic Era the current geologic era, which began 65.5 million years ago; also called the *Age of Mammals* **mass extinction** an episode during which large numbers of species become extinct	**Mesozoic Era** the geologic era that lasted from 251 million to 65.5 million years ago; also called the *Age of Reptiles*

1. Compare What do the start of the Mesozoic Era and the start of the Cenozoic Era have in common?

_____

2. Summarize Complete the table below to identify the periods of the Mesozoic Era. For each period, describe at least one major life-form that evolved during the period or was dominant during that period.

Period	Major Life-Forms

3. Explain What do many scientists think caused the mass extinction of the dinosaurs?

_____

_____

_____

4. Identify What is one major geologic development during the Mesozoic Era? What is one major geologic development during the Cenozoic Era?

_____

_____

5. Identify Relationships How could you identify the boundary between the Cretaceous and Tertiary Periods in a rock sample? Explain your answer.

_____

_____

_____

CHAPTER 10 Plate Tectonics

SECTION 1 Continental Drift

KEY IDEAS

As you read this section, keep these questions in mind:

• What is Wegener's hypothesis of continental drift?

• What is sea-floor spreading?

• How does paleomagnetism support the idea of sea-floor spreading?

• How does sea-floor spreading provide a mechanism for continental drift?

What Is Continental Drift?

Alfred Wegener was a German scientist who studied maps of the continents. He noticed that some of the continents seem to fit together like puzzle pieces. For example, he thought that South America and Africa look like they could fit together.

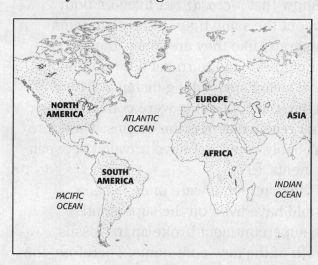

Wegener noticed that some of the continents looked like they could fit together.

The shapes of the continents gave Wegener an idea. He thought that the continents looked like they could fit together because they were once joined together. He made a hypothesis that the continents were once joined together into a single large continent. He called this large continent a *supercontinent*.

Wegener thought that the supercontinent began to break apart about 200 million years ago. Over time, the pieces slowly moved apart. They became the continents that we see today. Wegener's hypothesis is now known as **continental drift**. ☑

READING TOOLBOX

Describe Before you read this section, make a three-panel flip chart. Label the panels "Fossil evidence," "Rock evidence," and "Climate evidence." As you read, fill in information from the section describing the three kinds of evidence for Wegener's hypothesis.

LOOKING CLOSER
1. Identify On the map, circle the parts of South America and Africa that look like they fit together.

READING CHECK

2. Describe What is continental drift?

_____

_____

_____

_____

SECTION 1 **Continental Drift** *continued*

Critical Thinking

3. Explain Why was it important for Wegener to have evidence to support his hypothesis?

_____

_____

_____

_____

READING CHECK

4. Explain Why is it unlikely that *Mesosaurus* traveled between the continents?

_____

_____

_____

_____

LOOKING CLOSER

5. Identify On which three continents are *Glossopteris* fossils found?

_____

_____

_____

What Is the Evidence for Continental Drift?

The matching shapes of the continents support the idea of continental drift. However, there are also other pieces of evidence that support the hypothesis. These pieces of evidence include the following:

- fossil evidence
- rock evidence
- climate evidence

FOSSIL EVIDENCE FOR CONTINENTAL DRIFT

Some evidence that the continents were once joined comes from fossils. Remember that fossils are signs that living things once existed in an area. Wegener learned that fossils of similar animals and plants exist on continents that are far apart today. For example, fossils of *Mesosaurus*, an ancient animal, are found in South America and Africa. The fossils on both continents are identical.

The fossils show that *Mesosaurus* lived on both continents at about the same time. If the continents were always separate, like they are today, then *Mesosaurus* would have had to travel between them. It could not have swum such a long distance. There is no evidence that the continents were connected by land bridges that reached across the oceans. Therefore, *Mesosaurus* probably could not have traveled between separated continents. ☑

However, if the continents were once joined, *Mesosaurus* could have lived on the supercontinent. When the supercontinent broke apart, fossils remained on both of the new continents. Therefore, the *Mesosaurus* fossils and other similar fossils provide evidence for continental drift.

The locations of fossils of ancient life forms, such as *Mesosaurus* and *Glossopteris,* give evidence for continental drift.

SECTION 1 **Continental Drift** *continued*

ROCK EVIDENCE FOR CONTINENTAL DRIFT

Rocks also provide evidence for continental drift.
Similar rocks exist on continents that are far apart today.
Some mountains that exist on one continent seem to continue on another continent. If the continents were once
joined together, these similar rocks would line up. They
would form long mountain chains. Therefore, the rocks at
different places on Earth's surface give evidence that the
continents were once joined.

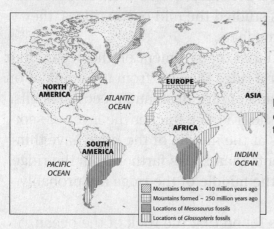

Rocks give evidence that the continents were once joined together.

CLIMATE EVIDENCE FOR CONTINENTAL DRIFT

Scientists think some of the continents had different climates long ago than they have today. They have
found signs that glaciers once existed in South America
and Africa. A glacier is a huge, slow-moving river of ice.
Today, most of South America and Africa are too hot for
glaciers to form. If the continents were once closer to
Earth's poles, they might have been much colder. ☑

Scientists have also found evidence that Antarctica
once had a much warmer climate. They have found fossils of tropical plants in Antarctica. If Antarctica had been
closer to the equator at one time, its climate would have
been warmer. Therefore, the evidence for ancient climates supports the idea that the continents have moved.

PROBLEMS WITH THE CONTINENTAL DRIFT HYPOTHESIS

Wegener had a lot of evidence to support the idea that
the continents were once joined. However, he could not
explain how they might have moved. He thought that the
continents might push through the ocean crust. Other
scientists showed that was impossible. Therefore, most
scientists did not accept Wegener's hypothesis.

LOOKING CLOSER

6. Compare On the map,
circle the continents that
match up based on fossil
evidence. Draw boxes around
the continents that match up
based on rock evidence.

READING CHECK

7. Explain Why is it unlikely
that glaciers existed in South
America and Africa recently?

_____

_____

_____

What Is Sea-Floor Spreading?

Wegener and other scientists living during the early 1900s thought that the ocean floor was smooth and flat. They thought it was all the same age and did not change very much over time. However, in the 1940s and 1950s, scientists began to learn that this idea is not true.

Scientists found long mountain ranges on the ocean floor. Many of these mountains run through the middle of the oceans. Therefore, scientists called them **mid-ocean ridges**. As scientists studied the mid-ocean ridges, they learned two surprising facts.

First, they learned that the sediment on the ocean floor is much thinner near a ridge than far from it. Sediment on the ocean floor is made of dirt, dust, and pieces of shells. The older the ocean floor is, the thicker the layer of sediment there is. Rocks at the middle of the ridge have thinner layers of sediments than rocks farther from the ridge. Therefore, rocks at the middle of the ridge are probably younger. ☑

Second, scientists found that the rock of the ocean floor is much younger than they thought. None of the rock on the ocean floor is older than 200 million years. (The oldest rocks on land are more than 4 billion years old.) Using radiometric dating, they also found that the rock near the ridge is younger than the rock farther away.

Talk About It

Discuss Look up the prefix *mid–* in a dictionary. With a partner, discuss why *mid–ocean ridge* is a good name for a line of mountains in the center of an ocean.

✓ READING CHECK

8. Explain How did finding thin sediment near the ridges tell scientists that the rocks at the ridge are very young?

_____

_____

_____

LOOKING CLOSER

9. Describe Fill in the missing terms to describe the sediment near the rift and the age of the rocks near the rift.

Rock close to the rift is _____ than rock far from the rift.

Sediment close to the rift is _____ than sediment far from the rift.

Mid-ocean ridge   Rift

Sediment

Oceanic crust

Lithosphere—

Magma

Asthenosphere—

Mid-ocean ridges are found in most oceans.

MID-OCEAN RIDGES AND SEA-FLOOR SPREADING

In the late 1950s, a scientist named Harry Hess made a new hypothesis. He knew that there are rifts, or valleys, running through the middle of mid-ocean ridges. He hypothesized that those rifts are cracks in Earth's crust. He thought that magma, or melted rock, could form below the crust and push up through the rift. When the melted rock cools and hardens, it forms new ocean crust.

The new crust forming at the rift makes the ocean floor wider. In other words, new crust pushes apart, or spreads, the sea floor on each side of the rift. Therefore, the process is known as **sea-floor spreading**. ☑

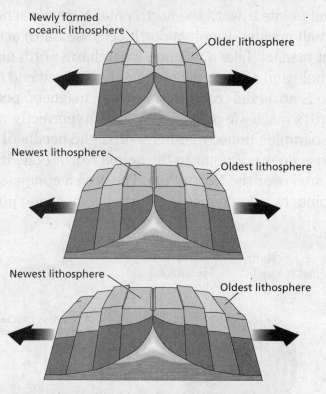

Newly formed oceanic lithosphere

Older lithosphere

Newest lithosphere

Oldest lithosphere

Newest lithosphere

Oldest lithosphere

As magma rises to the surface, the sides of the ridge spread apart. This process is called sea-floor spreading.

Sea-floor spreading makes the ocean floor on the two sides of a rift move apart. Hess thought that the moving sea floor might carry the continents. If that happened, then sea-floor spreading could explain how the continents move. Sea-floor spreading therefore gave more evidence for the continental drift hypothesis.

✓ READING CHECK

10. Explain Why is the process in which new crust forms called *sea-floor spreading?*

_____

_____

_____

LOOKING CLOSER

11. Apply Concepts Where in the bottom picture would you probably find the thickest sediment? Label that place on the picture.

What Is the Other Evidence for Sea-Floor Spreading?

As scientists studied the ocean floor in the 1950s and 1960s, they found more evidence for sea-floor spreading. One strong piece of evidence for sea-floor spreading is based on paleomagnetism. **Paleomagnetism** is the study of the magnetic properties of ancient rocks.

EARTH'S MAGNETIC FIELD

You probably know that you can use a compass to find which way is north. Most compass needles have one end painted red. The needle on the compass will spin until the red end points toward the north pole. A compass needle is a small magnet. It points north because Earth acts like a giant magnet. Like a magnet, Earth has a north magnetic pole and a south magnetic pole. The red end of the needle is attracted to Earth's northern magnetic pole. ☑

Earth's magnetic poles do not line up perfectly with the geographic poles. In other words, the needle of a compass does not point to the actual North Pole. It points to an area near the North Pole. The area a compass needle points to is known as the north geomagnetic pole.

READING CHECK

12. Explain Why does a compass needle point toward the north pole?

_____
_____
_____
_____

North
geomagnetic
pole

North
geographic
pole

A compass needle points to Earth's north geomagnetic pole.

LOOKING CLOSER

13. Identify Circle the spot on Earth that a compass needle points toward.

MAGNETIC REVERSALS

Earth's magnetic poles have not always been where they are today. Many times in the past, they have changed places. The northern magnetic pole moved to the south, and the southern magnetic pole moved to the north. Scientists call the times when the poles were in opposite places *magnetic reversals*. During a magnetic reversal, a compass needle points south, not north.

| SECTION 1 | **Continental Drift** continued |

PALEOMAGNETISM AND SEA-FLOOR SPREADING

Scientists have learned that some minerals are magnetic. They act like tiny compasses. When rock melts, the minerals can line up with Earth's magnetic field. When the melted rock cools and hardens, the minerals are stuck in place. If a magnetic reversal happens after the rock cools, the minerals cannot move to line up with the new magnetic field. Therefore, the rocks can show what Earth's magnetic field was like when they formed. ☑

Rocks that contain iron-rich minerals have magnetic properties. Scientists can study these properties to learn about Earth's magnetic field in the past. The study of these properties is called paleomagnetism.

Paleomagnetism gives more evidence for sea-floor spreading. When scientists study the magnetic fields in the rocks on the sea floor, they see a pattern. The rocks close to a mid-ocean ridge have normal magnetic fields. Farther from the ridge, the rocks have reversed magnetic fields. Even farther out, the fields are normal again. The pattern of normal and reversed fields is the same on both sides of the ridge.

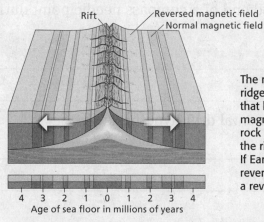

The rock that forms at the ridge forms a magnetic field that lines up with Earth's magnetic field. When that rock is pushed away from the ridge, new rock forms. If Earth's magnetic field is reversed, the new rock has a reversed magnetic field.

READING CHECK

14. Explain How can magnetic minerals show the direction of Earth's magnetic field in the past?

_____

_____

_____

_____

_____

_____

LOOKING CLOSER

15. Describe What happened to Earth's magnetic field from 1 million years ago to 2 million years ago?

_____

_____

_____

_____

As new crust forms at a mid-ocean ridge, the magnetic minerals line up with Earth's magnetic field. The older crust moves away from the ridge as new crust forms. When a magnetic reversal happens, the minerals in the new crust line up with the reversed magnetic field. However, the minerals in the older crust cannot move. They are frozen in place. Over time, "stripes" of rock form with normal and reversed magnetic fields.

Section 1 Review

SECTION VOCABULARY

continental drift the hypothesis that a single large landmass broke up into smaller land-masses to form the continents, which then drifted to their present locations	**paleomagnetism** the study of the alignment of magnetic minerals in rock, specifically as it re-lates to the reversal of Earth's magnetic poles; *also* the magnetic properties that rock acquires during formation
mid-ocean ridge a long, undersea mountain chain that has a steep, narrow valley at its center, that forms as magma rises from the asthenosphere, and that creates new oceanic lithosphere (sea floor) as tectonic plates move apart	**sea-floor spreading** the process by which new oceanic lithosphere (sea floor) forms when magma rises to Earth's surface at mid-ocean ridges and solidifies, as older, existing sea floor moves away from the ridge

1. Explain How does sea-floor spreading support the hypothesis of continental drift?

_____

_____

2. Infer Scientists once thought that all of the ocean floor was very old. Did they probably expect to find very thick sediment or very thin sediment on the ocean floor? Explain your answer.

_____

_____

3. Describe In which direction would the red end of a compass needle point during a magnetic reversal?

_____

_____

4. Explain How do fossils support the continental drift hypothesis?

_____

_____

_____

5. Describe What did scientists observe when they studied the magnetic fields of rocks on the sides of mid-ocean ridges?

_____

_____

_____

CHAPTER 10 | Plate Tectonics
SECTION
2 **The Theory of Plate Tectonics**

As you read this section, keep these questions in mind:
• What is the theory of plate tectonics?
• What are the three types of plate boundaries?
• What are three causes of plate movement?

What Is Plate Tectonics?

After Harry Hess described the idea of sea-floor spreading, scientists found more evidence that continents can move. They used the evidence to develop a new theory: the theory of plate tectonics. The theory of **plate tectonics** explains how continents move and change shape.

THE LITHOSPHERE AND ASTHENOSPHERE

Remember that Earth's outer layer is called the *crust*. The layer underneath the crust is called the *mantle*. The top part of the mantle is very stiff and brittle. Together, the crust and this upper, stiff part of the mantle form the **lithosphere**. ☑

The lithosphere includes only the very top part of the mantle. The layer of the mantle below the lithosphere is called the **asthenosphere**. Unlike the rock in the lithosphere, the rock in the asthenosphere is soft. It is solid, but it is so hot and soft that it can flow, like chewing gum. Scientists say that the asthenosphere is made of plastic rock. *Plastic* means "flexible and able to flow."

Summarize After you read this section, create a concept map that uses all the vocabulary terms.

READING CHECK

1. Identify What are the parts of the lithosphere?

_____

_____

_____

_____

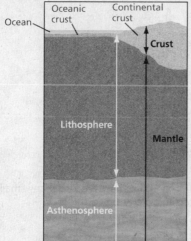

Oceanic crust | Continental crust
Ocean
Crust
Lithosphere
Mantle
Asthenosphere

The lithosphere is hard. It includes the crust and the top part of the mantle. The asthenosphere is soft. It can move slowly.

LOOKING CLOSER
2. Describe Which is thicker, the lithosphere or the crust?

_____

_____

TECTONIC PLATES

The lithosphere is broken up into large pieces called tectonic plates. The tectonic plates move slowly over the asthenosphere. As the tectonic plates move, they carry the continents with them. Therefore, the movement of tectonic plates explains the movement of continents. ☑

What Happens Where Tectonic Plates Touch?

Tectonic plates are like puzzle pieces. The places where they touch are called plate boundaries. Earthquakes and volcanoes are more common at plate boundaries than anywhere else.

EARTHQUAKES AND VOLCANOES

At plate boundaries, tectonic plates rub together. The plates do not rub together smoothly, though. Instead, they stick together, like two pieces of sandpaper. The movements of the plates cause pressure on the plate boundaries. When the pressure gets too high, the rock breaks. The breaking rock releases energy that makes the ground shake. The shaking is an earthquake.

Almost all earthquakes happen at plate boundaries. Scientists have special tools that can record where earthquakes happen. They can draw those locations on a map. When they draw the locations on a map, they see that most earthquakes happen in certain areas. These areas are the same as the plate boundaries.

Volcanoes are also more common on plate boundaries. Like earthquakes, volcanoes are most common in certain areas. The areas where earthquakes and volcanoes are most likely show where the plate boundaries are.

There are about 15 large tectonic plates on Earth. There are also many smaller plates. This map shows many of the tectonic plates on Earth.

✓ READING CHECK

3. Describe What is a tectonic plate?

_____

_____

Talk About It

Model Make a model of how an earthquake happens. Discuss your model with a partner. Describe how your model shows what happens during an earthquake.

LOOKING CLOSER

4. Infer Circle two areas on the map that probably have a lot of earthquakes or volcanoes.

SECTION 2 **The Theory of Plate Tectonics** *continued*

TYPES OF PLATE BOUNDARIES

Not all plate boundaries are the same. There are three types of plate boundaries:
- divergent boundaries, where plates move apart
- convergent boundaries, where plates move together
- transform boundaries, where plates slide past each other ☑

What Happens at a Divergent Boundary?

To *diverge* means "to move apart." At a **divergent boundary**, two plates move away from each other. Mid-ocean ridges are divergent boundaries. However, divergent boundaries can also form on land.

Divergent boundaries are places where new lithosphere forms. At a mid-ocean ridge, melted rock, or magma, rises up from the asthenosphere. It flows into the rift between the plates. When the magma cools and hardens, it forms new lithosphere.

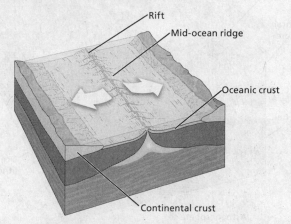

New lithosphere forms at divergent boundaries.
Most divergent boundaries are under the oceans.

What Happens at a Convergent Boundary?

To *converge* means "to come together." At a **convergent boundary**, two plates move toward each other. In other words, the plates collide. The collision of the plates can have different effects.

The effects of the collision depend on what kinds of lithosphere are colliding. There are two main types of lithosphere: oceanic lithosphere and continental lithosphere. Oceanic lithosphere is thin and dense. Continental lithosphere is thick and not very dense. ☑

✓ READING CHECK

5. Identify What are the three types of plate boundaries?

_____

_____

_____

Critical Thinking

6. Apply Concepts If one plate at a divergent boundary is moving north, in which direction is the other plate probably moving?

_____

✓ READING CHECK

7. Compare Name two ways continental lithosphere is different from oceanic lithosphere.

_____

_____

_____

_____

SECTION 2 **The Theory of Plate Tectonics** *continued*

OCEANIC-CONTINENTAL COLLISIONS

At some convergent boundaries, oceanic lithosphere meets continental lithosphere. The oceanic lithosphere is denser than the continental lithosphere. Therefore, the oceanic lithosphere sinks beneath the continental lithosphere. The oceanic lithosphere sinks into the asthenosphere. The sinking of the lithosphere into the asthenosphere is called *subduction*. ☑

As part of the lithosphere sinks into the asthenosphere, the heat and pressure on the lithosphere become greater. The high heat and pressure squeeze water out of the sinking lithosphere. The water mixes with the rock in the asthenosphere and makes the rock melt. The melted rock rises through the crust and erupts. Thus, volcanoes are common at plate boundaries where oceanic lithosphere sinks beneath continental lithosphere.

☑ **READING CHECK**

8. Define What is subduction?

_____

_____

_____

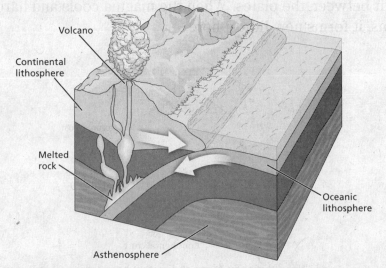

When oceanic lithosphere meets continental lithosphere, the oceanic lithosphere sinks into the asthenosphere. The Andes Mountains in South America are an example of this kind of convergent boundary.

LOOKING CLOSER

9. Identify Where does the magma that is erupting at this convergent boundary come from?

_____

_____

As the oceanic lithosphere sinks, it rubs against the continental lithosphere on the other plate. The rubbing produces pressure that can make the rock slip and break, causing earthquakes. Thus, large earthquakes are common at plate boundaries where oceanic lithosphere collides with continental lithosphere.

SECTION 2 **The Theory of Plate Tectonics** *continued*

CONTINENTAL-CONTINENTAL COLLISIONS

At some convergent boundaries, two pieces of continental lithosphere collide. Because continental lithosphere is not very dense, it does not easily sink into the asthenosphere. Therefore, when two pieces of continental lithosphere collide, both pieces crumple up and form very tall mountains. The tallest mountains in the world, the Himalaya Mountains, are found at this kind of convergent boundary. ☑

Volcanoes are not very common at this type of convergent boundary. Earthquakes are common. However, the earthquakes are not as large as those at continental-oceanic boundaries.

OCEANIC-OCEANIC COLLISIONS

At some convergent boundaries, oceanic lithosphere meets oceanic lithosphere. Subduction happens at these convergent boundaries. One of the pieces of oceanic lithosphere sinks beneath the other one. The sinking lithosphere gives off water, just like at a continental-oceanic convergent boundary.

The water causes the asthenosphere to melt and form magma. The magma rises through the lithosphere and erupts. Therefore, volcanoes are common at oceanic-oceanic convergent boundaries. Earthquakes are also common, because of the pressure produced when the sinking lithosphere rubs against the other lithosphere.

An *island arc* is a chain of volcanic islands. Island arcs are common at this kind of convergent boundary. Japan is an example of an island arc.

Type of Convergent Boundary	Description	Example
Continental-oceanic	continental lithosphere collides with oceanic lithosphere; volcanoes and earthquakes common; mountains form	Andes Mountains
Oceanic-oceanic	oceanic lithosphere collides with oceanic lithosphere; volcanoes and earthquakes common; chain of islands forms	Japan
Continental-continental	continental lithosphere collides with continental lithosphere; earthquakes common; very tall mountains form	Himalaya Mountains

✓ READING CHECK

10. Explain Why doesn't continental lithosphere sink into the asthenosphere?

_____

_____

_____

LOOKING CLOSER

11. Compare At what two types of convergent boundaries are you likely to find volcanoes?

_____

_____

SECTION 2 **The Theory of Plate Tectonics** *continued*

What Happens at a Transform Boundary?

At a **transform boundary**, two tectonic plates slide past each other. As the plates slide past each other, they stick and press together. When the pressure gets too high, the rock breaks and causes an earthquake. Therefore, earthquakes are common at transform boundaries. Volcanoes are not common at transform boundaries.

The San Andreas fault in California is an example of a transform boundary. Transform boundaries are also common along mid-ocean ridges. Transform boundaries break most mid-ocean ridges into short segments.

LOOKING CLOSER

12. Describe Draw arrows on the diagram to show the directions the plates are moving.

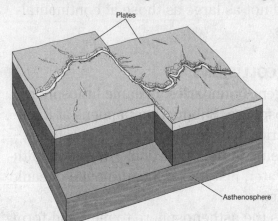

Plates

Asthenosphere

At a transform boundary, plates slide past each other. They do not move apart or together.

What Makes Tectonic Plates Move?

Scientists are still not sure why the tectonic plates move. However, they think that three main factors cause the plates to move. Those three factors are mantle convection, ridge push, and slab pull.

MANTLE CONVECTION

Suppose you put a pot of water on a hot stove. The water at the bottom of the pot will heat up first. As it heats up, it becomes less dense. The less dense water rises to the top of the pot. Cooler, denser water sinks toward the bottom to replace the rising water. The movement of the water is an example of convection. During *convection*, denser material sinks, and less dense material rises. ☑

Scientists think the rock in Earth's mantle can convect, just like the water in the pot. Hot rock rises toward the surface, and colder rock sinks. Scientists think the movement of the mantle might be one of the reasons the plates move. As the mantle moves, it may carry the plates along.

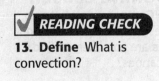

READING CHECK

13. Define What is convection?

_____

_____

_____

_____

SECTION 2 **The Theory of Plate Tectonics** *continued*

RIDGE PUSH

Convection in the mantle is not the only reason the plates move. At mid-ocean ridges, new crust forms. The new crust pushes the older crust away from the ridge. This process is called *ridge push*. Scientists think ridge push might also cause plates to move.

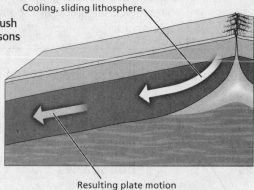

Scientists think ridge push may be one of the reasons the plates move.

Cooling, sliding lithosphere

Resulting plate motion

LOOKING CLOSER

14. Explain What causes ridge push?

_____

_____

_____

_____

SLAB PULL

Most scientists think that mantle convection and ridge push cause only a little bit of plate motion. They think pulling forces where plates converge are the main forces that make the plates move. Subduction happens at most convergent boundaries. Remember that during subduction, one plate sinks into the asthenosphere. Scientists think that, as the edge of the plate sinks, it pulls the rest of the plate along with it. This process is called *slab pull*.

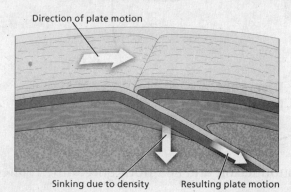

Direction of plate motion

Sinking due to density   Resulting plate motion

Scientists think that slab pull is the main reason the plates move.

LOOKING CLOSER

15. Explain Why does the edge of the plate sink?

_____

_____

Section 2 Review

SECTION VOCABULARY

asthenosphere the solid, plastic layer of the mantle beneath the lithosphere

convergent boundary the boundary between tectonic plates that are colliding

divergent boundary the boundary between tectonic plates that are moving away from each other

lithosphere the solid, outer layer of Earth that consists of the crust and the rigid upper part of the mantle

plate tectonics the theory that explains how large pieces of the lithosphere, called *plates*, move and change shape

transform boundary the boundary between tectonic plates that are sliding past each other horizontally

1. Compare Complete the Venn diagram to compare the three types of plate boundaries.

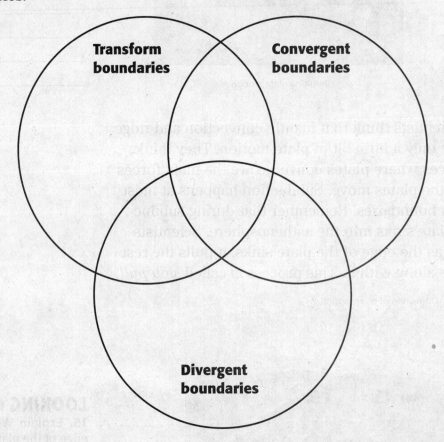

2. Describe Relationships How are subduction and sea-floor spreading related to ridge push and slab pull?

_____

_____

_____

_____

CHAPTER 10 | Plate Tectonics
SECTION 3 | The Changing Continents

As you read this section, keep these questions in mind:

• How do the movements of tectonic plates change Earth's surface?

• How have the movements of tectonic plates affected Earth's climate and life?

• What is the supercontinent cycle?

How Do Continents Change Shape?

Tectonic plates are always moving. The movements of the plates change Earth's surface and affect its climate. One of the ways plate movements affect Earth's surface is by changing the shapes of the continents.

The continents have not always looked the way they look today. In the future, they will look different, too. There are two main ways continents change: rifting and accretion.

READING TOOLBOX

Clarify As you read this section, underline any words or phrases you do not understand. Work with a partner to figure out what the underlined words and phrases mean.

RIFTING

At a divergent boundary, tectonic plates move apart. Today, most divergent boundaries are under the oceans. However, divergent boundaries can also exist on continents. For example, there is a divergent boundary in eastern Africa.

At the East African Rift Valley, the continent is breaking into pieces, or rifting. **Rifting** is the process in which a continent breaks apart. You can also use the word *rifting* to describe what happens at a mid-ocean ridge.

The East African Rift is getting wider each year.

LOOKING CLOSER

1. Infer Draw arrows on the picture to show which directions the plates are probably moving.

ACCRETION

Continents can also change shape by growing larger. A continent can grow larger if a volcano on it erupts. Continents can also grow by accretion. In the process of *accretion*, new lithosphere is added to the edge of a continent. The new lithosphere that is added is called a terrane. A **terrane** is a piece of lithosphere that has a different geologic history from the lithosphere around it.

Scientists have studied the geologic history of the rocks on continents. They have learned that the centers of most continents are more than 540 million years old. These very old, central parts of the continents are called *cratons.*

The edges of the continents are made up of different terranes. The terranes have formed over time at convergent boundaries. As one tectonic plate sinks beneath another at a convergent boundary, terranes on the sinking plate are scraped off. They stick to the edge of the continent on the other plate.

Critical Thinking

2. Infer How do geologists likely identify a terrane?

_____

_____

_____

_____

_____

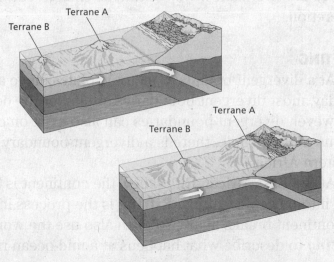

LOOKING CLOSER

3. Identify Label the continent on the diagrams.

Moving plates carry terranes with them. When a plate sinks into the asthenosphere, the terranes on it are scraped off. They become part of the continent.

Many different structures can make up terranes. Some terranes are volcanoes that have erupted on the ocean floor. Other terranes are made up of coral or rock that forms along beaches and on islands. Some terranes are made up of pieces of continental crust.

SECTION 3 **The Changing Continents** *continued*

IDENTIFYING TERRANES

A terrane may change a lot when it is scraped off onto a continent. Scientists can identify terranes by looking for three features.

1. A terrane has different rocks and fossils than other terranes or cratons.
2. Large faults, or cracks in rock, divide a terrane from other terranes or cratons.
3. The rocks in a terrane generally have different magnetic properties than the rocks in other terranes.

How Do Continental Movements Affect Earth?

The movements of the plates do not affect only the shapes of the continents. As the plates move, the continents also move. Mountains form and are broken down. Continents move closer to or farther from the equator. These changes and movements can affect Earth's climate. They can also affect life on Earth.

EFFECTS ON CLIMATE

The map below shows how the water in the oceans moves. You can see that the positions of the continents affect how the ocean water moves.

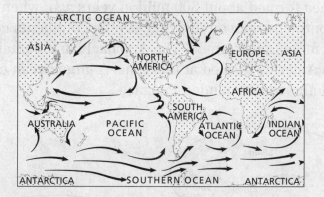

The movements of ocean water affect Earth's climate. Cool ocean water that flows near a continent can make the continent cooler. Warm water flowing near a continent can make the continent warmer.

The positions of the continents affect the movement of ocean water. The movement of ocean water affects climate. Therefore, as the continents move, climate can change.

Critical Thinking
4. Infer What do you think is the reason that there are large faults in places where terranes meet?

_____

_____

_____

_____

_____

Talk About It
Apply Concepts With a partner, talk about how the movement of ocean water would be different if the continents were in different places.

SECTION 3 **The Changing Continents** *continued*

EFFECTS ON LIFE

· When a continent breaks apart or a mountain forms, groups of living things can be separated. For example, one group of mice might be split into two groups. The two groups will live in different environments. Over time, they may evolve, or change, into new types of living things. In this way, plate tectonics can affect life. ☑

How Have the Continents Changed Over Time?

Alfred Wegener thought that all the continents had once been joined into a single supercontinent. Scientists have found evidence that he was correct. However, scientists today think that there may have been more than one supercontinent. They think the continents have joined and broken apart many times over Earth's history.

The process in which the continents come together, form a supercontinent, and then break apart again is called the **supercontinent cycle**. Right now, the continents are broken apart. Over millions of years, the continents will move together and form another supercontinent.

PANGAEA

The most recent supercontinent was called **Pangaea**. Pangaea formed about 300 million years ago, when the continents moved together. As the continents collided, mountains formed. The Appalachian mountains in North America formed at this time. A large ocean called **Panthalassa** surrounded Pangaea.

450 million years ago

225 million to 200 million years ago

About 450 million years ago, the continents were separated. They moved together and formed the supercontinent Pangaea.

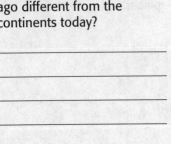

READING CHECK

5. Explain How can plate tectonics affect life?

_____
_____
_____
_____
_____

Talk About It

Discuss Look up the word *cycle* in a dictionary. With a partner, discuss why the supercontinent cycle is considered a cycle.

LOOKING CLOSER

6. Compare How were the continents 450 million years ago different from the continents today?

_____
_____
_____
_____
_____
_____

SECTION 3 **The Changing Continents** *continued*

THE BREAKUP OF PANGAEA

About 200 million years ago, Pangaea began to break apart. At first, a large rift split Pangaea into two pieces. Scientists call the pieces Laurasia and Gondwanaland. Over time, Laurasia and Gondwanaland also began to break apart. Laurasia broke into pieces that became North America, Europe, and Asia. Gondwanaland broke into pieces that became South America, Africa, India, Australia, and Antarctica. ☑

About 50 million years ago, India collided with Asia. The Himalaya Mountains began to form. India and Asia are still moving together today. Thus, the Himalaya Mountains are still growing.

READING CHECK

7. Identify Which continents did Laurasia form?

_____

_____

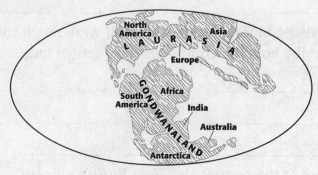

160 million to 140 million years ago

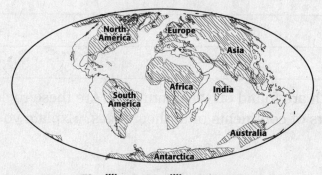

70 million to 50 million years ago

LOOKING CLOSER

8. Illustrate Look closely at the map showing the continents 160 million to 140 million years ago. Draw lines to show where the continents broke apart to form the Atlantic Ocean.

By about 160 million years ago, Pangaea had broken into two large pieces. Over time, those pieces broke apart to form the modern continents. The dark lines in the second map show where the continents are today.

SUPERCONTINENT OF THE FUTURE

Scientists can use information about how the plates are moving to predict what Earth will look like in the future. They think that in about 250 million years, the continents will form a new supercontinent. Africa will collide with Europe and Asia. North America and South America will collide with Africa. Australia and Antarctica will come together.

Section 3 Review

SECTION VOCABULARY

Pangaea the supercontinent that formed 300 million years ago and that began to break up 200 million years ago	**supercontinent cycle** the process by which supercontinents form and break apart over millions of years
Panthalassa the single, large ocean that covered Earth's surface during the time the supercontinent Pangaea existed	**terrane** a piece of lithosphere that has a unique geologic history and that may be part of a larger piece of lithosphere, such as a continent
rifting the process by which Earth's crust breaks apart; can occur within continental crust or oceanic crust	

1. Compare Describe the difference between Pangaea and Panthalassa.

_____

_____

2. Describe The continents that existed before Pangaea formed were much smaller than the continents today. Describe how the continents have grown larger.

_____

_____

_____

3. Explain How can the movements of the continents affect Earth's climate?

_____

_____

_____

4. Infer The oldest rocks on Earth are found on the continents. Are these rocks most likely found in the centers of continents or at their edges? Explain your answer.

_____

_____

5. Describe Relationships Describe how convergent and divergent boundaries are related to the supercontinent cycle.

_____

_____

_____

_____

CHAPTER 11 Deformation of the Crust
SECTION 1 How Rock Deforms

KEY IDEAS

As you read this section, keep these questions in mind:
- What is isostasy?
- What are the three main types of stress?
- How are folds and faults alike and different?

What Is Isostasy?

Mountain ranges are proof that the shape of Earth's surface is constantly changing. These changes are caused by deformation. **Deformation** is the bending and breaking of Earth's crust.

Deformation can happen when the weight of some part of Earth's crust changes. If the lithosphere becomes thicker and heavier, it sinks down into the asthenosphere. If the lithosphere becomes thinner and lighter, it rises in the asthenosphere.

The vertical movement of the lithosphere depends on two opposing forces. One is the force of gravity, which pulls the lithosphere down. The other is the buoyant force of the asthenosphere, which pushes up on the lithosphere. When these two forces are balanced, the lithosphere and asthenosphere are in a state of **isostasy**. ☑

When the weight of the lithosphere changes, the lithosphere sinks or rises until the forces balance again. The movement of the lithosphere puts forces on the rock in it. These forces can cause deformation.

READING TOOLBOX

Summarize As you read this section, underline sentences that relate to the Key Idea questions. When you finish reading, write a short answer to each Key Idea question using the underlined information.

✓ READING CHECK

1. Explain What are the two forces that must balance out to maintain a state of isostasy?

_____

_____

_____

LOOKING CLOSER
2. Explain Why are the mountains shrinking from image to image?

_____

_____

A Gravitational force
Original elevation
Continental lithosphere
Buoyant force

B New elevation

C Final elevation

As erosion wears away the crust, the lithosphere becomes lighter and rises.

TYPES OF ISOSTATIC ADJUSTMENTS

An *isostatic adjustment* happens when Earth's lithosphere rises or sinks to maintain isostasy. Isostatic adjustments are happening all the time in Earth's crust. For example, a mountain goes through isostatic adjustments as it erodes. Over millions of years, wind, water, and ice wear away the rock. The mountain becomes shorter and lighter. As the mountain shrinks, it rises in a process called *uplift*. ☑

The opposite of uplift is *subsidence*. During subsidence, the lithosphere becomes heavier. It sinks into the asthenosphere. Subsidence is common in places where large rivers flow into oceans. Large rivers generally carry large amounts of sediment, including mud, sand, and gravel. When the river flows into the ocean, the sediment drops onto the ocean floor. The extra weight of the sediment makes the ocean floor sink.

Isostatic adjustments can also happen when glaciers grow or shrink. A *glacier* is a huge river of ice. Glaciers can hold huge amounts of water. Therefore, they are very heavy. The weight of the ice makes the lithosphere beneath the glacier sink. At the same time, the ocean floor rises because the weight of the ocean water is less. The water has moved onto land and has been frozen in the glacier. ☑

When the glacier melts, the water returns to the ocean. The extra weight of the water causes the ocean floor to sink. At the same time, the land that was covered with ice rises because the weight of the crust has decreased.

READING CHECK

3. Describe What happens in the process of uplift?

_____

_____

_____

READING CHECK

4. Explain Why does the ocean floor rise when large glaciers form?

_____

_____

_____

_____

Isostatic Adjustments

Cause	Effect
Wind, water, and ice carry away rock from mountains.	The mountains become lighter, and uplift occurs.
Rivers deposit sediment on the ocean floor.	The ocean floor becomes heavier, and subsidence occurs.
Glaciers form as ice and snow build up.	The weight of the glacier causes subsidence under the glacier. The decreased weight of ocean water causes uplift in the oceans.
Glaciers melt as the climate gets warmer.	The decreased weight of the glacier causes uplift on land. The increased weight of ocean water causes subsidence in the oceans.

SECTION 1 **How Rock Deforms** *continued*

What Kinds of Stress Can Act on Rocks?

As Earth's lithosphere moves, the rock in the crust is squeezed, stretched, and twisted. These actions put force on the rock. **Stress** is the amount of force applied to a given area of rock. Stress occurs when the lithosphere sinks and is squeezed by the weight of rock above it. It also occurs when the rock in the crust rises and is stretched out. The movement of tectonic plates past one another can also produce stress.

There are three main types of stress: compression, tension, and shear stress. *Compression* is a type of stress that squeezes rock. Compression can change the shape of a rock or reduce the amount of space the rock takes up. Compression is a common kind of stress in places where tectonic plates are moving together.

Tension is the opposite of compression. *Tension* is stress that stretches rock. Tension can make rock longer and thinner. Tension is a common kind of stress in places where tectonic plates are moving apart.

Shear stress deforms rock by pushing its different parts in opposite directions. Sheared rock can bend, twist, or break apart as it moves past other rocks. Shear stress is a common kind of stress in places where tectonic plates slide past each other. ☑

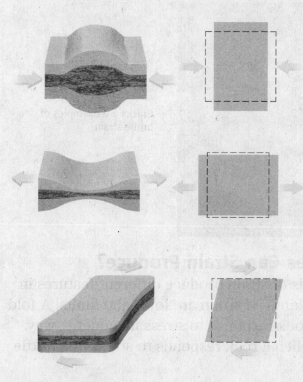

The pictures on the left show how different kinds of stress can affect rock layers. The pictures on the right show how the kinds of stress can affect a square block. The dotted lines show the original shape of each block.

Critical Thinking

5. Apply Concepts Which type of stress is probably most common in places where new mountains are forming?

_____

_____

READING CHECK

6. Identify Which kind of stress causes rock to twist?

_____

_____

LOOKING CLOSER

7. Identify Label the pictures to indicate which pictures show compression, which show tension, and which show shear stress.

THE EFFECT OF STRESS ON ROCKS

Stress can cause deformation. Deformation that is caused by stress is called **strain**. Changes in shape and size are examples of strain.

Strain is not always permanent. If the stress is applied slowly, the rock might go back to its original shape when the stress is removed. However, if too much stress is put on the rock, the strain may become permanent.

There are two main types of permanent strain: brittle and ductile. Rocks that break or fracture under stress are *brittle*. Cracks and breaks in rock are types of brittle strain. In contrast, *ductile* rocks respond to stress by bending without breaking. Folds and bends in rock are types of ductile strain. ☑

The type of strain a rock shows depends on several factors. These factors include temperature, pressure, the composition of the rock, and how fast the stress is applied.

Near Earth's surface, where temperature and pressure are low, brittle strain is most common. Brittle strain is also more common when a lot of stress is applied quickly. At higher temperature and pressure, ductile strain is more common. Small amounts of stress applied over long periods of time can also cause ductile strain.

READING CHECK

8. Identify Which type of strain can cause a rock to stretch?

_____
_____

LOOKING CLOSER

9. Describe Name two sets of conditions that might have produced the strain in the picture.

_____
_____
_____
_____
_____
_____

Cracks are examples of brittle strain.

What Features Can Strain Produce?

Different kinds of strain produce different features in rock. Two main kinds of strain are folds and faults. A fold occurs when a rock responds to stress in a ductile way. A fault occurs when a rock responds to stress in a brittle way.

CHARACTERISTICS OF FOLDS

A **fold** is a bend in a rock layer. Most folds form when rocks are compressed. As compression acts on the rock, the rock layers wrinkle and fold over themselves. Some folds also form because of shear stress.

Folds have different parts. They have sloping sides called *limbs*. The limbs meet at the bend, or *hinge*, of the rock layers.

Folds can be symmetrical or asymmetrical. If a fold can be sliced in two identical halves, it is symmetrical. The dividing line is called the *axial plane*. However, most folds are not symmetrical.

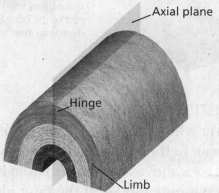

Axial plane

Hinge

Limb

Folds can have many different shapes. Many folds are bent vertically. However, some are overturned and seem to be lying on their sides. Folds can be open or very tight. The limbs can be even, or one can be steeper than the other. The hinge can be a smooth bend or a sharp point. Each fold is unique because it formed under a unique combination of conditions.

Folds can vary in size as well as shape. Some are smaller than your hand. Others cover thousands of square kilometers. Some folds are so large that they form ridges and valleys.

TYPES OF FOLDS

Geologists classify folds based on their characteristics. There are three main kinds of folds: anticlines, synclines, and monoclines. In an *anticline*, the oldest rocks are in the middle of the fold. In a *syncline*, the oldest rocks are on the outside of the fold. In a *monocline*, the two limbs are horizontal or almost horizontal. The pictures on the next page show examples of these kinds of folds. ☑

LOOKING CLOSER

10. Describe Is this fold symmetrical or asymmetrical? How do you know?

_____

_____

_____

_____

READING CHECK

11. Identify What are the three main kinds of folds?

_____

_____

_____

SECTION 1 | **How Rock Deforms** *continued*

Anticline

The oldest rocks are on the inside of an anticline. Most anticlines are arch shaped.

LOOKING CLOSER

12. Analyze Processes Why would a syncline be more likely to have a bowl shape?

_____

_____

_____

_____

_____

Syncline

The oldest rocks are on the outside of a syncline. Most synclines are bowl shaped.

Monocline

Monoclines form when one part of the crust is lifted relative to another part.

CHARACTERISTICS OF FAULTS

Faults form when rock deforms in a brittle way. A **fault** is a break in the body of a rock along which the surrounding rock moves. The *fault plane* is the plane along which the rock moves. If the fault plane is not vertical, the rock above the fault plane is known as the *hanging wall*. The rock below the fault plane is called the *footwall*. ☑

✓ READING CHECK

13. Define What is the hanging wall?

_____

_____

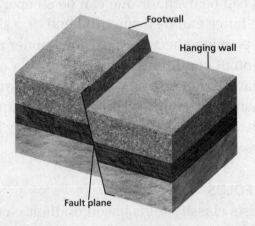

Footwall

Hanging wall

Fault plane

Like folds, faults can vary greatly in size. Small faults may affect only a few layers of rock found in a small region. Other faults are thousands of kilometers long. These large faults are often composed of smaller, connected faults, rather than a single fault.

SECTION 1 How Rock Deforms *continued*

TYPES OF FAULTS

There are two main types of faults: normal faults and reverse faults. In a *normal fault*, the hanging wall moves down relative to the footwall. In a *reverse fault*, the hanging wall moves up relative to the footwall. A *thrust fault* is a type of reverse fault in which the fault plane is almost horizontal.

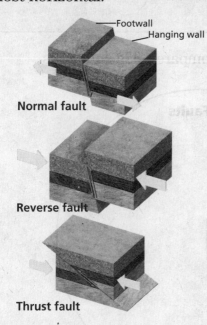

Footwall
Hanging wall

Most normal faults form when rock is under tension.

Normal fault

Most reverse faults form when rock is under compression.

Reverse fault

A thrust fault is a type of reverse fault.

Thrust fault

14. Describe Label the hanging wall and the footwall in the pictures of the reverse fault and the thrust fault.

In some faults, the rock does not move up and down. Instead, it moves horizontally. The two pieces of rock slide past one another. This type of fault is called a *strike-slip fault*. The rock in a strike-slip fault moves parallel to the direction of the fault's length. The fault plane in a strike-slip fault may be vertical or tilted.

Strike-slip faults are most commonly found at transform boundaries, where tectonic plates grind past each other. They may also occur at fracture zones between segments of mid-ocean ridges.

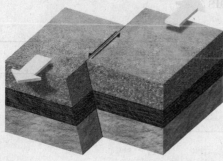

Strike-slip faults are common in areas that have shear stress acting on them.

15. Compare How is a strike-slip fault different from a normal fault?

_____

_____

_____

_____

_____

Name _____ Class _____ Date _____

Section 1 Review

SECTION VOCABULARY

deformation the bending, tilting, and breaking of Earth's crust; the change in the shape of rock in response to stress	**isostasy** a condition of gravitational and buoyant equilibrium between Earth's lithosphere and asthenosphere
fault a break in a body of rock along which one block slides relative to another; a form of brittle strain	**stress** the amount of force per unit area that acts on a rock
fold a form of ductile strain in which rock layers bend, usually as a result of compression	**strain** any change in a rock's shape or volume caused by stress

1. Compare Complete the Venn diagram below to compare folds and faults.

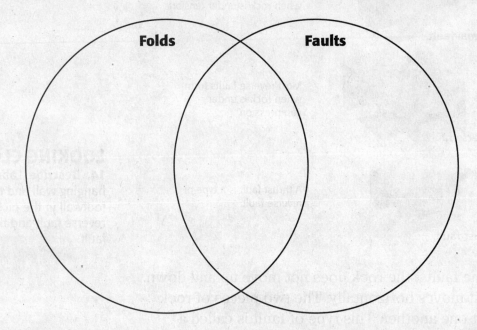

2. Apply Concepts What would you expect a rock that has experienced tension to look like?

_____

_____

3. Infer About 20,000 years ago, many areas in northern North America were covered with glaciers. Since then, the glaciers have melted. The lithosphere in many of these areas is now experiencing uplift. Why is this?

_____

_____

4. Describe How can a geologist tell if a fold is a syncline or an anticline?

_____

_____

CHAPTER 11 Deformation of the Crust

SECTION 2 How Mountains Form

KEY IDEAS

As you read this section, keep these questions in mind:

• What kinds of plate collisions form mountains?

• What are four main types of mountains?

• How do folded and fault-block mountains form?

What Is a Mountain Range?

A **mountain range** is a group of mountains that have similar ages, shapes, and sizes, and that are close together. The mountains in a mountain range all formed in a similar way. Mount Everest, Earth's highest mountain, is part of the Great Himalaya Range. Mount St. Helens, a volcanic mountain in the northwest United States, is part of the Cascade Range.

Groups of nearby mountain ranges form *mountain systems*. For example, the Appalachian mountain system is found in eastern North America. It is made up of the Great Smoky, Blue Ridge, Cumberland, Green, and White mountain ranges. ☑

Mountain systems, in turn, are part of even larger systems called *mountain belts*. Two of Earth's major mountain belts are the circum-Pacific belt and the Eurasian-Melanesian belt. Many well-known mountain systems are part of these two belts.

Both of these belts are located along convergent plate boundaries. The location of the belts is evidence that many mountains form as a result of tectonic plate collisions. The types of plates that collide affect the mountains that form.

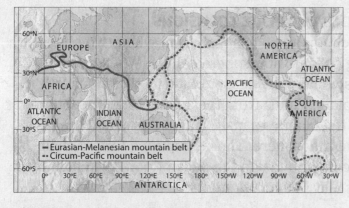

This map shows two of Earth's main mountain belts.

READING TOOLBOX

Predict Before reading this section, write each heading in your journal. Below each subheading, write one or two sentences about what you think you will learn in that subsection. As you read, write down what you learn.

✓ READING CHECK

1. Describe What is a mountain system?

_____

_____

LOOKING CLOSER

2. Apply Concepts The Cascade Range is in western North America. Along which mountain belt is the Cascade Range located?

_____

_____

SECTION 2 **How Mountains Form** *continued*

How Do Mountains Form?

Mountains generally form when the lithospheres of two tectonic plates collide. Remember that there are two main kinds of lithosphere: oceanic and continental. The type of lithosphere at the edge of each of the colliding plates affects the type of mountains that form.

OCEANIC-CONTINENTAL PLATE COLLISIONS

Some mountains form when oceanic lithosphere and continental lithosphere collide. Oceanic lithosphere is denser than continental lithosphere. Therefore, when they collide, the oceanic lithosphere *subducts*, or sinks, beneath the continental lithosphere. The continental lithosphere is uplifted, so tall mountains form. ☑

The subduction of the oceanic lithosphere can cause some of the mantle to melt. This produces magma that can erupt and form volcanic mountains. Mountains can also form at these plate boundaries when pieces of crust are scraped off the ocean lithosphere. These pieces of crust, which are called *terranes*, become part of the continent.

✔ **READING CHECK**

3. Explain Why does oceanic lithosphere subduct below continental lithosphere?

_____

_____

_____

LOOKING CLOSER

4. Identify What two processes probably helped to form the mountains in the picture?

_____

_____

_____

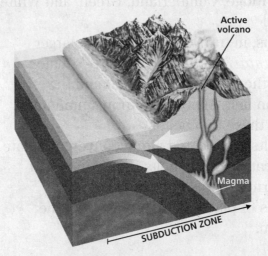

Active volcano

Magma

SUBDUCTION ZONE

Mountains and volcanoes form where an oceanic plate sinks beneath a continental plate. The Andes Mountains formed in this way.

OCEANIC-OCEANIC PLATE COLLISIONS

Volcanic mountains can also form when two plates containing oceanic lithosphere collide. When two oceanic plates collide, the denser plate subducts beneath the other plate. Fluids from the subducting lithosphere can cause the mantle to melt. Magma rises and breaks through the lithosphere. These eruptions form a chain of volcanic mountains on the ocean floor. The chain of mountains is called an *island arc*.

SECTION 2 **How Mountains Form** *continued*

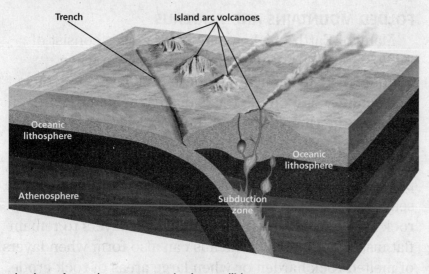

Island arcs form where two oceanic plates collide.
The Mariana Islands in the Pacific Ocean are an example of such an island arc.

CONTINENTAL-CONTINENTAL PLATE COLLISIONS

In some areas, two continental plates collide.
Continental lithosphere is less dense than the
asthenosphere. Therefore, continental lithosphere cannot
subduct. When two continental plates collide, the
lithosphere on both plates is pushed up. The continental
lithosphere is very thick. Therefore, continental-
continental plate collisions produce extremely tall
mountains. ☑

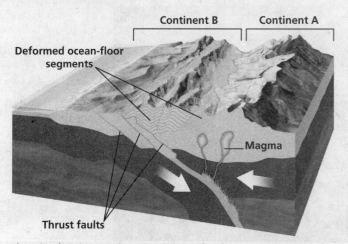

The Himalaya Mountains are an example of a mountain range that is forming where
two continental plates collide. Although magma forms where continents collide, it
generally does not erupt.

What Are the Different Types of Mountains?

Mountains are more than just elevated parts of Earth's
crust. They also contain important evidence of the
stresses that created them. Geologists classify mountains
based on their shapes and the ways they form.

LOOKING CLOSER

5. Describe What process
forms the mountains in
island arcs?

_____

_____

✓ **READING CHECK**

6. Explain Why do
continental-continental plate
collisions produce very tall
mountains?

_____

_____

_____

_____

SECTION 2 **How Mountains Form** *continued*

FOLDED MOUNTAINS AND PLATEAUS

Many of Earth's highest mountain ranges consist of folded mountains. **Folded mountains** form when tectonic plate movements squeeze rock layers together. The compression on the rocks makes them fold. Parts of the Alps, the Himalayas, and the Appalachians are folded mountains.

The stresses that form folded mountains can also form plateaus. A *plateau* is a large, flat area of rock high above sea level. They can form when thick, horizontal layers of rock are slowly uplifted. This allows the layers to remain flat instead of folding. Plateaus can also form when layers of melted rock harden or when large areas of rock erode. Many plateaus are found near folded mountains.

FAULT-BLOCK MOUNTAINS AND GRABENS

In places where parts of Earth's crust have been stretched and broken into large blocks, **fault-block mountains** can form. These mountains form when faulting causes blocks of rock to tilt and drop relative to other blocks. The higher blocks become mountain peaks. The Sierra Nevada range in California consists of many fault-block mountains.

The Sierra Nevada range contains many fault-block mountains.

The faulting that results in fault-block mountains can also form long, narrow valleys called *grabens*. Grabens and fault-block mountain ranges generally occur together. The mountains form when one block of rock rises relative to other blocks. Grabens form when one block slips downward. A famous graben found in the United States is Death Valley in California.

Critical Thinking

7. Apply Concepts What type of strain is probably most common in folded mountains?

_____

_____

LOOKING CLOSER

8. Explain How did the peaks of these mountains form?

_____

_____

_____

_____

_____

_____

DOME MOUNTAINS

Dome mountains are not as common as folded mountains or fault-block mountains. **Dome mountains** form when magma rising through Earth's crust pushes rock layers up, but does not erupt. Dome mountains may also form when tectonic forces gently uplift rock layers. Dome mountains are generally round and have gently sloping sides.

This dome mountain is part of the Hudson Highlands in New York.

LOOKING CLOSER
9. Describe What is the defining feature of this mountain?

_____

_____

VOLCANIC MOUNTAINS

Mountains that form when magma erupts onto Earth's surface are called *volcanic mountains*. Most volcanic mountains are part of mid-ocean ridges along divergent plate boundaries. The peaks of these mountains sometimes rise above sea level to form islands. Volcanic mountains are also common in places where oceanic-oceanic and oceanic-continental plate collisions happen.

Other volcanic mountains form at *hot spots*. Most hot spots are far from plate boundaries. At a hot spot, hot, solid rock rises through the lithosphere. When the rock melts, the magma can erupt and form islands. Scientists are still not sure exactly what causes hot spots to form.

Talk About It
Apply Concepts Choose a mountain range in the United States. Use the Internet or library to learn how the mountain range formed. Share what you learn with a partner or a small group.

Types of Mountains

Type of Mountain	Description	Example
Folded mountains	mountains formed by compression and folding of the crust	Alps, Appalachian Mountains, Himalaya Mountains
Fault-block mountains	mountains formed when blocks of rock move along large faults	Sierra Nevada
Dome mountains	small, round mountains formed when magma pushes rock layers up	Black Hills, Adirondack Mountains
Volcanic mountains	mountains formed when lava erupts on Earth's surface	Hawaiian Islands, Mid-Atlantic Ridge, Cascade Range

LOOKING CLOSER
10. Infer The Hawaiian Islands are in the middle of a tectonic plate. What feature probably formed the Hawaiian Islands?

Section 2 Review

SECTION VOCABULARY

dome mountain a circular or elliptical, almost symmetrical elevation or structure in which the stratified rock slopes downward gently from the central point of folding	**folded mountain** a mountain that forms when rock layers are squeezed together and uplifted
fault-block mountain a mountain that forms where faulting breaks Earth's crust into large blocks, which causes some blocks to drop down relative to other blocks	**mountain range** a series of mountains that are closely related in orientation, age, and mode of formation

1. Describe What characteristics do the mountains in a mountain range have in common?

_____

_____

2. Identify What are three types of plate collisions that can form mountains?

_____

_____

3. Compare What are the main differences between mountains that form where two continents collide and mountains that form where an oceanic plate collides with a continental plate?

_____

_____

_____

4. Describe What is one difference between the way that folded mountains and fault-block mountains form?

_____

_____

_____

5. Apply Concepts A geologist is studying a mountain. The mountain is small and round. Its sides are not very steep. How did the mountain most likely form? Explain your answer.

_____

_____

_____

CHAPTER 12 **Earthquakes**
SECTION 1

How and Where Earthquakes Happen

KEY IDEAS

As you read this section, keep these questions in mind:

• What is elastic rebound?

• What are the similarities and differences between body waves and surface waves?

• How does the structure of Earth's interior affect seismic waves?

• Why do most earthquakes happen at plate boundaries?

What Makes Earthquakes Happen?

Remember that a *fault* is a crack in rock. If there is pressure on the rock around a fault, the rock is under stress. Friction along the fault keeps the rock from moving. The stress can build up. Eventually, the stress becomes too high. The rock moves suddenly along the fault. It releases a great deal of energy. The energy makes the ground shake. The shaking is an **earthquake**.

Elastic rebound is important in causing earthquakes. **Elastic rebound** happens when a rock that is deformed goes back to its original shape. The diagram below shows an example of elastic rebound.

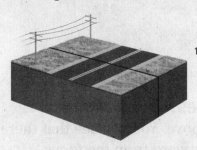

1. Two blocks of crust are pressed together at a fault. They are under stress, but they do not move because friction holds them in place.

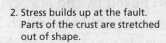

2. Stress builds up at the fault. Parts of the crust are stretched out of shape.

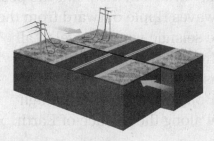

3. When the stress gets large enough, the blocks of crust slip past each other. The movement of the crust releases energy, which causes an earthquake. Each piece of crust snaps back to its original shape, but the two pieces of crust have moved past each other.

READING TOOLBOX

Organize As you read this section, create a concept map using the following terms: *P wave, surface wave, seismic wave, S wave, Love wave, body wave, Rayleigh wave, earthquake, focus, epicenter, fault,* and *movement.*

LOOKING CLOSER

1. Compare How does the road in the middle figure look different from the road in the top figure? Why is it different?

_____

_____

_____

_____

_____

FOCUS AND EPICENTER

When rock moves along a fault, the first motion on the fault is generally underground. The **focus** (plural, *foci*) of an earthquake is the point where the first motion occurs. The energy an earthquake releases moves outward in all directions from the focus. The **epicenter** of an earthquake is the point on Earth's surface directly above the focus. ☑

Scientists group earthquakes based on how deep their foci are. A *shallow-focus earthquake* has a focus less than 70 km below Earth's surface. An *intermediate-focus earthquake* has a focus between 70 km and 300 km below Earth's surface. A *deep-focus* earthquake has a focus more than 300 km below Earth's surface.

READING CHECK

2. Describe What is the difference between the epicenter and the focus?

_____

_____

_____

_____

Talk About It

Visualize Use an atlas or map to find two places on Earth that are about 70 km apart and two places that are about 300 km apart. Talk with a partner about how this information can help you understand shallow-focus, intermediate-focus, and deep-focus earthquakes.

LOOKING CLOSER

3. Identify Label the epicenter on the figure.

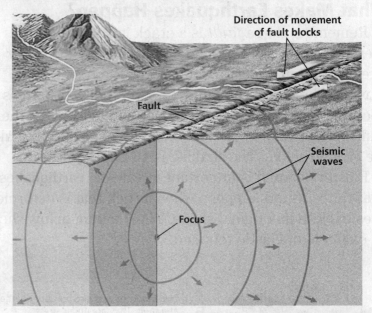

The vibrations of an earthquake start at the focus and spread out.

What Are Seismic Waves?

Look again at the figure above. You can see that there are seismic waves moving outward from the focus. *Seismic waves* are vibrations caused by the energy released in an earthquake. When a pebble falls into a pond, small waves ripple outward from the point the pebble hits. Similarly, seismic waves ripple outward from the focus of an earthquake. The seismic waves travel in all directions from the focus through the rock around it.

There are two main types of seismic waves: body waves and surface waves. **Body waves** travel through rock. **Surface waves** travel along the surface of Earth.

SECTION 1 **How and Where Earthquakes Happen** *continued*

TYPES OF BODY WAVES

There are two types of body waves: P waves and S waves. **P waves** cause rocks to move back and forth, parallel to the direction that the wave is moving. **S waves** cause rocks to move side to side, perpendicular to the direction that the wave is moving. The picture and table below give more information about P waves and S waves.

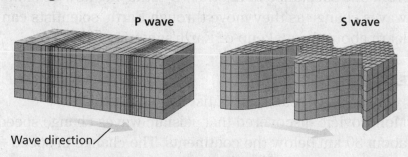

P wave   S wave

Wave direction

LOOKING CLOSER
4. Describe Draw arrows on the pictures to show the direction the ground moves when each type of wave passes.

Type of Wave	Other Names	Other Facts
P wave	• primary wave • compression wave	• fastest seismic waves • can move through solids, liquids, and gases
S wave	• secondary wave • shear wave	• slower than P waves • can move only through solids

SURFACE WAVES

Surface waves move along Earth's surface. Surface waves move more slowly than body waves, but surface waves can cause more damage. Most surface waves form in one of two ways:

• movement along a fault that is close to the surface

• change in the way rock moves when a body wave reaches Earth's surface

There are two main types of surface waves: Love waves and Rayleigh waves. The diagram below shows how Love waves and Rayleigh waves move the ground.

Critical Thinking
5. Compare How are a Love wave and an S wave the same? How are they different?

_____

_____

_____

_____

_____

_____

_____

_____

Rayleigh wave   Love wave

Wave direction

A Rayleigh wave moves the ground in a rolling, up-and-down motion.

A Love wave moves rock back and forth. It also causes rock to twist.

SECTION 1 **How and Where Earthquakes Happen** *continued*

What Can Seismic Waves Tell Us About Earth's Structure?

Scientists study seismic waves to learn more about Earth's structure. Seismic waves move at different speeds in different substances. In addition, the direction in which a seismic wave travels changes when it moves from one substance to another. By studying how seismic waves change as they move through Earth, scientists can learn about the makeup of Earth's interior. ☑

EARTH'S LAYERS

In 1909, a Croatian scientist named Andrija Mohorovičić discovered that seismic waves change speed about 30 km below the continents. The change in speed happens suddenly. The place where this change happens is where the crust and mantle meet. Today, scientists call this boundary the *Mohorovičić discontinuity*, or just the *Moho*. Below the continents, the Moho is about 30 km deep. Below the oceans, it is about 10 km deep.

Scientists have been able to use seismic waves to learn about other layers inside Earth. They now know that Earth has three main compositional zones: the crust, mantle, and core. Earth has five main structural zones: the lithosphere, asthenosphere, mesosphere, outer core, and inner core.

SHADOW ZONES

Remember that seismic waves change speed and direction as they move through Earth. Those changes can bend the waves in specific ways. The bending of the waves produces shadow zones. **Shadow zones** are areas on Earth's surface where waves from an earthquake cannot be detected.

☑ **READING CHECK**

6. Explain Why can scientists use seismic waves to learn about Earth's interior?

_____

_____

_____

Critical Thinking

7. Make Connections Why do the S waves in the diagram stop when they reach the liquid outer core?

_____

_____

The shadow zones for different earthquakes are different.

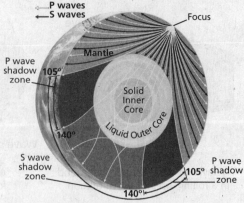

Where Do Earthquakes Happen?

Most earthquakes happen near the boundaries between plates. The movements of the plates put stress on the rock in the plates. The stress can cause the rock to slip and cause earthquakes.

Some earthquakes happen in the oceans. Others happen on land. The table below summarizes the environments where earthquakes can happen.

Type of Environment	Description	Example
Convergent oceanic	places where an oceanic plate collides with another oceanic plate or with a continental plate	Andes Mountains, Aleutian Islands
Divergent oceanic	places where two oceanic plates move apart	Mid-Atlantic Ridge
Continental	places where two continental plates collide, move apart, or slide past each other	San Andreas Fault, Himalaya Mountains

FAULT ZONES

Most faults exist in groups. An area that contains a lot of faults that are close together is called a **fault zone**. Fault zones can exist at any kind of plate boundary. One example of a fault zone is the North Anatolian fault zone in Turkey. Movement of the crust along the faults in this fault zone produces many earthquakes in Turkey. ☑

EARTHQUAKES AWAY FROM PLATE BOUNDARIES

Most earthquakes happen at plate boundaries. However, earthquakes can also happen far from plate boundaries. For example, in 1811 and 1812, several large earthquakes happened near New Madrid, Missouri. New Madrid is far from any plate boundaries.

Scientists are not sure why these earthquakes happened. However, they have discovered a very old fault zone underneath New Madrid. The fault zone is more than 600 million years old. It is buried under many layers of rock and sediment. Scientists think the New Madrid earthquakes may have happened when rock around the fault zone moved. However, they are not sure what made the rock move, or whether it might move again in the future.

Talk About It

Review With a partner, talk about the different types of plate boundaries that you have learned about. Discuss how the information you know about plate boundaries relates to the information in this section.

✓ READING CHECK

8. Define What is a fault zone?

_____

_____

_____

Section 1 Review

SECTION VOCABULARY

body wave a seismic wave that travels through the body of a medium	**P wave** a primary wave, or compression wave; a seismic wave that causes particles of rock to move in a back-and-forth direction parallel to the direction in which the wave is traveling
earthquake a movement or trembling of the ground that is caused by a sudden release of energy when rocks along a fault move	**shadow zone** an area on Earth's surface where no direct seismic waves from a particular earthquake can be detected
elastic rebound the sudden return of elastically deformed rock to its undeformed shape	**surface wave** a seismic wave that travels along the surface of a medium and that has a stronger effect near the surface of the medium than it has in the interior
epicenter the point on Earth's surface directly above an earthquake's starting point, or focus	
fault zone a region of numerous, closely spaced faults	**S wave** a secondary wave, or shear wave; a seismic wave that causes particles of rock to move in a side-to-side direction perpendicular to the direction in which the wave is traveling
focus the location within Earth along a fault at which the first motion of an earthquake occurs	

1. Describe Relationships How is elastic rebound related to earthquakes?

_____

_____

_____

2. Explain Why do most earthquakes happen at plate boundaries?

_____

_____

_____

3. Compare Describe three differences between P waves and S waves.

_____

_____

_____

4. Describe What are shadow zones, and why do they exist?

_____

_____

_____

_____

CHAPTER 12 Earthquakes
SECTION
2 Studying Earthquakes

KEY IDEAS

As you read this section, keep these questions in mind:

• What tool do scientists use to measure and record earthquakes?

• How do scientists find the epicenter of an earthquake?

• What scales do scientists use to describe the magnitude and intensity of an earthquake?

How Do Scientists Record Earthquakes?

Seismology is the study of earthquakes and seismic waves. Scientists who study seismology are called *seismologists*. Seismologists use many different tools to study earthquakes. One of the most important of these tools is a seismograph.

A **seismograph** is a machine that senses vibrations caused by seismic waves. Modern seismographs can detect vibrations in three directions. They can detect north-south vibrations, east-west vibrations, and up-down vibrations.

Seismographs record seismic wave vibrations on a chart called a **seismogram**. Most modern seismograms are produced by computers. The seismograph detects motion and changes it into electrical signals. The computer interprets the electrical signals and creates the seismogram.

Because P waves move more quickly than other seismic waves, a seismograph records P waves first. S waves travel more slowly than P waves, so the seismograph records S waves second. Surface waves are the slowest-moving waves. A seismograph records them last.

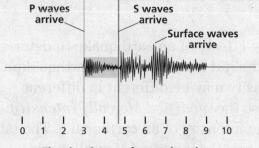

This seismogram shows when the three types of waves hit after an earthquake.

READING TOOLBOX

Outline As you read this section, write an outline of the information in the section. Use the heads and subheads as a guide. Make sure to include all of the vocabulary words.

Talk About It

Use Word Parts Use a dictionary to look up the meaning of the word parts *seism-, -ology, -graph,* and *-gram.* With a partner or small group, talk about how you can use these meanings to help you remember what *seismology, seismograph,* and *seismogram* mean.

LOOKING CLOSER

1. Estimate About how many minutes apart were the P waves and S waves of this earthquake?

_____

_____

_____

When scientists study an earthquake, they measure its magnitude and intensity. An earthquake's **magnitude** is its strength. An earthquake's **intensity** is the amount of damage that it causes.

Critical Thinking

2. Infer How do you think magnitude and intensity are related?

_____

_____

_____

MAGNITUDE

Scientists find out an earthquake's magnitude by measuring how much the ground moved. They use magnitude scales to describe the magnitude. The two main magnitude scales are the *Richter scale* and the *moment magnitude scale*. These scales are not objects, like a scale you use to weigh yourself. Instead, they are ways of classifying the strength of an earthquake.

For most of the 1900s, scientists used the Richter scale to describe magnitude. However, the moment magnitude scale is more accurate for large earthquakes. Therefore, today, most scientists use the moment magnitude scale. ☑

The moment magnitude of an earthquake is expressed as a number. The larger an earthquake's moment magnitude is, the stronger the earthquake is. For example, the largest earthquake that has ever been recorded had a moment magnitude of 9.5.

✓ **READING CHECK**

3. Identify What scale do most scientists today use to describe the magnitude of an earthquake?

_____

_____

LOOKING CLOSER

4. Apply Concepts Was the earthquake in northern Pakistan in 2005 stronger or weaker than an earthquake with a magnitude of 7.4?

_____

_____

This boy is standing in front of piles of rubble after an earthquake in northern Pakistan in 2005. The earthquake had a moment magnitude of 7.6. It killed more than 86,000 people, and it left more than 3 million people homeless.

INTENSITY

Scientists use the effects of an earthquake to determine the earthquake's intensity. Unlike an earthquake's magnitude, its intensity may be different in different places. Scientists use the *modified Mercalli intensity scale* to describe the intensity of an earthquake. The table on the next page shows the modified Mercalli scale.

SECTION 2 **Studying Earthquakes** *continued*

Modified Mercalli Intensity Scale

Intensity	Description
I	felt by almost no one
II	felt by a few people who are not moving
III	felt by most people who are inside; feels like a large truck driving by
IV	felt by many people; dishes and windows rattle; feels like something has hit the building
V	felt by nearly everyone; some objects break; some objects fall over
VI	felt by everyone; some heavy objects move; slight damage to some structures
VII	slight to moderate damage to some buildings
VIII	serious damage to ordinary buildings; buildings may partially collapse
IX	serious damage to earthquake-resistant buildings
X	many structures destroyed; railroad tracks bend
XI	almost all structures destroyed; bridges destroyed
XII	total destruction; objects thrown into the air

Several factors affect the intensity of an earthquake in an area, including

- soil type
- distance to the epicenter
- length and magnitude of the earthquake
- types of buildings and other structures in the area

Because areas have different characteristics, they may experience different earthquake intensities.

How Do Scientists Find the Epicenter of an Earthquake?

Scientists use seismograms to identify the epicenter of an earthquake. Remember that P waves travel more quickly than S waves do. As the waves travel farther from the epicenter, the time between them increases. At a seismograph that is close to the epicenter, the P waves and S waves will be close together. At a seismograph that is far from the epicenter, the P waves and S waves will be farther apart.

Seismologists use computers to study the seismograms from different places. The computers use complex calculations to figure out how far each place is from the epicenter. The computers use this information to figure out where the epicenter is.

LOOKING CLOSER

5. Describe An earthquake happens in an area. Almost everyone in the area feels the earth shake, but no buildings are damaged. What is the intensity of the earthquake in that area?

Talk About It

Reason Talk with a partner or small group about how different factors might affect the intensity of an earthquake. Support your ideas with evidence. If you wish, use the Internet or library to learn more about the factors that affect the intensity of an earthquake. Present your findings to your partner or small group.

Name _____ Class _____ Date _____

Section 2 Review

SECTION VOCABULARY

intensity in Earth science, the amount of damage caused by an earthquake	**seismogram** a tracing of earthquake motion that is recorded by a seismograph
magnitude a measure of the strength of an earthquake	**seismograph** an instrument that records vibrations in the ground

1. Describe Relationships How are a seismograph and a seismogram related?

_____

_____

2. Explain Two different cities experienced the same earthquake. In one city, scientists said that the earthquake had a level V intensity. In the other city, scientists said that the earthquake had a level VII intensity. Explain how this could be true.

_____

_____

_____

_____

3. Describe How do scientists find the location of an earthquake's epicenter?

_____

_____

_____

4. Apply Concepts An earthquake affected the towns of Quakeville and Shaketown. Quakeville was closer to the epicenter than Shaketown was. The seismogram on the left is from Quakeville. The picture on the right shows part of the seismogram from Shaketown. Complete the seismogram from Shaketown.

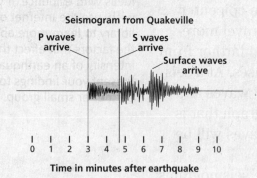

Seismogram from Quakeville

P waves arrive   S waves arrive   Surface waves arrive

0 1 2 3 4 5 6 7 8 9 10
Time in minutes after earthquake

Seismogram from Shaketown

3 4 5 6 7 8 9 10 11 12 13
Time in minutes after earthquake

SECTION 3 | # Earthquakes and Society

KEY IDEAS

As you read this section, keep these questions in mind:

- How are tsunamis and earthquakes related?
- How can a large earthquake affect buildings?
- How can you stay safe during an earthquake?
- How do scientists predict earthquake risks?

What Effects Can an Earthquake Have?

Very few people are harmed directly by the ground's movement during an earthquake. Most injuries happen for one of the following reasons:

- Buildings collapse.
- Objects and broken glass fly through the air.
- Electric wire and gas lines break.
- Dams collapse and cause a flood.

Many earthquakes cause the ground to rise or fall suddenly. If the epicenter is under the ocean, the ocean water in that area can also rise or fall suddenly. The movement causes a series of waves that get higher and higher as they reach land. Together, these waves form a **tsunami**. Tsunamis can be extremely harmful. They can destroy buildings, roads, and other structures. ☑

DESTRUCTION OF BUILDINGS

Buildings can be damaged by earthquakes. Buildings with weak walls can collapse. Very tall buildings may sway and tip over. Buildings that are built on loose soil can also sway and fall.

How Can You Stay Safe During an Earthquake?

Earthquakes can happen anywhere in the world. However, they are more common in certain places. People who live in those places should have plans for what to do in case an earthquake happens. The table on the next page describes things you can do to stay safe before, during, and after an earthquake.

> **READING TOOLBOX**
>
> **Take Notes** As you read this section, make two-column notes to summarize the main ideas. Use the headings to help you think of topics for the first column of the table.

> ☑ **READING CHECK**
>
> **1. Connect** How are tsunamis related to earthquakes?
>
> _____
>
> _____
>
> _____

SECTION 3 **Earthquakes and Society** *continued*

Before an Earthquake	Make an earthquake kit.	Include • bottled water • batteries • a radio • flashlights • canned food
	Make a plan.	• Find safe places in each room. • Decide on a meeting place.
	Make your home safe.	• Put heavy things near the floor. • Learn how to turn off the gas, water, and electricity.
During an Earthquake	Stay safe indoors.	• Stand in a doorway. • Crouch under a desk or table. • Stay away from windows and heavy furniture.
	Stay safe in a car.	• Move away from tall buildings, tunnels, power lines, or bridges. • Stop the car and stay in it.
After an Earthquake	Be careful.	• Check for fires. • Wear shoes near broken glass. • Avoid power lines that have fallen. • Be prepared for *aftershocks*, or weaker earthquakes that come after a strong earthquake.

LOOKING CLOSER

2. Apply Concepts If you are in your classroom during an earthquake, what should you do?

_____

_____

_____

_____

Critical Thinking

3. Infer How could scientists prevent harm if they were able to predict earthquakes?

_____

_____

_____

_____

_____

✓ **READING CHECK**

4. Define What is a seismic gap?

_____

_____

_____

How Can Scientists Predict Earthquakes?

People have tried to predict earthquakes for many years. If scientists could predict when an earthquake would happen, they could save more lives. Scientists today use several different methods to try to predict earthquakes. However, none of these methods is very accurate.

SEISMIC GAPS

Active faults have many earthquakes each year. A part of an active fault that hasn't had a strong earthquake in a long time is called a **seismic gap**. Some scientists think that if an active fault hasn't had a strong earthquake in a long time, it will have one soon. In other words, they think that strong earthquakes are more likely to happen in seismic gaps.

Scientists study the earthquakes that happen on active faults. They use this information to identify seismic gaps and to make predictions about where earthquakes might happen. ☑

SECTION 3 **Earthquakes and Society** *continued*

FORESHOCKS

Foreshocks are small earthquakes that happen before a much larger earthquake. Some foreshocks come a few seconds before the earthquake. Others can come a few weeks before the earthquake. ☑

In 1975, scientists in China recorded foreshocks near the city of Haicheng. Everyone left the city. The next day, there was a major earthquake. The earthquake destroyed parts of the city, but most people stayed safe because of the warning of the foreshock. However, this was the only recorded time that foreshocks helped predict an earthquake.

5. Define What is a foreshock?

_____

_____

_____

CHANGES IN ROCKS

Before an earthquake, the rocks around the fault zone are under a lot of stress. The ground may tilt. Rocks may crack or break into pieces. Water or natural gas may fill the cracks. Scientists cannot yet use this information to predict earthquakes. However, they hope that in the future they will be able to use these clues to predict when an earthquake will happen.

EARTHQUAKE-HAZARD LEVELS

Many earthquakes do not have foreshocks or other clues. Therefore, scientists cannot make exact predictions about earthquakes. However, scientists can use past earthquakes to estimate where future earthquakes are likely to happen. A place that has had a lot of strong earthquakes in the past has a high earthquake-hazard level. A place that has had few or no earthquakes has a lower hazard level.

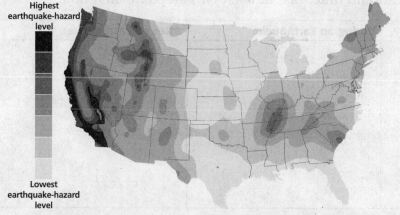

Highest earthquake-hazard level

Lowest earthquake-hazard level

This map shows the earthquake-hazard levels of places in the United States.

LOOKING CLOSER

6. Explain Put a star next to a state with a high earthquake hazard level. Circle a state that has a very low earthquake hazard level.

Section 3 Review

SECTION VOCABULARY

seismic gap an area along a fault where relatively few earthquakes have occurred recently but where strong earthquakes are known to have occurred in the past	tsunami a giant ocean wave that forms after a volcanic eruption, submarine earthquake, or landslide

1. Explain What causes a tsunami?

_____

_____

_____

2. Describe What are seismic gaps, and why are they important?

_____

_____

_____

3. Identify What are two ways an earthquake can damage a building?

_____

_____

4. Infer Scientists examined the rocks at a fault zone, and they predicted that an earthquake might happen there. What do you think they found?

_____

_____

_____

5. Identify In the table below, list steps that people who live in areas that have high earthquake-hazard levels should take. List at least two steps in each box.

Before an Earthquake	During an Earthquake	After an Earthquake

CHAPTER 13 | Volcanoes

SECTION 1

Volcanoes and Plate Tectonics

As you read this section, keep these questions in mind:

- What three conditions can cause magma to form?
- What is volcanism?
- What are three tectonic settings where volcanoes form?
- How can magma form plutons?

How Does Magma Form?

Remember that Earth has three compositional layers: the crust, the mantle, and the core. Even though the rock in the mantle is very hot, most of it is solid. It is solid because it is under a great deal of pressure from the weight of the rock above it. The graph below shows how pressure and temperature in the mantle are related.

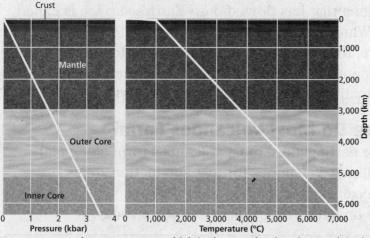

Crust
Mantle
Outer Core
Inner Core

Pressure (kbar) 0 1 2 3 4

Temperature (°C) 0 1,000 2,000 3,000 4,000 5,000 6,000 7,000

Depth (km) 0 1,000 2,000 3,000 4,000 5,000 6,000

Temperature and pressure are very high in the mantle. Therefore, rock in the mantle usually stays below its melting point.

Sometimes, however, the rock in the mantle can melt. When it does, it forms magma. **Magma** is melted rock under Earth's surface. There are three main conditions that can cause rock to melt:

- The temperature rises until it is higher than the rock's melting point.
- The pressure on the rock decreases, and its melting point also decreases.
- Water or other fluids seep into the rock and lower its melting point. ☑

Summarize As you read this section, underline the main ideas. When you finish reading, write a short summary of the section using the underlined ideas.

LOOKING CLOSER

1. Explain Temperatures in the lower mantle are very high. Why doesn't the rock in the lower mantle melt?

_____

_____

_____

_____

_____

2. Explain Why can adding water to hot, solid rock make the rock melt?

_____

_____

_____

HOW MAGMA AFFECTS ROCK

Because magma is less dense than solid rock, magma rises toward Earth's surface. As magma moves upward, it can affect the rock around it. For example, the heat from the magma may melt the rock around it. The melted rock becomes more magma.

The magma can also enter cracks in the rock and break off pieces of solid rock. The solid rock may melt and become magma. Sometimes, the pieces of rock the magma breaks off do not melt completely. When the magma cools, these pieces of rock become trapped in the newly formed igneous rock. ☑

How Does a Volcano Form?

Magma rises toward Earth's surface because magma is less dense than the solid rock that surrounds it. As the magma rises, it may collect in a *magma chamber* under Earth's surface. It may also flow out of an opening in Earth's surface called a *vent*.

Magma that has flowed onto Earth's surface is called **lava**. When lava flows through a vent onto Earth's surface, the vent is called a **volcano**. **Volcanism** is the movement of magma onto Earth's surface. A volcano can be a small hole in the ground or a huge mountain.

Where Do Most Volcanoes Form?

Like earthquakes, most volcanoes form along plate boundaries. Volcanoes form at subduction zones, mid-ocean ridges, and hot spots. The map below shows places on land where volcanoes occur today.

READING CHECK

3. Explain Why do some igneous rocks contain pieces of other rocks?

_____

_____

_____

_____

_____

_____

LOOKING CLOSER

4. Identify Where do most volcanoes form?

_____

_____

	Ring of Fire
▲	Active volcano
	Plate boundary

Many active volcanoes exist in the Pacific Ring of Fire. The Pacific Ring of Fire is also one of Earth's major earthquake zones.

SECTION 1 **Volcanoes and Plate Tectonics** *continued*

SUBDUCTION ZONES

Many volcanoes form along *subduction zones*, which are areas where one tectonic plate sinks under another. Some subduction zones form when two oceanic plates collide, and one sinks beneath the other. The figure below shows how this type of subduction forms volcanoes.

Talk About It
Apply Concepts With a partner, talk about what you have already learned about subduction zones. Discuss how that information relates to the information in this section.

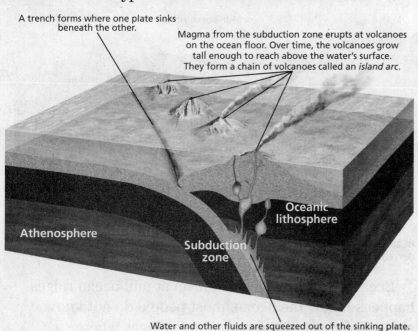

A trench forms where one plate sinks beneath the other.

Magma from the subduction zone erupts at volcanoes on the ocean floor. Over time, the volcanoes grow tall enough to reach above the water's surface. They form a chain of volcanoes called an *island arc*.

Athenosphere

Oceanic lithosphere

Subduction zone

Water and other fluids are squeezed out of the sinking plate. They move into the mantle rock and cause it to melt. The magma rises toward the surface.

Volcanoes are common at subduction zones.

The Aleutian Islands are a row of islands in the North Pacific Ocean. They formed along a subduction zone. Japan also formed along a subduction zone. The main island of Japan used to be a row of smaller volcanic islands. As more magma reached the surface, the islands joined together into one large piece of land. ☑

Some subduction zones form when an oceanic plate and a continental plate collide. The denser oceanic plate sinks beneath the continental plate. Water and fluids are squeezed out of the sinking plate. They make the mantle rock melt, just as they do when two oceanic plates collide. The magma rises to the surface and erupts on the continental plate.

Because the continental crust is very thick, the mountains that form are generally very tall. The Andes Mountains and the Cascade Mountains are examples of volcanic mountains that formed in this way.

LOOKING CLOSER
5. Describe What causes the rock in the mantle to melt at a subduction zone?

_____

_____

_____

_____

✓ **READING CHECK**
6. Explain Why is Japan a single landmass, and not a chain of islands?

_____

_____

_____

SECTION 1 **Volcanoes and Plate Tectonics** *continued*

MID-OCEAN RIDGES

Most of Earth's volcanoes are not found on land. They are under the oceans, at mid-ocean ridges. Remember that a *mid-ocean ridge* is a place where two plates are moving apart. Where the plates move apart, magma can erupt to form new crust.

LOOKING CLOSER

7. Explain Why does magma form at mid-ocean ridges?

_____

_____

_____

_____

Mid-ocean ridge

Sediment

Oceanic crust

Lithosphere

Magma

Asthenosphere

As the plates at a mid-ocean ridge move apart, the pressure on the mantle below decreases. The decrease in pressure causes some of the mantle rock to melt.

Because most of the volcanism at mid-ocean ridges happens below the ocean, most people do not know about it. However, there are some places where mid-ocean ridges rise above the ocean surface. Iceland is an example. Large *fissures*, or cracks, exist in Iceland. Half of Iceland is on the North American plate, and half is on the European plate. The fissures have formed where the two plates are moving apart.

HOT SPOTS

Some volcanoes do not form at plate boundaries. Instead, these volcanoes form over mantle plumes. A *mantle plume* is a column of solid, hot rock in the mantle. As the plume rises toward the surface, the pressure on it decreases. Some of the rock melts. The magma rises to the surface and breaks through Earth's crust, forming a volcano. A place where a mantle plume erupts on Earth's surface is called a **hot spot**.

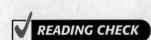
READING CHECK

8. Describe What happens as a tectonic plate moves over a mantle plume?

_____

_____

Mantle plumes do not move very much. However, the plate over the plume does move. As the plate drifts away from the plume, the magma stops flowing through the volcano. Another volcano forms over the plume. As the plate continues to move, a chain of volcanoes forms, as shown on the next page. ☑

SECTION 1 **Volcanoes and Plate Tectonics** *continued*

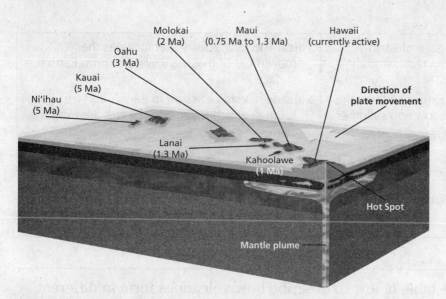

The Hawaiian Islands formed over a hot spot. The ages of the islands are shown in Ma, or millions of years.

LOOKING CLOSER
9. Estimate About how many years did it take for the hot spot to move from Ni'ihau to Hawaii?

_____

_____

Some mantle plumes are long and shaped like a horizontal line. Magma from these plumes erupts through Earth's crust in many places along the line. This forms a line of volcanoes.

What Is a Pluton?

When magma does not reach Earth's surface, it may cool and solidify inside the crust. This process forms a *pluton*. Plutons can vary in size and shape. For example, *dikes* are small, narrow plutons. They may be only a few centimeters wide. Dikes form when magma cuts through rock layers as it rises. Very large plutons are called *batholiths*. A batholith has an area of at least 100 km².

Critical Thinking
10. Apply Concepts What type of rock is a pluton made of?

_____

Devils Tower in Wyoming is an example of a pluton. It rises above the ground around it because the rock around it has been worn away.

Section 1 Review

SECTION VOCABULARY

hot spot a volcanically active area of Earth's surface, commonly far from a tectonic plate boundary	**volcanism** any activity that includes the movement of magma toward or onto Earth's surface
lava magma that flows onto Earth's surface; the rock that forms when lava cools and solidifies	**volcano** a vent or fissure in Earth's surface through which magma and gases are expelled
magma liquid rock produced under Earth's surface	

1. Define In your own words, define *volcanism*.

_____

_____

2. Describe Complete the table below to describe how volcanoes form in different areas.

Place Where Volcanoes Form	Description	Why Magma Forms There
Subduction zones		
	A mantle plume rises to the surface.	
	Two plates move apart.	As the plates move apart, the pressure on the rock below decreases. The decreased pressure causes the rock to melt.

3. Compare What is the main difference between how a pluton forms and how a volcano forms?

_____

_____

4. Apply Concepts The map below shows the locations of many volcanoes. On the map, circle three volcanoes that are probably found at hot spots.

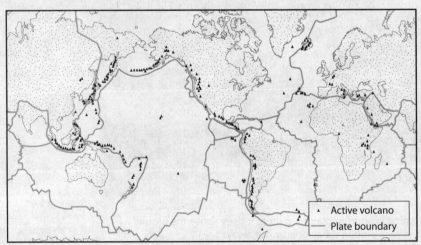

SECTION 2 | Volcanic Eruptions

KEY IDEAS

As you read this section, keep these questions in mind:

- How does the composition of magma affect volcanic eruptions and lava flow?
- What are the five major types of pyroclastic material?
- What are the three main types of volcanic cones?
- How does a caldera form?
- What are three events that may signal a volcanic eruption?

What Are the Two Types of Magma?

When magma cools, it hardens into volcanic rock. Scientists study the composition of volcanic rocks to understand the material in Earth's crust and mantle. Scientists classify magma based on its composition. There are two main types of magma: mafic and felsic.

Type of Magma	Composition	Color	Where It Is Commonly Found
Mafic	high in magnesium and iron	generally dark	oceanic crust
Felsic	high in silicate minerals	generally light	continental crust

Felsic magma is also more viscous than mafic magma. A *viscous* fluid is thick, so it does not flow easily. Magma's viscosity affects what happens when a volcano erupts.

What Are the Two Main Types of Eruptions?

Volcanic eruptions can be quiet or explosive. Mafic lava usually causes quiet eruptions. Felsic lava usually causes explosive eruptions.

QUIET ERUPTIONS

Most eruptions on the ocean floor form from mafic magma. Therefore, eruptions on the ocean floor are generally quiet. During a quiet eruption, magma flows down the sides of the volcano like a river. Geologists classify the magma from quiet eruptions by the shapes it forms when it cools. The table on the next page shows a few of these shapes.

READING TOOLBOX

Summarize When you finish reading this section, create a concept map using the following terms: *mafic lava, volcanic ash, lapilli, pahoehoe, felsic lava, aa, volcanic bomb, pyroclastic material, shield volcano, volcanic dust,* and *volcanic block.*

Critical Thinking

1. Contrast How could you tell the difference between a mafic rock and a felsic rock by looking at them?

_____

_____

_____

Critical Thinking

2. Explain What is the most likely reason that felsic magma usually causes explosive eruptions?

_____

_____

_____

SECTION 2 **Volcanic Eruptions** *continued*

LOOKING CLOSER
3. Describe What does pahoehoe look like when it cools?

_____

_____

Type of Lava	What It Forms From	What Happens to It When It Cools
Pahoehoe	hot, fluid, mafic lava	It has a smooth, ropelike texture.
Aa	the same material as pahoehoe, but with more gas in it	The crust breaks into sharp pieces.
Blocky lava	mafic lava that is more viscous than the lava that forms pahoehoe	It breaks into large chunks.

EXPLOSIVE ERUPTIONS

Explosive eruptions are much less common than quiet eruptions. However, explosive eruptions can be much more destructive. During an explosive eruption, hot ash, gas, and rocks shoot out of the volcano.

The lavas that produce explosive eruptions are generally felsic lavas. Felsic lavas often contain a lot of trapped gases, such as water vapor and carbon dioxide. The gas in the lava creates pressure inside the volcano, like the bubbles in a can of soda. The pressure can make the volcano erupt explosively. In an explosive eruption, chunks of lava fly through the air. These chunks are called **pyroclastic material**. ☑

How Do Scientists Classify Pyroclastic Material?

Some kinds of pyroclastic material form when solid lava breaks apart and is thrown into the air. Other kinds of pyroclastic material form when liquid lava flies through the air and hardens. Scientists classify pyroclastic material based on its size. The table below shows the five main types of pyroclastic material.

✓ **READING CHECK**

4. Identify Which type of lava is pyroclastic material usually made from?

_____

_____

Talk About It

Apply Concepts Use a meterstick to identify how large the four types of pyroclastic material are. As a class, discuss what each of the materials would look like. Find objects in the classroom that are as big as one of the types of material.

Type of Material	Description
Volcanic dust	Volcanic dust is made of pieces of solid rock that are less than 0.25 mm in diameter.
Volcanic ash	Volcanic ash is made of pieces of solid rock that are less than 2 mm in diameter. Volcanic dust is a type of volcanic ash.
Lapilli	Lapilli are pieces of solid rock that are between 2 mm and 64 mm in diameter. They generally fall to the ground near the vent.
Volcanic blocks	Volcanic blocks are pieces of solid rock that are more than 64 mm in diameter. They are the largest type of pyroclastic material.
Volcanic bombs	Volcanic bombs form when large chunks of lava fly out of a volcano and cool in the air. They can have many different shapes.

What Are the Three Main Types of Volcanoes?

Quiet and explosive eruptions produce different types of volcanoes. During quiet eruptions, lava flows out of the vent to create a volcanic cone. During explosive eruptions, pyroclastic material piles up around the vent. There are three main types of volcanoes: shield volcanoes, cinder cones, and composite volcanoes. ☑

SHIELD VOLCANOES

Shield volcanoes form from quiet eruptions of hot, mafic lava. The lava spreads out over a wide area, and layers of lava build up. Therefore, a shield volcano has a wide base, and its sides have a very gentle slope. Although shield volcanoes have a gentle slope, they can still be very large. The volcanoes in the Hawaiian Islands are shield volcanoes.

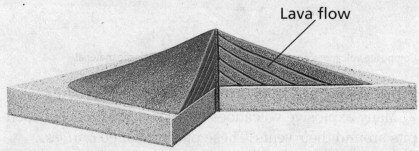

Lava flow

Quiet eruptions of thin, fluid lava form shield volcanoes.

CINDER CONES

Cinder cones form from small, explosive eruptions. They have very steep slopes, and they are made of pyroclastic material. Cinder cones are generally very small. Parícutin volcano in Mexico is an example of a cinder cone volcano.

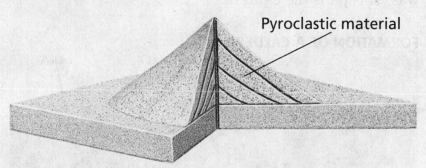

Pyroclastic material

Pyroclastic material that builds up during explosive eruptions can form a cinder cone.

✔️ **READING CHECK**

5. Identify What are the three main kinds of volcanoes?

_____

_____

_____

Critical Thinking

6. Describe From where do you think the shield volcano got its name?

_____

_____

_____

_____

_____

LOOKING CLOSER

7. Explain Which type of volcanic eruption produces cinder cone volcanoes?

_____

_____

COMPOSITE VOLCANOES

Composite volcanoes form when a volcano has both explosive eruptions and quiet eruptions. During a quiet eruption, lava flows down the sides of the cone. When an explosive eruption occurs, pyroclastic material falls all around the vent. Therefore, composite volcanoes contain layers of hardened lava and layers of pyroclastic material.

Composite volcanoes generally have a gentle slope near the base, but a steeper slope near the vent. Mount St. Helens is an example of a composite volcano.

LOOKING CLOSER

8. Identify What two materials are composite volcanoes made of?

_____

_____

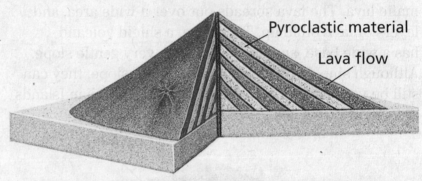

Composite volcanoes contain both lava flows and pyroclastic material.

How Are Calderas and Craters Different?

Many explosive volcanoes have circular, funnel-shaped pits around their vents. These pits are called *craters*. They form when pyroclastic material builds up around the vent. As wind and water wear away the rock around the edge of the crater, the crater becomes larger.

Some volcanoes contain large, deep depressions called calderas. A caldera is different from a crater. When the magma chamber beneath a volcano empties, the volcano may collapse. A deep pit forms where the volcanic cone was. This pit is the **caldera**.

FORMATION OF A CALDERA

Talk About It

Describe Processes Talk with a partner about the process shown in the figures. Together, discuss what is shown in each part of the figure.

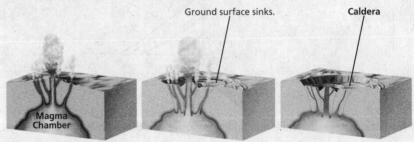

Ground surface sinks.

Caldera

Magma Chamber

SECTION 2 **Volcanic Eruptions** *continued*

Can Scientists Predict Volcanic Eruptions?

Scientists cannot always predict where or when a volcano will erupt. However, by studying volcanoes, scientists have been able to identify some clues about when an eruption may happen.

One way scientists predict volcanic eruptions is by studying the earthquakes that happen near a volcano. Just before an eruption, the earthquake activity around a volcano may change. This can happen for any of the following reasons:

• Magma moving upward puts increasing pressure on the surrounding rock.

• The temperature inside the rocks can change.

• Rocks near the volcano can break as magma moves through them.

Scientists also study the gases that rise from the volcano. Just before an eruption, volcanoes often give off more gas. The composition of the gas may also change before an eruption.

These scientists are taking samples of gases that are coming from a volcano.

LOOKING CLOSER
9. Infer Why are these scientists probably wearing protective clothing?

_____

_____

_____

Scientists also study the shape and size of a volcano to figure out whether it may erupt. Before an eruption, rising magma can cause the volcano's sides to bulge. The movement of magma can also cause the ground to tilt slightly. Scientists can use special instruments to measure these changes. ☑

Scientists need to identify patterns in earthquake activity, released gases, and land tilt to be able to make these predictions. Unfortunately, only a few active volcanoes have been studied for long enough for these methods to work. In addition, volcanoes that have been inactive for years may erupt without warning. Therefore, scientists generally cannot accurately predict volcanic eruptions.

✓ **READING CHECK**

10. Explain Why might the volcano's sides bulge before an eruption?

_____

_____

_____

Section 2 Review

SECTION VOCABULARY

caldera a large, circular depression that forms when the magma chamber below a volcano partially empties and causes the ground above to sink	**mafic** describes magma or igneous rock that is rich in magnesium and iron and that is generally dark in color
felsic describes magma or igneous rock that is rich in feldspars and silica and that is generally light in color	**pyroclastic material** fragments of rock that form during a volcanic eruption

1. Explain Why does felsic lava produce explosive eruptions more often than mafic lava does?

_____

_____

_____

2. Compare Give one similarity and one difference between lapilli and volcanic blocks.

_____

_____

3. Describe How do calderas form?

_____

_____

_____

4. Infer Which would be more likely to increase the steepness of a volcanic cone—a quiet eruption or an explosive eruption? Explain your answer.

_____

_____

_____

5. Explain Scientists today are studying many active volcanoes around the world. They are even studying volcanoes that have not erupted for hundreds or thousands of years. What is the most likely reason they are studying these volcanoes?

_____

_____

_____

CHAPTER 14 | Weathering and Erosion

SECTION 1
Weathering Processes

KEY IDEAS

As you read this section, keep these questions in mind:

• What are three agents of mechanical weathering?

• How do mechanical and chemical weathering processes compare?

• What are four chemical reactions that decompose rock?

What Is Weathering?

Most rocks deep in Earth's crust form under conditions of high temperatures and pressure. Over time, movements of tectonic plates lift these rocks to Earth's surface. The rocks at Earth's surface experience different conditions. Surface rocks are exposed to much lower temperatures and pressures. Surface rocks are also exposed to the gases and water in Earth's atmosphere.

Conditions on Earth's surface cause rocks to change. The rocks may break down physically or change chemically. Such change in rocks at Earth's surface is called **weathering**. There are two main types of weathering:

• mechanical weathering

• chemical weathering ☑

What Is Mechanical Weathering?

In the process of **mechanical weathering**, rocks break down by physical means. Mechanical weathering changes the physical appearance of a rock. However, it does not change the chemical composition of the rock.

Common *agents*, or causes, of mechanical weathering are ice, plants and animals, gravity, running water, and wind. These agents produce different forms of mechanical weathering, such as

• exfoliation

• ice wedging

• abrasion

• cracks and scrapes

READING TOOLBOX

Identify Examples As you read, list examples of weathering processes. Look for signal words that introduce examples. Signal words may include the following:

• for example

• such as

✓ READING CHECK

1. Identify What are the two main types of weathering?

_____

_____

Critical Thinking

2. Make Connections Name one agent of weathering that would not be common in a desert. Explain your answer.

_____

_____

_____

_____

EXFOLIATION

In the process of *exfoliation*, outer layers of a rock peel away. For example, erosion may expose granite beneath Earth's surface. When the granite is exposed, there is less pressure on it. As a result, the granite expands. Cracks called *joints* develop in the rock. The rock breaks into curved sheets that peel away from the underlying rock. ☑

ICE WEDGING

Ice wedging happens when water flows into cracks in rock and then freezes. When water freezes, its volume increases by about 10%. The increased volume of water puts pressure on the surrounding rock. Over time, the ice thaws and refreezes many times. Cycles of freezing and thawing widen the cracks in the rock. Finally, the rock splits apart. The figure below shows the process of ice wedging.

Rocks in the northern United States often experience ice wedging.

Ice wedging generally happens at high elevations and in cold climates. It also happens in places where the temperature regularly moves above and below freezing.

ABRASION

Abrasion happens when rocks collide with other rocks. The collisions wear away rock surfaces. Gravity, running water, and wind can all cause abrasion.

Gravity causes loose soil and rocks to move down the side of a hill or mountain. The rocks break as they fall. Running water carries rock particles that scrape against other rocks. Scraping wears away the rock surfaces. Wind lifts and carries small particles. The particles hit rock surfaces and wear them away.

✔ **READING CHECK**

3. Explain How can erosion cause exfoliation?

_____

_____

_____

_____

LOOKING CLOSER

4. Summarize How does ice wedging weather rock?

_____

_____

_____

_____

Talk About It

Apply Concepts With a partner, discuss how different agents of weathering can affect objects that you see every day. Give specific examples.

SECTION 1 **Weathering Processes** *continued*

PLANT AND ANIMAL ACTIVITY

Plants and animals can also cause mechanical weathering. As plants grow, their roots grow and spread out. The growing roots put pressure on rocks and cause cracks. Over time, the roots of larger plants move into the cracks and make them bigger.

Animals can affect rocks by digging. Rabbits, ants, worms, and many other animals move soil. When animals move soil, they expose new rock surfaces to weathering. Exposing rocks affects how quickly they change over time.

As the gray wolf digs in the soil to make a den, it increases the rate of weathering.

LOOKING CLOSER

5. Explain How is this animal affecting the weathering process?

_____
_____
_____

What Is Chemical Weathering?

In the process of **chemical weathering**, rocks break down because of chemical reactions with the environment. Chemical reactions act on the minerals in rock. These reactions commonly happen between rock, water, carbon dioxide, oxygen, and acids or bases. Chemical weathering changes both the chemical composition of rock and how the rock looks. ☑

Acids are substances that form *hydronium ions*, H_3O^+, in water. Hydronium ions can cause bonds in minerals to break. *Bases* are substances that form *hydroxide ions*, OH^-, in water. Chemical reactions with acids or bases can change the structures of minerals and cause new minerals to form. Different chemical reactions produce different forms of chemical weathering. Common types of chemical reactions involved in chemical weathering include

- oxidation
- hydrolysis
- carbonation

✓ **READING CHECK**

6. Describe What are two results of chemical weathering on rocks?

_____
_____
_____

OXIDATION

In **oxidation**, elements combine with oxygen. Oxidation commonly happens in rocks that have iron-rich minerals. In such rocks, the iron, Fe, combines quickly with oxygen, O_2, that is dissolved in water. The reaction produces iron oxide, Fe_2O_3, or rust.

LOOKING CLOSER
7. Identify What is produced when iron combines with oxygen?

_____

_____

$$4Fe + 3O_2 \rightarrow 2Fe_2O_3$$

Rocks that contain iron oxide tend to have a reddish color. For example, the soil in some parts of the southeastern United States is red because of iron oxide.

HYDROLYSIS

In **hydrolysis**, minerals react chemically with water. For example, the mineral feldspar reacts chemically with water. In this reaction, hydronium ions replace other atoms in the feldspar crystals. This chemical change changes the feldspar into a kind of clay called *kaolin*.

Minerals that are affected by hydrolysis typically dissolve in water. Water can carry the dissolved minerals to lower layers of rock in a process called *leaching*. Leaching can cause minerals to collect in a thin layer under Earth's surface.

Talk About It
Use Word Roots Use a dictionary to look up the roots *hydro-*, *oxi-*, and *carbon*. With a partner, discuss how these roots are related to the meanings of the chemical weathering processes.

CARBONATION

When carbon dioxide, CO_2, dissolves in water, H_2O, a weak acid called *carbonic acid*, H_2CO_3, forms.

LOOKING CLOSER
8. Identify What two substances react to form carbonic acid?

_____

_____

$$H_2O + CO_2 \rightarrow H_2CO_3$$

Carbonic acid has more hydronium ions than pure water does. These additional ions speed up the process of hydrolysis. Some minerals can combine with carbonic acid to form minerals called carbonates. Minerals become carbonates in the process of **carbonation**.

For example, carbonic acid reacts with calcite, a mineral in limestone. This reaction produces calcium bicarbonate. Calcium bicarbonate dissolves easily in water. For this reason, limestone weathers away relatively quickly.

SECTION 1 **Weathering Processes** *continued*

Rain, weak acids, and air chemically weather rock.

The bonds between mineral grains weaken as weathering continues.

Sediment forms from the weathered rock.

Critical Thinking

9. Make Connections What is the role of chemical weathering in the rock cycle?

_____

_____

_____

_____

_____

ORGANIC ACIDS

Some organisms naturally produce acids that cause chemical weathering. For example, mosses and lichens grow on rocks and produce weak acids. These acids seep into the rock and make cracks. Over time, the cracks cause the rock to break apart.

ACID PRECIPITATION

Rain, sleet, and snow are all forms of precipitation. Natural precipitation is slightly acidic because it combines with small amounts of carbon dioxide. Burning fossil fuels sends more carbon dioxide into the air. It also releases compounds called nitrogen oxides and sulfur oxides. These compounds combine with water in the atmosphere to form nitric acid, nitrous acid, or sulfuric acid. The acids fall to Earth as **acid precipitation**. ☑

Acid precipitation weathers some rock faster than regular precipitation does. It has damaged many monuments and sculptures, as shown below. Acid precipitation was common in some cities between 1940 and 1990. New laws to reduce air pollution have helped reduce the amount of acid precipitation in the United States.

✓ **READING CHECK**

10. Summarize How does acid precipitation form?

_____

_____

_____

_____

_____

_____

Acid precipitation damaged this stone lion in England.

Section 1 Review

SECTION VOCABULARY

abrasion the grinding and wearing away of rock surfaces through the mechanical action of other rock or sand particles	**hydrolysis** a chemical reaction between water and another substance to form two or more new substances
acid precipitation precipitation, such as rain, sleet, or snow, that contains a high concentration of acids, often because of the pollution of the atmosphere	**mechanical weathering** the process by which rocks break down into smaller pieces by physical means
carbonation the conversion of a compound into a carbonate	**oxidation** the process by which a metallic element combines with oxygen
chemical weathering the process by which rocks break down as a result of chemical reactions	**weathering** the natural process by which atmospheric and environmental agents, such as wind, rain, and temperature changes, disintegrate and decompose rocks

1. Compare What is the difference between mechanical weathering and chemical weathering?

_____

_____

2. Identify List three agents of mechanical weathering.

_____

3. Explain How do plants and animals help weather rocks and soil?

_____

_____

4. Compare Complete the table to compare oxidation, hydrolysis, and carbonation.

	Oxidation	Hydrolysis	Carbonation
Substance that the mineral reacts with	oxygen		
Example of process			Calcite reacts with carbonic acid to form calcium bicarbonate.

5. Understand Relationships How can power plants that burn fossil fuels affect chemical weathering processes?

_____

_____

_____

CHAPTER 14 Weathering and Erosion
SECTION
2 | Rates of Weathering

KEY IDEAS

As you read this section, keep these questions in mind:

• How does rock composition affect weathering rate?

• How does surface area affect weathering rate?

• How do climate and topography affect weathering rate?

What Affects the Rate of Weathering?

In general, mechanical and chemical weathering processes happen very slowly. For example, a layer of limestone that is 150 m thick could take 30 million years to dissolve through carbonation.

However, not all rocks weather at the same rate. The rate of weathering depends on many factors, such as

• rock composition

• amount of exposure

• climate

• topography ☑

How Does Rock Composition Affect the Rate of Weathering?

The materials that make up a rock affect the rate of weathering. Some rocks are softer and less resistant to weathering. That is, they weather more easily. Other rocks are harder and more resistant to weathering. They weather much more slowly.

In many cases, a single rock mass may be made up of several different kinds of rock. The different rocks may weather at different rates. In the process of **differential weathering**, softer rock wears away and leaves harder rock behind. For example, quartz is a hard mineral that resists weathering. For this reason, rock that contains quartz will not weather as quickly as rock without quartz. ☑

How easily a rock weathers depends mostly on the material that holds the rock particles together. For example, the particles in some sandstones are held together with strong silicate minerals. These sandstones resist weathering longer than sandstones without silicates.

READING TOOLBOX

Graphic Organizer As you read, create a spider map. Label the center oval "Factors that affect the rate of weathering." Fill in the map with the factors explained in this section.

✓ **READING CHECK**

1. List Name three factors that affect the rate of weathering.

_____

_____

_____

✓ **READING CHECK**

2. Identify How does quartz affect a rock's resistance to weathering?

_____

_____

_____

SECTION 2 **Rates of Weathering** *continued*

How Does Exposure Affect the Rate of Weathering?

The amount a rock is exposed to weathering agents helps determine the rate of weathering. Rocks weather faster when they are more exposed to weathering agents. Surface area and openings in the rock determine how much a rock is exposed. ☑

SURFACE AREA

A rock's *surface area* is the part of the rock that is exposed to air, water, and other weathering agents. Surface area increases as a rock breaks into smaller pieces.

For example, imagine a rock is a cube with six sides exposed, as shown below. The areas of the six sides add up to the total surface area of the cube.

Now imagine the rock breaks into eight smaller cubes. The amount of material stays the same. However, the rock's total surface area doubles. The rock is exposed in more places, so it will weather faster.

To find the surface area of a cube, add up the surface areas of the six faces, or sides.

If the cube breaks into smaller cubes, more total faces will be exposed. Total surface area has increased.

FRACTURES AND JOINTS

Recall that *joints* are areas of weakness in a rock, and *fractures* are breaks in a rock. Fractures and joints increase the surface area of the rock. The increased surface area speeds up the weathering process.

Fractures and joints also allow water to flow into the rock. The water may break the rock through ice wedging. Water also chemically weathers the rock exposed in the fracture or joint. The chemical weathering removes rock material and makes the opening in the rock weaker.

SECTION 2 **Rates of Weathering** *continued*

How Does Climate Affect the Rate of Weathering?

Climate also affects how fast rock weathers. Rates of weathering are highest in climates that have periods of hot and cold weather. Regular freezing and thawing can cause ice wedging. Chemical weathering can then act quickly on the fractured rock. When temperature rises, the chemical reactions accelerate, or speed up. Rates of weathering are also high in warm, humid climates. The moisture in the air easily weathers exposed surfaces.

The lowest rates of weathering occur in hot, dry climates. The lack of water limits many weathering processes, such as carbonation and ice wedging. Weathering is also slow in very cold climates.

How Does Topography Affect the Rate of Weathering?

Topography is the elevation and shape of the surface of land. Temperatures at high elevations are generally low. For this reason, ice wedging is more common at high elevations than at low elevations.

Weathering may happen more quickly on steep slopes, such as mountains. Gravity and heavy rain cause rocks to slide down the mountains. The rocks hit each other and break apart. As rocks fall away, new surfaces are exposed to weathering.

How Do Plants and Animals Affect the Rate of Weathering?

Plants and animals can affect the rate of weathering. The table below gives examples of activities that disturb or break rocks.

Activities that Affect the Rate of Weathering

	Activity	Effect
Humans	construction	exposes new rock surfaces
	mining	exposes rock to strong acids
	recreational activities	exposes new rock surfaces
Other animals	biological waste	causes chemical weathering
	digging	exposes new rock surfaces
Plants	growth of roots	breaks apart rock

Talk About It
Make Connections With a partner, discuss the climate you live in. What do you think the rate of weathering is like in your climate?

Critical Thinking
6. Infer Would ice wedging be more common in the mountains or at sea level? Explain your answer.

_____
_____
_____
_____

LOOKING CLOSER
7. Identify Name two human activities that affect the rate of weathering.

_____

Section 2 Review

SECTION VOCABULARY

differential weathering the process by which softer, less weather-resistant rocks wear away at a faster rate than harder, more weather-resistant rocks

1. **Analyze Conclusions** A geologist finds a sharp, jagged rock formation. She concludes that the formation is a result of differential weathering. What does the geologist mean?

_____

_____

_____

_____

2. **Identify** In which climates is the rate of weathering the fastest? Why?

_____

_____

3. **Describe** What are two ways that topography can affect the rate of weathering?

_____

_____

4. **Explain** How does surface area affect the rate of weathering?

_____

_____

_____

5. **Analyze Processes** Imagine that you want to protect an important stone monument from weathering by moving it to an area with a different climate. What type of climate would you choose? Explain your answer.

_____

_____

_____

6. **Apply Concepts** Think of some outdoor activities that you do for fun. Describe how one of these activities might affect the rocks around you.

_____

_____

_____

_____

CHAPTER 14 | Weathering and Erosion
SECTION 3 Soil

KEY IDEAS

As you read this section, keep these questions in mind:

• How does soil form?

• How does parent rock affect soil composition?

• What are the layers of mature residual soils?

• What types of soil form in arctic and tropical climates?

How Does Soil Form?

Weathering forms a layer of rock fragments that covers much of Earth's surface. This layer is called *regolith*. The solid, unweathered rock that lies beneath the regolith is called *bedrock*. The upper rock fragments in regolith weather to form a layer of fine particles. These particles are an important component of soil. **Soil** is a mixture of minerals, water, gases, and the remains of organisms.

Much of the material in soil comes from weathered rock. The original rock that produced the weathered material is called the *parent rock*.

The characteristics of soil depend on its parent rock. Some soil forms and stays directly over its parent rock. This soil is *residual soil*. Sometimes, wind and water carry soil particles away from their parent rock. Such soil is called *transported soil*. Transported soil may have different characteristics than the rock underneath it. ☑

Soil composition refers to the materials that make up soil. The color of soil is related to the soil's composition. For example, black soils are generally rich in organic material. Soil moisture can also affect color. Moist soils are generally darker than dry soils.

Rock particles in soil can be grouped by size, as shown below.

Particle Type	Diameter of Particle
Clay	less than 0.002 mm
Silt	from 0.002 mm to 0.05 mm
Sand	from 0.05 mm to 2 mm

The amount of clay, silt, and sand in a soil determines the soil's *texture*.

READING TOOLBOX

Ask Questions Before you read this section, create a three-column chart. Fill in the first two columns of the chart with what you already know about soil and what you want to know about soil. After you read the section, fill out the last column in the chart with what you learned about soil. Discuss your chart with a partner.

✓ READING CHECK

1. Compare How do residual soil and transported soil differ?

_____

_____

_____

LOOKING CLOSER
2. Identify Which type of soil particle is largest?

_____

SECTION 3 **Soil** *continued*

What Is a Soil Profile?

Residual soils typically develop distinct layers over time. Scientists use a soil profile to study the layers of soil. A **soil profile** is a cross section of, or slice through, soil and its bedrock. The different layers of soil are called **horizons**.

Residual soils generally have three main horizons. The *A horizon*, or *topsoil*, is a mixture of organic materials and small rock particles. Most organisms that live in soil live in the A horizon. When the organisms die, their remains decay. Decay produces **humus**, a dark, organic material. ☑

The *B horizon*, or *subsoil*, has minerals from the topsoil, clay, and sometimes humus. In dry climates, minerals collect in the B horizon as water evaporates.

The *C horizon* has partially weathered bedrock. The first stages of mechanical and chemical change happen in this layer. The figure below shows a soil profile.

Soil Horizons of Residual Soils

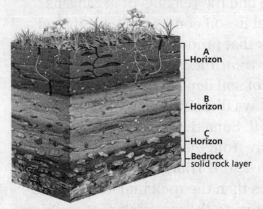

As it sinks into the ground, water carries minerals to lower layers of soil.

How Does Climate Affect Soil?

Climate determines the weathering processes that happen in an area. These weathering processes affect soil composition.

TROPICAL SOILS

In humid tropical climates, where it is hot and rainy, chemical weathering happens quickly. Thick soils called *laterites* form. Heavy rains remove minerals and nutrients from the topsoil, making the topsoil layer thin. However, tropical climates also have dense plant life. These plants add organic material to the soil. As a result, a thin layer of humus covers the B horizon. ☑

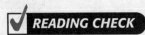

READING CHECK

3. Describe Describe the characteristics of the A horizon.

_____

_____

LOOKING CLOSER

4. Identify What lies under the C horizon?

_____

_____

READING CHECK

5. Explain How does dense plant growth affect the soil in tropical climates?

_____

_____

_____

SECTION 3 **Soil** *continued*

TEMPERATE SOILS

In temperate climates, temperatures range between low and high, and rainfall is moderate. Both chemical and physical weathering are important in temperate regions. Temperate soils have the thickest A horizon.

Two main soil types form in temperate climates: pedalfer and pedocal. *Pedalfer* soils form in areas with more than 65 cm of rain per year. Pedalfer soils contain iron, clay, and quartz. *Pedocal* soils form in areas with less than 65 cm of rain per year. Pedocal soils contain large amounts of calcium carbonate. ☑

DESERT AND ARCTIC SOILS

Desert and arctic regions do not get much rain. In these climates, chemical weathering happens slowly. The soil forms mainly by mechanical weathering. For this reason, the soil is thin and made up mostly of regolith. Desert and arctic regions have relatively little plant or animal life, so their soils have little humus.

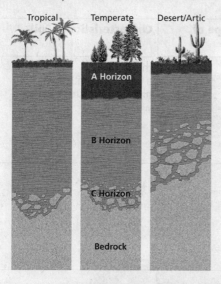
Tropical   Temperate   Desert/Artic

A Horizon

B Horizon

C Horizon

Bedrock

Tropical climates produce thick, infertile soils. Temperate climates produce thick, fertile soils. Desert and arctic climates produce thin soils.

✔ READING CHECK

6. Identify The Gulf Coast states generally receive more than 65 cm of rain per year. Which kind of soils would you expect to find in this region?

_____

LOOKING CLOSER

7. Compare How is tropical soil different from temperate soil?

_____

_____

_____

How Does Topography Affect Soil?

Topography, or the shape of the land, also affects soil formation. As rainwater runs down a slope, it washes away topsoil. As a result, the soil on the slope is thin. The soil at the top and bottom of the slope is thicker.

Topsoil on a slope is often too thin to support dense plant life. For this reason, the soil is poor and lacks humus. The land at the bottom of slopes often has thick, wet soil. The soil supports organisms and is rich in humus.

Section 3 Review

SECTION VOCABULARY

horizon a horizontal layer of soil that can be distinguished from the layers above and below it **humus** dark, organic material formed in soil from the decayed remains of plants and animals	**soil** a loose mixture of rock fragments and organic material that can support the growth of vegetation **soil profile** a vertical section of soil that shows the layers, or horizons

1. Identify List the three main layers in mature residual soils.

_____

2. Explain How does weathering help form soil?

_____

_____

3. Explain How does the composition of the parent rock affect soil composition?

_____

_____

4. Compare Complete the table to compare soils in different climates.

	Characteristics of Climate	Most Important Type of Weathering	Characteristics of Soil
Tropical		chemical	thin topsoil; a layer of humus; high rates of chemical weathering
Temperate	cool to warm; moderate amounts of rain		
Desert and arctic			

5. Apply Concepts Which climate would likely be best for growing crops with deep roots? Explain your answer.

_____

_____

SECTION 4 Erosion

As you read this section, keep these questions in mind:

- What is erosion, and what are four agents of erosion?
- What are four farming methods that conserve soil?
- How does gravity contribute to erosion?
- What are the three major landforms shaped by weathering and erosion?

What Is Erosion?

Weathering causes rock particles to break away from rock. However, the rock particles do not always stay near the parent rock. Forces in the environment may move the particles to other places. This process, in which Earth materials are moved from one place to another, is called **erosion**. The most common agents of erosion are

- gravity
- wind
- glaciers
- water

How Does Erosion Affect Soil?

Tiny particles of rock that form during weathering mix with water, air, and humus to form soil. Soil erodes constantly, but soil erosion is normally a slow process. New soil forms fast enough to replace eroding soil. However, living and nonliving factors can upset this natural balance. When this happens, soil erodes quickly before new soil can replace it.

Some scientists think that soil erosion is the greatest environmental problem today. Erosion removes fertile topsoil and makes it harder to grow crops.

Certain farming techniques can accelerate, or speed up, soil erosion. For example, some farmers plow long, narrow rows called *furrows*. Furrows on slopes channel water from rainfall, washing away the soil. Over time, the furrows become larger. They form deep ditches, or gullies. This type of soil erosion is called *gullying*. Gullying can ruin farmland.

Determine Cause and Effect As you read, make a chart showing the causes and effects of erosion. When you are finished, compare your chart with a partner's.

Critical Thinking

1. Identify Relationships What is the relationship between weathering and erosion?

_____

_____

_____

_____

_____

_____

Critical Thinking

2. Make Connections What is the relationship between soil erosion and hunger?

_____

_____

_____

_____

_____

_____

SECTION 4 **Erosion** *continued*

SHEET EROSION

In the process of **sheet erosion**, wind and water remove layers of topsoil. Over time, erosion may expose the surface of the subsoil.

Sheet erosion may happen in places where heavy rains wash away layers of topsoil. During dry periods, wind can also cause sheet erosion. Wind carries the loose, dry soil away in clouds of dust and sand. These soil particles may form large dust storms. ☑

RESULTS OF SOIL EROSION

Constant erosion makes it harder for soil to support life. The flowchart below shows how erosion affects the fertility of soil.

Erosion removes the A horizon, which contains fertile humus.

↓

The B horizon is less fertile because it does not have much humus. The B horizon is difficult to farm.

↓

The B horizon has no plant life to protect it from more erosion.

↓

Erosion continues to remove layers of soil. Over time, erosion may remove all the soil.

EFFECTS OF HUMAN ACTIVITIES ON EROSION RATES

Human activities affect how quickly soil erodes. Farming techniques and construction projects can increase the rate of erosion. For example, people remove plants to build houses and roads. Without plants for protection, the topsoil erodes more quickly. New soil cannot form fast enough. In some areas, it may take thousands of years for new topsoil to form.

Human actions can also reduce or prevent soil erosion. *Soil conservation* involves taking steps to prevent soil erosion.

✓ READING CHECK

3. Describe What kind of conditions can lead to sheet erosion?

_____

_____

_____

_____

LOOKING CLOSER

4. Describe What makes the B horizon at risk for erosion?

_____

_____

_____

_____

_____

_____

SECTION 4 **Erosion** *continued*

What Are Some Methods of Soil Conservation?

People have begun to understand how human activities affect the environment. Now, many people are trying to protect soil through soil conservation. For example, some land development projects are leaving trees and plants in place when possible. Other projects are adding plants to the soil to prevent erosion. Farmers also use soil conservation methods to prevent erosion. Some of these methods are

- contour plowing
- strip-cropping
- terracing
- crop rotation

CONTOUR PLOWING

Farmers around the world use different planting methods to reduce soil erosion. In the *contour plowing* method, farmers plow in curved bands. These bands follow the contour, or shape, of the land. Contour plowing prevents water from flowing straight down slopes. Therefore, this method helps prevents gullying. ☑

STRIP-CROPPING

Farmers may also use *strip-cropping* to prevent erosion. In this method, farmers plant crops in alternating bands, as shown below. For example, a farmer may plant rows of corn in one band. Then the farmer plants a *cover crop*, such as alfalfa, next to the corn. A cover crop fully covers the surface of the land. This cover crop slows the runoff of rainwater and protects the soil. ☑

Contour Plowing   Strip-Cropping

Talk About It

Discuss With a partner, talk about land use in your community. What activities may be damaging the soil? What activities may be helping the soil?

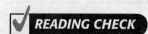 **READING CHECK**

5. Describe How does contour plowing help conserve soil?

_____

_____

_____

READING CHECK

6. Identify Give an example of a cover crop.

_____

TERRACING

Normally, the soil on hillsides is thin because of erosion. However, farmers can use *terracing* to farm on slopes. In this method, farmers build steplike ridges, or terraces, that follow the shape of a sloped field. Terraces slow the movement of water down the slope. Slowing the water prevents soil from washing away quickly. Many farmers in Asia use terracing to grow rice. ☑

7. Explain What is one advantage of terracing?

_____

_____

_____

Terraced fields such as these help slow runoff and prevent rapid soil erosion.

CROP ROTATION

In *crop rotation*, farmers change the type of crop they plant each year. One year, a farmer may plant a crop that will be harvested, or picked. The next year, the farmer may plant a cover crop. The cover crop is not harvested. Instead, it helps to slow runoff and hold the soil in place. Other types of crop rotation help keep the soil fertile. ☑

8. Identify What are two functions of cover crops?

_____

_____

_____

What Is the Role of Gravity in Erosion?

Gravity causes rock fragments to move down a slope. This movement of fragments down a slope is called **mass movement**. Some mass movements happen quickly. Others happen very slowly. The most destructive mass movements happen quickly.

Types of Mass Movement

Fast Mass Movements	Slow Mass Movements
• rockfalls	• solifluction
• landslides	• creep
• mudflows	
• slumps	

ROCKFALLS AND LANDSLIDES

The fastest kind of mass movement is a *rockfall*. In a rockfall, rock falls from a steep cliff. The rocks in rockfalls can be tiny fragments or giant boulders.

In a *landslide*, masses of loose rock and soil suddenly fall down a slope. In large landslides, loose blocks of bedrock fall. This happens on very steep slopes. Small landslides often happen on the steep hills next to highways. Heavy rainfall, volcanic eruptions, and earthquakes can cause landslides.

An earthquake in El Salvador caused this landslide.

MUDFLOWS AND SLUMPS

The quick movement of a large amount of mud forms a *mudflow*. Mudflows happen in mountain regions because of volcanic eruptions or heavy rainfall. Mudflows move down slopes and valleys. The mud typically spreads out in a fan shape at the base of the slope.

Sometimes, a large block of soil and rock falls downhill in one piece. The block then slides along the slope of the surface. This movement is a *slump*. Slumping happens on very steep slopes. Water and loss of friction cause the soil and rock to slip downhill.

SOLIFLUCTION

Many slopes do not seem to change. However, such slopes often experience slow mass movements. Slow mass movements actually move more rock material overall than landslides. One form of slow mass movement is solifluction. In **solifluction**, soil that is soaked with water flows over hard or frozen layers of soil.

Solifluction happens in arctic and mountain climates, where the subsoil is always frozen. Water from the topsoil cannot flow into the frozen subsoil. As a result, the surface layer becomes muddy and flows slowly downhill.

Critical Thinking

9. Compare What is the difference between a rockfall and a landslide?

_____

_____

_____

_____

Critical Thinking

10. Infer Solifluction can also happen in warmer areas where the subsoil is made of hard clay. Why would subsoil with hard clay likely lead to solifluction?

_____

_____

_____

SECTION 4 **Erosion** *continued*

CREEP

Another form of slow mass movement is creep. **Creep** is the slow downhill movement of weathered rock material. Soil creep moves the most soil of all types of mass movements. Factors such as water between rock particles, growing plants, burrowing animals, and freezing and thawing cause soil creep. All of these factors help loosen particles, which allows gravity to pull the particles downhill.

The rock fragments form piles as they collect at the base of a slope. These piles are called *talus*. Talus weathers into smaller fragments that move farther down the slope. The fragments wash into gullies and streams. Eventually, the gullies and streams carry the particles into rivers. ☑

The movement of rock fragments downhill caused these talus cones to form at the base of the Canadian Rockies.

How Does Erosion Affect Landforms?

The physical features on Earth's surface are called **landforms**. Weathering and erosion help shape three major landforms: mountains, plains, and plateaus. They also shape minor landforms such as hills, valleys, and dunes.

EROSION OF MOUNTAINS

Mountains go through different stages over time. First, tectonic forces form mountains by lifting Earth's crust. The forces cause mountains to rise. The mountains rise faster than they are eroded. The mountains are generally rugged and have sharp peaks.

Over time, forces stop uplifting the mountains. Weathering and erosion wear down the rugged peaks. The mountains become rounded and have gentle slopes. Eventually mountains become low hills. Such features are called *peneplains*, which means "almost flat." ☑

These mountains in the Andes are still being uplifted.

The Appalachian Mountains have been eroded over millions of years.

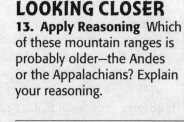

LOOKING CLOSER
13. Apply Reasoning Which of these mountain ranges is probably older—the Andes or the Appalachians? Explain your reasoning.

_____

_____

_____

_____

_____

_____

_____

EROSION OF PLAINS AND PLATEAUS

A *plain* is a flat landform near sea level. A *plateau* is a wide, flat landform that has a high elevation. A plateau experiences much more erosion than a plain. Young plateaus typically have deep valleys that separate the wide, flat regions.

Plateaus weather in different ways. In dry climates, rocks that are resistant to weathering form plateaus with flat tops. Over time, erosion may split the plateaus into smaller areas called *mesas*. Mesas erode into even smaller formations called *buttes*. In dry areas, buttes and mesas have steep walls and flat tops. In wet climates, humidity and precipitation weather landforms into round shapes. ☑

READING CHECK

14. Sequence Which landform develops first—a mesa or a butte? Explain.

_____

_____

_____

Ancient rivers carved plateaus into mesas. The mesas eventually eroded into the buttes of Monument Valley in Arizona.

Section 4 Review

SECTION VOCABULARY

creep the slow downhill movement of weathered rock material	**mass movement** the movement of a large mass of sediment or a section of land down a slope
erosion a process in which the materials of Earth's surface are loosened, dissolved, or worn away and transported from one place to another by a natural agent, such as wind, water, ice, or gravity	**sheet erosion** the process by which water flows over a layer of soil and removes the topsoil
landform a physical feature of Earth's surface	**solifluction** the slow, downslope flow of soil saturated with water in areas surrounding glaciers at high elevations

1. Define In your own words, define *erosion*.

_____

_____

2. Organize Complete the spider map below to identify and describe four methods of soil conservation. Be sure to include how each method protects soil.

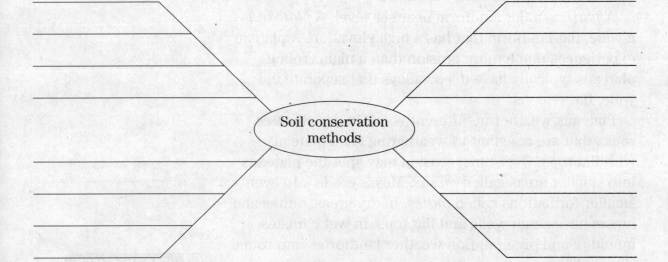

Soil conservation methods

3. Identify What are three major landforms shaped by weathering and erosion?

_____

4. Explain How does gravity cause erosion? Give two examples.

_____

_____

5. Apply Ideas Imagine that you wanted to grow grapes on a hillside. What farming method or methods would you use? Explain your answer.

_____

_____

CHAPTER 15 River Systems

SECTION 1 The Water Cycle

As you read this section, keep these questions in mind:
- What are the stages of the water cycle?
- What factors affect an area's water budget?
- What are two ways to conserve water?

How Does Water Move Through the Earth System?

Water covers more than two-thirds of Earth's surface. It flows in rivers and streams. It is stored in lakes, oceans, and icecaps. It even flows through rock below Earth's surface. In Earth's atmosphere, water exists as an invisible gas called *water vapor*. Liquid water also exists in the atmosphere as small particles in clouds and fog.

Re-read Read the section through once. Then, read the section again, and write the answers to the Key Ideas questions as you find them. You may wish to write the answers or additional notes in the text margin.

The water in the Earth system changes constantly from one form to another. Earth's water also moves constantly. Water vapor in the atmosphere changes to liquid water and falls as rain. Rivers flow into oceans. Water escapes from oceans as vapor and enters the atmosphere. The movement of water between the atmosphere and the land and oceans is called the **water cycle**.

The water cycle can happen because water can change states. You know that freezing is a change from a liquid to a solid. Melting is a change of state from a solid to a liquid. Two other changes of state important to the water cycle are evaporation and condensation.

LOOKING CLOSER
1. Analyze Graphics Give an example from the photo of each state of water (solid, liquid, gas).

_____

_____

2. Calculate Each year about 500,000 km³ of water evaporates into the atmosphere. About 86% of this water evaporates from the oceans. How much water in km³ evaporates from other sources?

_____

_____

Critical Thinking

3. Identify Relationships What is the relationship between condensation and evaporation?

_____

_____

_____

_____

4. Identify List four forms of precipitation.

_____

_____

EVAPOTRANSPIRATION

The process in which liquid water changes into water vapor is called *evaporation*. Most water evaporates from the ocean. Water also evaporates from lakes, streams, and the soil. Another way water vapor enters the atmosphere is by transpiration. In *transpiration*, plants release water vapor from their leaves. **Evapotranspiration** is the total loss of water from an area through evaporation and transpiration.

CONDENSATION

Condensation is the change of state from a gas to a liquid. As air rises in the atmosphere, it cools. Some of the water vapor in the cooler air condenses. The tiny water droplets that form through condensation make up clouds.

PRECIPITATION

Water that moved into the atmosphere returns to Earth in the process of *precipitation*. During precipitation, liquid or solid water falls from clouds to the ground. The word **precipitation** also refers to any form the water takes as it falls to Earth from clouds. Rain, snow, sleet, and hail are all forms of precipitation.

Most precipitation falls on Earth's oceans. The rest falls on land and becomes runoff or groundwater. Eventually, almost all of this water returns to the atmosphere through evapotranspiration, and the cycle continues. ☑

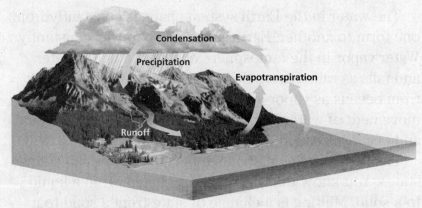

Evapotranspiration, condensation, and precipitation make up the water cycle.

What Is a Water Budget?

Earth has a *water budget*, which is much like a financial budget. In Earth's water budget, precipitation is like income. Evapotranspiration and runoff are like expenses. Overall, Earth's water budget is balanced. The amount of water that moves into the atmosphere is about the same as the amount of precipitation. However, a local water budget is generally not balanced. A *local water budget* is the water budget of a certain area. ☑

Factors That Affect a Local Water Budget

Factor	Effect
Temperature	In general, lower temperatures decrease evapotranspiration. Higher temperatures in warm seasons increase evapotranspiration.
Number of plants	Plants reduce runoff, but increase evapotranspiration.
Wind	High winds increase the rate of evapotranspiration.
Rainfall	When precipitation is greater than evapotranspiration, the result is wet soil and, sometimes, flooding. When evapotranspiration is greater than precipitation, the soil becomes dry.

A local water budget can change with seasons. The factors that affect a local water budget can also vary from place to place.

Why Is Conserving Water Important?

On average, each person in the United States uses about 95,000 L of water each year. People use water for bathing, washing clothes and dishes, watering lawns, drinking, and flushing away wastes. Industry also uses a great deal of water. Most of the water that cities and industries use returns to rivers and oceans as wastewater. Some of this wastewater contains harmful materials, such as toxic chemicals and metals.

Earth has a great deal of water. However, only a very small amount is fresh water that humans and other organisms need. There are two main ways humans can make sure there is enough fresh water for the future. One way is through water conservation, or using water wisely.

Another way to protect future water supplies is to find new ways to get fresh water. In one such method, called **desalination**, salt is removed from ocean water. This method is very expensive. Thus, the best way to protect the supply of fresh water is to use water wisely.

✓ READING CHECK

5. Explain In your own words, explain what is meant by a balanced water budget.

_____

_____

_____

_____

_____

Talk About It

Apply Ideas In a small group, talk about where on Earth desalination might be most useful. What kinds of conditions exist in such a place? What other sources of fresh water exist in these places?

Section 1 Review

SECTION VOCABULARY

condensation the change of state from a gas to a liquid	**precipitation** any form of water that falls to Earth's surface from the clouds; includes rain, snow, sleet, and hail
desalination a process of removing salt from ocean water	**water cycle** the continuous movement of water between the atmosphere, the land, and the oceans
evapotranspiration the total loss of water from an area, which equals the sum of the water lost by evaporation from the soil and other surfaces and the water lost by transpiration from organisms	

1. Compare How are the processes of condensation and precipitation different?

_____

_____

_____

2. Identify What are two ways water reaches the oceans?

_____

_____

3. Apply Concepts Describe five ways you can conserve water.

_____

_____

_____

_____

_____

_____

4. Explain Why are most local water budgets unbalanced?

_____

_____

_____

5. Analyze Processes Why do most precipitation and evaporation happen over the oceans?

_____

_____

_____

CHAPTER 15 **River Systems**

SECTION 2 **Stream Erosion**

As you read this section, keep these questions in mind:

- How does a river develop?
- What factors affect a river's ability to erode its channel?
- How do erosive factors affect the development of a river channel?
- What are the parts of a river system?

What Are the Parts of a Stream?

A *stream* is a body of water that flows over the land. A stream has three main parts: a channel, banks, and a bed.

Part	Description
Channel	the narrow groove in the ground in which a stream flows
Banks	the edges of the channel that rise above the water level
Bed	the part of the channel below the water level

There are three main characteristics of streams that affect the stream's ability to erode land. These three factors are stream load, stream discharge, and gradient. ☑

As it flows downhill, a stream carries soil, pieces of rocks, and dissolved minerals. These materials that a stream carries are called the **stream load**. The larger a stream's load is, the greater the stream's ability to erode its channel is. Stream load has three parts: suspended load, bed load, and dissolved load.

Suspended load is made up of fine sand and silt. These fine particles do not sink because the water is moving so quickly. *Bed load* is made up of heavier materials, such as coarse sand, gravel, and pebbles. *Dissolved load* is the minerals that are carried in liquid solution. ☑

The volume of water that moves along the stream bed in a given time period is called the stream's **discharge**. The faster a stream flows, the higher its discharge is. The greater a stream's discharge, the heavier a load it can carry. A fast-moving stream carries more sediment and larger particles than a slow-moving stream does.

The speed of the stream also affects how the stream widens its channel. Fast-moving streams erode their channels more quickly than slow-moving streams do.

READING TOOLBOX

Outline Before you read this section, write each of the headings in your notebook. As you read, use the headings to create an outline of the section.

READING CHECK

1. List What are the three main stream erosive factors?

_____

_____

_____

READING CHECK

2. Compare How is dissolved load different from suspended load?

_____

_____

_____

_____

SECTION 2 **Stream Erosion** *continued*

Critical Thinking

3. Predict A particular stream flows at a very high speed. What kind of gradient does the stream most likely have?

_____

_____

_____

Math Skills

4. Calculate You can use the following equation to calculate the discharge of a stream or river:

discharge =
speed of the water ×
cross-sectional area of the
channel

Suppose a river moves 1.5 m/s through a cross-sectional area of 520 m². What is the discharge of water that the river carries? Express your answer in cubic meters per second (m³/s).

_____

STREAM GRADIENT

The speed of a stream affects the stream load and how quickly the stream erodes its channel. The speed of a stream depends mainly on gradient. **Gradient** is the steepness of the stream's slope.

Near the *headwaters*, or beginning of a stream, the gradient is generally steep. Near the *mouth*, or where the stream enters a larger body of water, the gradient is flatter. A flatter gradient makes the stream slower. A flatter gradient also decreases the stream's ability to erode its channel.

How Does a River Channel Develop?

Over time, a stream channel erodes and becomes wider and deeper. When a stream becomes longer and wider, it is called a *river*.

MEANDERING CHANNELS

A river that has a low gradient typically has more bends than a river with a steep gradient has. As gradient decreases, the speed of the water decreases. When water speed decreases, the river is less able to erode into its bed. Instead, the energy of the water flowing through the channel erodes the banks. Erosion of the banks produces a winding pattern of wide curves called **meanders**. The figure below shows how meanders form.

LOOKING CLOSER

5. Analyze Diagrams On the diagram, label the area where water is moving fastest and the area where water is moving slowest.

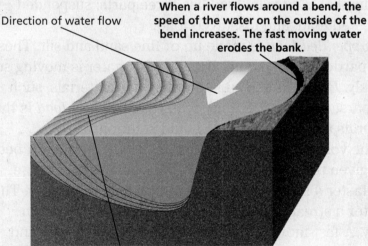

Direction of water flow

When a river flows around a bend, the speed of the water on the outside of the bend increases. The fast moving water erodes the bank.

The speed of the water on the inside of the bend decreases. The decrease in speed causes the river to deposit sediment on the inside of the bend. The deposited sediment is called a *bar*.

Over time, erosion and deposition make the bends in the river sharper.

SECTION 2 **Stream Erosion** *continued*

BRAIDED STREAMS

Most rivers have a single channel. However, under certain conditions, sediment bars between a river's banks can divide the river into several channels. The water in the separate channels may join around the sediment bars. A stream or river made up of multiple channels that divide and rejoin is called a **braided stream**. In general, a high gradient and a large sediment load can cause a braided stream to form. ☑

What Are the Parts of a River System?

A river system is made up of a main stream and smaller streams that feed into it. The figure below shows a general river system.

✔ **READING CHECK**

6. Identify What are the main factors that cause a braided stream to form?

_____

_____

Water runs off land and into the tributaries. The land from which water runs off into a stream is a **watershed**.

Ridges or elevated areas that separate watersheds are called *divides*.

Watershed

A small stream that feeds into the main stream is called a **tributary**.

River

LOOKING CLOSER

7. Describe Relationships What is the relationship between a tributary and a stream?

_____

_____

River systems change continuously because of erosion. In a process called *headward erosion*, channels become longer at their upper ends. They branch out where runoff enters the streams. Erosion of slopes can make a watershed larger. A stream in a watershed with a high rate of erosion may capture a stream from another watershed. This process is called *stream piracy*. The stream that has been captured drains into its new river system.

Section 2 Review

SECTION VOCABULARY

braided stream a stream or river that is composed of multiple channels that divide and rejoin around sediment bars	**stream load** the materials other than the water that are carried by a stream
discharge the volume of water that flows within a given time	**tributary** a stream that flows into a lake or into a larger stream
gradient the change in elevation over a given distance	**watershed** the area of land that is drained by a river system
meander one of the bends, twists, or curves in a low-gradient stream or river	

1. **Summarize Relationships** Complete the concept map below to describe streams and river systems. Use the following terms in your concept map: *braided stream, stream load, suspended load, dissolved load, bed load, meander, stream gradient, tributaries,* and *watershed.*

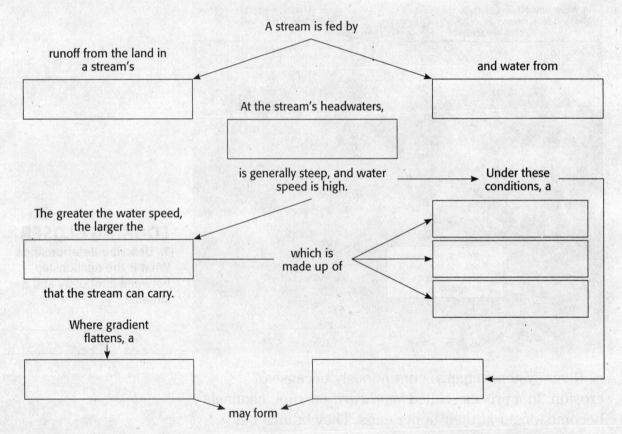

2. **Explain** What are the effects of stream discharge and gradient on the ability of a river to erode its channel?

_____

_____

_____

CHAPTER 15 River Systems

SECTION 3 Stream Deposition

As you read this section, keep these questions in mind:

• What are two types of stream deposition?

• What are advantages and disadvantages of living in a floodplain?

• What are three methods of flood control?

• What are the stages in the life cycle of a lake?

What Are Two Types of Stream Deposition?

Recall that the total load a stream can carry depends on how fast the stream is moving. When the speed of the stream decreases, the load the stream can carry decreases. The stream deposits some of its stream load. A stream may deposit sediment on land or in water.

When a stream empties into a large body of water such as a lake or ocean, the stream's speed decreases. The stream deposits sediment at its mouth. The sediments typically form a triangular shape. This triangular-shaped deposit at the mouth of a stream is called a **delta**. ☑

This delta is in Prince William Sound in Alaska.

When a stream flows down a steep slope and reaches a flat plain, the speed of the stream decreases suddenly. The stream deposits sediment on the plain at the bottom of the slope. The deposits form a fan-shaped deposit called an **alluvial fan**.

What Is a Floodplain?

If a large volume of water enters a stream suddenly, the stream may overflow its banks. The overflow of water is called a *flood*. The flood water covers the valley floor. The part of the valley floor that may be covered with water during a flood is called a **floodplain**. ☑

READING TOOLBOX

Make Notecards Before you read this section, write each Key Ideas question on a separate notecard. As you read, write the answers on the back of the notecards. After you read, compare your cards with a partner's and make corrections as needed.

✓ READING CHECK

1. Describe Under what conditions does a delta form?

_____

_____

_____

_____

✓ READING CHECK

2. Explain How are a river or stream and its floodplain related?

_____

_____

_____

_____

SECTION 3 **Stream Deposition** *continued*

Critical Thinking

3. Compare During a flood, how does the deposition of coarse sediments differ from the deposition of finer sediments?

_____

_____

_____

_____

LOOKING CLOSER

4. Describe How is flooding helpful to farmers?

_____

_____

_____

_____

LOOKING CLOSER

5. Synthesize Text and Graphics Identify one direct method and one indirect method of flood control.

_____

_____

_____

NATURAL LEVEES

When a stream overflows its banks and spreads over the floodplain, the stream loses speed. As it loses speed, the stream deposits coarse sediments along the banks of the channel. As the sediments collect, they form a raised bank called a *natural levee.*

FINER FLOOD SEDIMENTS

Not all the sediments a steam deposits during a flood form levees. Flood water carries fine sediments farther out onto the floodplain. After many floods, the fine sediments help produce rich soils. The table below describes advantages and disadvantages of living in a floodplain.

Advantages	Disadvantages
• Floodplains give people easy access to the river for shipping, fishing, and transportation. • Fine sediments produce rich soils that are good for farming.	• Flooding can cause damage to property. • People can drown in flood waters or catch diseases carried by flood water.

How Do Human Activities Affect Flooding?

Plants, such as trees and grass, protect the ground surface from erosion. The plants can take in water that would otherwise run off. Activities such as logging, farming, and constructing buildings remove plants. Without plants to cover the ground, erosion happens more easily, and flooding is more likely to happen.

Because floods can be dangerous and damaging to property, people try to control flooding. Many methods of flood control involve building structures that change the way water flows. The table below describes three of these structures. People can also control floods indirectly. Indirect methods include conserving forests and soils to prevent excess runoff.

Direct Methods of Flood Control

Structure	How It Is Helpful
Dams	The runoff that collects behind a dam can be used to produce electricity. People can also use the water for drinking, bathing, and farming.
Artificial levees	They act like high river banks to block rising water.
Floodways	When the volume of river water increases, these overflow channels carry away excess water.

What Are the Stages of a Lake's Life Cycle?

Not all streams flow from the land to the ocean. Sometimes, water from a stream collects in a low spot in the land and forms a lake. The land the lake water sits in is called its *basin*. Most water in lakes comes from precipitation and the melting of ice and snow. Water from springs, rivers, and runoff can also enter lakes.

Although a lake is not alive, scientists may speak about a lake's life cycle. The life cycle of a lake stretches from when the lake forms to when it disappears. Compared to many other bodies of water, a lake has a relatively short life cycle.

Lakes can disappear because their water evaporates or drains away. Although evaporation happens constantly, precipitation generally replaces what was lost. However, if the climate in the area becomes drier, evaporation may be greater than precipitation. ☑

Lakes can also disappear when their basins fill with sediment. Streams that feed a lake and runoff from land carry sediments into the lake. Over time, the sediments can build up and fill in the lake. Organic matter from plants may collect on the bottom of a shallow lake. As this organic matter builds up, a bog or swamp may form. The lake basin may eventually become dry land.

Talk About It

Extend Concepts What are some other situations in which people might talk about the "life cycle" of a nonliving thing? In a small group, talk about your ideas.

☑ READING CHECK

6. Explain Why don't typical rates of evaporation for an area cause a lake to dry up?

_____

_____

_____

Life Cycle of a Lake

Precipitation collects in a shallow spot in the land called a depression, forming a lake.

The lake loses water as water drains away or evaporates. The lake may also start to fill with sediment.

As the lake loses water, the lake basin may eventually become dry land. A lake may also fill completely with sediments and plant material.

LOOKING CLOSER

7. Summarize What two processes generally cause a lake to become dry land?

_____

_____

Section 3 Review

SECTION VOCABULARY

alluvial fan a fan-shaped mass of rock material deposited by a stream when the slope of the land decreases sharply	**floodplain** an area along a river that forms from sediments deposited when the river overflows its banks
delta a fan-shaped mass of rock material deposited at the mouth of a stream	

1. Compare How is a delta different from an alluvial fan?

_____

_____

2. Identify What are three direct methods people can use to control floods?

_____

_____

_____

3. Describe Describe one advantage and one disadvantage of living in a floodplain.

_____

_____

_____

4. Summarize Describe three ways human activities can affect the size and number of floods that happen in an area.

_____

_____

_____

_____

5. Analyze Ideas In spring, floods are common in rivers with headwaters in areas with cold, snowy winters. Explain why this is so.

_____

_____

_____

6. Propose Solutions Suppose you had to choose a material for an artificial levee. What characteristic should the material have? Explain your answer.

_____

_____

_____

CHAPTER 16 Groundwater

SECTION 1

Water Beneath the Surface

KEY IDEAS

As you read this section, keep these questions in mind:

• What are two properties of aquifers?

• How is the water table related to the land surface?

• How are wells, springs, and artesian formations related?

• What are two features formed by hot groundwater?

What Is Groundwater?

Some of Earth's fresh water is in streams and lakes, but much of it is found underground. Surface water seeps through the soil and into the upper layers of Earth's crust. It settles into the spaces between underground rocks. This water is called **groundwater**. A layer of rock or sediment that holds groundwater is called an **aquifer**.

How Does Water Flow Through an Aquifer?

Groundwater flows downward because of gravity, but water flows through some aquifers more easily than others. Aquifers have two main properties that affect water flow: porosity and permeability. ☑

Pores are open spaces between the particles in a rock or sediment. **Porosity** is the percentage of a rock or sediment that pores take up. A rock with high porosity is said to be more *porous* than one with low porosity. Three main factors affect porosity:

• sorting

• particle size

• particle shape

Well-sorted sediment contains particles that are all about the same size. Poorly sorted sediment contains particles of different sizes. In general, well-sorted sediments are more porous than poorly sorted sediments.

If you fill a jar with pebbles, there will be open spaces between the pebbles. If you pour sand into the jar, the sand fills the spaces between the pebbles. The mixture of sand and pebbles is less porous because it is poorly sorted.

READING TOOLBOX

Take Notes As you read this section, create combination notes that express information about groundwater in words and pictures or diagrams.

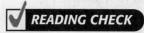

READING CHECK

1. Explain What are the two properties of an aquifer that affect water flow?

_____

_____

SECTION 1 **Water Beneath the Surface** *continued*

LOOKING CLOSER

2. Identify Which of these pictures represents an aquifer with high porosity? Which represents an aquifer with low porosity?

_____

_____

_____

Well sorted

Well sorted

Poorly sorted

Particle packing also affects porosity. If the particles in an aquifer are packed together tightly, there are few spaces between them. Therefore, the aquifer is less porous. If the particles are loosely packed, the spaces between them are larger. Therefore, the aquifer is more porous.

The shape of the particles affects porosity as well. If the particles have an irregular shape, the aquifer will have a higher porosity.

Critical Thinking

3. Make Connections Can a material have a high porosity but a low permeability? Explain your answer.

_____

_____

_____

_____

PERMEABILITY

If the open spaces in the rock layer are connected, water can move through the rock. A rock's ability to let water pass through is called **permeability**. Rock that water cannot flow through is called *impermeable*.

The size and sorting of rock particles affects permeability. Rock made of large, well-sorted particles tends to have a high permeability. For example, sandstone is very permeable. Limestone may be permeable if it contains cracks that are connected to each other. Clay is made of flat, very small particles. The particles stick tightly together and prevent water from moving between them. Therefore, clay is impermeable.

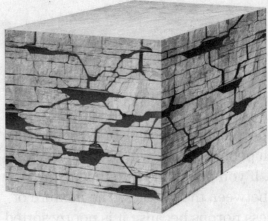

This rock is permeable because its pores are connected to each other. Therefore, water can flow easily between the pores.

What Are the Parts of an Aquifer?

Gravity pulls rainwater down through the soil and into the spaces within an aquifer. Some aquifers lie just below the soil. Scientists divide these aquifers into two zones: the zone of saturation and the zone of aeration.

The *zone of saturation* is the area where most of the water collects. The spaces between particles in the zone of saturation are filled with only water. The top of the zone of saturation is called the **water table**. The *zone of aeration* is the area that rainwater passes through to reach the zone of saturation.

Talk About It

Infer Use a dictionary to look up the meaning of the word *saturated*. With a partner, discuss why the zone of saturation has that name.

Groundwater soaks into the ground, passes through the zone of aeration, and collects in the zone of saturation.

LOOKING CLOSER
4. Identify Label the water table in the figure.

The zone of aeration has three layers. The top layer of the zone of aeration is the soil moisture region. This layer is made of grains of topsoil. Each grain is surrounded by a thin layer of water.

The second layer takes up most of the zone of aeration. In this layer, the pores between particles contain both water and air.

The bottom layer of the zone of aeration is the *capillary fringe*. Small amounts of water move upward from the zone of saturation, through the capillary fringe, to the zone of aeration. The water moves upward because it is attracted to the particles in the capillary fringe. The pores in the capillary fringe contain both air and water. However, they contain more water than the pores in the main part of the zone of aeration. ☑

READING CHECK
5. Define What is the capillary fringe?

_____
_____
_____
_____

SECTION 1 **Water Beneath the Surface** *continued*

The top of the zone of saturation is the water table. The capillary fringe pulls water upward from the zone of saturation.

LOOKING CLOSER

6. Identify Circle the area in the figure that has the least amount of water per volume of rock.

The depth of the water table is not the same all the time or in all places. For example, the water table can rise closer to the surface during heavy rainfall. It can fall farther from the surface during a drought. In wet regions, the water table may be just below the surface. In dry regions, the water table may be hundreds of meters below the surface.

In most areas, there is only one water table. However, in some areas, the main water table is covered with a layer of impermeable rock. The rock layer blocks water from reaching the main zone of saturation. Therefore, water collects on top of the impermeable rock. This creates a second water table, called a *perched water table*.

Critical Thinking

7. Predict If a region receives a lot of rainfall, will the water table in the region probably rise or fall?

_____

_____

MOVEMENT OF GROUNDWATER

Groundwater moves downhill, just as surface water does. If an aquifer is nearly flat, the groundwater moves slowly. If the aquifer has a steep slope, the groundwater moves more quickly. The steepness of the aquifer is called its *gradient*.

How Can People Protect Groundwater?

Although groundwater is renewable, it takes a long time for it to renew itself. Groundwater moves slowly. Therefore, the water that we take from aquifers may not renew itself for hundreds or thousands of years.

In many places, groundwater is the only source of fresh water. Therefore, some communities try to conserve groundwater. For example, they might monitor the level of the water table. They might clean and re-use wastewater. They might also prevent people from pumping too much water out of the aquifer.

SECTION 1 Water Beneath the Surface *continued*

POLLUTION

People can also have an effect on whether pollution enters an aquifer. For example, people can be careful not to pollute water in a recharge zone. A *recharge zone* is an area where water travels through permeable rock to reach an aquifer. Pollution in a recharge zone can enter an aquifer. A recharge zone can become polluted by fertilizers, chemicals in underground tanks, or leaking sewage systems. ☑

How Are Wells and Springs Different?

Groundwater reaches Earth's surface through wells and springs. A *well* is a hole that people dig that reaches below the level of the water table. A *spring* is a natural flow of groundwater to Earth's surface. Wells and springs are classified into two groups: ordinary and artesian.

ORDINARY WELLS

People dig wells to bring groundwater to Earth's surface. Ordinary wells work only if they reach permeable rock below the water table. If the rock is not permeable enough, it will take a long time for the groundwater to be replaced.

When water is pumped from a well, a *cone of depression* forms. At a cone of depression, the water table becomes much lower. If too much water is removed, the cone of depression may drop below the well. If that happens, the well will dry up. The cone of depression may also cause nearby wells to dry up.

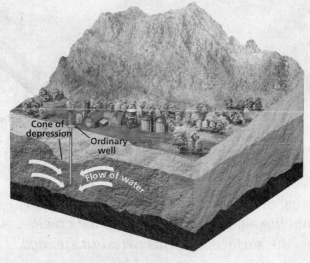

A cone of depression forms in the water table around an ordinary well.

Cone of depression
Ordinary well
Flow of water

READING CHECK

8. Explain Why is it important to keep a recharge zone clean?

_____

_____

_____

_____

_____

LOOKING CLOSER

9. Predict What would happen if the cone of depression dropped below the bottom of the well?

_____

_____

ORDINARY SPRINGS

Ordinary springs are generally found in areas with uneven ground. In one spot, the ground is lower than the water table. Groundwater flows along the slope of the water table. When the water table meets Earth's surface, water flows out and forms a spring.

Ordinary springs may not flow continuously. If the water table drops below the level of the spring, the spring will dry up. For example, many springs go dry during a drought. ☑

ARTESIAN WELLS AND SPRINGS

In some places, a layer of permeable rock is found between two sloping layers of impermeable rock. This arrangement of rock is called an **artesian formation**. The permeable rock is an aquifer. The top layer of impermeable rock is called the *caprock*.

Water enters the aquifer from a recharge zone, where the permeable rock is not covered by impermeable rock. It then flows downhill through the aquifer. As the water flows downhill, the weight of the water above it puts pressure on it. When a well is drilled in the caprock, the pressure forces the water up through the well. Therefore, people do not need to pump water out of an artesian well. It flows upward on its own.

READING CHECK

10. Describe What would happen to an ordinary spring if the water table dropped below the level of the spring?

_____

_____

Talk About It

Evaluate What are the advantages and disadvantages of ordinary wells and artesian wells? Discuss your answers with a partner.

LOOKING CLOSER

11. Identify Label the ordinary and artesian wells in the diagram.

Cone of depression

Aquifer

Caprock

Water table

In an artesian formation, the aquifer is covered by caprock. When a well is drilled through the caprock, pressure forces the groundwater upward.

In some places, there are natural cracks in the caprock. Water from the aquifer flows through the cracks. When it reaches the surface, it forms *artesian springs*.

SECTION 1 **Water Beneath the Surface** *continued*

How Do Hot Springs Form?

The water from most springs is cool. However, rock below Earth's surface can be very hot. Therefore, water that flows through deep aquifers may be very hot. When this water reaches the surface, it can form a *hot spring*. ☑

In some areas, chemically weathered rock mixes with hot water from the springs. When this happens, a *mud pot* forms. Mud pots look like puddles of bubbling clay.

✓ **READING CHECK**

12. Explain What heats the water in a hot spring?

_____

_____

How Do Geysers Form?

A *geyser* is a type of hot spring that erupts from time to time. A geyser has one or more underground chambers. It also has a vent that connects the chambers to Earth's surface.

Hot rocks surround the underground chambers, so the water in them gets very hot. However, the water does not boil. Its boiling point is very high because it is under a lot of pressure. When the water near the vent finally begins to boil, it produces steam. The steam pushes the water to the surface, where it explodes out of the vent. ☑

That water is no longer pushing down on the water in the chambers. Therefore, the water in the chambers is under less pressure. The water's boiling point goes down, so it begins to boil. It turns to steam and explodes through the vent. After the eruption, the groundwater begins to collect and the process begins again.

✓ **READING CHECK**

13. Explain Why does the water in a geyser take so long to boil?

_____

_____

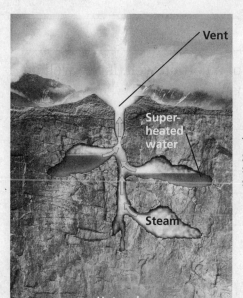

The water in a geyser's chambers gets superheated. When the pressure decreases, the water turns to steam and erupts to the surface.

LOOKING CLOSER

14. Describe What caused the water in the bottom chamber to turn to steam?

_____

_____

Section 1 Review

SECTION VOCABULARY

aquifer a body of rock or sediment that stores groundwater and allows the flow of groundwater	**permeability** the ability of a rock or sediment to let fluids pass through its open spaces, or pores
artesian formation a sloping layer of permeable rock sandwiched between two layers of impermeable rock and exposed at the surface	**porosity** the percentage of the total volume of a rock or sediment that consists of open spaces
groundwater the water that is beneath Earth's surface	**water table** the upper surface of underground water; the upper boundary of the zone of saturation

1. Compare How are the rock layers in an artesian formation different from the rock layers in an ordinary aquifer?

_____

_____

2. Identify What are the two properties of an aquifer that affect the flow of groundwater?

_____

3. Describe Name the two zones of groundwater, and describe their characteristics.

_____

_____

4. Apply Concepts During a hot summer, an ordinary spring in an area dries up. What most likely happened to cause the spring to dry up?

_____

_____

5. Infer A person must use a pump to get water out of a certain well. Is the well an ordinary well or an artesian well? Explain your answer.

_____

_____

_____

6. Identify What are two land features caused by hot groundwater?

_____

_____

Groundwater and Chemical Weathering

KEY IDEAS

As you read this section, keep these questions in mind:
- How does water chemically weather rock?
- How do caverns and sinkholes form?
- What are two features of karst topography?

How Does Groundwater Cause Chemical Weathering?

As water moves through soil or other organic matter, it combines with carbon dioxide. This combination forms carbonic acid. Carbonic acid is a weak acid, but it can chemically weather rock. As the acid passes through permeable rock, it can dissolve the minerals in the rock. Those minerals then mix with the groundwater.

Water that contains high levels of dissolved minerals is called *hard water*. Water that contains lower levels of dissolved minerals is called *soft water*. Many people do not like to use hard water for the following reasons:

- More soap is needed to produce suds in hard water than in soft water.
- Hard water can have a slight taste of metal.
- Hard water can damage some home appliances because it leaves behind mineral deposits. ☑

What Structures Are Formed by Chemical Weathering?

Chemical weathering can form new structures in two ways. First, it can dissolve rock. The dissolved rock can form new structures. Second, groundwater can deposit dissolved minerals to create new structures.

Chemical weathering especially affects rocks, such as limestone, that contain a lot of calcite. Although limestone is not porous, it contains many cracks. As groundwater flows through these cracks, carbonic acid dissolves the limestone. The cracks become larger. Over a long period of time, a cavern may form. A **cavern** is a large cave that may be connected to many smaller caves.

READING TOOLBOX

Organize On a separate piece of paper, create a spider map to summarize the landforms created by chemical weathering.

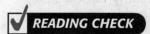
READING CHECK

1. Define What is hard water?

_____

_____

_____

Talk About It

Investigate Learn more about an area that has a lot of caverns. How did the caverns form? What type of rock are they made of? Share your findings with the class.

STALACTITES AND STALAGMITES

Caverns beneath the water table fill with water. Caverns that are above the water table do not. However, water still passes through caverns above the water table.

Groundwater that contains dissolved calcite may drip from the cavern's ceiling. When it does, some of the calcite is deposited on the ceiling. These deposits form a structure that hangs from the ceiling like an icicle. This structure is called a *stalactite*.

Water that falls to the cave floor can also leave deposits behind. The deposits form a structure that looks like an upside-down icicle. This structure is called a *stalagmite*. Sometimes, a stalactite and a stalagmite join together to form a *column*. ☑

✔ **READING CHECK**

2. Identify How does a column form in a cavern?

_____

_____

The stalactites and stalagmites in this picture formed from mineral deposits.

LOOKING CLOSER

3. Identify Circle a stalagmite in this picture.

LOOKING CLOSER

4. Contrast How are subsidence sinkholes and collapse sinkholes different?

_____

_____

_____

_____

SINKHOLES

A circular depression, or pit, that forms when land collapses is called a **sinkhole**. There are three types of sinkholes, which are described in the table below.

Type of Sinkhole	How It Forms
Dissolution sinkhole	Groundwater flows through cracks in rock and dissolves the rock. The dissolved material is carried away and leaves behind a pit.
Subsidence sinkhole	Groundwater flows through cracks in rock and dissolves it. Sediment slowly settles into the larger cracks. A depression forms where the sediment was.
Collapse sinkhole	Groundwater flows through cracks in rock and dissolves it, forming a cavern. The cavern cannot support the rock and sediment in its roof, so the roof collapses. Collapse sinkholes can cause a lot of damage.

The cavern under this highway collapsed to form a sinkhole.

NATURAL BRIDGES

When the roof of a cavern collapses in several places, a line of sinkholes forms. The rock in between two sinkholes forms an arch. The arch is called a *natural bridge*. When a natural bridge first forms, it is thick. Eventually, erosion causes the bridge to become thinner. If it gets too thin, it may collapse.

What Is Karst Topography?

When groundwater chemically weathers limestone or other rock in a region, the region may change. Many features such as caverns, sinkholes, and natural bridges can form. The topography of this type of region is called **karst topography.** Some examples of places in the United States with karst topography are Kentucky, Tennessee, Indiana, Florida, and Puerto Rico.

Karst topography most commonly forms in humid regions that have limestone near the surface. Precipitation in those regions becomes groundwater, which flows through the limestone. The water dissolves the limestone and enlarges cracks in the ground through chemical weathering. Caverns and sinkholes form as these cracks get larger.

Karst topography can also form in areas with dry climates. Groundwater may exist below the ground in dry areas. The groundwater can erode the rock below the surface.

Section 2 Review

SECTION VOCABULARY

cavern a natural cavity that forms in rock as a result of the dissolution of minerals; also a large cave that commonly contains many smaller, connecting chambers	**sinkhole** a circular depression that forms when rock dissolves, when overlying sediment fills an existing cavity, or when the roof of an underground cavern or mine collapses
karst topography a type of irregular topography that is characterized by caverns, sinkholes, and underground drainage and that forms on limestone or other soluble rock	

1. Describe How are sinkholes different from caverns?

_____

_____

2. Compare Use the Venn diagram below to compare stalactites and stalagmites.

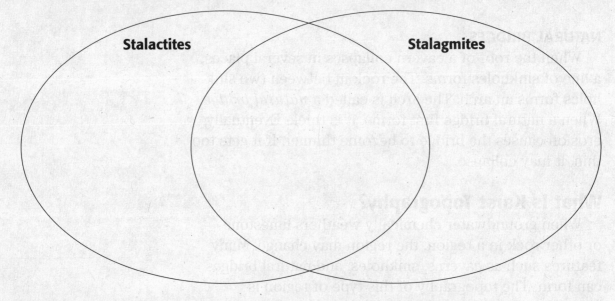

Stalactites   **Stalagmites**

3. Apply Concepts How could acid rain make sinkholes more common?

_____

_____

_____

4. Identify What are two common features of karst topography?

_____

_____

5. Infer When the water in a bathtub is hard, a layer of scum may form on the sides of the bathtub. What is the scum made of?

_____

_____

_____

CHAPTER 17 | Glaciers

SECTION 1

Glaciers: Moving Ice

KEY IDEAS

As you read this section, keep these questions in mind:

- How do glaciers form?
- How are the two glacier types alike and different?
- How do glaciers move?
- What are the features of glaciers?

How Do Glaciers Form?

A **glacier** is a large, compact mass of moving ice. Natural forces compact snow into glaciers in a similar way to how you make a snowball by squeezing snow.

Glaciers are found at high elevations and in polar regions. In these areas, snow stays on the ground all year long. Ice and snow build up and form a permanent mass called a *snowfield*.

At high elevations, snowfields can be found above a certain elevation known as the *snowline*.

Temperatures in these areas remain near or below 0 °C. The low temperatures generally cause snow to build up every year instead of melting. Parts of the snowfield do occasionally melt and then refreeze. Over time, this process changes the snow into grainy ice called *firn*. ☑

In deep layers of snow and firn, the top layers press down and flatten the ice beneath. The pressure of the top layers also squeezes air from between the ice grains. The snow and firn continue to build up, forming a glacier. As the glacier becomes bigger and heavier, it eventually begins to move downhill under its own weight.

A glacier's size depends on how much snow builds up and how much ice is lost through melting. When new snow piles up faster than it melts, the glacier gets bigger. When snow and ice melt more quickly than new snow is added, the glacier shrinks.

READING TOOLBOX

Summarize As you read this section, highlight sentences that relate to the Key Ideas questions. When you finish reading, write a short answer to each Key Ideas question using the underlined information.

LOOKING CLOSER

1. Explain How can you tell that the snow and ice in the picture is not simply due to cold weather?

_____

_____

_____

✓ READING CHECK

2. Describe How does firn form?

_____

_____

_____

ALPINE AND CONTINENTAL GLACIERS

There are two types of glaciers: alpine and continental. An **alpine glacier** is a narrow, wedge-shaped mass of ice. Alpine glaciers form in mountainous areas. The mountains around them limit them to a small area.

In contrast, a **continental glacier** is a huge sheet of ice that is not confined by surrounding landforms. Continental glaciers, or *ice sheets*, can cover millions of square kilometers and can be thousands of meters thick. Today, continental glaciers can be found only in Greenland and Antarctica. If these glaciers melted, they would raise the worldwide sea level by more than 50 meters. ☑

READING CHECK

3. Infer Why do you think today's continental glaciers exist only in Greenland and Antarctica?

_____

_____

_____

_____

A Comparison of Alpine and Continental Glaciers

Alpine Glaciers	Continental Glaciers
• are narrow and wedge shaped • are found in mountainous regions • are confined to a small area by surrounding topography	• are broad and may cover millions of square kilometers • are found only in Greenland and Antarctica • are not limited by surrounding topography

How Do Glaciers Move?

Both rivers and glaciers flow downward due to the force of gravity. In fact, glaciers are sometimes called "rivers of ice." However, rivers and glaciers move in different ways. Unlike the water in a river, the ice in a glacier moves very slowly. In a single year, some glaciers may travel only a few centimeters. The ice in glaciers also cannot flow easily around barriers. Glaciers move through two basic processes: basal slip and internal plastic flow.

BASAL SLIP

READING CHECK

4. Explain In the process of basal slip, why does the ice beneath the glacier melt?

_____

_____

_____

_____

_____

_____

Many glaciers move through the process of **basal slip**. Basal slip happens because the weight of a glacier exerts pressure that lowers the melting point of the ice. The ice melts where the glacier touches the ground.

The water mixes with sediment beneath the glacier. This mixture acts as a lubricant between the ice and the ground, making the glacier slide forward. Glaciers can move by sliding over this thin layer of water and sediment. ☑

SECTION 1 | Glaciers: Moving Ice *continued*

INTERNAL PLASTIC FLOW

Glaciers can also move by a process called **internal plastic flow**. In this process, pressure deforms the ice grains under a glacier. The grains then slide over each other, causing the glacier to flow slowly.

The rate of flow varies in different parts of the glacier. The slope of the ground and the thickness and temperature of the ice determine the flow rate. The edges of a glacier move more slowly than the center because of friction with the rock beneath. For the same reason, the top layers of the glacier flow more quickly than the bottom layers. ☑

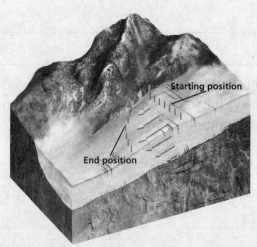

Measurement stakes driven into an alpine glacier move as the glacier flows. Their start and end positions show how the central part of the glacier moves more quickly than the edges.

What Are the Main Features of Glaciers?

Although a glacier flows, low pressure on the glacier's surface ice causes the ice to remain brittle. The glacier flows unevenly beneath the surface. As tension builds, large cracks, called **crevasses**, can form on the surface.

A continental glacier moves outward in all directions from its center. Certain parts of the glacier may eventually stretch out over the ocean and form *ice shelves*. Sometimes, large blocks of ice called *icebergs* break off from the ice shelves. The icebergs then drift into the ocean. Most of an iceberg is below the surface of the water and is therefore not visible from the surface.

☑ **READING CHECK**

5. Identify In the process of internal plastic flow, which parts of the glacier will move most quickly?

_____

_____

_____

LOOKING CLOSER

6. Explain Based on the figure, how can you tell that the center of the glacier has moved more quickly than the edges?

_____

_____

_____

_____

_____

Section 1 Review

SECTION VOCABULARY

alpine glacier a narrow, wedge-shaped mass of ice that forms in a mountainous region and that is confined to a small area by surrounding topography	**crevasse** in a glacier, a large crack or fissure that results from ice movement
	glacier a large mass of moving ice
basal slip the process that causes the ice at the base of a glacier to melt and the glacier to slide	**internal plastic flow** the process by which glaciers flow slowly as grains of ice deform under pressure and slide over each other
continental glacier a massive sheet of ice that may cover millions of square kilometers, that may be thousands of meters thick, and that is not confined by surrounding topography	

1. Describe In your own words, describe how crevasses form.

_____

_____

2. Infer Glaciers shrink and grow depending on how much snow and ice they lose or gain. Scientists study glaciers for evidence of climate change. Why might glaciers be good indicators of climate change?

_____

_____

_____

_____

3. Explain Why are glaciers called "rivers of ice"?

_____

_____

4. Compare What is one significant difference between basal slip and internal plastic flow?

_____

_____

_____

5. Explain What is the relationship between an ice sheet, an ice shelf, and an iceberg?

_____

_____

CHAPTER 17 Glaciers

SECTION 2 Glacial Erosion and Deposition

KEY IDEAS

As you read this section, keep these questions in mind:

• What landscape features does glacial erosion produce?

• What landscape features does glacial deposition produce?

• How do glacial lakes form?

What Landscape Features Does Glacial Erosion Produce?

Glaciers formed many of the landforms that exist in the northern United States and Canada. Large lakes, solitary boulders on flat plains, and jagged ridges are just a few examples. Glaciers produced these landforms through the processes of erosion and deposition.

Like rivers, glaciers can erode the landscape into new shapes. Also, rivers and glaciers can both pick up and carry rocks and sediment. However, landforms produced by glaciers are very different from those made by rivers.

A moving glacier may loosen and pull out rock from the bedrock. The glacier drags that rock across the bedrock, leaving long, parallel grooves in the bedrock. The grooves show the direction of the glacier's movement.

Direction of glacier movement

Grooves

The grooves in the bedrock point in the direction that the glacier is moving.

READING TOOLBOX

Categorize This section has a lot of information about different landscape features. Organize this information by creating a table. As you read, list all of the landscape features in your notebook. Then, classify each feature by writing down its size, shape, and location, as well as how it formed.

LOOKING CLOSER

1. Infer The grooves in the bedrock are parallel to the direction of the glacier's movement. However, they don't tell the whole story. What evidence indicates that the glacier in the figure was moving right to left instead of left to right?

_____

_____

_____

_____

LANDFORMS

Glaciers have shaped many mountain ranges and other landforms through erosion. The process of erosion begins in the upper end of a valley where an alpine glacier forms. As the glacier moves through a river valley, rock from the valley walls breaks off. Losing rock makes the valley walls steeper.

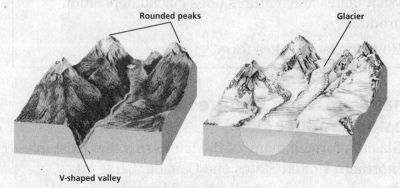

The advance of a glacier changes the shape of a river valley.

The moving glacier also pulls blocks of rock from the valley floor. These actions produce a bowl-shaped depression called a **cirque**. Sharp, jagged ridges called **arêtes** form between cirques. When several arêtes join, they form a sharp, pyramid-like peak called a **horn**. ☑

As the glacier flows through a valley, it also picks up large amounts of rock. These rock fragments become embedded in ice. Remember that large rocks can carve grooves in the bedrock. The rocks in a glacier may also smooth the bedrock, like sandpaper makes wood smooth.

Glaciers can also slide over rock projections, making one side of the rock rounded. The rounded side of one of these landforms, called *roches moutonnées*, faces the direction the glacier came from. The ice pulls rock away from the other side, making that side steep and jagged.

LOOKING CLOSER

2. Describe How did the V-shaped valley on the left become the U-shaped valley on the right?

_____

_____

_____

_____

_____

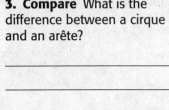

READING CHECK

3. Compare What is the difference between a cirque and an arête?

_____

_____

_____

_____

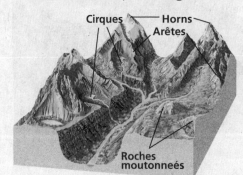

Cirques, arêtes, horns, and roches moutonnées are some of the landscape features formed by glacial erosion.

SECTION 2 **Glacial Erosion and Deposition** *continued*

VALLEYS

In addition to creating individual landforms, glaciers also change the overall shape of valleys through erosion. Many valleys have a V shape because rivers carved them out of the rock. As a glacier scrapes away a valley's walls and floor, this V shape changes to a U shape. Glacial erosion is the only process that forms U-shaped valleys. Therefore, scientists can look for this shape to determine whether or not a glacier has eroded a valley. ☑

Smaller glaciers in nearby valleys may flow into a main alpine glacier. These smaller glaciers cannot cut as deeply into the rock as the main glacier can. As a result, the valleys created by the smaller glaciers are not as deep as the main valley. When the ice melts, the smaller valley is suspended high above the main valley floor. These valleys are called *hanging valleys*. When a stream flows from a hanging valley, a waterfall forms.

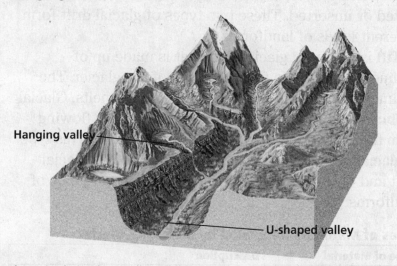

Hanging valley

U-shaped valley

The main glacier changes the valley from a V shape to a U shape. Smaller glaciers can create hanging valleys.

CONTINENTAL GLACIAL EROSION

Continental glaciers erode the landscape differently than alpine glaciers do. As they move, continental glaciers smooth and round exposed rock surfaces. This process produces a smooth, level landscape. Rocks carried at the base of the continental glacier also scratch and groove rock surfaces. These scratches and grooves lie parallel to the direction of the glacier's movement.

✓ **READING CHECK**

4. Explain Why is the presence of a U-shaped valley evidence that glaciers once existed in an area?

_____

_____

_____

LOOKING CLOSER

5. Infer When a stream flows out of a hanging valley, it forms a waterfall. Why do you think this happens?

_____

_____

_____

_____

What Landscape Features Does Glacial Deposition Produce?

Glaciers also change landscapes through the process of deposition. Deposition occurs when a glacier melts. As it melts, the glacier deposits much of the material that it has collected. This material may range in size from fine sediment to large rocks.

Large rocks that a glacier carries from a distant source are called **erratics**. A glacier can carry an erratic over very long distances. As a result, the composition of an erratic is typically different from that of the bedrock.

Other landforms can also develop as glaciers melt and deposit sediment. The general term for all sediments that a glacier deposits is **glacial drift**. Remember that a sample of sorted sediments is made up of particles that are about the same size. Unsorted sediments are made up of particles of a variety of sizes. Glacial drift can be either sorted or unsorted. These two types of glacial drift form different kinds of landforms.

Till is unsorted glacial drift that is made up of sediments that come from the base of the glacier. The sediments are left behind when the glacier melts. Glacial drift can also be sorted into layers by streams flowing from the melted ice, also known as *meltwater*. This type of glacial drift is called *stratified drift*. Sorted glacial drift and unsorted glacial drift create different kinds of landforms. ☑

✓ READING CHECK

6. Identify Which term refers to glacial drift that is not sorted?

_____

_____

Types of Materials Deposited by a Melting Glacier

Type of Material	Description
	the general term for all sediment that has been carried by a glacier
	large rock or boulder carried over a long distance by a glacier
	glacial drift that has been deposited directly by the melting glacier; unsorted sediment
	glacial drift that has been deposited by streams flowing from the melted ice of the glacier; sediment that has been sorted into layers by the streams

LOOKING CLOSER

7. Summarize Complete the table to summarize the information from the text.

SECTION 2 **Glacial Erosion and Deposition** *continued*

TILL DEPOSITS

When a glacier deposits till, the resulting landforms are called moraines. A **moraine** is a ridge of unsorted sediment found on the ground or on the glacier. There are several different types of moraines.

A *lateral moraine* lies along the sides of an alpine glacier. It typically looks like a long ridge bordering the glacier. When two or more alpine glaciers join, their lateral moraines combine and form a *medial moraine.* ☑

Any unsorted material that is left beneath the glacier when the ice melts is called *ground moraine.* The soil of a ground moraine is typically very rocky. A continental glacier may sometimes push ground moraine into clusters called drumlins. *Drumlins* are long, low mounds of till. They are generally tear shaped. The longer axes of these drumlins are parallel to the direction the glacier moved.

Terminal moraines are small ridges of till that lie at the leading edge of a melting glacier. Terminal moraines have many depressions. These depressions often contain lakes or ponds.

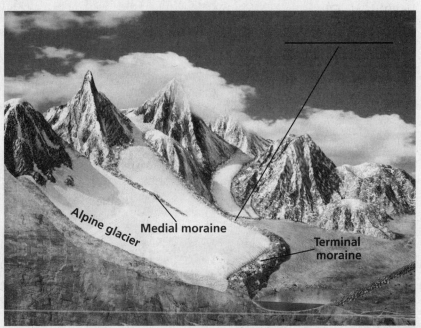

Moraines are one group of landforms formed by glacial deposition.

☑ **READING CHECK**

8. Describe How do lateral moraines form a medial moraine?

_____

_____

_____

Critical Thinking

9. Apply Concepts How could you determine how the glacier that formed a drumlin was moving?

_____

_____

_____

_____

_____

_____

_____

LOOKING CLOSER

10. Identify On the figure, label the unidentified landform.

SECTION 2 **Glacial Erosion and Deposition** *continued*

OTHER FEATURES FORMED BY GLACIAL DEPOSITION

In addition to moraines, glacial deposition can also form other landforms. When a glacier melts, streams of meltwater flow from its edges, surface, and underside. The melted ice carries glacial drift and deposits it in front of the glacier. This deposit forms a large *outwash plain.* An outwash plain lies in front of the glacier's terminal moraine. Many of the streams formed by the glacier's melted ice run across the plain.

Most outwash plains contain many small depressions called **kettles**. A kettle forms when a chunk of glacial ice becomes buried in the glacial drift. As the ice melts, a hole forms in the drift. Eventually, the drift collapses into the hole and forms a depression. Kettles often fill with water, forming kettle lakes.

When continental glaciers recede, they may leave behind eskers. **Eskers** are long, winding ridges of gravel and sand. These ridges consist of stratified drift that were deposited by streams of meltwater. Some extend for many kilometers. They may resemble raised, winding roadways. ☑

READING CHECK

11. Define What is an esker?

_____

_____

_____

LOOKING CLOSER

12. Synthesize Text and Graphics On the figure, locate and label a drumlin and an erratic.

Land that has been glaciated can contain many landforms, such as erratics, drumlins, and kettles.

How Do Glacial Lakes Form?

Glacial lakes can form in several different ways. Lake basins may form where glaciers erode surfaces and leave depressions in the bedrock. Other lakes may form as a result of deposition rather than erosion. Many lakes form in the uneven surfaces of ground moraines. In addition, long, narrow lakes called *finger lakes* can form where terminal and lateral moraines block existing streams. ☑

HISTORY OF THE GREAT LAKES

The Great Lakes of North America formed as a result of erosion and deposition. Glacial erosion widened and deepened existing valleys. Moraines then blocked off the ends of these valleys. As the glacier melted, the meltwater was trapped, forming the Great Lakes.

SALT LAKES

Salt lakes are a special kind of glacial lake. Like other glacial lakes, these lakes formed during the last glacial advance. However, topographic and climate changes resulted in changes to the structure of these lakes. Unlike other glacial lakes, salt lakes no longer have outlet streams that allow water to leave the lake. Water can leave the lake only by evaporation.

When the water from the lakes evaporates, salt that was dissolved in the water is left behind. Thus, the water becomes increasingly salty. Salt lakes typically form in dry climates, where evaporation is rapid and there is little precipitation.

Streams and rivers carry dissolved minerals to the Great Salt Lake in Utah, but there are no streams to carry water and minerals out of the lake. Water evaporates from the lake, but minerals are left behind.

> **✓ READING CHECK**
>
> **13. Describe** How do finger lakes form?
>
> _____
>
> _____
>
> _____
>
> _____

> **LOOKING CLOSER**
>
> **14. Explain** How do minerals such as salt become concentrated in the Great Salt Lake?
>
> _____
>
> _____
>
> _____
>
> _____

Section 2 Review

SECTION VOCABULARY

arête a sharp, jagged ridge that forms between cirques	**horn** a sharp, pyramid-like peak that forms because of the erosion of cirques
cirque a deep and steep bowl-like depression produced by glacial erosion	**kettle** a bowl-shaped depression in a glacial drift deposit
erratic a large rock transported from a distant source by a glacier	**moraine** a landform that is made from unsorted sediments deposited by a glacier
esker a long, winding ridge of gravel and coarse sand deposited by glacial meltwater streams	**till** unsorted rock material that is deposited directly by a melting glacier
glacial drift rock material carried and deposited by glaciers	

1. **Describe** In your own words, describe how a kettle forms.

_____

_____

2. **Compare** Rivers and glaciers can both erode the surrounding landscape. Name one similarity between how rivers and glaciers erode the landscape. Then, name one difference.

_____

_____

3. **List** What are some features you would expect to find in a valley that was eroded by an alpine glacier?

_____

_____

4. **Compare** How are erratics different from glacial drift?

_____

_____

_____

5. **Describe** What is one way in which a glacial lake can form?

_____

_____

6. **Explain** Why are salt lakes more common in dry climates than in wet ones?

_____

_____

_____

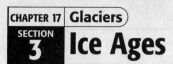

CHAPTER 17 | **Glaciers**

SECTION 3 | **Ice Ages**

KEY IDEAS

As you read this section, keep these questions in mind:

• What are the characteristics of the glacial and interglacial periods within an ice age?

• What theory best explains ice ages?

What Is an Ice Age?

Continental glaciers once covered much more of Earth's surface than they do today. Glaciers grow and cover more land during an ice age. An **ice age** is a long period during which climate cools. Ice ages most likely begin with a slow decrease in global temperatures. A drop of only 5 °C may be enough to start an ice age.

The earliest known ice age began 800 million years ago. The most recent ice age began 4 million years ago. The growth of glaciers in this most recent ice age reached its peak about 18,000 years ago.

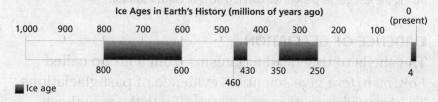

Ice Ages in Earth's History (millions of years ago)

■ Ice age

What Are Glacial and Interglacial Periods?

Continental glaciers advance (grow) and retreat (shrink) several times during an ice age. They advance during colder periods and retreat during warmer periods. A cooler period when glaciers advance is called a *glacial period*. A warmer period when glaciers retreat is called an *interglacial period*. Currently, Earth is in an interglacial period of the most recent ice age.

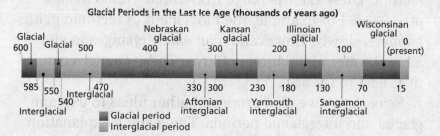

Glacial Periods in the Last Ice Age (thousands of years ago)

■ Glacial period
■ Interglacial period

READING TOOLBOX

Outline Use the headings in this section to create an outline in your notebook. As you read, use the details under each of the headings to fill in your outline. Remember to watch for details that relate directly to the Key Ideas.

LOOKING CLOSER

1. Interpret Graphics The most recent ice age began 4 million years ago. When did the previous ice age end?

_____

_____

LOOKING CLOSER

2. Interpret Graphics How many glacial periods have there been in the past 600,000 years?

_____

_____

SECTION 3 **Ice Ages** *continued*

GLOBAL GLACIATION

Glaciation is the process in which an area becomes covered by glaciers. During the last glacial period, glaciers covered about one-third of Earth's surface. In some places, the ice was several kilometers thick. So much water was locked in the ice that the sea level was about 140 meters lower than it is today. As a result, the coastlines of the continents extended much farther than they do now. ☑

☑ **READING CHECK**

3. Explain Why did the coastlines of the continents once extend farther than they do now?

_____

_____

_____

LOOKING CLOSER

4. Infer Why do you think so many of the glaciers in the last glacial period were grouped around the poles?

_____

_____

_____

_____

Critical Thinking

5. Infer If you discovered a marine fossil that coiled its shell to the left, what would that tell you about the time period the organism lived in?

_____

_____

_____

During the last glacial period, ice covered 30% of Earth's surface.

Extent of continental glaciation
Extent of sea ice
Current land mass

EVIDENCE OF GLACIATION

The shells of tiny dead organisms from a group called *Foraminifera* give scientists evidence of past glaciations. The temperature of ocean water affects the way these organisms form their shells. Those that lived in warmer water coiled their shells to the right. Those that lived in cooler water coiled their shells to the left. The amount of dissolved oxygen in the ocean also affected the shells. Oxygen amounts depend on water temperatures.

What Are the Causes of Glaciation?

The glaciation of Earth's surface is caused by several factors. These factors range from rapid events to slow processes. For example, the movement of tectonic plates happens slowly. However, it can cause changes in global air and water circulation patterns. These changes can then lead to ice ages.

Scientists have also proposed other ideas to explain glacial and interglacial periods. The leading explanation is the Milankovitch theory.

SECTION 3 Ice Ages *continued*

THE MILANKOVITCH THEORY

Milutin Milankovitch observed that some climate changes happen in cycles. He thought changes in Earth's movement relative to the sun caused these cycles. The **Milankovitch theory** states that three cyclical changes in Earth's orbit and axis tilt cause climate changes.

First, the shape of Earth's orbit, or *eccentricity*, changes from circular to oval and back again. This change happens every 100,000 years. The second change happens in the tilt of Earth's axis. Every 41,000 years, the tilt varies between 22.2° and 24.5°. The final change is the circular motion, or *precession*, of Earth's axis. Precession makes the axis wobble and change its position. Earth's axis traces a complete circle every 25,700 years.

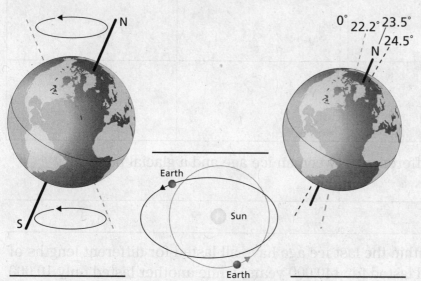

These three diagrams show the changes in Earth's movement predicted by the Milankovitch theory.

Milankovitch calculated how these factors affect the amount of sunlight that reaches Earth's surface. Changes in the distribution of energy affect global temperatures. These changes can cause periods of glacial advance or retreat. Scientists have found marine fossil evidence that supports this theory.

OTHER EXPLANATIONS

Other scientists have suggested different causes of glacial periods. Some scientists think that changes are caused by varying amounts of energy produced by the sun. Others think that glacial periods start when volcanic dust blocks sunlight.

Math Skills

6. Estimate The current tilt of Earth's axis is 23.5°. Remember that the tilt moves from 24.5° to 22.2° every 41,000 years. Estimate how many years will pass before Earth's tilt reaches 22.2°.

_____

LOOKING CLOSER

7. Analyze Diagrams The diagrams show the three changes in Earth's movement predicted by the Milankovitch theory. Based on the information in the text, label each diagram with the correct name.

Talk About It

Apply Concepts Choose a scientific theory that explains the causes of glacial periods. Use the Internet or library to learn more about that theory. Share what you learn with a partner or a small group.

Section 3 Review

SECTION VOCABULARY

ice age a long period of climatic cooling during which the continents are glaciated repeatedly	**Milankovitch theory** the theory that cyclical changes in Earth's orbit and in the tilt of Earth's axis occur over thousands of years and cause climatic changes

1. Summarize Fill in the table below to summarize the main components of the Milankovitch theory.

Motion	What It Affects	How Often It Occurs	Description of Motion
Eccentricity			
Tilt			
Precession			

2. Compare What is the difference between an ice age and a glacial period?

_____

_____

3. Infer Glacial periods within the last ice age have all lasted for different lengths of time. One glacial period lasted for 140,000 years, while another lasted only 10,000 years. Using the Milankovitch theory, explain why you think these lengths are so different.

_____

_____

_____

_____

_____

4. Describe Other than the Milankovitch theory, what is a possible explanation for the cause of Earth's glacial periods?

_____

_____

CHAPTER 18 Erosion by Wind and Waves
SECTION 1 Wind Erosion

KEY IDEAS

As you read this section, keep these questions in mind:

• What are two ways that wind erodes land?

• How do the two types of wind deposits compare?

How Does Wind Shape Land?

Wind has energy. This energy can move a sailboat or turn a windmill. It can also carry sand or dust particles from one place to another. These particles shape the land through erosion and deposition.

How Does Wind Move Sand and Dust?

Sand and dust are different types of particles. *Sand* is fragments of weathered rock and minerals. Most grains of sand are made of quartz. Other common minerals in sand are mica, feldspar, and magnetite.

Dust is made up of tiny particles that are smaller than sand grains. Most dust particles are tiny fragments of rocks and minerals. Other sources of dust are plants, animals, bacteria, and pollution. ☑

SAND MOVEMENT

Sand particles can be heavy. Therefore, wind cannot keep sand in the air. Instead, wind rolls sand grains along the ground.

Sand can also move by jumps and bounces called **saltation**. Saltation happens when rolling sand grains collide and some bounce into the air. The sand grains in the air move a short distance and then fall. The falling sand grains hit other sand grains. During saltation, sand grains move in the same direction that the wind blows.

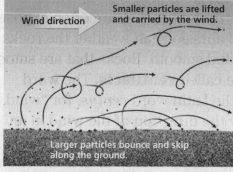

Wind direction — Smaller particles are lifted and carried by the wind.

Most sand grains rise less than 1 m above the ground during saltation.

Larger particles bounce and skip along the ground.

READING TOOLBOX

Take Notes As you read this section, use a four-corner fold to compare the different types of sand dunes. Label the outer flaps with the types of dunes. Describe each dune underneath the correct flap.

✔ READING CHECK

1. Compare How are sand and dust different?

_____

_____

_____

_____

_____

LOOKING CLOSER

2. Describe How does wind move sand by saltation?

_____

_____

_____

_____

DUST MOVEMENT

Dust particles are very small and light. Therefore, wind can carry dust particles through the air. Dust from volcanic eruptions can stay in the air for many years. In some areas, strong winds lift large amounts of dust and create dust storms. ☑

What Are the Effects of Wind Erosion?

Wind erosion happens all over the world. However, wind erosion has the greatest effect on deserts and coastlines. These areas have fewer plants to hold the soil in place. Also, deserts have thin, dry soil. The wind can easily blow the soil away. Moist soil is heavier and sticks together. As a result, moist soil is more difficult to move.

Wind erosion causes many changes at Earth's surface. Three features that form from wind erosion are

- desert pavement
- deflation hollows
- ventifacts ☑

DEFLATION

One common form of wind erosion is deflation. In the process of **deflation**, wind removes the top layer of fine, dry soil. The wind leaves behind larger rock particles. Deflation forms a surface of small rocks called *desert pavement* or *stone pavement*. Desert pavement protects underlying land from erosion.

Deflation is a serious problem for farmers because it blows away the best soil for growing crops. As the topsoil blows away, a shallow pit may form. This pit is called a *deflation hollow*. A deflation hollow may grow to be several kilometers wide and up to 20 m deep.

VENTIFACTS

Small rocks on deserts and beaches are often exposed to wind abrasion. Wind abrasion can weather the rocks until they become flat and smooth. Rocks that are smooth from wind abrasion are called **ventifacts**. The word *ventifact* comes from the Latin word *ventus*, for "wind."

Ventifacts can show the direction of the wind in an area. If the wind usually blows in one direction, the smooth surfaces of ventifacts will face in that direction.

READING CHECK

3. Identify Name two natural events that can add dust to the air.

_____

_____

READING CHECK

4. Identify What is one feature that forms from wind erosion?

_____

Talk About It

Use Root Words With a partner, use a dictionary to find two other words based on the Latin word *ventus.* How can this root help you remember the meaning of the words?

SECTION 1 **Wind Erosion** *continued*

LIMITS OF WIND EROSION

Most wind erosion happens near the ground, where saltation occurs. Wind erosion also happens very slowly. As a result, wind erosion has a limited effect on large masses of rock.

What Are the Effects of Wind Deposition?

The wind deposits, or drops, particles when it cannot carry them anymore. Over time, more particles drop and cover the deposited particles. Pressure and chemical weathering can bind these particles together. This compaction and cementation is one way sedimentary rocks can form.

Wind deposition can also affect the landforms on Earth's surface. Two landforms that form through wind deposition are dunes and loess deposits. ☑

DUNES

Wind deposits can create piles of sand called **dunes**. Dunes form in places with dry, sandy soil and strong winds. Dunes commonly form in deserts and along the shores of oceans and lakes.

A dune forms in stages, as shown below. First, a barrier slows the speed of the wind. This causes sand to collect on both sides of the barrier. Over time, the wind deposits more sand. The dune grows and buries the original barrier.

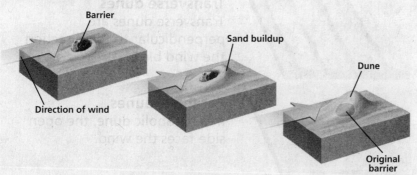

Barrier · Sand buildup · Dune · Direction of wind · Original barrier

Dune formation begins with a barrier, such as a rock, a fence, or some grass. Over time, sand builds up and covers the barrier.

Critical Thinking

5. Apply Ideas Why might rocks on a beach erode more quickly than the top of a sea cliff?

_____

_____

_____

_____

✓ **READING CHECK**

6. Identify What are two landforms that can form through wind deposition?

_____

_____

LOOKING CLOSER

7. Summarize How do sand dunes form?

_____

_____

_____

_____

_____

SECTION 1 **Wind Erosion** *continued*

TYPES OF DUNES

Wind affects the shape of sand dunes. In general, the blowing wind forms a gentle slope on the side of the dune facing the wind. This side of the dune is called the *windward* side. As wind blows sand over the top of the dune, the sand collects on the other side. The side of the dune away from the wind is the *slipface.* The buildup of sand on the slipface creates a steep slope. ☑

Wind can form different types of sand dunes, as shown below. In some cases, wind blows around the ends of the dune and forms two long points. This gives the dune a crescent, or moon, shape. Both *barchan dunes* and *parabolic dunes* have a crescent shape. A barchan dune has its open side away from the wind. A parabolic dune has its open side facing the wind.

In areas with large amounts of sand, the wind may form long ridges of sand. These ridges are called *transverse dunes*. Transverse dunes form at right angles to the wind direction. *Longitudinal dunes* also form in ridges. However, longitudinal dunes are parallel to the wind direction.

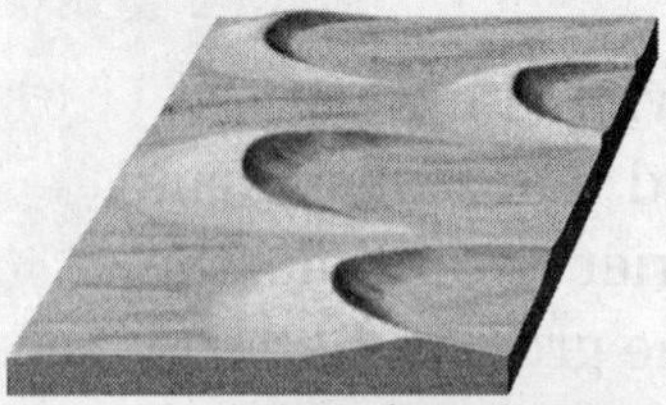

✓ **READING CHECK**

8. Explain Which side of a sand dune generally has the steeper slope? Why?

_____

_____

_____

_____

Barchan dunes
In a barchan dune, the open side faces away from the wind.

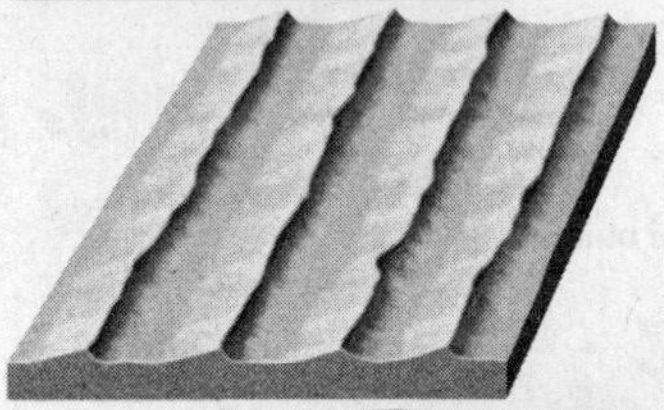

Transverse dunes
Transverse dunes are perpendicular to the direction the wind blows.

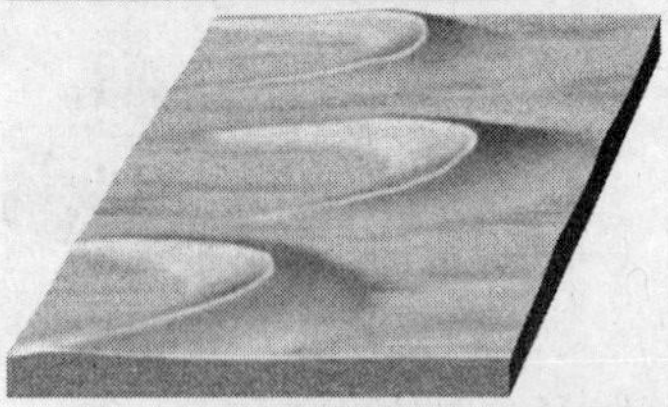

Parabolic dunes
In a parabolic dune, the open side faces the wind.

Longitudinal dunes
Longitudunal dunes are parallel to the direction the wind blows.

LOOKING CLOSER
9. Describe Draw an arrow on each picture to show the direction the wind is blowing.

DUNE MIGRATION

The movement of dunes is called *dune migration*. If the wind generally blows in the same direction, dunes will move in the direction of the wind.

Dune migration happens when wind blows sand over the top of the dune. The sand builds up on the slipface of the dune. Over time, the sand continues to move from one side of the dune to the other.

In flat areas, dunes migrate until they reach a barrier. People often build fences or plant trees to stop dunes from covering highways and farmland.

LOESS

Wind carries dust higher and farther than it carries sand. Wind may deposit dust in very thin layers. Fine-grained sediment that is deposited by the wind is called **loess**. Loess is made of fine sediments of quartz, feldspar, clay, and other minerals. Most loess is deposited in thin layers. However, very thick layers of loess called *loess deposits* also form in some areas. ☑

Loess is soft and erodes easily. It sometimes forms steep bluffs, as shown below. Loess deposits are very fertile. They can form good soil for growing crops.

These loess deposits are in Vicksburg, Mississippi.

A deep layer of loess covers areas in northern China. The material in this deposit came from the Gobi Desert, in Mongolia. Deposits of loess also exist in central Europe. North America has loess deposits in Oregon, Washington, and many midwestern states. These deposits probably formed from the dust from dried glacial lakes.

Critical Thinking

10. Analyze Processes Why does planting grass and trees prevent dunes from covering roads?

_____

_____

_____

✓ **READING CHECK**

11. Describe What is loess?

_____

_____

_____

Section 1 Review

SECTION VOCABULARY

deflation a form of wind erosion in which fine, dry soil particles are blown away	**saltation** the movement of sand or other sediments by short jumps and bounces that is caused by wind or water
dune a mound of wind-deposited sand that moves as a result of the action of wind	**ventifact** any rock that is pitted, grooved, or polished by wind abrasion
loess fine-grained sediments of quartz, feldspar, hornblende, mica, and clay deposited by the wind	

1. **Organize** Complete the concept map to show how wind affects Earth's surface. Use the terms *dunes*, *deposition*, *ventifacts*, *erosion*, *loess*, and *desert pavement*.

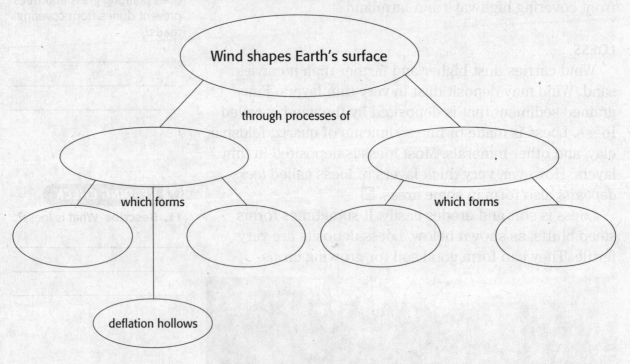

2. **Compare** How are dunes and loess deposits similar? How are they different?

_____

_____

3. **Explain** Why does wind erosion have a major effect on deserts?

_____

_____

_____

4. **Evaluate Methods** Suppose you visited a desert and marked the location of a sand dune. If you came back the next year, would the dune be in the same place? Explain your answer.

_____

_____

Wave Erosion

KEY IDEAS

As you read this section, keep these questions in mind:

- What are six features that wave erosion forms?
- How do beaches form?
- What features form from the movement of sand along a shore?

How Do Waves Shape the Shoreline?

Wind creates waves and currents by blowing over bodies of water. These waves and currents affect shorelines. *Shorelines* are the places where the water and the land meet.

Wave erosion changes the shape of a shoreline. The force of waves may break off pieces of rock and throw the pieces back against the shore. The rocks collide in the moving water. This type of mechanical weathering breaks large rocks into small stones and sand.

Storms are another major cause of shoreline erosion. Storms create large, powerful waves. These waves release large amounts of energy on the shoreline. A storm can change the appearance of a shoreline in one day. ☑

Chemical weathering also affects the rock along a shoreline. Waves push salt water and air into cracks in the rock. Chemicals in the air and water react with the rock. These chemical reactions widen the cracks. The wide cracks expose more of the rock to weathering.

What Features Do Waves Form?

Waves create features, or landforms, by eroding land and depositing sediment. Wave deposition forms beaches. Wave erosion forms many different features, such as

- sea cliffs
- sea caves
- sea arches
- sea stacks
- terraces. ☑

READING TOOLBOX

Summarize As you read this section, make two-column notes to describe the features that form from wave erosion and deposition. In the first column, write the name of each feature. When you finish reading, write a short description of each feature in the second column. You may use words, drawings, or both in your descriptions.

☑ READING CHECK

1. Describe How do storms affect shorelines?

_____

_____

_____

☑ READING CHECK

2. List Name three features that form from wave erosion.

_____

_____

_____

Critical Thinking

3. Apply Concepts Quartz is a hard mineral. Would a sea cliff made of quartz form a headland or a bay? Why?

_____

_____

_____

LOOKING CLOSER

4. Describe How does a sea cave become a sea arch?

_____

_____

_____

SEA CLIFFS

In some places, waves hit directly against rock. The waves slowly erode the base of the rock. Finally, the rock collapses to form a steep *sea cliff*.

The rate of sea cliff erosion depends on the wave energy and the hardness of the rock. Soft rock, such as limestone, erodes quickly. Harder rock, such as granite, erodes slowly. Hard rock formations that stretch out from shore are called **headlands**. Areas with softer rock form *bays*.

SEA CAVES, ARCHES, AND STACKS

As waves continue to strike cliffs and headlands, they form new land features. The chart below shows how these features form.

Waves erode the base of a cliff and form a large hole called a *sea cave*.

↓

Over time, waves cut completely through the cliff and form a *sea arch*.

↓

Finally, the top of the arch may collapse. This forms an offshore column called a *sea stack*.

TERRACES

Wave erosion generally leaves a flat area of rock underwater at the base of a sea cliff. This flat area is called a *wave-cut terrace*. Waves may deposit eroded material around the wave-cut terrace to form a *wave-built terrace*.

How Do Beaches Form?

A **beach** is a deposit of sediment along an ocean or lake shore. Beaches form where more sediment collects than erodes. After a beach forms, the rate of deposition and the rate of erosion may change.

BEACH COMPOSITION

Beaches are made of different sizes and types of materials. In general, smaller particles have traveled farther before deposition. The composition of beach materials depends on the minerals in the source rock.

Some beaches may have pieces of shells and coral. Other beaches may have large pebbles.

Talk About It

Make Connections Think of a beach you have visited or seen in a picture. What was the beach composition like? Describe it to a partner.

SECTION 2 **Wave Erosion** *continued*

BERMS

Each wave that reaches the beach moves sand slightly. The sand builds up to form a sloping surface. During high tides or storms, waves deposit sand at the top of this slope. As a result, most beaches have a raised section called a *berm*. ☑

The berm changes shape in different seasons. In winter, the berm is high and steep. This is because storms remove sand from the side of the berm facing the sea. The waves deposit this sand offshore to form a long underwater ridge called a *sand bar*. In the summer, waves may move the sand back to the shore. The beach gets wider, and the berm has a gentler slope.

✔ READING CHECK

5. Define What is a berm?

_____

_____

_____

What Are Longshore-Current Deposits?

The direction of waves along a shore determines how the waves move sediment. Most waves approach the shore at an angle. Then, the waves retreat at a right angle to the shore. As a result, waves move sand grains in a zig-zag motion. ☑

Waves moving at an angle to the shoreline create longshore currents. In a **longshore current**, water moves parallel to and near the shoreline. Longshore currents move sand parallel to the shoreline.

Sand moves along a shoreline until the shoreline changes direction at a bay or a headland. Here, the longshore current slows. Waves deposit sand at the far end of the headland, as shown below. These deposits may form spits and tombolos. A *spit* is a long, narrow deposit of sand connected to the shore. A *tombolo* is a ridge of sand that connects an offshore island to the mainland.

✔ READING CHECK

6. Describe How do waves move at a shoreline?

_____

_____

_____

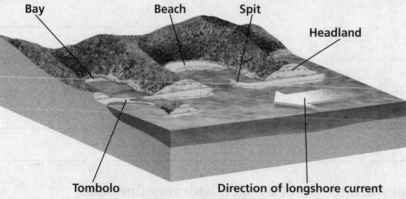

Sand drifts down a shoreline in the direction of the longshore current.

LOOKING CLOSER
7. Identify What are two features that longshore currents form?

_____

_____

Section 2 Review

SECTION VOCABULARY

beach an area of the shoreline that is made up of deposited sediment	**longshore current** a water current that travels near and parallel to the shoreline
headland a high and steep formation of rock that extends out from shore into the water	

1. Explain How do spits form? Use the term *longshore current* in your answer.

_____

_____

2. Summarize Describe one type of weathering process that shapes shorelines.

_____

_____

3. Explain How do beaches form?

_____

_____

4. Compare Complete the table below to compare sea arches, sea caves, and sea stacks.

	Sea Cave	Sea Arch	Sea Stack
Forms from			wave erosion
Description		a sea cliff with a hole that cuts completely through its base	

5. Compare What is the difference between a wave-cut terrace and a wave-built terrace?

_____

_____

6. Identify Relationships How do seasonal changes affect beaches?

_____

_____

7. Make Inferences What can you infer about a beach with very fine sand?

_____

_____

Coastal Erosion and Deposition

KEY IDEAS

As you read this section, keep these questions in mind:
- How do changes in sea level affect coastlines?
- What are the features of a barrier island?
- How do humans affect coastal land?

What Affects Coastlines?

Coastlines are areas where land meets the ocean. Coastlines extend from shallow water to several kilometers inland. Many factors affect coastlines, including changes in sea level and movement of coastal land. Human activities also change coastlines.

How Do Absolute Sea-Level Changes Affect Coastlines?

Absolute sea level rises or falls when the amount of water in the ocean changes. Changes in sea level either cover or expose coastlines.

The absolute sea level on Earth has changed over time. During the last glacial period, some ocean water was frozen in continental ice sheets. Over time, parts of the ice sheets have melted. This has added more water to the oceans. As a result, the sea level has risen about 1 mm per year for the last 5,000 years. ☑

In the distant future, the ice sheets could melt completely. If this happened, the sea level would rise more than 50 m. The oceans would cover many coastal areas, including New York, Los Angeles, and Miami.

Sea Level Change in Past 35,000 Years

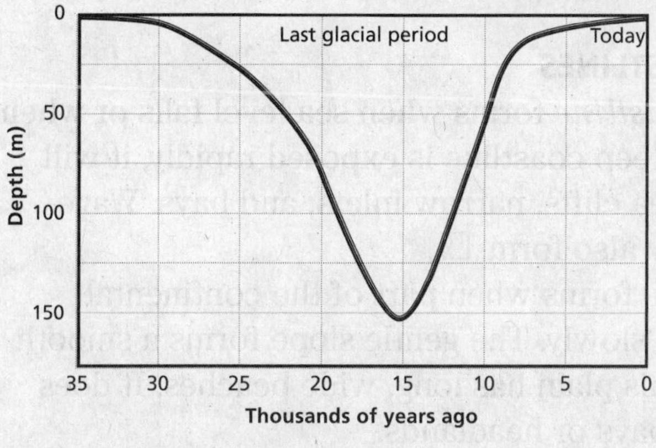

Last glacial period   Today

Depth (m)

Thousands of years ago

This graph shows how sea level has changed over the past 35,000 years.

READING TOOLBOX

Take Notes Use two-column notes to learn and review concepts from this section. Write main ideas in the left column and detailed notes in the right column.

✓ READING CHECK

1. Explain Why was absolute sea level lower during the last glacial period?

_____

_____

_____

LOOKING CLOSER

2. Interpret About how many meters has sea level risen from 15,000 years ago to today?

_____

_____

SECTION 3 **Coastal Erosion and Deposition** *continued*

Critical Thinking

3. Compare How is relative sea level different from absolute sea level?

_____

_____

_____

_____

_____

How Do Relative Sea-Level Changes Affect Coastlines?

Relative sea-level changes happen when land near the coast changes. Changes in coastal land may result from large-scale geologic processes or local coastal changes. For example, movements of Earth's crust can raise and lower coastlines.

SUBMERGENT COASTLINES

A *submergent coastline* forms when sea level rises or when land sinks. On a submergent coastline, valleys become bays and inlets. The high land that divided the valleys becomes headlands. The tops of tall mountains or hills may become islands. Beaches on submergent coastlines are short, narrow, and rocky.

New features can form along submergent coastlines. When ocean water floods glacial valleys, fiords form. *Fiords* are deep, narrow bays with steep walls. Ocean water may also cover the mouth of a river valley to form a wide, shallow bay. This type of bay is an **estuary**. In an estuary, fresh water mixes with salt water from the ocean.

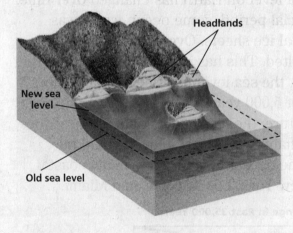

Headlands

New sea level

Old sea level

The features of a submergent coastline erode over time as sea level rises.

LOOKING CLOSER

4. Identify What is one feature of a submergent coastline?

_____

_____

_____

EMERGENT COASTLINES

An *emergent coastline* forms when sea level falls or when land rises. If a steep coastline is exposed rapidly, it will erode to form sea cliffs, narrow inlets, and bays. Wave-cut terraces may also form. ☑

A gentle slope forms when part of the continental shelf is exposed slowly. The gentle slope forms a smooth coastal plain. This plain has long, wide beaches. It does not have many bays or headlands.

 **READING CHECK**

5. Describe How does an emergent coastline form?

_____

_____

_____

SECTION 3 **Coastal Erosion and Deposition** *continued*

BARRIER ISLANDS

Sometimes sea level rises over a flat coastal plain. The shoreline moves inland and separates dunes from the old shoreline. These dunes form barrier islands. **Barrier islands** are long, narrow ridges of sand that are parallel to the shore. Barrier islands can be 3 to 30 km offshore. They can be more than 100 km long. The shallow water between the barrier island and the shoreline is a **lagoon**.

Barrier islands can also form from storms and waves. Storms may separate a sand spit from the shore and form a barrier island. Waves may pile up ridges of sand from the sea bottom and form a barrier island.

Many natural forces affect barrier islands. Waves, currents, and winds cause barrier islands to migrate toward the shoreline. Winds blowing toward the shore create a line of dunes on the island. Large waves from storms greatly erode barrier islands. Storm waves wash sand from the ocean side to the inland side of the island. Some barrier islands are eroding at a rate of 20 m per year.

Critical Thinking
6. Make Predictions How would a season of heavy storms affect a barrier island?

_____

_____

_____

Santa Rosa Island is a barrier island off the coast of Florida.

LOOKING CLOSER
7. Identify Circle the lagoon in this picture.

How Can Humans Affect Coastlines?

Humans use coastal lands for fishing, shipping, land development, and recreation. These activities can damage coastal areas in many ways. For example, ships and oil wells near the shoreline may cause oil spills. Waste from industry and coastal towns can pollute the coastline. This pollution can harm living things, including people.

Many people want to protect coastal areas. These people may work with the government to make rules that protect the coastline.

Talk About It
Express a Viewpoint Do you think it is important to protect coastal areas? Why or why not? Discuss your opinions with a partner.

Section 3 Review

SECTION VOCABULARY

barrier island a long ridge of sand or narrow island that lies parallel to the shore **estuary** an area where fresh water from rivers mixes with salt water from the ocean; the part of a river where the tides meet the river current	**lagoon** a small body of water separated from the sea by a low, narrow strip of land

1. Describe What are two features of a barrier island?

_____

_____

2. Summarize How can an increase in relative sea level affect a coastline? Give two examples.

_____

_____

3. Explain How do wind and waves affect barrier islands?

_____

_____

4. Describe What are two ways that humans affect coastlines?

_____

_____

_____

5. Predict Consequences How would coastlines change if Earth began a new glacial period? Explain your answer.

_____

_____

_____

6. Apply Concepts A scientist is studying a coastline in an area. The scientist finds estuaries and islands in the area. Describe how these features may have formed.

_____

_____

_____

CHAPTER 19 The Atmosphere
SECTION 1
Characteristics of the Atmosphere

As you read this section, keep these questions in mind:

- What is Earth's atmosphere made of?
- How do the two types of barometers work?
- What are the layers of the atmosphere?
- What are two problems related to air pollution?

What Is the Atmosphere?

The **atmosphere** is the layer of gases that surrounds Earth. The atmosphere is a mixture of elements and compounds. We generally call that mixture *air*. The atmosphere protects Earth from the sun's radiation. It also helps keep Earth's temperature stable.

THE COMPOSITION OF THE ATMOSPHERE

The atmosphere is made up of three main gases: nitrogen, N_2; oxygen, O_2; and argon, Ar. The atmosphere contains very small amounts of many other gases, such as carbon dioxide, CO_2, and water vapor, H_2O. The graph below shows the composition of Earth's atmosphere.

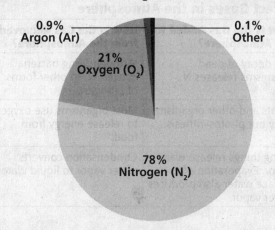

0.9%
Argon (Ar)

0.1%
Other

21%
Oxygen (O_2)

78%
Nitrogen (N_2)

This graph shows the composition of dry air at sea level. The percentage shown for each gas is the percentage of the volume of the air that is made up of that gas.

NITROGEN IN THE ATMOSPHERE

Bacteria in soil and water called *nitrogen-fixing bacteria* constantly remove nitrogen from the atmosphere. They change the nitrogen gas into a form plants can use. When animals eat the plants, the nitrogen moves into the animals' bodies. When organisms decay, the nitrogen in their bodies moves back into the atmosphere.

READING TOOLBOX

Summarize Select two colored pencils or pens. As you read this section, use one color to underline the main ideas in the section. Use the other color to underline the details related to each main idea. When you finish reading, write an outline of the section using the information you underlined.

LOOKING CLOSER

1. Identify What percentage of dry air is made up of nitrogen gas, N_2?

_____

_____

SECTION 1 | **Characteristics of the Atmosphere** *continued*

OXYGEN IN THE ATMOSPHERE

For most living things, oxygen is the most important gas in the atmosphere. Plants, animals, and other organisms use oxygen to release energy from food. They take oxygen from the air to carry out this process.

Plants also add oxygen to the atmosphere. In the process of *photosynthesis*, plants use energy from sunlight to make food from carbon dioxide and water. One of the products of this process is oxygen gas, which enters the atmosphere. ☑

WATER VAPOR IN THE ATMOSPHERE

When water evaporates, it forms an invisible gas called *water vapor*. Plants and animals also give off water vapor as part of their life processes. Water vapor in the atmosphere can condense and turn into liquid water. The liquid water may remain in the atmosphere in clouds. It may also fall to the ground as precipitation.

The amount of water vapor in the air changes over time. The time of day, season, and location affect the amount of water vapor in the air. Air may contain as much as 4% water vapor. Air that contains less than 1% water vapor is called *dry air*.

Processes That Affect Gases in the Atmosphere

Gas	How Is the Gas Added to the Atmosphere?	How Is the Gas Removed from the Atmosphere?
Nitrogen, N_2	The decay of dead organisms releases N_2.	Nitrogen-fixing bacteria convert N_2 to other forms of nitrogen.
Oxygen, O_2	Plants and other organisms carry out photosynthesis.	Most organisms use oxygen to release energy from food.
Water vapor, H_2O	Living things release water vapor. Evaporation of surface water also produces water vapor.	Condensation converts water vapor to liquid water.

OZONE IN THE ATMOSPHERE

A small amount of oxygen in the atmosphere is present as **ozone**, O_3. Ozone in the upper atmosphere forms the *ozone layer*. The ozone layer protects Earth's surface from harmful radiation. However, certain chemicals can damage the ozone layer. These chemicals include *chlorofluorocarbons*, or CFCs, and nitrogen oxide.

☑ **READING CHECK**

2. Identify What process adds oxygen to the atmosphere?

_____

_____

Critical Thinking

3. Think Logically The amounts of oxygen and nitrogen in the atmosphere are almost constant. What can you infer about the rates of the processes that add nitrogen to the atmosphere and that remove nitrogen from the atmosphere? What can you infer about the rates of the processes that add oxygen to the atmosphere and that remove oxygen from the atmosphere? Explain your answer.

_____

_____

_____

_____

_____

_____

_____

_____

_____

SECTION 1 **Characteristics of the Atmosphere** *continued*

PARTICULATES IN THE ATMOSPHERE

The atmosphere is made up mainly of gases. However, it also contains tiny particles of liquids and solids. These particles of solids and liquids are called *particulates*. Large particulates may stay in the atmosphere for only a short time. However, smaller particulates may stay in the atmosphere for years. The table below describes some of the sources of particulates in the atmosphere.

Type of Particulate	Description
Volcanic dust	tiny particles of rock that are thrown into the atmosphere during volcanic eruptions
Pollen	particles of pollen that are carried by the wind
Mineral crystals	tiny crystals of salt and other minerals from the oceans or soil
Ash from fires	ashes that form when objects burn and that are carried by the wind
Bacteria	tiny organisms that can be carried by the wind

What Is Atmospheric Pressure?

The atmosphere is many kilometers thick. The weight of the air in the atmosphere presses down on Earth's surface. The force on an area of land from all the air above it is called **atmospheric pressure**. Atmospheric pressure acts in all directions: up, down, and sideways. ☑

Earth's gravity keeps 99% of the air in the atmosphere within 32 km of the surface. Atmospheric pressure is highest near Earth's surface. As altitude increases, there is less and less air pressing down from above. Therefore, atmospheric pressure decreases with altitude.

Temperature and water vapor can also affect atmospheric pressure. In general, as temperature increases, atmospheric pressure decreases. This happens because the particles in a warm gas are farther apart than the particles in a cool gas are. As the particles move farther apart, the pressure on a given amount of area decreases.

Increasing the amount of water vapor in the air can also decrease atmospheric pressure. Water molecules weigh less than molecules of nitrogen or oxygen. Therefore, air that contains water vapor produces less pressure than dry air does. For example, the pressure in a desert may be higher than the pressure near an ocean at the same temperature.

Critical Thinking

4. Apply Reason Why do you think small particulates can stay in the atmosphere longer than large particulates can?

_____

_____

_____

_____

✓ READING CHECK

5. Identify What produces atmospheric pressure?

_____

_____

Talk About It

Explain Make a drawing or model to explain why adding water vapor to air can decrease atmospheric pressure. Share your drawing or model with a partner. Explain what it shows. Discuss any differences between your models.

MEASURING ATMOSPHERIC PRESSURE

Three common units used to describe atmospheric pressure are atmospheres (atm), millimeters of mercury (mm Hg), and millibars (mb). *Standard atmospheric pressure* is the pressure of dry air at sea level. It is equal to 1 atm, 760 mm Hg, or about 1,000 mb. ☑

Scientists use a tool called a *barometer* to measure atmospheric pressure. There are two main types of barometers: mercurial barometers and aneroid barometers. The diagram below shows how a *mercurial barometer* works.

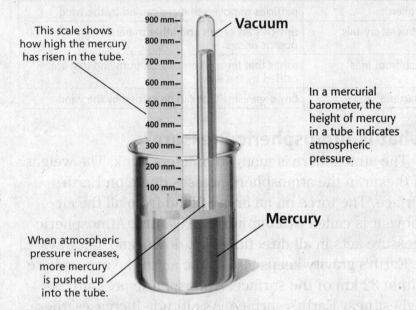

This scale shows how high the mercury has risen in the tube.

900 mm
800 mm
700 mm
600 mm
500 mm
400 mm
300 mm
200 mm
100 mm

Vacuum

In a mercurial barometer, the height of mercury in a tube indicates atmospheric pressure.

Mercury

When atmospheric pressure increases, more mercury is pushed up into the tube.

Mercurial barometers were common in the past. However, because mercury is harmful, most scientists no longer use them. Instead, they use aneroid barometers. An *aneroid barometer* contains a sealed metal container. Most of the air inside the container is sucked out before the container is sealed. When atmospheric pressure changes, the sides of the container bend inward or bulge outward. The movements of the container's sides move a pointer, which indicates the atmospheric pressure on a scale.

Barometers can also act as altimeters. An *altimeter* is a tool that measures altitude, or height above sea level. Remember that atmospheric pressure decreases as altitude increases. Therefore, as a barometer is carried to higher altitudes, the pressure reading it shows will decrease.

☑ **READING CHECK**

6. Identify What are three units used to describe atmospheric pressure?

_____

_____

_____

LOOKING CLOSER

7. Predict What happens to the level of mercury in the tube when atmospheric pressure decreases?

_____

_____

Critical Thinking

8. Apply Concepts Do the sides of the container in an aneroid barometer probably bend inward or outward when air pressure outside the barometer increases? Explain your answer.

_____

_____

_____

What Are the Layers of the Atmosphere?

Remember that atmospheric pressure decreases as altitude increases. The temperature of the atmosphere also changes with altitude. However, it does not constantly decrease with altitude like pressure does. There are three altitudes at which temperature changes suddenly. Scientists divide the atmosphere into four layers based on these changes. The diagram below shows the temperature and pressure in each layer of the atmosphere. ☑

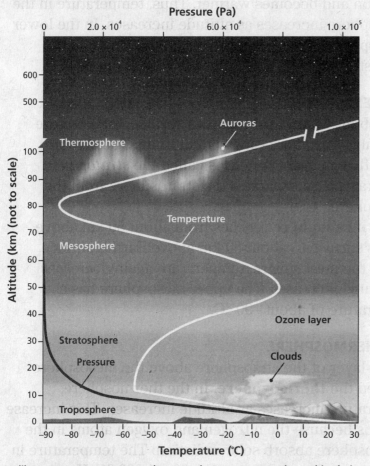

Unlike pressure, temperature does not decrease constantly as altitude increases.

THE TROPOSPHERE

The **troposphere** is the layer of the atmosphere that is closest to Earth's surface. All of the weather on Earth happens within the troposphere. Almost all of the water vapor and carbon dioxide in the atmosphere are in this layer. Within the troposphere, temperature decreases steadily as altitude increases. The troposphere reaches to about 12 km above Earth's surface.

✓ **READING CHECK**

9. Describe What do scientists base the division of the atmosphere on?

_____

_____

LOOKING CLOSER

10. Interpret Graphics At what altitude does the minimum atmospheric temperature occur?

_____

11. Describe Which layer of the atmosphere is thickest?

_____

THE STRATOSPHERE

At about 12 km above Earth's surface, temperature suddenly stops decreasing as altitude increases. The area in which this sudden change happens is called the *tropopause*. The tropopause separates the troposphere from the stratosphere.

The **stratosphere** reaches from above 12 km above Earth's surface to about 50 km above Earth's surface. Most of the ozone in Earth's atmosphere is in the stratosphere. Ozone in the stratosphere absorbs solar radiation and becomes warmer. Thus, temperature in the stratosphere increases as altitude increases. In the lower stratosphere, the temperature is about –60 °C. In the upper stratosphere, the temperature is about 0 °C. ☑

THE MESOSPHERE

At about 50 km above Earth's surface, temperature suddenly stops increasing with altitude. The area in which this change happens is called the *stratopause*. The stratopause separates the stratosphere from the mesosphere.

The **mesosphere** reaches from about 50 km above Earth's surface to about 80 km above Earth's surface. Within the mesosphere, temperature again decreases as altitude increases. The upper mesosphere has a temperature of about –90 °C.

THE THERMOSPHERE

The layer of the atmosphere above the mesosphere is called the **thermosphere**. In the thermosphere, temperature increases as altitude increases. This increase happens because the nitrogen and oxygen atoms in the thermosphere absorb solar radiation. The temperature in the thermosphere may be as high as 1,000 °C. However, because there are so few atoms in the thermosphere, temperature is very difficult to measure. ☑

✔ **READING CHECK**

12. Describe How does temperature change with altitude in the stratosphere?

_____

_____

_____

✔ **READING CHECK**

13. Identify Why does temperature increase as altitude increases in the thermosphere?

_____

_____

Layers of the Atmosphere

Layer	As Altitude Increases, Pressure . . .	As Altitude Increases, Temperature . . .
Troposphere	decreases	decreases
Stratosphere	decreases	increases
Mesosphere	decreases	decreases
Thermosphere	decreases	increases

SECTION 1 **Characteristics of the Atmosphere** *continued*

THE IONOSPHERE AND THE EXOSPHERE

The thermosphere is the uppermost layer of the atmosphere. Scientists often divide the thermosphere into two layers, the ionosphere and the exosphere.

The *ionosphere* is the lower part of the thermosphere. It reaches from about 80 km to about 400 km above Earth's surface. Within the ionosphere, solar radiation can break apart atoms and molecules to form ions. The ions can interact with the solar radiation to form auroras. *Auroras* are bright lights that seem to flow through the sky. ☑

The *exosphere* is the layer of the thermosphere that reaches from above the ionosphere into outer space. Scientists are not sure where the upper boundary of the thermosphere is. Therefore, they have different definitions for where the edge of the exosphere lies.

☑ **READING CHECK**

14. Describe What causes auroras to form?

_____

_____

_____

What Is Air Pollution?

An *air pollutant* is any substance in the air that is harmful to living things. *Air pollution* is a general term for all air pollutants. Natural processes, such as volcanic eruptions, can cause air pollution. However, today, most of the air pollution in the atmosphere comes from human actions. For example, burning fossil fuels produces a great deal of air pollution.

Air pollution can cause many problems. One common problem caused by air pollution is smog. *Smog* is an air pollutant that forms when exhaust from vehicles reacts with sunlight.

Sometimes, weather can make air pollutants more harmful. One example of this process is a temperature inversion. The flow chart below describes how a temperature inversion forms.

A layer of warm air forms above a layer of cool, polluted air. The warm air is less dense than the cool air.

↓

The warm air stops the cool air from rising and leaving the area.

↓

The cool, polluted air is trapped close to the ground.

LOOKING CLOSER

15. Explain Why can't the cool air in a temperature inversion move away?

_____

_____

_____

Section 1 Review

SECTION VOCABULARY

atmosphere a mixture of gases that surrounds a planet, moon, or other celestial body	**stratosphere** the layer of the atmosphere that lies between the troposphere and the mesosphere and in which temperature increases as altitude increases; contains the ozone layer
atmospheric pressure the force per unit area that is exerted on a surface by the weight of the atmosphere	
mesosphere the coldest layer of the atmosphere, between the stratosphere and the thermosphere, in which temperature decreases as altitude increases	**thermosphere** the uppermost layer of the atmosphere, in which temperature increases as altitude increases; includes the ionosphere
ozone a gas molecule that is made up of three oxygen atoms	**troposphere** the lowest layer of the atmosphere, in which temperature drops at a constant rate as altitude increases; the part of the atmosphere where weather conditions exist

1. Compare Complete the Venn diagram below to compare the stratosphere and the troposphere.

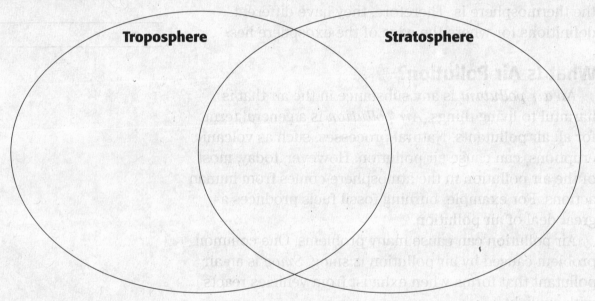

2. Describe How does an aneroid barometer measure atmospheric pressure?

_____

_____

_____

3. Identify Name the three most abundant gases in the atmosphere, and identify the percentage of the atmosphere that each makes up.

_____

_____

4. Apply Concepts Why is air pollution often worse in cities than in rural areas?

_____

_____

SECTION 2 Solar Energy and the Atmosphere

KEY IDEAS

As you read this section, keep these questions in mind:

• How does radiant energy reach Earth?

• How do visible light and infrared energy warm Earth?

• What are conduction, convection, and radiation?

What Is Radiation?

Almost all the heat in Earth's atmosphere comes from energy from the sun. The sun's rays heat the gases in the atmosphere directly. They also heat the land and oceans. The heat from the land and oceans can warm the atmosphere.

Energy from the sun travels to Earth in the form of radiation. *Radiation*, or radiant energy, is energy that travels as waves. Visible light, radio waves, and X rays are examples of radiation. Waves that carry energy as radiation are called *electromagnetic waves*. ☑

Scientists often model electromagnetic waves as long chains of peaks and valleys. The distance from one peak to the next is the *wavelength* of the wave. Different types of radiation have different wavelengths. Gamma rays, X rays, and ultraviolet rays have the shortest wavelengths. Radio waves and microwaves have the longest wavelengths.

The wavelength of a wave of visible light determines the color of the light. Red light waves have the longest wavelengths of all the colors of visible light. Blue light waves have the shortest wavelengths of all the colors of visible light.

The **electromagnetic spectrum** is the complete range of all possible wavelengths for electromagnetic waves. The electromagnetic spectrum includes all forms of radiation, as shown below.

The Electromagnetic Spectrum

Radio/TV————————►	◄Microwaves◄—Infrared—►	◄	Visible light	◄Ultraviolet►◄—X rays—►◄—Gamma rays

10^4 10^3 10^2 10^1 10^0 10^{-1} 10^{-2} 10^{-3} 10^{-4} 10^{-5} 10^{-6} 10^{-7} 10^{-8} 10^{-9} 10^{-10} 10^{-11} 10^{-12} 10^{-13} 10^{-14}
Wavelength (m)

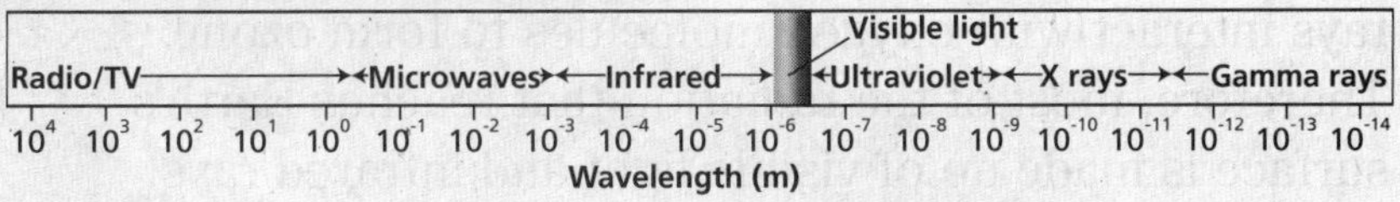

READING TOOLBOX

Ask Questions As you read this section, write down any questions you have about the information. Share your questions with a partner. Together, try to figure out the answers to your questions.

✓ READING CHECK

1. Identify What are three examples of radiation?

_____

_____

_____

Critical Thinking

2. Use Logic
Electromagnetic waves with long wavelengths have less energy than those with short wavelengths. Which form of radiation probably has more energy—X rays or radio waves? Explain your answer.

_____

_____

_____

_____

SECTION 2 **Solar Energy and the Atmosphere** *continued*

What Happens to Solar Radiation When It Reaches Earth?

Radiation that comes from the sun is called *solar radiation*. Solar radiation includes almost all forms of radiation. Earth's atmosphere interacts with the different forms of radiation in different ways. About 30% of the solar radiation that reaches Earth is reflected back into space. The atmosphere absorbs about 20% of the radiation. Earth's land and oceans absorb the remaining 50% of the radiation.

LOOKING CLOSER
3. Synthesize Text and Graphics Label the diagram to show the percentage of solar radiation that is reflected; absorbed by clouds, dust, and gas; and absorbed by Earth's surface.

Solar energy, 100%

Solar energy reflected by clouds, dust, air, and Earth's surface

Solar energy absorbed by clouds, dust, and gases

Solar energy absorbed by Earth's surface

REFLECTION AND ALBEDO

Solar radiation can reflect off land, water, ice, clouds, and even the gas molecules in the air. *Reflection* happens when an electromagnetic wave strikes a surface and bounces off.

Critical Thinking
4. Reason The grass in a field reflects about 15% of the radiation that hits it. What is the albedo of the grass?

_____

Different surfaces reflect different amounts of radiation. For example, the smooth surface of a lake reflects more radiation than a field of dark soil does. The fraction of solar radiation that a surface reflects is the surface's **albedo**. Because Earth reflects about 30% of the solar radiation that reaches it, Earth's albedo is about 0.3.

ABSORPTION

The upper atmosphere absorbs most of the short-wavelength radiation in solar radiation. Gases in the mesosphere and thermosphere absorb X rays, gamma rays, and ultraviolet rays. In the stratosphere, ultraviolet rays interact with oxygen molecules to form ozone. Therefore, most of the radiation that reaches Earth's surface is made up of visible light and infrared rays. Objects on the surface absorb this radiation.

HOW ABSORPTION KEEPS EARTH WARM

When an object absorbs radiation, the particles in the object gain energy and move faster. The faster particle motion increases the object's temperature. The particles give off some of their energy in the form of infrared rays.

Earth's atmosphere allows most visible light to pass through. However, infrared rays cannot easily pass through the atmosphere. Instead, gases such as carbon dioxide absorb the infrared rays and become warmer. Therefore, scientists often say that Earth's atmosphere "traps" heat near Earth's surface.

The atmosphere prevents heat from leaving Earth. A greenhouse used in gardening also "traps" heat. Therefore, the process in which the atmosphere prevents energy from leaving Earth is often called the **greenhouse effect**. ☑

❶ Solar radiation passes through the atmosphere and warm's Earth's surface.

❷ The surface gives off heat. Some of the heat escapes into space.

❸ Gases in the atmosphere absorb most of the heat.

HUMANS AND THE GREENHOUSE EFFECT

Some gases, such as carbon dioxide and methane, absorb heat much more easily than other gases. Gases that absorb heat easily are called *greenhouse gases*. Most scientists think that human actions are increasing the amount of greenhouse gases in the atmosphere. For example, when people burn fossil fuels, carbon dioxide enters the atmosphere. ☑

Scientists think the increase in greenhouse gases may be causing the greenhouse effect to increase. As more greenhouse gases enter the atmosphere, it traps more heat. As a result, Earth becomes warmer.

The greenhouse effect is very important for life on Earth. Without it, Earth would be too cold for living things to survive. However, if the greenhouse effect is too strong, Earth may become too warm. The increased temperatures may harm ecosystems and living things.

✓ **READING CHECK**

5. Define What is the greenhouse effect?

_____

_____

_____

✓ **READING CHECK**

6. Identify What is one way human actions can affect the atmosphere?

_____

_____

_____

What Factors Affect Earth's Surface Temperatures?

Not all areas on Earth are the same temperature all the time. For example, areas near the poles are generally much colder than areas near the equator. The tops of mountains are generally cooler than areas at lower altitudes. Latitude, altitude, time of year, and bodies of water nearby all affect an area's temperature.

The most important factor affecting an area's temperature is latitude. Earth is a sphere. Therefore, the sun's rays do not hit all parts of Earth's surface at the same angle, as shown below.

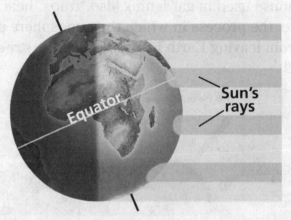

Near the equator, the energy in sunlight is concentrated in a small area. Near the poles, the energy is spread out over a much larger area. Thus, the sunlight is much less intense. This is the main reason that temperatures tend to decrease as you move away from the equator.

Look again at the figure above. You can see that Earth is tilted. This tilt is what causes the seasons. As Earth moves around the sun, the tilt causes different parts of Earth to receive different amounts of sunlight.

For example, in January, the Northern Hemisphere is tilted away from the sun. Therefore, it receives less sunlight, and temperatures are lower. At the same time, the Southern Hemisphere is tilted toward the sun. It receives more sunlight, so temperatures are higher.

The amount of water vapor in the air also affects an area's temperature. Water vapor stores energy. Areas at high altitudes tend to have thinner air. There is less water vapor to store energy. Therefore, areas at high altitudes tend to warm quickly during the day but cool quickly at night.

SECTION 2 **Solar Energy and the Atmosphere** *continued*

BODIES OF WATER

Water bodies, such as lakes and oceans, can store a great deal of energy. They can release this energy slowly when temperatures are low. Therefore, areas that are near large bodies of water tend to have moderate temperatures. Unlike areas far from water, they tend to be cooler in the summer and warmer in the winter. ☑

What Are Conduction and Convection?

Radiation is not the only way energy can move from place to place. Two other forms of energy transfer are conduction and convection.

During **conduction,** energy moves between objects that are touching. Collisions between the particles in the objects transfer energy. The particles in solids are close together. Therefore, solids generally conduct energy well. However, gases are generally not good conductors. Therefore, conduction is not the main way that energy moves in the atmosphere. Only a few centimeters of air near the ground can be heated by conduction.

Convection transfers most of the energy in the atmosphere. During **convection,** matter rises or sinks because of differences in density. For example, warm air is less dense than cool air. Therefore, warm air rises into the atmosphere. At the same time, cool air sinks toward the ground.

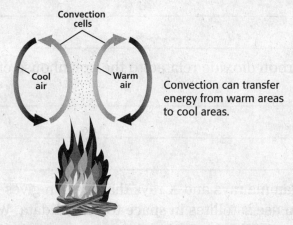

Convection cells

Cool air

Warm air

Convection can transfer energy from warm areas to cool areas.

As the warm air moves, it carries energy with it. Therefore, convection moves energy from warmer areas to cooler areas. Convection carries heat from Earth's surface into the atmosphere. It also carries heat from the equator to the poles.

✓ **READING CHECK**

8. Explain Why do areas near the oceans tend to have more moderate temperatures than areas far from the oceans?

_____

_____

_____

_____

LOOKING CLOSER

9. Explain Why does the air directly above the fire rise?

_____

_____

_____

Section 2 Review

SECTION VOCABULARY

albedo the fraction of solar radiation that is reflected off the surface of an object	**electromagnetic spectrum** all of the frequencies or wavelengths of electromagnetic radiation
conduction the transfer of energy as heat through a material	**greenhouse effect** the warming of the surface and lower atmosphere of Earth that occurs when carbon dioxide, water vapor, and other gases in the air absorb and reradiate infrared radiation
convection the movement of matter due to differences in density that are caused by temperature variations; can result in the transfer of energy as heat	

1. Compare How is convection different from conduction?

_____

_____

_____

2. Explain How does solar radiation reach Earth?

_____

3. Describe How does visible light cause Earth's surface to become warmer?

_____

_____

_____

4. Apply Concepts Most deserts heat up quickly during the day, but cool off quickly at night. What is the most likely reason for this?

_____

_____

_____

5. Describe Relationships How is carbon dioxide related to the greenhouse effect?

_____

_____

_____

6. Infer Some scientists study the gamma rays and X rays that the sun gives off. These scientists generally have to use satellites in space to collect data. Why can the scientists not collect their data on Earth's surface?

_____

_____

_____

_____

CHAPTER 19 **The Atmosphere**
SECTION **3** **Atmospheric Circulation**

KEY IDEAS

As you read this section, keep these questions in mind:

• What is the Coriolis effect?

• What are three global wind belts, and how are they related to global air circulation?

• What are two factors that form local wind patterns?

What Is the Coriolis Effect?

Air near Earth's surface generally moves from the equator toward the poles. This movement happens because air tends to move from areas with high pressure to areas with low pressure. High-pressure areas form where cold air sinks toward Earth's surface. Low-pressure areas form where warm air rises.

The air in the atmosphere does not move straight from the equator to the poles. Instead, it tends to move along curved paths. Water in the oceans also tends to move along curved paths as it moves from the equator toward the poles. The curving of the paths of water and air is called the **Coriolis effect**. ☑

The Coriolis effect happens because Earth rotates on its axis. Each point on Earth makes one complete rotation every day. Areas near the equator must travel farther and faster than areas near the poles. Air or water near the equator is moving east faster than air or water near the poles. When air or water moves north or south, its path seems to bend because of this difference in speed.

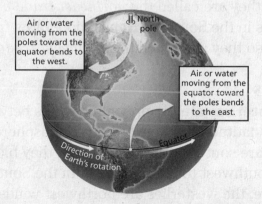

Air or water moving from the poles toward the equator bends to the west.

North pole

Air or water moving from the equator toward the poles bends to the east.

Direction of Earth's rotation

Equator

The Coriolis effect is important only for large bodies of air or water that move quickly over long distances.

READING TOOLBOX

Draw Diagrams As you read this section, circle important terms and phrases. When you finish reading, draw a diagram to define or describe each term or phrase.

☑ READING CHECK

1. Define What is the Coriolis effect?

_____

_____

_____

Critical Thinking

2. Apply Concepts In which direction would air moving north from Antarctica bend?

_____

SECTION 3 Atmospheric Circulation *continued*

What Are Prevailing Winds?

Remember that *convection* is the movement of matter because of density differences. *Convection cells* form in the atmosphere as air rises and sinks. There are six main convection cells in Earth's atmosphere. Each convection cell is related to an area on Earth's surface called a *wind belt*. Within a wind belt, the winds tend to blow in one main direction. Winds in a wind belt that blow in one main direction are *prevailing winds*.

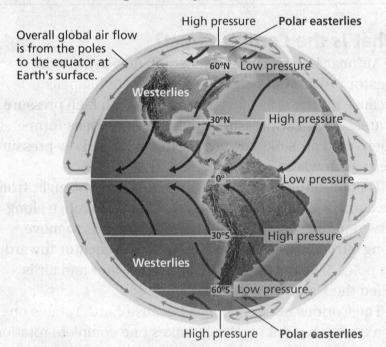

LOOKING CLOSER

3. Apply Concepts What is the overall direction of air flow in the upper atmosphere?

_____

_____

_____

TRADE WINDS

The prevailing winds between the equator and 30°N or 30°S latitude are the **trade winds**. The trade winds in the Northern Hemisphere blow from the northeast. Therefore, they are called the *northeast trade winds*. The trade winds in the Southern Hemisphere blow from the southeast, so they are called the *southeast trade winds*. ☑

☑ **READING CHECK**

4. Explain Why are the trade winds in the Northern Hemisphere called northeast trade winds?

_____

_____

_____

WESTERLIES

The **westerlies** are the prevailing winds between 30° and 60° latitude. In the Northern Hemisphere, the westerlies are southwest winds. That is, they blow from the southwest to the northeast. In the Southern Hemisphere, the westerlies are northwest winds. They blow from the northwest to the southeast. The westerlies are the main winds that blow in most of the United States.

POLAR EASTERLIES

The prevailing winds that blow between 60° latitude and the poles are the **polar easterlies**. The polar easterlies are strongest in the Southern Hemisphere, where they blow off of Antarctica.

THE DOLDRUMS AND HORSE LATITUDES

The area where the trade winds meet is called the *doldrums*. In the doldrums, winds are very weak. They do not blow in any specific direction. Atmospheric pressure in the doldrums is generally low. ☑

The areas where the trade winds meet the westerlies are called the *horse latitudes*. Winds in the horse latitudes are also generally weak. Atmospheric pressure in the horse latitudes is generally high.

✓ **READING CHECK**

5. Define What is the doldrums?

_____

_____

JET STREAMS

There are narrow bands of fast-moving winds in the upper troposphere and lower stratosphere. These winds are called **jet streams**. They can be up to 100 km wide and about 2–3 km thick. The winds in jet streams can be as fast as 400 km/h.

What Causes Local Winds?

The winds in an area do not always blow in the direction of the prevailing winds. Many local factors can affect the winds in an area. Two factors that can produce local winds are water bodies and mountains. The table below describes the effects of these factors.

Factors That Cause Local Winds

Factor	Effect
Water bodies, such as oceans	Sunlight heats land more quickly than it heats water. Therefore, during the day, the land near a water body tends to be warmer than the water. The air above the land is also warmer and has a lower pressure. Therefore, a *sea breeze* blows from the water toward the land. At night, the land is cooler than the water. The air above the land is cooler and has a higher pressure. Therefore, a *land breeze* blows from the land toward the water.
Mountains	During the day, warm air from the base of the mountain rises. The warm air moves up the mountain and forms a *valley breeze*. At night, cold air from the top of the mountain sinks toward the ground. It forms a *mountain breeze*.

LOOKING CLOSER

6. Explain Why do sea breezes form?

_____

_____

_____

_____

_____

Section 3 Review

SECTION VOCABULARY

Coriolis effect the curving of the path of a moving object from an otherwise straight path due to Earth's rotation	**trade winds** prevailing winds that blow from east to west from 30° latitude to the equator in both hemispheres
jet stream a narrow band of strong winds that blow in the upper troposphere	**westerlies** prevailing winds that blow from west to east between 30° and 60° latitude in both hemispheres
polar easterlies prevailing winds that blow from east to west between 60° and 90° latitude in both hemispheres	

1. Apply Concepts A friend tells you that the water in the sink spins as it goes down the drain because of the Coriolis effect. Is your friend right? Explain your answer.

_____

_____

2. Identify What are the three main global wind belts?

_____

3. Identify On the diagram below, label the northeast trade winds, the southeast trade winds, the doldrums, and the horse latitudes.

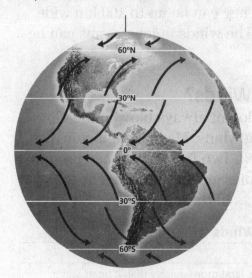

4. Infer What causes the cold air at the top of a mountain to sink at night?

_____

_____

5. Explain Why is a lake cooler than the land near it during the day, but warmer than the land during the night?

_____

_____

_____

CHAPTER 20 Water in the Atmosphere

SECTION 1

Atmospheric Moisture

As you read this section, keep these questions in mind:

• How does energy affect the changing forms of water?

• What are absolute and relative humidity, and how are they measured?

• What happens when the temperature of air decreases to the dew point?

How Does Water Change Phases?

Water can exist in three different *phases*, or states. The gas phase is called *water vapor*. The solid phase is called *ice*. The liquid phase is just called *water*.

Water changes phase when it absorbs or loses heat energy. For example, molecules of ice move very little and are packed together tightly. When the ice absorbs energy, the molecules begin to move more quickly. They break out of their positions and slide past each other. The ice melts and becomes liquid water.

When the water absorbs more energy, the molecules move even more quickly. The molecules that move the fastest escape from the liquid in a process called *evaporation*. When the water evaporates, it changes to water vapor. ☑

LATENT HEAT

Latent heat is the heat that is absorbed or released by a substance when it changes phase. For example, when water vapor *condenses*, or changes into a liquid, energy is released. This energy is latent heat. Similarly, latent heat is absorbed when ice thaws and is released when water freezes.

Summarize As you read this section, underline the main ideas. When you finish reading, write a short summary of the section using the underlined ideas.

READING CHECK

1. Describe What happens when molecules in liquid water absorb energy?

_____

_____

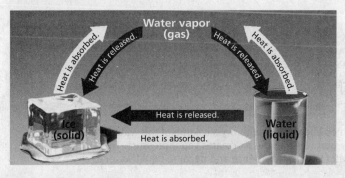

Water exists in three states, or phases. As it changes from one phase to another, water either absorbs or releases heat energy.

LOOKING CLOSER

2. Identify Is heat released or absorbed when ice melts?

READING CHECK

3. Explain How does most water enter the atmosphere?

Critical Thinking

4. Contrast How is sublimation different from evaporation?

LOOKING CLOSER

5. Predict What will happen to some of the water vapor in the second figure?

EVAPORATION AND SUBLIMATION

Most water enters the atmosphere through evaporation. The oceans near the equator receive a lot of solar energy. Therefore, a lot of water in those oceans evaporates into the atmosphere. Most of the water vapor in the atmosphere comes from those oceans. ☑

Water vapor also evaporates and enters the atmosphere from lakes, ponds, streams, and soil. Plants release water into the atmosphere through a process called *transpiration.* Animals give off water vapor when they breathe out. Volcanoes and burning fuels also release small amounts of water vapor into the atmosphere.

Usually, ice changes to a liquid before it turns to water vapor. However, sometimes ice changes directly to water vapor without becoming a liquid. This process is called **sublimation**. Sublimation generally happens when the air is dry and the temperature is below freezing.

What Is Humidity?

The water vapor in the air is called *humidity.* Humidity is controlled by the rate of condensation and the rate of evaporation. The *rate of condensation* is a measure of how quickly water vapor condenses. The *rate of evaporation* is a measure of how quickly liquid water evaporates.

The temperature of the air determines the rate of evaporation. Water evaporates faster at higher temperatures. The rate of condensation is determined by vapor pressure, as the figure below shows. *Vapor pressure* is the pressure that water vapor in the air puts on an object. When vapor pressure is high, the rate of condensation is high.

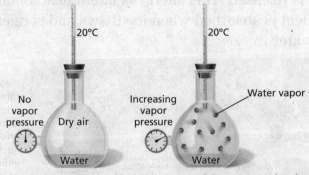

When water comes into contact with dry air, some of the water molecules evaporate. The water vapor in the air creates vapor pressure. The vapor pressure causes some water vapor to condense and become liquid water again.

THE DEW POINT

When the rate of condensation equals the rate of evaporation, the air is *saturated* with water vapor. The temperature at which air is saturated is called the **dew point**. Air can cool below its dew point when it touches a cold surface. For example, grass, leaves, and other objects near the ground lose heat at night. Their surface temperatures drop. When air comes into contact with these objects, it cools. It can cool enough to reach its dew point.

At temperatures below the dew point, liquid water droplets can form from the water in the air. When air comes into contact with cool grass, it can reach its dew point. If it does, liquid water droplets form on the grass from the vapor in the air. These droplets are called *dew*.

The dew on this spider web formed when the air dropped below the dew point.

If the dew point falls below the freezing temperature of water, frost may form. *Frost* is water vapor that changes directly into solid ice crystals. Frost is not frozen dew. Unlike frost, frozen dew looks like clear beads of ice. Frozen dew is very uncommon.

ABSOLUTE HUMIDITY

One way to express the amount of moisture in the air is by calculating absolute humidity. **Absolute humidity** is a measure of the actual amount of water vapor in the air. You can calculate absolute humidity using the following equation:

$$\text{absolute humidity} = \frac{\text{mass of water vapor (grams)}}{\text{volume of air (cubic meters)}}$$

LOOKING CLOSER
6. Identify Why did the air condense when it touched the spider web?

_____

_____

_____

Math *Skills*

7. Calculate In 2 m³ of air, there is 30 g of water vapor. What is the absolute humidity of the air?

_____

MIXING RATIO

Absolute humidity depends on the volume of air. When the temperature or pressure of air changes, its volume can also change. Its mass, however, does not change. Therefore, meteorologists prefer to express the moisture in air by using the *mixing ratio*.

The mixing ratio is the ratio of the mass of water vapor to the mass of dry air. For example, the air in moist regions might have 18 g of water vapor in 1 kg of air. Therefore, the mixing ratio would be 18 g/kg. Because the mixing ratio uses only units of mass, it is not affected by temperature or pressure changes. ☑

RELATIVE HUMIDITY

Scientists also express the amount of water vapor in the air by measuring relative humidity. To calculate relative humidity, scientists first measure the amount of water vapor in the air. Then, they determine the amount of water vapor necessary to reach saturation. **Relative humidity** is the ratio of those two numbers.

For example, at 25 °C, air is saturated when it contains 20 g of water vapor per 1 kg of air. If air that is 25 °C contains 5 g of water vapor per 1 kg of air, the relative humidity is 5/20, or 25%.

How Do Meteorologists Measure Humidity?

Meteorologists can use humidity measurements to predict weather conditions. They can measure relative humidity using any of these instruments:

• an electrical hygrometer

• a psychrometer

• a dew cell

• a hair hygrometer

An electrical hygrometer uses a thin film to measure humidity. The humidity in the surrounding air affects the film's ability to absorb or release water vapor. The amount of water vapor in the film affects the film's ability to conduct electricity. Scientists can measure the film's ability to conduct electricity. They can then use those measurements to figure out the humidity of the air.

✓ READING CHECK

8. Explain Why do scientists often express humidity as a mixing ratio rather than as absolute humidity?

_____

_____

_____

_____

Math *Skills*

9. Calculate If 1 kg of air at 25 °C contains 10 g of water vapor, what is the relative humidity of the air?

_____

SECTION 1 **Atmospheric Moisture** *continued*

PSYCHROMETER

A psychrometer also measures humidity. It contains two thermometers. The bulb of one thermometer is covered with a wet cloth. The other thermometer bulb is dry. As air passes through the wet-bulb thermometer, some water in the cloth evaporates. Evaporation requires energy, so heat energy is released and the cloth cools. The wet-bulb thermometer shows the cloth's temperature. ☑

If humidity is low, the water evaporates more quickly. Therefore, the temperature reading on the wet-bulb thermometer is much lower than the reading on the dry-bulb thermometer. If the air is saturated, no water evaporates. Therefore, the temperatures are the same.

READING CHECK

10. Describe Why is the wet-bulb thermometer in a psychrometer cooler than the dry-bulb thermometer?

_____

_____

_____

_____

_____

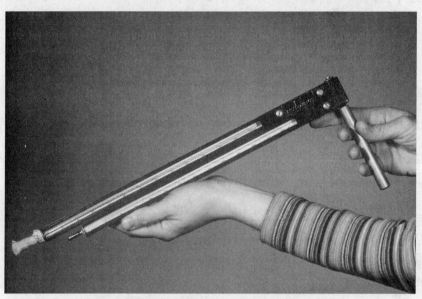

A psychrometer measures the difference in temperature between a wet-bulb and a dry-bulb thermometer. That measurement can be used to calculate humidity.

LOOKING CLOSER

11. Identify Label the wet-bulb thermometer and the dry-bulb thermometer.

OTHER METHODS FOR MEASURING HUMIDITY

The table below describes two other instruments that scientists use to measure humidity.

Instrument	Description
Dew cell	uses electrical resistance to determine the dew point
Hair hygrometer	uses a hair to measure humidity; high humidity makes the hair longer

Scientists can use electrical hygrometers to measure humidity high in the atmosphere. Scientists attach the hygrometer to a weather balloon. The balloon carries the hygrometer high into the air.

Section 1 Review

SECTION VOCABULARY

absolute humidity the mass of water vapor per unit volume of air that contains the water vapor, usually expressed as grams of water vapor per cubic meter of air	**relative humidity** the ratio of the amount of water vapor in the air to the amount of water vapor needed to reach saturation at a given temperature
dew point at constant pressure and water vapor content, the temperature at which the rate of condensation equals the rate of evaporation	**sublimation** the process in which a solid changes directly into a gas (the term is sometimes also used for the reverse process)
latent heat the heat energy that is absorbed or released by a substance during a phase change	

1. Compare What is the difference between absolute humidity and relative humidity?

_____

_____

_____

2. Describe What happens when the temperature of air decreases to below the dew point?

_____

_____

3. Identify What are four instruments that scientists use to measure humidity?

_____

4. Explain Name two phase changes of water that involve the release of heat.

_____

5. Describe Relationships Complete the table below to summarize processes that affect water vapor in the air. Use the terms *condensation, evaporation*, and *temperature* to complete the table.

If . . .	Then . . .
. . . vapor pressure increases . . .	. . . rate of _____ increases.
_____ decreases . . .	. . . rate of evaporation decreases.
. . . rate of _____ is greater than rate of condensation . . .	. . . evaporation occurs.
. . . rate of condensation is greater than rate of evaporation . . .	_____ occurs.

6. Infer In general, the cooler the air is, the less water vapor it must contain to be saturated. What will most likely happen to relative humidity if air temperature decreases, but no water vapor enters or leaves the air?

_____

CHAPTER 20 Water in the Atmosphere
SECTION 2 Clouds and Fog

As you read this section, keep these questions in mind:

• What conditions are necessary for clouds to form?

• What are the four processes of cooling that can lead to the formation of clouds?

• What are the characteristics of the three major types of clouds?

• What are four ways in which fog can form?

How Do Clouds Form?

A **cloud** is a collection of water droplets or ice crystals in the air. A cloud forms when water vapor condenses around small particles in the air. These particles are called **condensation nuclei** (singular, *condensation nucleus*). The troposphere contains millions of tiny particles that act as condensation nuclei. They may be particles of dust, ice, or salt suspended in the air.

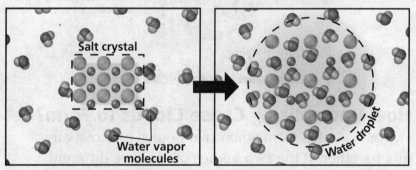

Water molecules condense around the salt crystal. More water molecules condense around the original small droplet.

In order for clouds to form, the air must be saturated with water vapor. The air is saturated with water vapor when it has reached its dew point. Remember that when the temperature drops below the dew point, water droplets can form. These droplets condense around the condensation nuclei.

Therefore, in order for clouds to form, the air's temperature must drop below its dew point. There are four ways that air cools enough that clouds form: adiabatic cooling, mixing, lifting, and advective cooling. ☑

READING TOOLBOX

Predict Before reading this section, write each heading on a piece of paper. Below each heading, write what you think you will learn.

LOOKING CLOSER
1. Identify What is the condensation nucleus in this figure?

_____

_____

READING CHECK

2. Identify What are four ways that air cools enough for clouds to form?

_____

_____

_____

How Does Adiabatic Cooling Cause Clouds to Form?

As a body of air rises, the atmospheric pressure on it decreases. Because of the lower pressure, the molecules in the body of air move farther apart. Therefore, fewer molecules collide with each other and the air becomes cooler. This process is called **adiabatic cooling**. ☑

The air close to Earth is warmer and less dense than the air high in the atmosphere. Therefore, the air close to Earth rises. As it rises, it becomes cooler because of adiabatic cooling. When it cools below the dew point, the vapor in the air condenses and clouds form. The altitude at which this happens is called the *condensation level*.

3. Explain Why does air cool when it rises?

_____

_____

_____

_____

_____

_____

LOOKING CLOSER

4. Identify What is the condensation level in the figure?

_____

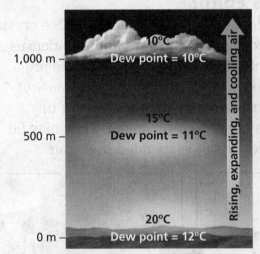

In this figure, the temperature and the dew point are the same at an altitude of 1,000 m. Above that altitude, condensation begins and clouds form.

How Does Mixing Cause Clouds to Form?

Some clouds form when two bodies of moist air mix together. If the two bodies of air have different temperatures, the mixing will cause the temperature of the air to change. The mixed body of air may cool to below its dew point. When that happens, clouds form.

How Does Lifting Cause Clouds to Form?

When air is forced to rise, it expands and cools. If it cools to below its dew point, clouds will form.

There are two main situations that force air to rise. First, a moving body of air can meet sloping ground, such as a mountain. When this happens, the air will be forced upward. Second, a body of cold, dense air can push a less dense body of air upward. When that happens, storm clouds often form.

SECTION 2 **Clouds and Fog** *continued*

How Does Advective Cooling Cause Clouds to Form?

When a body of air moves over a cold surface, the cold surface absorbs heat from the air. This causes the air to cool. If the temperature of the air falls below its dew point, clouds can form. This process is called **advective cooling**. ☑

How Do Scientists Classify Clouds?

Clouds are classified by shape and by altitude. The three main cloud shapes are stratus clouds, cirrus clouds, and cumulus clouds.

STRATUS CLOUDS

A **stratus cloud** is relatively thin and flat. The word *stratus* means "sheetlike." Stratus clouds form when a layer of warm, moist air lies above a layer of cool air. When the warm air reaches its dew point, wide stratus clouds form. Stratus clouds cover large areas of sky and often block out the sun. ☑

Very little precipitation falls from most types of stratus clouds. However, *nimbostratus* clouds can cause heavy precipitation.

CIRRUS CLOUDS

A **cirrus cloud** looks like it is made of thin strands. Cirrus clouds form at altitudes above 6,000 m. Because the air is so cold at such high altitudes, cirrus clouds are made of ice crystals. Because cirrus clouds are thin, light can pass through them easily.

These wispy cirrus clouds form high in the atmosphere.

✓ **READING CHECK**

5. Define When does advective cooling occur?

_____

_____

✓ **READING CHECK**

6. Describe What shape is a stratus cloud?

_____

_____

_____

LOOKING CLOSER

7. Infer What are the clouds in this picture made of?

_____

SECTION 2 **Clouds and Fog** *continued*

CUMULUS CLOUDS

A **cumulus cloud** has a dark bottom and a puffy top that looks like a cotton ball. The word *cumulus* means "piled." Cumulus clouds form when warm, moist air rises and cools. As the cooling air reaches its dew point, clouds form.

On hot, humid days, cumulus clouds can be very tall. High storm clouds, called *cumulonimbus clouds*, can form. The prefix *nimbo-* and the suffix *-nimbus* mean "rain." Cumulonimbus clouds often form before a thunderstorm.

Critical Thinking

8. Contrast What is the main way that these cumulus clouds are different from the cirrus clouds on the previous page?

_____

_____

_____

These fluffy cumulus clouds look like cotton balls in the sky.

ALTITUDE AND CLOUD TYPES

Scientists also classify clouds by their altitude, or height. There are three main altitude groups: low clouds, middle clouds, and high clouds. Scientists use prefixes to indicate the height of a cloud. The table below summarizes the three different altitude groups.

LOOKING CLOSER

9. Identify At what altitude would a cirrostratus cloud probably be found?

_____

_____

Cloud Group	Altitude	Prefix	Example
Low	0–2,000 m	*strato-*	stratocumulus
Middle	2,000–6,000 m	*alto-*	altostratus
High	above 6,000 m	*cirro-*	cirrocumulus

You can understand a lot about a cloud by its name. For example, you can divide the word *cirrostratus* into the prefix *cirro-* and the root *stratus*. The prefix shows that a cirrostratus cloud must have a high altitude. The *stratus* root shows that it is relatively thin and flat.

The figure on the next page shows several different types of clouds.

SECTION 2 **Clouds and Fog** *continued*

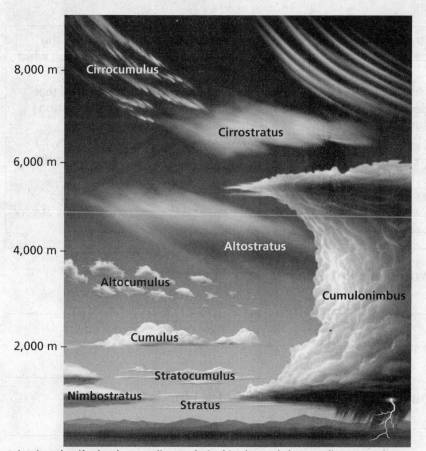

Scientists classify clouds according to their altitudes and shapes. The name of a cloud can give you clues about what type of cloud it is.

Talk About It
Classify With a partner, discuss the different clouds in the figure. What does the name of each cloud tell you about the cloud's properties? Use the information on the previous page to help you.

Critical Thinking
10. Apply Concepts Which two clouds in the figure probably produce a lot of precipitation?

_____

_____

_____

How Does Fog Form?

Fog is similar to clouds because it forms when water vapor in the air condenses. However, fog forms very near Earth's surface. The table below describes four types of fog and how they form.

Type of Fog	Cause	Description
Radiation fog	The ground becomes cooler at night, so the air near the ground cools.	• thickest in valleys because dense, cold air sinks • thick around cities because water condenses on dust and smoke particles
Advection fog	Warm, moist air moves across a cool surface.	forms along coasts because the air over the water is cooler than the air over the land
Upslope fog	Air rises and cools as it passes along sloping land.	forms near mountains and other sloping land
Steam fog	Cool air moves over a warm body of water.	forms over rivers and other bodies of water

Critical Thinking
11. Connect Why might advection fog and advective cooling share the same root?

_____

_____

_____

Section 2 Review

SECTION VOCABULARY

adiabatic cooling the process by which the temperature of an air mass decreases as the air mass rises and expands	**condensation nucleus** a solid particle in the atmosphere that provides the surface on which water vapor condenses
advective cooling the process by which the temperature of an air mass decreases as the air mass moves over a cold surface	**cumulus cloud** a low-level, billowy cloud that commonly has a top that resembles cotton balls and a dark bottom
cirrus cloud a feathery cloud that is composed of ice crystals and that has the highest altitude of any cloud in the sky	**fog** water vapor that has condensed very near the surface of Earth because air close to the ground has cooled
cloud a collection of small water droplets or ice crystals suspended in the air, which forms when the air is cooled and condensation occurs	**stratus cloud** a gray cloud that has a flat, uniform base and that commonly forms at very low altitudes

1. Describe In your own words, describe adiabatic cooling.

_____

_____

_____

2. Explain Why must the air drop below its dew point for clouds to form?

_____

_____

3. Describe What are two situations that can cause lifting?

_____

_____

4. Apply Concepts Fill in the spaces in the table to describe different types of clouds.

Name	Altitude	Shape	Precipitation?
Cirrostratus			no
Altocumulus		puffy	
Nimbostratus	low		
Cumulonimbus	low to middle		

5. Compare How is radiation fog different from advection fog?

_____

_____

_____

CHAPTER 20 | Water in the Atmosphere
SECTION 3 | Precipitation

KEY IDEAS

As you read this section, keep these questions in mind:

• What are the four forms of precipitation?

• What are two processes that cause precipitation?

• How is precipitation measured?

• How can rain be produced artificially?

What Are the Forms of Precipitation?

Any moisture that falls to Earth's surface is called **precipitation**. There are four main forms of precipitation: rain, snow, sleet, and hail.

RAIN

Rain is liquid precipitation. Raindrops are normally between 0.5 and 5 mm in diameter. If the raindrops are smaller than 0.5 mm in diameter, the rain is called *drizzle*.

SNOW

Snow is the most common form of solid precipitation. *Snow* consists of particles of ice. Sometimes these particles fall as pellets (tiny spheres) or tiny ice crystals. Other times, the ice crystals combine to form snowflakes. Snowflakes are generally largest when the temperature is near 0 °C. They are smaller at lower temperatures. ☑

SLEET

Sleet forms when rain falls through a layer of freezing air near Earth's surface. The rain freezes into sleet, or clear ice pellets. Sometimes, the rain does not freeze until it hits a surface near the ground. When it does, it forms a thick layer of ice called *glaze ice* or *freezing rain*.

The glaze ice on this flower formed when rain froze near the ground.

READING TOOLBOX

Organize As you read this section, create a concept map using the following terms: *rain, glaze ice, sleet, supercooling, precipitation, drizzle, coalescence, snow,* and *hail.*

✔ **READING CHECK**

1. Explain How does a snowflake form?

_____

_____

_____

Critical Thinking

2. Compare How is glaze ice different from sleet?

_____

_____

_____

_____

_____

HAIL

Hail is solid precipitation in the form of lumps of ice. Hail usually forms in cumulonimbus clouds. Convection currents in the clouds carry raindrops to high levels, where the raindrops freeze. The hailstones fall and begin to melt. If the hailstones are lifted upward again, another layer of ice forms on them. The cycle continues until they become too heavy for the convection currents to carry them. When that happens, they fall to the ground as hail. ☑

What Causes Precipitation?

Most cloud droplets have a diameter of about 20 μm (micrometers)—smaller than the period at the end of this sentence. A droplet must increase in diameter by about 100 times to fall as precipitation. Two processes cause cloud droplets to grow large enough to fall as precipitation: coalescence and supercooling.

COALESCENCE

Large cloud droplets fall more quickly than small cloud droplets. As large droplets fall, they collide with smaller droplets. These droplets combine with the larger droplet in a process called **coalescence**. ☑

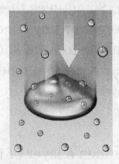

During coalescence, large cloud droplets collide and combine with smaller droplets. The resulting droplets are large enough to fall as rain.

SUPERCOOLING

Precipitation also forms through **supercooling**. When there are not enough freezing nuclei in a cloud, water droplets cannot freeze. Instead, they become supercooled. Supercooled water droplets may have a temperature as low as –40 °C. When they finally do condense onto freezing nuclei, they form large ice crystals very quickly. They become heavy enough to fall to Earth's surface.

If the ice crystals pass through warmer air as they fall, they can melt. This process can form huge raindrops that are common in summer thunderstorms.

SECTION 3 Precipitation *continued*

How Do Scientists Measure Precipitation?

Meteorologists use many instruments to measure precipitation. For example, they might use a meterstick to measure the depth of snow. They also might use a *rain gauge* to measure rainfall. One type of rain gauge looks like a cup with measurements on it. Rain falls in the cup, and the gauge can be used as a measuring cup.

DOPPLER RADAR

Scientists can also use Doppler radar images to get information about precipitation. Meteorologists use Doppler radar by bouncing radio waves off rain or snow. They time how long the waves take to return. In this way, they can detect the location, direction of movement, and intensity of the precipitation. This information can help warn people of an approaching storm.

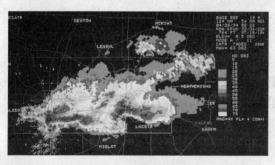

This Doppler radar image shows information about a thunderstorm system over northern Texas. The darkest colors on the image show the areas of heaviest rainfall.

What Is Cloud Seeding?

When there is a drought, scientists may try to force clouds to release precipitation. **Cloud seeding** is the process of adding materials to a cloud so that rain will fall.

There are two main methods of cloud seeding. In one method, scientists add silver iodide crystals to a cloud. These crystals act as condensation nuclei so that raindrops will form. The crystals can be dropped from a plane or shot from the ground. A second method of cloud seeding uses powdered dry ice. The dry ice particles act as freezing nuclei so that ice crystals will form. When the ice crystals fall, they may melt and form raindrops. ☑

Cloud seeding does not always work. In some cases, seeded clouds produce more rain than unseeded clouds. In other cases, unseeded clouds produce the same amount of rain, or even more rain. Scientists are trying to understand why this happens so that cloud seeding can become more successful.

Critical Thinking

5. Infer Rain is a form of liquid precipitation. How does this help explain why rain cannot be measured with a meterstick?

_____

_____

_____

_____

LOOKING CLOSER

6. Identify Circle the locations on the image that have the heaviest rainfall.

✔ READING CHECK

7. Compare How are the two methods of cloud seeding similar? How are they different?

_____

_____

_____

_____

_____

_____

Section 3 Review

SECTION VOCABULARY

cloud seeding the process of introducing freezing nuclei or condensation nuclei into a cloud in order to cause rain to fall	**precipitation** any form of water that falls to Earth's surface from the clouds; includes rain, snow, sleet, and hail
coalescence the formation of a large droplet by the combination of smaller droplets	**supercooling** a condition in which a substance is cooled below its freezing point, condensation point, or sublimation point without going through a change of state

1. Identify What are four forms of precipitation?

_____

_____

2. Contrast How is rain different from the other forms of precipitation?

_____

_____

_____

3. Explain Why are coalescence and supercooling important?

_____

_____

_____

_____

4. Infer If the convection currents in a cloud were very weak, would the hailstones that come from the cloud be large or small? Explain your answer.

_____

_____

_____

_____

5. Explain How do scientists use Doppler radar to measure precipitation?

_____

_____

_____

_____

6. Explain How can scientists create precipitation artificially?

_____

_____

_____

_____

CHAPTER 21 | **Weather**

SECTION
1 **Air Masses**

As you read this section, keep these questions in mind:

• How does an air mass form?

• What are the four main types of air masses?

• How do air masses affect North America's weather?

How Does Air Move?

Remember that air moves from areas of high pressure to areas of low pressure. In general, surface air moves from the poles toward the equator. At high altitudes, warm air flows from the equator toward the poles. These motions happen because the equator is generally warmer than the poles. Because the air at the equator is warmer, air pressure there is low. Air pressure at the poles is higher, because the air there is colder.

The movements of air in the atmosphere create global wind belts. The Northern Hemisphere and the Southern Hemisphere each have three wind belts. Earth's rotation can influence the direction of these wind belts through the *Coriolis effect*.

What Is an Air Mass?

Air does not move much when air pressure differences are small. The air may stay in one place or move very slowly over an area. If this happens, the air takes on the temperature and humidity of that region. A large body of air with similar temperature and moisture is an **air mass**.

Scientists classify air masses by their *source regions*, or the areas in which they form. Scientists use two-letter symbols to describe air masses. The first letter in the symbol indicates whether the air mass is dry or moist. The second letter indicates whether the air mass is warm or cold.

Source Region	Type of Air	Symbol
Continental	dry	c
Maritime	moist	m
Tropical	warm	T
Polar	cold	P

READING TOOLBOX

Summarize As you read this section, underline or circle the vocabulary words and other important terms. After you read the section, create a concept map using the terms you underlined or circled.

Critical Thinking

1. Explain How does pressure affect the movement of surface air?

_____

_____

_____

_____

LOOKING CLOSER

2. Identify Where do warm air masses form?

_____

SECTION 1 **Air Masses** *continued*

CONTINENTAL AIR MASSES

Continental air masses form over large bodies of land, such as northern Asia and the southwestern United States. Continental air masses have very low humidity because they form over land. In general, continental air masses bring dry weather when they move into other regions. ☑

There are two types of continental air masses: *continental polar* (cP) and *continental tropical* (cT). Continental polar air masses are dry and cold. Continental tropical air masses are dry and warm.

MARITIME AIR MASSES

Maritime air masses form over large bodies of water, such as the Atlantic and Pacific Oceans. These air masses usually have higher humidity than continental air masses do. Maritime air masses bring precipitation and fog when they move to a new region.

There are two types of maritime air masses: *maritime polar* (mP) and *maritime tropical* (mT). Maritime polar air masses are moist and cold. Maritime tropical air masses are moist and warm.

What Air Masses Affect North America?

An air mass usually brings the weather of its source location. However, an air mass may change as it moves away from its source location. For example, cold dry air may become warm and moist as it moves from land to a warm ocean. The lower layers of the air become warm and rise. As the air rises, clouds and precipitation may form.

The air masses that affect the weather of North America come from six places. The table below shows the sources, movements, and weather of these air masses.

Air Masses in North America

Air Mass	Source Region	Movement	Weather
cP	polar regions in Canada	south-southeast	cold and dry
mP	polar Pacific; polar Atlantic	southeast; south-southwest	cold and moist
cT	southwestern United States	north-northeast	warm and dry
mT	tropical Pacific; tropical Atlantic	northeast; north-northwest	warm and moist

✓ READING CHECK

3. Explain How do continental air masses affect the weather of a region?

_____

_____

Critical Thinking

4. Draw Conclusions Which type of maritime air mass forms over the Arctic Ocean? Why?

_____

_____

_____

_____

LOOKING CLOSER

5. Describe What type of weather does the continental polar air mass bring?

_____

_____

SECTION 1 **Air Masses** *continued*

TROPICAL AIR MASSES

Continental tropical air masses form over the deserts of the southwestern United States. These air masses bring dry, hot weather in the summer. They do not form in winter.

Maritime tropical air masses form over the Atlantic Ocean, the Caribbean Sea, and the Gulf of Mexico. These air masses bring mild, cloudy weather to the eastern United States in winter. In summer, they bring hot, humid weather and storms.

Maritime tropical air masses also form over the Pacific Ocean. During summer, they do not usually reach the Pacific coast. In winter, maritime tropical air masses bring precipitation to the coast and the Southwest.

POLAR AIR MASSES

Continental polar air masses form over ice and snow in northern Canada. These air masses move into the northern United States. In summer, they bring cool, dry weather. In winter, they bring very cold weather.

Maritime polar air masses form over the North Pacific Ocean and reach the Pacific coast. In winter, they bring rain and snow. In summer, they bring cool, often foggy weather. These air masses lose their moisture as they move over the Rocky Mountains. As a result, they can bring cool and dry weather to the central United States.

Maritime polar air masses also form over the Atlantic Ocean. These air masses usually move east toward Europe. Sometimes, they move west over eastern Canada and the United States. In winter, they bring cold, cloudy weather and snow. In summer, they bring cool weather and fog.

6. Infer How is summer in the southwestern United States different from summer in the southeastern United States?

_____

_____

_____

Talk About It

Apply Concepts Look at the map below. Which air masses affect the weather where you live? How do they affect the weather? Discuss your ideas with a partner.

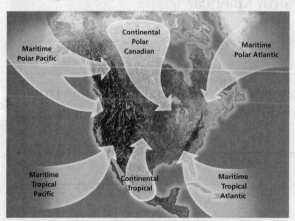

The air masses that affect the weather in North America are named according to their source regions.

LOOKING CLOSER

7. Identify Which air mass brings dry, hot weather in the summer?

_____

_____

Section 1 Review

SECTION VOCABULARY

air mass a large body of air throughout which temperature and moisture content are similar	

1. Explain How does an air mass form?

_____

_____

2. List What are the four main types of air masses?

_____

3. Compare Use the charts below to compare the types of maritime and continental air masses.

	Continental Polar	Continental Tropical
Symbol	cP	
Weather		

	Maritime Polar	Maritime Tropical
Symbol		
Weather	moist and cold	

4. Describe How do tropical air masses affect North America?

_____

_____

5. Describe How do polar air masses affect North America?

_____

_____

6. Make Predictions Suppose a continental polar air mass replaced a maritime tropical air mass. How would temperature and humidity change? Explain your answer.

_____

_____

_____

CHAPTER 21 | Weather
SECTION 2 | Fronts

As you read this section, keep these questions in mind:

- What weather patterns do warm and cold fronts bring?
- How does a midlatitude cyclone form?
- How do hurricanes, thunderstorms, and tornadoes form?

What Is a Front?

Air masses have different densities. Cool air masses are denser than warm air masses. These density differences keep the air masses separate. As a result, a boundary forms between the air masses. This boundary is a *front*. A typical front is several hundred kilometers long. Some fronts may be several thousand kilometers long. ☑

In the middle latitudes, changes in weather happen along fronts. The middle latitudes are the regions between the tropical and polar regions. Tropical regions do not have fronts because tropical air masses do not have large differences in temperature.

What Are the Types of Fronts?

One air mass must collide with another air mass to form a front. The type of front that forms depends on how the air masses move.

COLD FRONTS

A **cold front** forms when a cold air mass pushes under a warm air mass. The moving cold air lifts the warm air. If the warm air is moist, clouds will form. The front moves in the direction the cold air mass was moving.

Cold fronts can move at different speeds. Fast-moving cold fronts lift warm air more quickly than slow-moving cold fronts do. The speed of a cold front affects the weather conditions along the front, as shown below.

Types of Cold Fronts

Speed of Front	Resulting Weather Conditions
Fast	large clouds; short, violent storms; chance of a long line of heavy thunderstorms called a *squall line*
Slow	weaker storms; lighter precipitation

READING TOOLBOX

Make Comparisons As you read this section, make a chart to compare midlatitude cyclones, hurricanes, and tornadoes. Include information about size, wind speed, and duration for each event.

READING CHECK

1. Define What is a front?

_____

_____

_____

LOOKING CLOSER

2. Identify Which type of cold front may form a squall line?

_____

_____

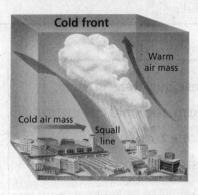

Cold front

Warm air mass

Cold air mass

Squall line

Large cumulus and cumulonimbus clouds usually form along fast-moving cold fronts.

LOOKING CLOSER
3. Describe What type of weather commonly forms along cold fronts?

_____

_____

WARM FRONTS

A **warm front** forms when a warm air mass pushes a cold air mass. The less dense warm air rises over the cooler air. The front moves in the direction the warm air mass was moving. A warm front has a gentle slope. As a result, clouds may stretch ahead of the surface location, or *base*, of the front. A warm front causes precipitation over a large area. It sometimes causes violent weather.

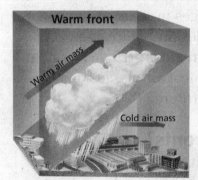

Warm front

Warm air mass

Cold air mass

Clouds may extend ahead of the base of a warm front.

LOOKING CLOSER
4. Compare How is the slope of a warm front different from the slope of a cold front?

_____

_____

STATIONARY AND OCCLUDED FRONTS

A **stationary front** forms when air masses move slowly or not at all. A stationary front causes weather similar to the weather of a warm front. An **occluded front** forms when a fast-moving cold front lifts a warm air mass completely off the ground.

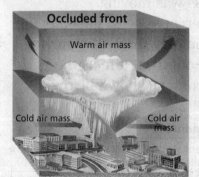

Occluded front

Warm air mass

Cold air mass

Cold air mass

An occluded front forms when a cold air mass lifts a warm air mass off the ground.

LOOKING CLOSER
5. Explain What happens to warm air as an occluded front forms?

_____

_____

How Do Cyclones Form?

A dome of cold air covers each of Earth's polar regions. This cold air meets the tropical air mass of the middle latitudes at the *polar front.*

Waves often form along the polar front, as shown below. A *wave* is a bend that forms in a cold front or a stationary front. This wave is the beginning of a low-pressure storm center called a midlatitude cyclone, or *wave cyclone.* **Midlatitude cyclones** are areas of low pressure that have rotating wind. The wind moves toward the rising air in the center.

Midlatitude cyclones strongly affect weather patterns in the middle latitudes. They usually last for several days. In North America, they usually travel east at about 45 km/h as they spin counterclockwise. The cyclones may lose energy as they pass over mountains.

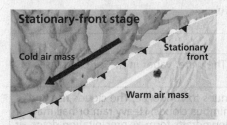

Stationary-front stage

Cold air mass

Stationary front

Warm air mass

Midlatitude cyclones start to form along a stationary front. Winds blow in opposite directions along the front.

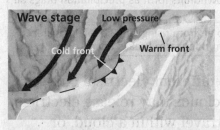

Wave stage Low pressure

Cold front Warm front

A *wave* forms when a bulge of cold air forms and moves slightly ahead of the rest of the front.

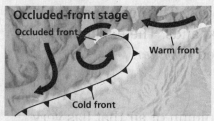

Occluded-front stage

Occluded front

Warm front

Cold front

The fast-moving part of the front moves up until it reaches the warm front. An occluded front forms.

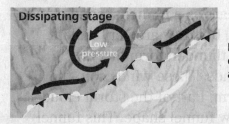

Dissipating stage

Low pressure

Eventually, the system loses most of its energy. The cyclone breaks apart.

Critical Thinking

6. Understand Relationships
Would a wave form along the equator? Why or why not?

_____

_____

_____

_____

Talk About It

Discuss Images With a partner, talk about what these images show. Work together to describe in your own words how a midlatitude cyclone forms.

LOOKING CLOSER

7. Identify Name three types of fronts shown in this midlatitude cyclone.

_____

_____

_____

ANTICYCLONES

Fronts can also cause anticyclones. The air in an *anticyclone* sinks and flows outward from a high-pressure center. In the Northern Hemisphere, air flows clockwise around an anticyclone. Anticyclones bring dry weather. If an anticyclone stays in one place, it may cause air pollution problems and drought. ☑

What Are Some Types of Severe Weather?

Severe weather is weather that can cause property damage and death. Severe weather includes thunderstorms, tornadoes, and hurricanes.

THUNDERSTORMS

A **thunderstorm** is a heavy storm with rain, thunder, lightning, and strong winds. Thunderstorms develop in three stages, as shown below.

Stage	Weather Conditions
Cumulus	Warm, moist air rises. The water vapor in the air condenses to form cumulus clouds.
Mature	The water vapor continues to condense. The clouds rise and become dark cumulonimbus clouds. Heavy rain or hail may fall from the clouds. Downdrafts form as precipitation drags air downward.
Dissipating	Strong downdrafts stop air from rising. The supply of water vapor decreases. The thunderstorm breaks apart.

Parts of a cloud can have different electrical charges. To make the charges equal, clouds may release electricity as *lightning*. Lightning can travel within a cloud, or between a cloud and the ground. The lightning heats the air, and the air quickly expands. The expanding air produces the loud noise called *thunder*.

TORNADOES

A **tornado** is a spinning column of air that has very high winds. A tornado appears as a funnel-shaped cloud. Tornadoes last a short time, but they are very violent.

A tornado forms when a thunderstorm meets high-altitude, horizontal winds. These winds spin the rising air in the thunderstorm. Part of the storm cloud may reach down in a narrow funnel shape. This funnel may or may not touch the ground. If the funnel does touch the ground, it generally moves in an irregular path. ☑

READING CHECK

8. Compare How are anticyclones different from midlatitude cyclones?

_____
_____
_____
_____

LOOKING CLOSER

9. Describe What causes a thunderstorm to break apart?

_____
_____
_____

READING CHECK

10. Explain How do tornadoes form?

_____
_____
_____
_____

SECTION 2 Fronts *continued*

HURRICANES

Tropical storms are intense storms that usually form in the tropics. Tropical storms are different from midlatitude cyclones in many ways. Tropical storms cover a smaller area. They do not have warm or cold fronts. Also, they are usually more violent than midlatitude cyclones. A tropical storm with winds that spiral in toward a low-pressure center is called a **hurricane**. A hurricane has wind speeds of 120 km/h or more.

Hurricanes develop over warm, tropical oceans. A hurricane starts when warm, moist air over the ocean quickly rises. The moisture condenses and releases a large amount of energy as *latent heat*. Latent heat is heat energy that is absorbed or released during a phase change.

A fully developed hurricane has thick bands of clouds. These clouds spin upward around the center, or eye, of the storm. Winds increase near the eye. However, the eye itself is a region of calm, sinking air.

Hurricanes are the most destructive storms on Earth. The most dangerous part of a hurricane is a storm surge. A *storm surge* is a rise in sea level with large waves. A storm surge can flood low coastal areas and cause people to drown. ☑

Scientists classify hurricanes using many factors. These factors include central pressure, wind speed, and storm surge. Scientists use these factors to rank hurricanes on the *Saffir-Simpson scale*, which has five categories. Category 1 storms cause the least damage. Category 5 storms cause the worst damage.

Critical Thinking

11. Draw Conclusions Why are hurricanes more likely to hit states along the Gulf of Mexico than states in the Northeast?

_____

_____

_____

_____

✓ READING CHECK

12. Explain Why is a storm surge so dangerous?

_____

_____

_____

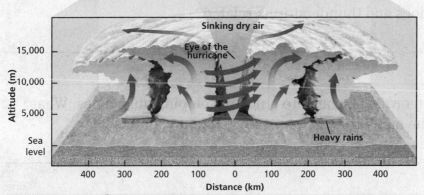

The arrows in this picture represent the movement of moist air. Air moves the fastest near the center of the hurricane.

LOOKING CLOSER

13. Identify How wide is the hurricane in this picture?

_____

Section 2 Review

SECTION VOCABULARY

cold front the front edge of a moving mass of cold air that pushes beneath a warmer air mass like a wedge	**stationary front** a front of air masses that moves either very slowly or not at all
hurricane a severe storm that develops over tropical oceans and whose strong winds of more than 120 km/h spiral in toward the intensely low-pressure storm center	**thunderstorm** a usually brief, heavy storm that consists of rain, strong winds, lightning, and thunder
midlatitude cyclone an area of low pressure that is characterized by rotating wind that moves toward the rising air of the central low-pressure region	**tornado** a destructive, rotating column of air that has very high wind speeds and that may be visible as a funnel-shaped cloud
occluded front a front that forms when a cold air mass overtakes a warm air mass and lifts the warm air mass off the ground and over another air mass	**warm front** the front edge of an advancing warm air mass that replaces colder air with warmer air

1. **Compare** How are the weather patterns produced by cold fronts and warm fronts similar? How are they different?

_____

_____

2. **Summarize** How does a midlatitude cyclone form?

_____

_____

3. **List** What are the three stages in the development of a thunderstorm?

_____

4. **Explain** What causes thunder during a thunderstorm?

_____

_____

5. **Explain** How are tornadoes and thunderstorms related?

_____

_____

6. **Evaluate Methods** A meteorologist wants to study developing hurricanes. What areas of Earth should the meteorologist observe? Explain your answer.

_____

_____

_____

CHAPTER 21 | Weather

SECTION 3 | Weather Instruments

KEY IDEAS

As you read this section, keep these questions in mind:

- What are four instruments that measure conditions in the lower atmosphere?
- How do scientists measure conditions in the upper atmosphere?
- How do computers help scientists understand weather?

How Do Scientists Observe Weather?

You may have seen scientists on the news talking about weather. Scientists who study weather are called *meteorologists*. Meteorologists study weather by measuring atmospheric pressure, humidity, temperature, wind speed, and precipitation. They use special instruments to make these measurements. They use the measurements to *forecast*, or predict, weather patterns. ☑

How Do Scientists Measure Conditions in the Lower Atmosphere?

Meteorologists can predict weather patterns by studying conditions in the lower atmosphere. Scientists use many instruments to measure these conditions.

AIR TEMPERATURE

A **thermometer** is an instrument that shows temperature. One type of thermometer has liquid inside a glass tube. The liquid rises and falls with the temperature, as shown below.

How a Common Thermometer Works

Temperature Change	Liquid Reaction
Increase ↑	Liquid expands and fills more of the tube.
Decrease ↓	Liquid contracts and fills less of the tube.

Another type of thermometer is an *electrical thermometer*. This thermometer uses changes in electric currents to measure temperature. A *thermistor* is a type of electrical thermometer that responds very quickly to temperature changes. For this reason, thermistors are useful where temperatures change quickly.

READING TOOLBOX

Make an Outline As you read, make an outline of this section. Use the headings "Lower Atmosphere Instruments" and "Upper Atmosphere Instruments" in your outline.

READING CHECK

1. Identify Name two conditions scientists measure when they observe weather.

_____

_____

LOOKING CLOSER

2. Describe What happens to the liquid in a thermometer when the temperature rises?

_____

_____

AIR PRESSURE, WIND SPEED, AND WIND DIRECTION

An instrument called a **barometer** detects atmospheric pressure, or air pressure. Changes in air pressure can affect air masses. A decrease in air pressure usually means that a front is approaching. ☑

An instrument called an **anemometer** determines wind speed. A typical anemometer has small cups attached to a center pole. The cups spin as the wind pushes against them. This spinning motion sends a signal that records the wind speed.

An instrument called a **wind vane** shows wind direction. Most wind vanes are arrow-shaped tools that turn freely on a pole. The wind blows the wind vane to point in the same direction as the wind.

Scientists may describe wind direction using one of 16 compass directions. Scientists may also describe wind direction in degrees, as shown below.

Direction the Wind Comes From	Description Using Compass Directions	Description Using Degrees
North	northerly	0°
East	easterly	90°
South	southerly	180°
West	westerly	270°

How Do Scientists Measure Conditions in the Upper Atmosphere?

Scientists study conditions in the upper atmosphere to better understand local and global weather patterns. Scientists use many instruments to measure these conditions.

A **radiosonde** is a package of instruments that rises into the upper atmosphere on a balloon. It measures conditions such as humidity, air pressure, and air temperature. The radiosonde sends the measurements as radio waves to a receiver. The receiver records the information.

Scientists track the path of the radiosonde balloon to measure high-altitude winds. When the balloon reaches a very high altitude, it expands and bursts. The radiosonde falls back to Earth on a parachute. ☑

✓ READING CHECK

3. Explain How can scientists use a barometer to predict weather patterns?

_____

_____

_____

_____

LOOKING CLOSER

4. Identify How would scientists describe the direction of a westerly wind in degrees?

_____

_____

✓ READING CHECK

5. Describe How does a radiosonde travel to and from the upper atmosphere?

_____

_____

_____

SECTION 3 **Weather Instruments** *continued*

RADAR

Radar stands for **ra**dio **d**etection **and r**anging. Radar uses reflected radio waves to measure the speed and location of objects. For example, water particles in the atmosphere reflect radar pulses. Therefore, radar can find precipitation and storms. One kind of radar, Doppler radar, can show the location, movement, and wind patterns of a storm.

WEATHER SATELLITES

Weather satellites carry important instruments that collect information about the atmosphere. In some regions, scientists cannot observe weather from the ground. Satellite images can give weather information for these regions, as shown below.

Satellite cloud images can help scientists measure wind speed and direction at the level of clouds. Satellite images of infrared energy can check cloud, land, and ocean temperatures at night. Satellite instruments can also measure sea conditions, such as currents and waves.

This satellite image shows Hurricane Wilma in 2005 as it approached Florida.

Critical Thinking

6. Compare Why are satellites useful for tracking hurricanes?

_____

_____

_____

_____

LOOKING CLOSER

7. Identify Where was this hurricane located?

_____

_____

COMPUTERS

Before computers, scientists had to solve difficult math equations to describe weather patterns. Now, scientists use powerful computers to understand the weather. These computers can solve equations and store weather data from around the world. Computers can also store weather records from the past. Computers help scientists to constantly improve weather forecasts and better understand the atmosphere.

Section 3 Review

SECTION VOCABULARY

anemometer an instrument used to measure wind speed	**radiosonde** a package of instruments that is carried aloft by a balloon to measure upper atmospheric conditions, including temperature, dew point, and wind velocity
barometer an instrument that measures atmospheric pressure	
radar a system that uses reflected radio waves to determine the velocity and location of objects	**thermometer** an instrument that measures and indicates temperature
	wind vane an instrument used to determine the direction of the wind

1. Identify What are four instruments that scientists use to measure conditions in the lower atmosphere?

_____

2. Describe What are two types of thermometers? Describe how each determines temperature.

_____

_____

3. Compare What is the difference between an anemometer and a wind vane?

_____

_____

4. List Name three instruments scientists use to study the upper atmosphere. Describe how one of the instruments helps scientists learn about the upper atmosphere.

_____

_____

_____

5. Explain How do computers help scientists understand weather?

_____

_____

6. Predict Consequences Think of the weather instruments discussed in this section. How would weather forecasts be different if scientists did not have these weather instruments?

_____

_____

_____

CHAPTER 21 | Weather)

SECTION
4 # Forecasting the Weather

As you read this section, keep these questions in mind:

• How do weather stations communicate weather data?

• How do meteorologists create weather maps?

• How do computer models help meteorologists forecast weather?

• What are three types of weather that meteorologists have tried to control?

When Did Weather Forecasting Begin?

People have tried to predict the weather for thousands of years. In many early cultures, people believed gods controlled the weather. Some people tried to use the positions of the moon and stars to predict weather.

Scientific weather predictions began with the invention of weather instruments, such as the thermometer. The invention of the telegraph in 1844 helped meteorologists share weather information. Over time, national weather services formed. ☑

How Do Meteorologists Collect Weather Data?

Weather observers are people who watch and record changes in weather conditions. Weather observers are at weather stations around the world. They report weather conditions regularly, often many times per hour. Weather observers record many things, including

• atmospheric pressure

• speed and direction of surface wind

• precipitation, temperature, and humidity

• type, amount, and height of clouds

• visibility and general weather conditions ☑

Automatic observing systems also record data. These systems, along with weather observers, send data to a collection center. Weather centers around the world share the data they collect.

Make a List As you read this section, list ways that meteorologists collect, display, and analyze weather data. Discuss your list with a partner.

✓ **READING CHECK**

1. Explain When did people begin to make scientific weather predictions?

_____

_____

✓ **READING CHECK**

2. Identify What are two things that weather observers record?

_____

_____

SECTION 4 **Forecasting the Weather** *continued*

How Do Weather Maps Show Weather Data?

Weather maps display data from weather stations. Weather maps help meteorologists understand the current weather and predict future weather. Meteorologists use symbols and colors to show weather data on a weather map. Meteorologists around the world use and understand these symbols. ☑

WEATHER SYMBOLS

Some weather maps have groups of symbols that show the weather conditions at weather stations. This group of symbols is called a **station model**. Weather symbols describe conditions such as cloud cover and wind speed. The figure below shows examples of weather symbols and a station model.

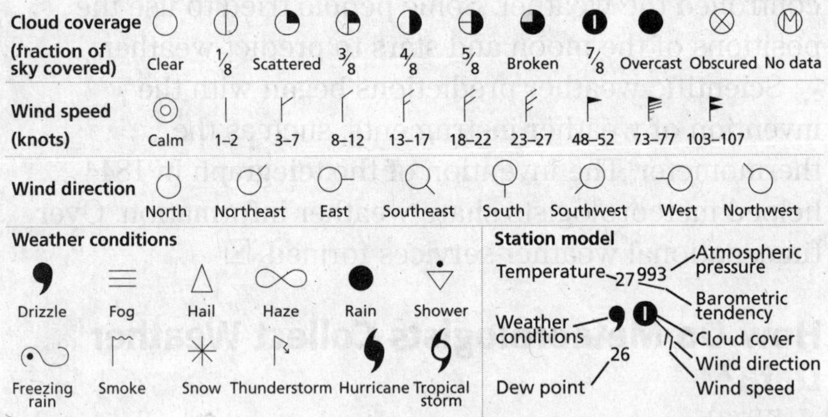

☑ **READING CHECK**

3. Explain Why do meteorologists use weather maps?

_____

_____

_____

_____

LOOKING CLOSER

4. List Identify three pieces of information you can get from a station model.

_____

_____

_____

The station model shows the air temperature and the dew point. The *dew point* is the temperature at which the condensation rate equals the evaporation rate. The dew point shows the level of humidity in the air.

The station model also includes the atmospheric pressure, a three-digit number in the upper right-hand section. This number describes pressure in millibars (mb). The line under the number may be flat or angled. This line shows whether the pressure is rising, falling, or steady.

Talk About It

Use Models Draw the symbols for weather conditions on index cards. With a partner, take turns showing the index cards and naming the weather condition. Then discuss which symbol describes the current weather conditions in your area.

SECTION 4 **Forecasting the Weather** *continued*

PLOTTING TEMPERATURE AND PRESSURE

Scientists use lines on weather maps to connect points of equal measurement. *Isotherms* are lines that connect points of equal temperature. *Isobars* are lines that connect points of equal atmospheric pressure. Scientists use the spacing and shape of isobars to understand the movement of wind, as shown below.

Isobar Spacing and Wind Speed

Spacing	Change in Pressure	Wind Speed
Close together	quick	high
Far apart	gradual	low

Isobars that form circles show areas of high or low air pressure. High-pressure centers are marked with an *H*. Low-pressure centers are marked with an *L*.

PLOTTING FRONTS AND PRECIPITATION

The table below shows the symbols used to represent fronts on a weather map.

Type of Front	Color	Example
Warm	red	━●━●━●━●━●━
Cold	blue	 ━▲━▲━▲━▲━
Occluded	purple OR red and blue	 ━▲━●━▲━●━
Stationary	red and blue	 ━▲━●━▲━●━

Weather maps can also show the types and amounts of precipitation in an area. Different weather maps show precipitation in different ways. Some maps use color to show the type of precipitation. Others use symbols to show type of precipitation, and color to show amount of precipitation.

How Do Meteorologists Forecast Weather?

Meteorologists use computers to mark weather systems on maps. The meteorologists compare the most recent weather map with older maps. This helps them track large weather systems and forecast the weather.

Copyright © Holt McDougal. All rights reserved.

LOOKING CLOSER
5. Compare Which would show stronger winds—widely spaced isobars or closely spaced isobars?

_____

_____

LOOKING CLOSER
6. Draw Next to each front symbol, or on a separate piece of paper, use colored pencils or markers to draw the symbols for the four types of fronts in their correct colors.

SECTION 4 **Forecasting the Weather** *continued*

WEATHER DATA

Doppler radar and satellite images give data about weather patterns. Meteorologists put these data into computers and create weather models. These models can show the possible weather conditions for many days. However, the models are based on general patterns. Meteorologists must interpret the models to make accurate forecasts. ☑

Meteorologists use many sets of data to make a forecast. Some computer models may be better at predicting certain weather conditions. Other computer models may be better at predicting weather in one area. Meteorologists must compare models to make an accurate forecast. If two or more models give the same information, meteorologists are more certain about the forecast.

TYPES OF FORECASTS

Meteorologists make different types of forecasts:

- *Nowcasts* use radar to track current weather conditions.
- *Daily forecasts* predict weather for a 48-hour period.
- *Extended forecasts* look ahead 3 to 5 days.
- *Medium-range forecasts* look ahead 3 to 7 days.
- *Long-range forecasts* look ahead weeks or months. ☑

Meteorologists can make accurate weather forecasts for 0 to 5 days. However, accuracy decreases with each day. Computers help meteorologists make extended forecasts. These computers analyze changes in air movements to predict future weather conditions.

SEVERE WEATHER WATCHES AND WARNINGS

Severe weather can destroy buildings and hurt people if they are not ready. For this reason, meteorologists try to forecast severe weather early. Meteorologists may *issue*, or give, warnings and watches when they forecast severe weather. Meteorologists issue a *watch* when weather conditions make severe weather possible. They give a *warning* when they expect severe weather within 24 hours.

Meteorologists use these alerts to tell people how to be safe during severe weather. The table on the next page shows some ways to be safe during severe weather.

✓ **READING CHECK**

7. Identify Name two weather instruments that provide data for computer models.

_____

_____

✓ **READING CHECK**

8. Identify Which type of forecast predicts tomorrow's weather?

_____

Critical Thinking

9. Infer Is severe weather more likely during a severe weather watch or during a severe weather warning?

_____

SECTION 4 **Forecasting the Weather** *continued*

Severe Weather Safety Tips

Type of Weather	How to Stay Safe
Thunderstorm	Listen to weather updates. Stay or go inside. Avoid electrical objects, running water, metal pipes, and phone lines. If you are outside, avoid tall objects and bodies of water. Get into a car, if possible.
Tornado	Listen to weather updates. Stay or go inside. Go to a basement or small, inner room or closet with no windows. Avoid areas with flying debris. If you are outside, lie in a low area. Protect your head and neck.
Hurricane	Listen to weather updates. Be ready to follow an evacuation route. Stay inside. Avoid areas with flying debris.
Blizzard	Listen to weather updates. Stay or go inside. Dress warmly. Avoid walking or driving in icy conditions.

LOOKING CLOSER

10. Summarize Name two things you should do to stay safe during a tornado.

_____

_____

_____

PREPARING FOR SEVERE WEATHER

People can prepare for severe weather by having a storm preparedness kit. This kit should include a radio, batteries, flashlights, rain gear, blankets, water, canned food, and medicine. People can also practice safety routes so that they know where to go during severe weather.

Can People Control the Weather?

Some meteorologists are studying ways to control rain, hail, and lightning. One method for producing rain is *cloud seeding*. In this process, scientists add certain particles to clouds. These particles cause precipitation to fall from the clouds. Cloud seeding can also prevent severe precipitation. Some scientists have used cloud seeding on possible hail clouds. This caused rain to fall instead of hail. ☑

✓ **READING CHECK**

11. Define What is *cloud seeding?*

_____

_____

_____

_____

HURRICANE CONTROL

Scientists have also seeded hurricanes. The scientists added frozen nuclei to hurricanes to reduce their intensity. This process does not always work. Most scientists have stopped trying to control hurricanes because the technology is limited.

LIGHTNING CONTROL

Some scientists have tried to control lightning. They added silver-iodide nuclei to possible lightning storms. However, scientists are not sure if this process really affects lightning.

Section 4 Review

SECTION VOCABULARY

station model a pattern of meteorological symbols that represents the weather at a particular observing station and that is recorded on a weather map

1. Explain How do weather stations communicate weather data? Use the term *station model* in your answer.

_____

_____

2. Organize Complete the concept map below with the terms *warning, isotherm, station model, isobar, watch,* and *weather map.*

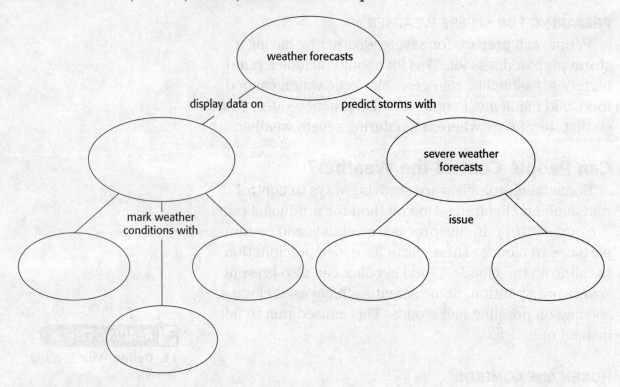

3. Describe How do meteorologists use computer models to forecast weather?

_____

_____

4. List Name three types of weather that meteorologists have tried to control.

_____

5. Make Inferences Why might people want to use cloud seeding to produce rain?

_____

_____

SECTION 1 Factors That Affect Climate

KEY IDEAS

As you read this section, keep these questions in mind:

- What are the two main characteristics of an area's climate?
- How does latitude determine the amount of solar energy that Earth receives?
- How do the different rates at which water and land are heated affect climate?
- What are the effects of topography on climate?

What Is Climate?

Weather and climate are not the same thing. *Weather* is the condition of the atmosphere at a particular time. **Climate** is the pattern of weather conditions for an area over a long period of time.

An area's climate has two main characteristics: temperature and precipitation. An area's average yearly temperature and precipitation can give you important information about the area's climate. However, the yearly range of temperatures and precipitation in an area is also important, as shown in the photo below.

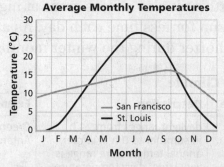

Average Monthly Temperatures

St. Louis and San Francisco have the same average yearly temperature. However, they have very different yearly temperature ranges.

The *yearly temperature range* of an area is the difference between the area's highest and lowest monthly average temperatures. Similarly, the *yearly precipitation range* of an area is the difference between the area's highest and lowest monthly average precipitation.

Several factors influence the temperature and precipitation levels of an area. The three factors that have the greatest influence on climate are latitude, heat absorption and release, and topography.

READING TOOLBOX

Ask Questions As you read this section, underline any ideas that you don't understand. When you finish reading, write several questions about the underlined ideas. Work in pairs to try to figure out the answers.

LOOKING CLOSER

1. Describe How are the yearly temperature ranges of St. Louis and San Francisco different from one another?

_____

_____

_____

_____

_____

_____

_____

SECTION 1 **Factors That Affect Climate** *continued*

How Does Latitude Affect Climate?

The most important factor that determines a region's climate is the region's latitude. Different latitudes on Earth receive different amounts of solar energy. ☑

SOLAR ENERGY

The more solar energy an area receives, the higher the average temperatures in the area will be. The angle at which the sun's rays hit Earth determines how much solar energy an area receives.

At the equator, the sun's rays hit Earth at a 90° angle. The sun's rays are concentrated on a small area. Therefore, temperatures at the equator are high. At higher latitudes, the sun's rays hit Earth at a smaller angle. Therefore, the sun's rays are spread out over a larger area. As a result, temperatures at higher latitudes are low. ☑

Earth's axis is tilted. Thus, the angle at which the sun's rays hit Earth changes as Earth orbits the sun. During winter in the Northern Hemisphere, the northern half of Earth tilts away from the sun. Therefore, the Northern Hemisphere receives less solar radiation, and temperatures are lower. At the same time, the Southern Hemisphere is tilted toward the sun, so its temperatures are higher.

During winter, Earth's tilt also causes areas at higher latitudes to face the sun for less time each day. As a result, the days are shorter during the winter months.

READING CHECK

2. Identify What is the most important factor that determines a region's climate?

_____

READING CHECK

3. Explain Why are temperatures high at the equator?

_____

_____

_____

_____

LOOKING CLOSER

4. Interpret Which region has the smallest yearly temperature range?

_____

_____

Effects of Latitude on Climate

Region	Latitude Range	Description	Examples
Polar regions	60°N–90°N and 60°S–90°S	daylight ranges from 24 h in summer to 0 h in winter; annual temperature range is very large; daily temperature range is very small	Greenland, Antarctica
Middle latitudes	about 20°N–60°N and about 20°S–60°S	daylight changes during the year, but less than in polar regions; yearly temperature range is smaller than in polar regions	most of North America and Europe
Equator	0° to about 20°N and 0° to about 20°S	daylight changes little during the year; yearly temperature range is smaller than in middle latitudes	parts of Africa and South America

SECTION 1 **Factors That Affect Climate** *continued*

GLOBAL WIND PATTERNS

Solar energy heats the air above Earth's surface. The warmer the surface is, the warmer the air above it is. Therefore, belts of cool, high-pressure air form near the poles. Belts of warm, low-pressure air form near the equator. These differences in air pressure produce global winds.

Global winds affect precipitation and temperature. Areas in different wind belts often have different climates. For example, the equatorial region is located in the *doldrums*. Within the doldrums, air rises and cools, making water vapor condense. Therefore, the equatorial region receives large amounts of precipitation.

In contrast, the *subtropical highs* exist between 20° and 30° latitude. Within the subtropical highs, air sinks. As it sinks, it becomes warmer and less humid. Therefore, the subtropical highs generally receive little precipitation.

In the middle latitudes, at 45° to 60° latitude, warm tropical air meets cold polar air. This produces large amounts of precipitation. In high-pressure areas above 60° latitude, air is cold and dry. Therefore, precipitation in these regions is low.

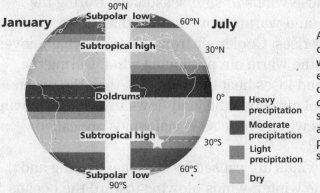

How Does Heat Absorption Affect Climate?

The amount of heat that air absorbs or releases depends on the temperature of the land or water beneath it. Land and water absorb and release heat differently.

Land is opaque and unmoving, so it heats more quickly than water. Surface water, on the other hand, is transparent and moves continuously. Waves and currents replace warm surface water with cooler water. This action prevents the surface temperature from increasing rapidly.

Critical Thinking

5. Apply Concepts Weather maps typically show areas of high pressure and low pressure. Why might a low-pressure area be more likely to have storms?

_____

_____

_____

_____

_____

_____

LOOKING CLOSER

6. Interpret South Africa (shown on the map with a star) is a country on the southern tip of the African continent. During which season will this country receive the most precipitation?

_____

SECTION 1 **Factors That Affect Climate** *continued*

SPECIFIC HEAT AND EVAPORATION

Even when it is not in motion, water warms more slowly than land. It also releases heat energy more slowly. This is because the specific heat of water is higher than that of land. **Specific heat** is the amount of energy needed to change the temperature of 1 g of a substance by 1 °C. ☑

The temperatures of land and water at the same latitude also vary because of differences in heat loss through evaporation. Evaporation affects water surfaces more than land surfaces, because water surfaces contain more water.

OCEAN CURRENTS

Warm and cold ocean currents can heat or cool the air above them. Therefore, ocean currents can affect an area's climate. For example, wind can blow warm air above a warm ocean current onto the nearby land. The warm air can make the land's climate warmer.

SEASONAL WINDS

In some areas, temperature differences between land and water cause winds to shift seasonally. During the summer, the land warms more quickly than the ocean. The warm air rises. Cooler air from over the ocean moves in to replace the warm air, producing wind. During the winter, the land loses heat more quickly than the ocean does. The cool air above the land flows toward the ocean and produces wind. These seasonal winds are called **monsoons**. ☑

Monsoon winds are caused by seasonal heating and cooling. In the winter, winds blowing toward the oceans can cause dry weather and droughts. In the summer, winds blowing toward the land bring moisture from the ocean. These summer winds can cause heavy rainfall and flooding.

READING CHECK

7. Explain Why does land heat more quickly than water?

_____

_____

READING CHECK

8. Define What is a monsoon?

_____

_____

_____

_____

LOOKING CLOSER

9. Identify Complete the table to describe summer and winter monsoon winds.

Effects of Seasonal Winds on Climate

Season	Direction the Monsoon Blows	Effects on Climate
Winter		Winter monsoon winds bring dry weather and droughts.
Summer	from ocean toward the land	

SECTION 1 **Factors That Affect Climate** *continued*

EL NIÑO–SOUTHERN OSCILLATION

The *El Niño–Southern Oscillation*, or *ENSO*, is a cycle of changing wind and water-current patterns. Every 3 to 10 years, **El Niño**, the warm-water phase of the ENSO, makes surface-water temperatures in some areas rise. The event changes the interaction of ocean and air. This change can alter global weather patterns.

During El Niño, some areas have more typhoons, cyclones, and floods. Droughts may strike other areas. The ENSO also has a cool-water phase called *La Niña*. La Niña can also affect weather patterns. For example, during La Niña, some areas experience more hurricanes. ☑

What Effect Does Topography Have on Climate?

The surface features of land, or *topography*, also influence climate. Topographical features, such as mountains, can control air flow through a region.

Changes in *elevation*, or height above sea level, can cause temperature changes. Temperature generally decreases as elevation increases. Even along the equator, high mountain peaks can be cold enough to be covered with snow.

Mountains can also influence climate by creating an effect called a *rain shadow*, as shown below. When a moving air mass comes into contact with a mountain range, the air rises and cools. The rising and cooling produces precipitation. The precipitation falls mainly on one side of the mountain. As a result, the air that flows down the other side is warmer and drier.

> **READING CHECK**
>
> **10. Explain** What is La Niña?
>
> _____
>
> _____

> **LOOKING CLOSER**
>
> **11. Infer** Which side of the mountain would you expect to have more vegetation? Why?
>
> _____
>
> _____
>
> _____
>
> _____
>
> _____

As air rises, it cools and releases moisture.

As air sinks, it compresses and warms.

Mountains cause air to rise, cool, and lose moisture as air passes over them. This process creates the rain shadow effect.

Section 1 Review

SECTION VOCABULARY

climate the weather conditions in an area over a long period of time **El Niño** the warm-water phase of the El Niño–Southern Oscillation; a periodic occurrence in the eastern Pacific Ocean in which the surface-water temperature becomes unusually warm	**monsoon** a seasonal wind that blows toward the land in the summer, bringing heavy rains, and that blows away from the land in the winter, bringing dry weather **specific heat** the quantity of heat required to raise a unit mass of homogenous material 1 K or 1 °C in a specified way, given constant pressure and volume

1. Identify What are the two main characteristics that describe the climate of an area?

_____

2. Explain How does the latitude of an area on Earth determine the amount of sunlight the area receives?

_____

_____

_____

3. Explain Why do areas near the poles receive little to no daylight during the winter?

_____

_____

_____

4. Compare What is the difference between El Niño and La Niña?

_____

_____

5. Describe How do monsoons form?

_____

_____

_____

_____

6. Define What is a rain shadow?

_____

_____

_____

_____

CHAPTER 22 | Climate)

SECTION 2 | Climate Zones

KEY IDEAS

As you read this section, keep these questions in mind:

• What are the characteristics of the three types of tropical climates?

• What are the characteristics of the five types of middle-latitude climates?

• What are the characteristics of the three types of polar climates?

• Why can city climates differ from rural climates?

What Are Climate Zones?

Climate zones are areas on Earth with different temperature ranges and amounts of precipitation. Earth has three major climate zones: tropical, middle-latitude, and polar. Each zone has a specific temperature range. The amount of precipitation within each zone varies. Therefore, each zone also has several types of climates.

What Are the Types of Tropical Climates?

Regions at or near the equator that have high temperatures have **tropical climates**. Tropical climates have an average monthly temperature of at least 18 °C, even during the coldest months. There are three main tropical climates, as shown below.

Characteristics of Tropical Climates

Climate	Temperature and Precipitation	Description
Rain forest	• small temperature range • annual rainfall of about 200 cm	• dense, lush vegetation • high biodiversity • examples: southeast Asia and the Amazon River basin in South America
Desert	• large temperature range • hot days and cold nights • annual rainfall of less than 25 cm	• little to no vegetation • organisms adapted to dry conditions • examples: north Africa, southwestern Asia
Savanna	• small temperature range • annual rainfall of about 50 cm • alternating wet/dry periods	• open grasslands with clumps of drought-resistant shrubs • examples: parts of the following areas: South America, Africa, southeast Asia, northern Australia

READING TOOLBOX

Summarize Relationships Create a cause-and-effect map to show the relationship between different climate conditions (cause) and amount and type of vegetation (effect). For example, one climate condition would be high temperatures and low rainfall. Another would be low temperatures and low precipitation.

LOOKING CLOSER

1. Compare Which area has a drier climate—northern Australia or north Africa?

_____

_____

2. Classify The country of Belize is located in Central America. Southern Belize receives about 160 cm of rain each year. In which tropical climate would you classify southern Belize? Explain.

_____

_____

_____

_____

What Are the Types of Middle-Latitude Climates?

Middle-latitude climates have more moderate temperatures than tropical climates. They have an average maximum temperature below 18 °C in the coldest month and above 10 °C in the warmest month. There are five main middle-latitude climates. ☑

☑ **READING CHECK**

3. Define What general conditions exist in a middle-latitude climate?

_____

_____

_____

_____

_____

LOOKING CLOSER

4. Contrast What is one difference between humid subtropical and Mediterranean climates?

_____

_____

_____

_____

Critical Thinking

5. Compare How are a Mediterranean climate and a savanna climate similar? How are they different?

_____

_____

_____

_____

_____

Characteristics of Middle-Latitude Climates

Climate	Temperature and Precipitation	Description
Marine west coast	• small annual temperature range • between 60 cm and 150 cm of precipitation each year	• deciduous trees and dense forests • mild winters and summers • example: the Pacific Northwest of the United States
Steppe	• large annual temperature range • annual precipitation of less than 40 cm	• drought-resistant vegetation • cold, dry winters • warm, wet summers • example: the Great Plains of the United States
Humid continental	• large annual temperature range • annual precipitation of greater than 75 cm	• wide variety of vegetation and evergreen trees • variable weather • example: the northeastern United States
Humid subtropical	• large annual temperature range • annual precipitation of 75–165 cm	• broadleaf and evergreen trees • high humidity • example: the southeastern United States
Mediterranean	• small annual temperature range • average annual precipitation of about 40 cm	• broadleaf and evergreen trees • long, dry summers • mild, wet winters • example: areas near the Mediterranean Sea and along the coast of central and southern California

What Are the Types of Polar Climates?

The climates in the polar regions are called **polar climates**. These climates all have very low temperatures. The table on the next page describes the three types of polar climates.

Characteristics of Polar Climates

Climate	Temperature and Precipitation	Description
Subarctic	• largest annual temperature range (63 °C) • annual precipitation of 25–50 cm	• evergreen trees • brief, cool summers • long, cold winters
Tundra	• average temperature below 4 °C • annual precipitation of about 25 cm	• treeless plains • nine months of temperatures below freezing
Polar icecap	• average temperature below 0 °C • low annual precipitation (less than 25 cm)	• few living things • temperatures below freezing all year • high winds • much of the land and ocean covered by thick sheets of ice year-round

What Are Local Climates?

The climate of a small area is called a **microclimate**. Microclimates are influenced by vegetation density and human-made structures. Human-made structures absorb solar energy and radiate it as heat. Vegetation does not radiate as much heat energy. Therefore, average temperatures may be a few degrees higher in cities than in rural areas.

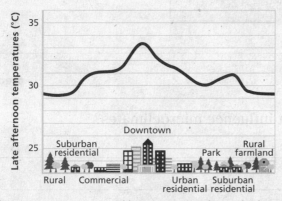

Urban areas have more pavement and less vegetation than suburban and rural areas have.

Elevation and bodies of water can also affect local climates. As elevation increases, the temperature in an area decreases. Water absorbs and releases heat more slowly than land. Therefore, water bodies can moderate the temperature of nearby land. Large bodies of water can also increase precipitation. Areas near water have a smaller range of temperatures and more precipitation than other locations at the same latitude.

Critical Thinking

6. Apply Concepts Certain areas in the state of Alaska experience high temperatures in summer and very low temperatures in winter. What type of climate do these areas have?

_____

_____

_____

LOOKING CLOSER

7. Analyze Relationships What is the general relationship between amount of paved surface and temperature?

_____

_____

_____

_____

_____

_____

Section 2 Review

SECTION VOCABULARY

microclimate the climate of a small area **middle-latitude climate** a climate that has an average maximum temperature below 18 °C in the coldest month and an average minimum temperature above 10 °C in the warmest month	**polar climate** a climate that is characterized by average temperatures that are near or below freezing **tropical climate** a climate characterized by high temperatures and heavy precipitation during at least part of the year

1. Compare On the graph below, write the names of the following climates to compare their relative temperatures and amounts of precipitation: humid continental, polar icecap, savanna, subarctic, tropical desert, tropical rain forest, tundra. One climate has already been placed on the graph for you.

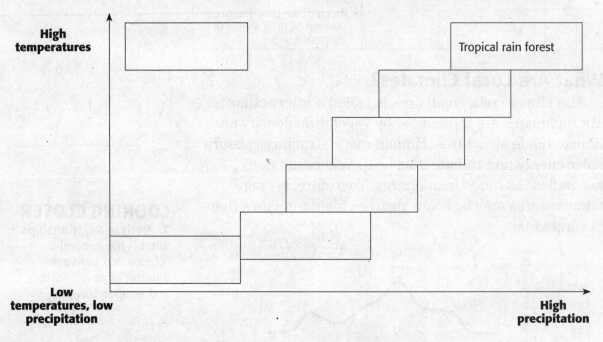

2. Identify What are four factors that influence microclimates?

_____

_____

3. Explain Why are cities often a few degrees warmer than surrounding rural areas?

_____

_____

_____

4. Apply Concepts The lowest average monthly temperature in an area is 12 °C. Its highest average monthly temperature is 17.5 °C. In which climate zone is the area most likely located?

_____

_____

CHAPTER 22 Climate

SECTION 3 Climate Change

As you read this section, keep these questions in mind:
- What are some methods of studying climate change?
- What factors may cause climate change?
- What are the possible effects of climate change?
- How can humans minimize their effect on climate change?

How Do People Study Climate Change?

Climatologists are scientists who study and compare past and present climates. They look for patterns that allow them to make predictions about future climates. Scientists also learn about climate change by looking at evidence left by past climates.

One way scientists study past climates is by observing samples of ice called *ice cores*. Typically, climatologists study ice that formed thousands of years ago. The scientists measure the concentration of gases in the ice. These gas concentrations give scientists information about the atmosphere when the ice formed. For examples, high CO_2 concentrations indicate a warmer climate. Decreases in CO_2 happen during ice ages.

The table below describes other methods scientists use study past climates.

Method	What Is Measured	How Measurements Are Interpreted	Length of Time Measured
Sea-floor sediment	^{18}O in shells	• high ^{18}O levels = cool water • lower ^{18}O levels = warm water	hundreds of thousands of years
Fossils	pollen types, leaf shapes, physical features of animals	• flower pollens/broad leaves = warm climates • evergreen pollens, small, waxy leaves = cool climates • physical adaptations to certain climates	millions of years
Tree rings	ring width	• thin rings = cool weather and/or less precipitation	hundreds to thousands of years
Speleothems	^{13}C and ^{18}O in stalagmites	• high ^{13}C levels = El Niño events • low ^{18}O levels = record of individual hurricanes	weeks to hundreds of years

READING TOOLBOX

Outline Create an outline that contains all of the headings in this section. As you read, underline information that relates to the Key Ideas. After you read, use the underlined text to fill in your outline.

LOOKING CLOSER

1. Interpret Tables Which method of studying past climates would allow scientists to learn more about what the climate was like 3 million years ago?

MODELING CLIMATES

Studying climate change is difficult because so many factors influence climate. Scientists use computers to build climate models. These models use huge amounts of data and sort out the variables that influence climate. With computer models, scientists can make a change in one variable to see how that variable affects other conditions. ☑

Climate models can simulate temperature, precipitation, wind patterns, and sea-level changes. As computers become more powerful, climate models will provide more useful information about the global climate system.

What Factors Can Cause Climate Change?

Computer models have helped scientists identify several possible causes of climate change. These causes, or factors, include changes in Earth's orbit, tectonic plate movements, volcanic activity, and human activity.

ORBITAL CHANGES

Recall that cyclic changes in the shape of Earth's orbit, axis tilt, and axis "wobble" can lead to climate change. These factors are described by the *Milankovitch theory*.

Each orbital change has its own effect on climate. Variations in Earth's orbit affect Earth's distance from the sun. This distance can affect temperatures on Earth's surface. Decreasing the tilt of Earth's axis decreases temperature differences between seasons. The wobble of Earth's axis can change the direction of Earth's tilt and reverse the seasons.

✓ **READING CHECK**

2. Explain Why do scientists use computer models to study climate change?

_____

_____

_____

_____

Critical Thinking

3. Infer When is the difference in seasonal temperatures greater—when the tilt of Earth's axis is at 23° or at 24°?

_____

_____

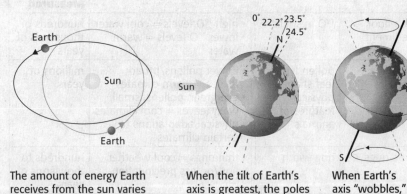

The amount of energy Earth receives from the sun varies more when Earth's orbit is more elongated.

When the tilt of Earth's axis is greatest, the poles receive more solar energy.

When Earth's axis "wobbles," the seasons may reverse.

SECTION 3 **Climate Change** *continued*

PLATE TECTONICS AND VOLCANIC ACTIVITY

The movements of continental plates over millions of years can affect climate. As the positions of continents change, winds and ocean currents change. Changes in wind and water flow affect global temperature and precipitation patterns. Therefore, the climate of a continent is not the same now as it was millions of years ago.

Large volcanic eruptions can also affect climates around the world. Sulfur and ash from eruptions decrease temperatures by reflecting sunlight back into space. These changes may last a few weeks or several years, depending on the strength of the eruption and how long it lasts. ☑

HUMAN ACTIVITY

The ways humans use land and chemicals that human activities produce can affect climate. Burning fossil fuels releases carbon dioxide, or CO_2, into the atmosphere. CO_2 is also released when trees are burned to clear land for agriculture and urban development. An increase in CO_2 concentrations may lead to an increase in global temperatures.

Deforestation also affects climate. Like other plants, trees take in CO_2 from the atmosphere. When too many trees are cut down, more CO_2 stays in the atmosphere. As scientists continue to study climate, they will learn more about how human activity affects climate change. ☑

READING CHECK

4. Explain How can a volcanic eruption affect global climates?

_____

_____

_____

READING CHECK

5. Describe How does vegetation help remove CO_2 from the atmosphere?

_____

_____

Farmers often clear forests to make places to plant their crops.

What Are the Possible Effects of Climate Change?

Scientists are concerned about the possible effects of climate change. Changes in the climate of one area can affect worldwide climates. Even short-term changes may lead to long-lasting effects that could affect life on Earth. Two possible effects of climate change are global warming and sea-level changes.

GLOBAL WARMING

Global temperatures have increased by about 1 °C over the last century. Scientists are trying to find out if this increase is a natural variation or the result of human activities. A gradual increase in average global temperatures is called **global warming**. ☑

Global warming could affect global climate. For example, some areas could have more evaporation, and become drier. Other areas might have more precipitation.

SEA-LEVEL CHANGES

Scientists predict that global temperatures could increase 2 °C to 4 °C during this century. An increase of only a few degrees could melt the polar icecaps and raise the sea level. This rise could cause flooding near coastlines. About 40% to 50% of the world's population lives near coastlines. People living near the coast would have to move, and there would be less agricultural land and fresh water available.

✔ **READING CHECK**

6. Define What is global warming?

_____

_____

_____

Critical Thinking

7. Infer Why do you think so much of the world's population lives near coastlines?

_____

_____

_____

_____

LOOKING CLOSER

8. Interpret Graphics If the sea rose by 3 m, which three states would lose the most area?

_____

_____

_____

If the sea level rises, shorelines could drift inland many miles.

SECTION 3 Climate Change *continued*

What Can People Do About Climate Change?

Many countries are working together to reduce the potential effects of global warming. Some countries have passed treaties and laws to reduce pollution. They are also monitoring and changing certain industrial practices. On a local level, some communities have started reforestation projects. During reforestation, people plant trees.

Many communities are working to prevent global warming by planting trees.

INDIVIDUAL EFFORTS

Each person can help reduce pollution that is caused by burning fossil fuels. Activities such as driving cars and using electricity increase the amount of CO_2 in the atmosphere. People can produce less CO_2 by turning off extra lights. People can also turn down the heat in the winter and reduce air conditioning use in the summer. Recycling is also helpful because less energy is needed to recycle some products than to create them from new resources.

TRANSPORTATION SOLUTIONS

Using public transportation and driving fuel-efficient vehicles can help reduce CO_2 emissions as well. A vehicle burns fuel more efficiently when it is properly tuned. When the tires of a car are properly inflated, the car uses less fuel. Driving at a consistent speed is another way to help a vehicle burn fuel more efficiently.

Recently, car manufacturers have begun to develop cars that are more fuel efficient. *Hybrid cars* use both gasoline and electricity. These cars release less CO_2 into the air than other cars do.

Critical Thinking

9. Identify Relationships What is the relationship between reforestation and decreasing global warming?

_____

_____

_____

_____

_____

_____

Talk About It

Identify Research some other ways that humans can help prevent global warming. Present your findings to the class.

Section 3 Review

SECTION VOCABULARY

climatologist a scientist who gathers data to study and compare past and present climates and to predict future climate change	**global warming** a gradual increase in the average global temperature

1. Explain What information can climatologists learn from fossils?

_____

_____

2. Evaluate Methods Climatologists look at many pieces of evidence to study climate change. These pieces of evidence can support each other. Describe one way in which scientists can use ice cores to check the results of a sea-floor sediment test. Then, identify the different information the two methods provide.

_____

_____

_____

_____

3. Compare Plate tectonics and orbital changes affect Earth's climate in different ways. What is one difference in the way the two processes affect climate change?

_____

_____

_____

4. Describe Relationships How does deforestation affect Earth's atmosphere?

_____

_____

5. Explain One potential effect of global warming is a change in Earth's sea levels. Why are many people concerned about such a change?

_____

_____

_____

6. Identify Name three ways that humans can reduce the potential effects of global warming.

_____

_____

CHAPTER 23 | The Ocean Basins

SECTION 1 | The Water Planet

What Is the Global Ocean?

Earth has more liquid water on its surface than any other planet in the solar system. In fact, 71% of Earth's surface is covered by liquid water. Most of Earth's water is found in its oceans. All the oceans on Earth are connected to each other. Therefore, scientists often refer to all the oceans on Earth as the **global ocean**. The global ocean is divided into five major oceans: the Atlantic, Pacific, Indian, Arctic, and Southern Oceans.

Ocean	Average Depth	Characteristics
Pacific	4.3 km	contains more than half the ocean water on Earth; contains the deepest point in the oceans on Earth (11 km below the surface)
Atlantic	3.8 km	covers about one-fifth of Earth's surface
Indian	3.9 km	is the warmest ocean
Southern	4.5 km	extends from the coast of Antarctica to 60°S latitude
Arctic	1.3 km	surrounds the North Pole

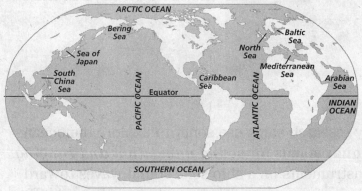

The global ocean is divided into many oceans and seas.

Seas are also part of the global ocean. The main difference between a sea and an ocean is that a **sea** is smaller than an ocean. Most seas are partially surrounded by land.

READING TOOLBOX

Outline As you read this section, create an outline of the section. Use the headings from the section in your outline.

LOOKING CLOSER

1. Compare In which ocean is the average water depth the greatest? In which ocean is the deepest point found?

_____

_____

_____

_____

LOOKING CLOSER

2. Identify Use five different colors to fill in the areas of each of the five oceans.

How Do Scientists Study the Oceans?

Oceanography is the study of different aspects of the oceans. For example, oceanographers may study plants and animals in the ocean, the ocean floor, or the water's chemical makeup. ☑

THE HISTORY OF OCEANOGRAPHY

Matthew F. Maury was an American naval officer who used naval records to learn about the ocean. In 1855, he published the first textbook about the oceans. From 1872 to 1876, a team of scientists studied the Atlantic, Indian, and Pacific Oceans. They conducted their research aboard a British navy ship called the HMS *Challenger*.

OCEANOGRAPHY TODAY

Today, there are many ships that study the oceans. For example, the *JOIDES Resolution* does scientific research by drilling into the ocean floor. At the beginning of this century, it was the largest and most advanced drilling ship in the world. Today, the Japanese ship *CHIKYU* is one of the most advanced drilling ships.

Scientists on the *JOIDES Resolution* drill into the floor of the ocean. By drilling into the ocean floor, they can learn about plate tectonics and the history of the oceans.

SONAR

Many research ships use sonar to explore the ocean floor. **Sonar** stands for *sound navigation and ranging*. Sonar instruments on a ship send sound waves toward the bottom of the ocean. The sound waves bounce off the ocean floor and return to the ship. Scientists measure how long it takes for the sound waves to return to the ship. They use this information to calculate the depth of the ocean floor. Then, they can create maps of the ocean floor. ☑

LOOKING CLOSER
4. Identify What are two things that scientists on the *JOIDES Resolution* study?

_____

_____

SECTION 1 **The Water Planet** *continued*

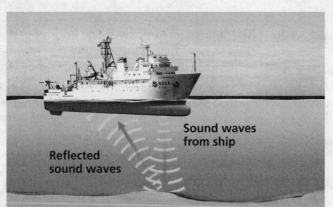

Sound waves from ship

Reflected sound waves

Ships use sonar equipment to send out sound waves. When the waves strike a solid object, they bounce off and return to the ship.

SUBMERSIBLES

Oceanographers also use underwater ships called *submersibles* to study the ocean. Some submersibles, such as bathyspheres and bathyscaphs, can carry people deep below the ocean's surface. A *bathysphere* stays connected to a research ship as the bathysphere dives to the ocean floor. A *bathyscaph* is a submarine that is not connected to a research ship. One of the most well-known bathyscaphs is *Alvin*, the submersible that discovered the *Titanic*.

Some modern submersibles are robots. They can take pictures, collect samples from the ocean floor, and perform other tasks. Because the robots do not have people on board, they can stay underwater for long periods of time. They can also travel to depths that would be dangerous for people.

UNDERWATER RESEARCH

Scientists have used submersibles to make amazing discoveries. Oceanographers used to think that no animals could live very deep in the water. Using submersibles, scientists have discovered unusual animals living on the ocean floor. For example, they found giant clams, blind white crabs, and giant tube worms.

This angler fish lives deep in the ocean. It can produce its own light, which attracts its prey to it.

Critical Thinking

6. Identify Why might scientists use a robot instead of a bathysphere or a bathyscaph?

_____

_____

_____

_____

_____

LOOKING CLOSER

7. Explain What feature helps the angler fish capture prey?

_____

_____

Section 1 Review

SECTION VOCABULARY

global ocean the body of salt water that covers nearly three-fourths of Earth's surface **oceanography** the scientific study of the ocean, including the properties and movements of ocean water, the characteristics of the ocean floor, and the organisms that live in the ocean	**sea** a large, commonly saline body of water that is smaller than an ocean and that may be partially or completely surrounded by land **sonar** *sound navigation and ranging,* a system that uses acoustic signals and returned echoes to determine the location of objects or to communicate

1. Identify What are the five major parts of the global ocean?

_____

_____

2. Identify What are two important events in the history of oceanography?

_____

_____

_____

3. Describe What is the main difference between a sea and an ocean?

_____

_____

4. Identify What are two ways that oceanographers study the ocean?

_____

_____

_____

5. Explain How do scientists use sonar to study the ocean?

_____

_____

_____

_____

_____

6. Describe What are three types of submersibles? Briefly describe each type.

_____

_____

_____

_____

_____

CHAPTER 23 The Ocean Basins
SECTION
2 Features of the Ocean Floor

KEY IDEAS

As you read this section, keep these questions in mind:

• What are the main features of the continental margins?

• What are the main features of the deep-ocean basin?

What Are the Parts of the Ocean Floor?

The ocean floor can be divided into two main parts: the continental margins and the deep-ocean basin. The **continental margins** are the shallow parts of the ocean floor that are made of continental crust. The **deep-ocean basin**, which is made of oceanic crust, begins at the edge of the continental margin. The deep-ocean basin is the deepest part of the ocean.

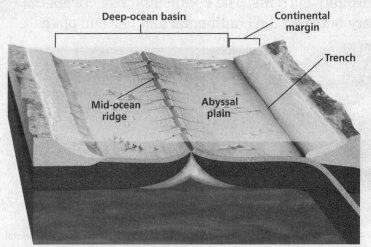

The two parts of the ocean floor are the deep-ocean basin and the continental margins.

What Are the Parts of the Continental Margins?

The continental crust and the oceanic crust do not meet at the shoreline. Instead, they meet beneath the ocean, at the continental margin. The continental margin is made of three main parts: the continental shelf, the continental slope, and the continental rise. ☑

The *continental shelf* is the part of the margin that begins at the shoreline and slopes gently toward the open ocean. It continues until the ocean floor begins to slope more steeply. The average depth of the water covering a continental shelf is about 60 m.

READING TOOLBOX

Organize When you finish reading this section, create a concept map that contains the following terms: *continental shelf, deep-ocean basin, continental margin, continental rise, abyssal plain, trench, mid-ocean ridge, continental slope,* and *seamount.*

LOOKING CLOSER

1. Identify What are two features found in the deep-ocean basin?

_____

_____

✓ READING CHECK

2. Describe Where do continental crust and oceanic crust meet?

_____

_____

SECTION 2 **Features of the Ocean Floor** *continued*

CONTINENTAL SLOPE

The continental slope is the steepest part of the continental margin. It begins at the edge of the continental shelf and continues down to the flattest part of the ocean floor. The boundary between the continental crust and the oceanic crust is at the base of the continental slope.

Submarine canyons can form in the continental shelf and continental slope. *Submarine canyons* are deep, V-shaped valleys. Some of these canyons form near the mouths of major rivers. Others form because of turbidity currents. *Turbidity currents* are very dense currents that carry a lot of sediment down the continental slopes.

CONTINENTAL RISE

The *continental rise* is the base of the continental slope. It is made of large piles of sediment, which form from turbidity currents. The continental rise covers the boundary between the continental and oceanic plates.

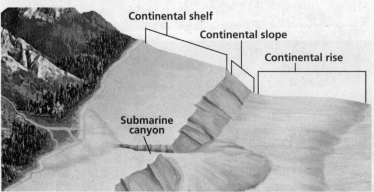

The continental margin is made of three parts: the continental shelf, the continental slope, and the continental rise.

What Are the Parts of the Deep-Ocean Basin?

Deep-ocean basins also have distinct features. The deep-ocean basin includes the abyssal plain, mid-ocean ridges, seamounts, and ocean trenches.

ABYSSAL PLAINS

The flat areas of the deep-ocean basin are called the abyssal plains. Abyssal plains cover about half the deep-ocean basins, and they are Earth's flattest regions. Layers of sediment cover the abyssal plains. Ocean currents and wind carry some sediment from the continental margins. Other sediment forms when organisms that live in the ocean settle to the ocean floor when they die. ☑

Talk About It

Learn Word Roots Use a dictionary or the Internet to learn the meaning of the prefix *sub-*. With a partner, talk about why submarine canyons are called *submarine canyons.*

LOOKING CLOSER

3. Identify Which part of the continental margin has the steepest slope?

_____

_____

 **READING CHECK**

4. Define What are abyssal plains?

_____

_____

SECTION 2 **Features of the Ocean Floor** *continued*

MID-OCEAN RIDGES

A mid-ocean ridge is a long mountain chain that forms on the floor of the ocean. Mid-ocean ridges form where tectonic plates move apart. A narrow rift, or crack, runs through the center of the ridge. Magma rises through the rift and cools to form new rock. The ridge is made of this new rock. As the new rock cools, it becomes denser and begins to sink.

As the direction of the oceanic plate changes, the ridges break into segments. These segments are called *fracture zones*.

SEAMOUNTS

A volcanic mountain on the ocean floor is called a *seamount*. Some seamounts form near hot spots. As lava continues to erupt at a seamount, the mountain gets taller. Seamounts that rise above the ocean's surface form volcanic islands. As the oceanic plate moves away from the hot spot, the islands sink and are eroded by waves. They become *guyots*, which are underwater seamounts with flat tops.

OCEAN TRENCHES

Long, narrow valleys in the deep-ocean basins are called *trenches*. Trenches form when one plate subducts under another plate. Earthquakes often happen near trenches, and volcanoes often form near trenches as well.

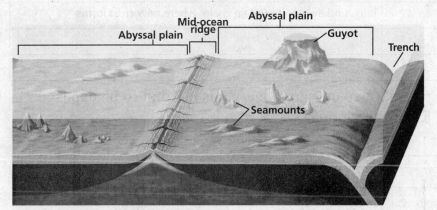

Most of the deep-ocean basin consists of abyssal plains. Several other features are common in the deep-ocean basin as well.

Critical Thinking

5. Compare How are mid-ocean ridges similar to volcanoes?

_____

_____

_____

_____

_____

_____

_____

Talk About It

Evaluate With a partner, discuss the different features of the deep-ocean basin. Which features do you think are most interesting? Why?

LOOKING CLOSER

6. Infer Which is probably older—the guyot or the seamounts near it? Explain your answer.

_____

_____

_____

_____

_____

Section 2 Review

SECTION VOCABULARY

abyssal plain a large, flat, almost level area of the deep-ocean basin **continental margin** the shallow sea floor that is located between the shoreline and the deep-ocean bottom **deep-ocean basin** the part of the ocean floor that is under deep water beyond the continent margin and that is composed of oceanic crust and a thin layer of sediment	**trench** a long, narrow, and steep depression that forms on the ocean floor as a result of subduction of a tectonic plate, that runs parallel to the trend of a chain of volcanic islands or the coastline of a continent, and that may be as deep as 11 km below sea level; also called an *ocean trench* or a *deep-ocean trench*

1. Identify What are the two main divisions of the ocean basin?

_____

2. Compare Describe one similarity and three differences between the continental slope and the continental rise.

_____

_____

_____

3. Explain How are turbidity currents related to submarine canyons?

_____

_____

4. Describe Complete the table below to describe features of the deep-ocean basin.

Feature	Description
	large, flat region
	long, underwater mountain chain; where new crust forms
Seamount	
Trench	

5. Apply Concepts Which part of the continental margin is the first to be exposed when sea level drops? Explain your answer.

_____

_____

_____

6. Explain How are seamounts and guyots related?

_____

_____

CHAPTER 23 The Ocean Basins

SECTION 3 Ocean-Floor Sediments

KEY IDEAS

As you read this section, keep these questions in mind:

• How do ocean-floor sediments form?

• How are ocean-floor sediments classified by their physical composition?

Where Do Ocean-Basin Sediments Come From?

Sediments cover the floor of the ocean. They can enter the ocean when

• a river carries them into the ocean

• the shoreline erodes and sediments are washed into the ocean

• organisms die and their remains sink to the ocean floor.

Scientists study samples of the sediments in the deep-ocean basin. They gather the samples by scooping sediments from the ocean floor or by collecting core samples. **Core samples** are cylinders of sediment that scientists collect by drilling into the ocean floor.

This scientist is studying a core sample aboard the research ship *JOIDES Resolution*.

Scientists have discovered that most sediments in the deep-ocean basin are lighter than sediments closer to shore. Heavier sediments like gravel and sand are usually deposited close to shore. Lighter sediments are usually carried by the water and deposited far from shore.

READING TOOLBOX

Organize As you read this section, create an idea wheel that describes categories of ocean-floor sediments.

LOOKING CLOSER

1. Identify What is the scientist in the figure looking at?

_____

_____

_____

Critical Thinking

2. Explain Why are heavier ocean sediments probably more likely to be found close to shore?

_____

_____

_____

INORGANIC SEDIMENTS

Inorganic sediments can be deposited in the deep-ocean basin in several ways. Some sediments are rock particles that a river carried into the ocean. Most of these sediments stay on the continental shelf. However, turbidity currents can carry some of them into the deep-ocean basin.

Other inorganic sediments reach the deep-ocean basin from the air. These sediments may be rock particles or volcanic dust. The wind carries the sediments until they fall into the ocean. Then they sink to the ocean floor.

Icebergs can also add sediments to the ocean floor. As a glacier moves across land, rock attaches itself to the glacier. When an iceberg breaks off from the glacier, it drifts into the ocean. As the iceberg melts, the rock particles sink to the ocean floor. ☑

Some sediments even come from meteorites. Most of a meteorite vaporizes when it enters Earth's atmosphere. However, some dust remains. That dust can fall into Earth's oceans and become ocean-floor sediment.

When substances that are dissolved in water crystallize, they can also form mineral deposits on the ocean floor. Some of these deposits are called **nodules**. Nodules are often found on the abyssal plain. They are mostly made of manganese, nickel, copper, and iron.

These nodules contain minerals. They are commonly found on the abyssal plains.

BIOGENIC SEDIMENTS

Sediments that are *biogenic* were originally produced by living organisms. They form from the remains of plants and animals in the ocean. In many places on the ocean floor, most of the sediments are biogenic.

☑ **READING CHECK**

3. Identify What are three ways that inorganic sediments can travel from land into the ocean?

_____

_____

_____

LOOKING CLOSER

4. Identify Where are nodules usually found?

_____

_____

How Do Scientists Classify Sediments?

Scientists classify sediments according to their composition. There are two main types of deep-ocean floor sediments: muds and ooze.

MUDS

Muds are made of very tiny particles of rock. Red clay is one type of mud that is commonly found on the abyssal plain. Red clay is made of clay particles mixed with silt, sand, and biogenic material. It can be red, but it can also be gray, blue, green, or yellow-brown.

OOZE

About 40% of the ocean floor is covered with soft, fine sediment called *ooze*. Ooze is mostly made of mud, but it also contains biogenic materials. For example, some ooze may contain the remains of tiny sea organisms. ☑

Scientists divide ooze into two categories: calcareous ooze and siliceous ooze. *Calcareous ooze* is made mostly of calcium carbonate. At depths between 3 km and 5 km, calcium carbonate dissolves in the ocean water. Therefore, calcareous ooze does not form below a depth of 5 km.

Siliceous ooze is made mostly of silicon dioxide. Siliceous ooze forms mainly from the shells of tiny organisms called radiolarians and diatoms. It can be found anywhere. However, the waters near Antarctica contain a lot of radiolarians and diatoms. Therefore, those areas contain a lot of siliceous ooze.

READING CHECK

5. Compare How is ooze different from mud?

_____

_____

Diatom   Radiolarian

Diatoms and radiolarians are important parts of biogenic sediments on the ocean floor. In these figures, both are magnified hundreds of times.

LOOKING CLOSER

6. Identify What do diatoms and radiolarians have in common?

_____

_____

_____

Section 3 Review

SECTION VOCABULARY

core sample a cylindrical piece of sediment, rock, soil, snow, or ice that is collected by drilling	**nodule** a lump of minerals that is made of oxides of manganese, iron, copper, or nickel and that is found in scattered groups on the ocean floor

1. Infer A scientist found that a core sample contained volcanic ash and dust. Where did the sediment probably come from? How did it probably get on the ocean floor?

_____

_____

_____

2. Describe Complete the flowchart to show how icebergs can add sediment to the deep-ocean basin.

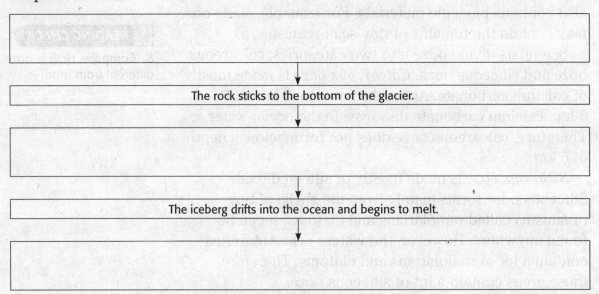

3. Compare How are nodules different from other types of inorganic sediments?

_____

_____

4. Identify What are biogenic sediments?

_____

5. Contrast List two differences between calcareous ooze and siliceous ooze.

_____

_____

_____

CHAPTER 24 Ocean Water

1 Properties of Ocean Water

KEY IDEAS

As you read this section, keep these questions in mind:
- What is the chemical composition of ocean water?
- What are the salinity, temperature, density, and color of ocean water?

What Are the Properties of Ocean Water?

Pure liquid water has no taste, smell, or color. However, the liquid water in the ocean is not pure. Many solids and gases dissolve in ocean water. Ocean water also contains small, solid particles and tiny organisms.

Ocean water is a complex mixture of chemicals. It supports many different *organisms*, or living things. Scientists study properties of ocean water to understand how the ocean, atmosphere, and land interact. Some properties of ocean water that scientists study are
- chemical composition
- salinity
- temperature
- density
- color. ☑

What Gases Dissolve in Ocean Water?

The two main gases in the atmosphere are nitrogen, N_2, and oxygen, O_2. Nitrogen and oxygen are also the main gases dissolved in ocean water. Other gases from the atmosphere are present in ocean water in small amounts. Ocean water also has a large amount of dissolved carbon dioxide, CO_2. ☑

SOURCES OF DISSOLVED GASES

The dissolved gases in ocean water come from many sources. Gases may enter ocean water from streams and rivers. Some gases come from volcanic eruptions under the ocean. Organisms in the ocean also release gases into ocean water. For example, marine organisms that carry out photosynthesis release oxygen into the ocean water. However, most gases in the ocean come from the atmosphere.

READING TOOLBOX

Analyze Comparisons As you read, list examples of comparisons in this section. Identify the objects or conecpts being compared and the signal word or phrase. Signal words for comparisons include *more than* and *less than*.

☑ READING CHECK

1. List Name three properties of ocean water.

_____

_____

_____

☑ READING CHECK

2. Identify What are the two main gases dissolved in ocean water?

_____

_____

SECTION 1 **Properties of Ocean Water** *continued*

Dissolved gases affect the chemical composition of ocean water.

LOOKING CLOSER

3. Identify On the diagram, label four sources of dissolved gases in the oceans.

TEMPERATURE AND DISSOLVED GASES

The temperature of water affects how much gas dissolves in the water. More gas can dissolve in cold water than in warm water. As a result, surface water in cold regions can hold more dissolved gas than water in warm regions can.

Gases can return to the atmosphere from the ocean. If the water temperature rises, the water releases extra gases into the atmosphere. For example, warm oceans near the equator release CO_2 into the atmosphere. Oceans in cooler regions dissolve large amounts of CO_2. Therefore, the ocean and the atmosphere constantly exchange gases as water temperature changes.

Critical Thinking

4. Apply Concepts Why would surface water in the North Atlantic Ocean probably have more dissolved gases than surface water in the Caribbean Sea?

_____

_____

_____

_____

THE OCEAN AS A CARBON SINK

The ocean contains more than 60 times as much carbon as the atmosphere does. The ocean may trap dissolved CO_2 for hundreds to thousands of years. The ocean is often called a *carbon sink* because it can store so much CO_2 ☑.

As a carbon sink, the ocean helps control Earth's climate. The amount of CO_2 in the air affects how the atmosphere traps heat from the sun. The ocean changes the amount of CO_2 in the air when it dissolves CO_2. Therefore, the ocean affects the movement of heat in Earth's atmosphere.

✓ READING CHECK

5. Explain Why is the ocean called a *carbon sink*?

_____

_____

_____

What Solids Dissolve in Ocean Water?

Ocean water is 96.5% pure water, or H_2O. Dissolved solids make up about 3.5% of the mass of ocean water. These dissolved solids are often called *sea salts*. Sea salts give the ocean its salty taste.

SECTION 1 **Properties of Ocean Water** *continued*

COMPOSITION OF DISSOLVED SOLIDS

About 75 chemical elements make up the sea salts in ocean water. The six most abundant elements in sea salts are chlorine, sodium, magnesium, sulfur, calcium, and potassium. Sodium and chlorine combine to form the salt halite. Halite makes up more than 85% of sea salt.

The remaining dissolved solids are made of other salts and minerals, as shown below. *Trace elements* are elements that exist in very small amounts. Gold, zinc, and phosphorous are trace elements in the ocean.

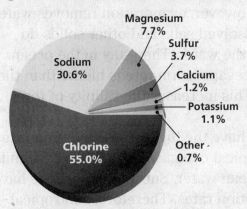

This chart shows the most abundant elements in the dissolved solids in ocean water.

LOOKING CLOSER

6. Identify What is the most abundant element in sea salts?

_____

_____

SOURCES OF DISSOLVED SOLIDS

The elements that form dissolved solids come from three main sources:

• volcanic eruptions

• chemical weathering of rock on land

• chemical reactions between water and new sea-floor rocks

Rivers carry about 400 billion kilograms of dissolved solids into the ocean each year. Most of these dissolved solids are salts. As water evaporates from the ocean, sea salts stay in the ocean. Rain and snow return a very small amount of these salts to the land.

What Is Salinity?

Salinity is a measure of the amount of dissolved solids in a liquid. For example, 1,000 g of ocean water may contain 35 g of solids. The salinity of this water would be written as 35 parts per thousand (ppt), or 35‰. Ten parts per thousand equals 1%. Thus, the ocean is about 3.5% salts. Fresh water is less than 0.1% salts. That is, it has a salinity of less than 1‰. ☑

✓ **READING CHECK**

7. Define What is salinity?

_____

_____

SECTION 1 **Properties of Ocean Water** *continued*

MEASURING SALINITY

Modern instruments measure salinity by recording the conductivity of water. *Conductivity* is a measure of how easily electricity moves through water. Electricity moves more easily through water with high salinity. ☑

What Affects the Salinity of Ocean Water?

Precipitation and evaporation rates affect the salinity of water. Precipitation, such as rain and snow, is made of fresh water. When precipitation falls, the fresh water enters the ocean. However, evaporation removes water from the ocean. Dissolved salts and other solids do not evaporate with the water. They stay in the ocean. In some places, the evaporation rate is higher than the precipitation rate. This increases the salinity of the surface water. ☑

Tropical regions have the highest precipitation rates. For this reason, tropical ocean water has lower salinity than subtropical ocean water. Subtropical regions have the highest evaporation rates. Therefore, subtropical oceans and seas tend to have the highest salinities.

The salinity of most ocean water ranges from 33‰ to 36‰. The global ocean has an average salinity of 34.7‰. However, salinity can vary greatly. For example, the Red Sea has a salinity of 40‰. The high salinity is due to the hot, dry climate around the Red Sea. This climate causes high levels of evaporation.

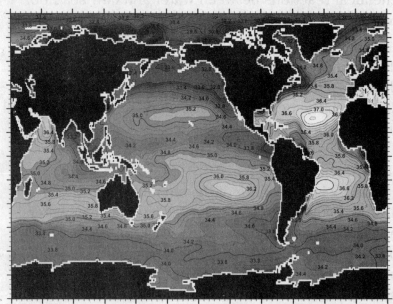

On this map, lighter ocean colors represent higher salinities.

Math *Skills*

10. Calculate What is the range of salinity in ocean water? Express your answer using percentages.

_____

_____

_____

LOOKING CLOSER

11. Identify Which ocean has a higher average salinity—the Pacific Ocean or the Atlantic Ocean?

_____

SECTION 1 **Properties of Ocean Water** *continued*

What Affects the Temperature of Ocean Water?

Solar energy and water movement affect ocean temperatures. The depth and location of ocean water also affect temperature. Scientists mark layers of ocean water based on depth and temperature. These layers include surface water, the thermocline, and deep water. ☑

SURFACE WATER

Waves and currents mix the water near the ocean's surface. This mixing action carries heat down to a depth of 100 m to 300 m. Therefore, the upper 100 m to 300 m of water has a fairly constant temperature. Temperature decreases only slightly as depth increases.

The temperature of surface water decreases as you move closer to the poles. The polar regions receive much less solar energy, or sunlight, than tropical regions do. As a result, polar surface water is much colder than tropical surface water. Tropical oceans can have a surface temperature of 30 °C. The surface temperature in polar oceans can drop to −1.9 °C.

Ocean water freezes at about −1.9 °C. As a result, large areas of sea ice form in polar oceans. A floating layer of sea ice that covers an area of the ocean surface is called **pack ice**. Pack ice can be up to 5 m thick. This layer of ice prevents the water underneath from freezing.

In the middle latitudes, the ocean surface temperature changes with the seasons. The ocean surface temperature may change by 10 °C to 20 °C between summer and winter.

The surface temperature of polar ocean water is below the freezing point of fresh water.

✓ READING CHECK

12. Identify What factors affect ocean temperature?

_____

_____

_____

Talk About It

Compare With a partner, compare the surface water temperatures in different areas of the world. As you discuss, use phrases such as *cooler than* and *warmer than* to make comparisons.

LOOKING CLOSER

13. Explain Why does sea ice form in polar oceans?

_____

_____

_____

THE THERMOCLINE

The thermocline is the layer of water under the surface layer. In the **thermocline**, the water temperature decreases sharply as depth increases. This decrease happens because the sun cannot directly heat ocean water below the surface layer.

The thermocline exists because the warm surface water cannot mix easily with the cold, dense water below. Thus, the thermocline separates the warm surface water and the cold deep water. The temperature of water below the thermocline decreases slowly. ☑

Changes in temperature or currents can affect the depth of the thermocline. These changes can even cause the thermocline to disappear. However, the thermocline is present under most of the ocean surface.

DEEP WATER

In the deep zones of the ocean, the water temperature is usually about 2 °C. The colder the water is, the denser it is. The density of cold, deep water controls the movement of deep ocean currents. This movement happens when the cold, dense water at the poles sinks. The water flows underneath warm water toward the equator.

✓ **READING CHECK**

14. Summarize Why does the thermocline form in ocean water?

_____

_____

LOOKING CLOSER

15. Compare In which zone does temperature decrease most slowly as depth increases?

_____

_____

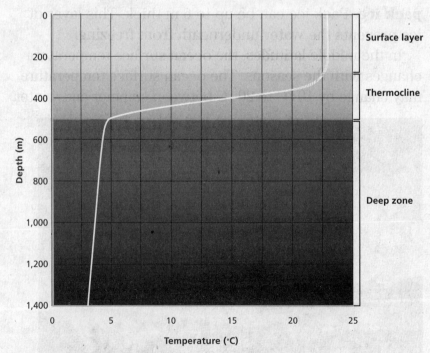

The temperature of ocean water decreases as depth increases.

SECTION 1 **Properties of Ocean Water** *continued*

What Affects the Density of Ocean Water?

Density is the amount of matter (mass) in a certain space (volume). For example, 1 g of pure water has a volume of 1 cm^3. Therefore, the density of water is 1 g/cm^3. Ocean water has a density between 1.020 g/cm^3 and 1.029 g/cm^3. Two main factors affect the density of ocean water: salinity and temperature. The table below summarizes the effects of these factors on density.

Factor	How It Affects Density
Salinity	Dissolved solids add mass to water, but do not increase its volume very much. Therefore, as salinity increases, density increases.
Temperature	Cold water is denser than warm water. Therefore, as temperature decreases, density increases.

Water temperature affects density more than salinity does. Therefore, the densest ocean water is in the polar regions. In these regions, the ocean surface is coldest. The cold, dense water sinks and moves through ocean basins near the ocean floor. ☑

What Is the Color of Ocean Water?

The color of ocean water depends on the way water absorbs or reflects sunlight. The sun produces white light, which includes all the visible wavelengths, or colors, of light. Water absorbs the white light from the sun. Generally, the water reflects only the blue wavelengths. Therefore, ocean water appears blue.

WHY OCEAN COLOR IS IMPORTANT

Substances or organisms in ocean water can affect the color of the water. For example, *phytoplankton* are tiny organisms in the ocean that carry out photosynthesis. Many other organisms eat phytoplankton. Phytoplankton absorb red and blue light, but reflect green light. Therefore, phytoplankton can affect the shade of blue of the ocean.

Scientists can study the color of the ocean to see if phytoplankton are present. Since phytoplankton need certain nutrients, these organisms can show scientists the health of the ocean. If the ocean color shows that no phytoplankton are present, the water may lack nutrients.

LOOKING CLOSER
16. Identify What two factors affect the density of ocean water?

_____

_____

READING CHECK
17. Explain Why does ocean water generally sink near the poles?

_____

_____

_____

_____

_____

Critical Thinking
18. Identify Relationships How would a decrease in phytoplankton affect other ocean organisms?

_____

_____

Section 1 Review

SECTION VOCABULARY

density the ratio of the mass of a substance to the volume of the substance; commonly expressed as grams per cubic centimeter for solids and liquids and as grams per liter for gases	**salinity** a measure of the amount of dissolved salts in a given amount of liquid
	thermocline a layer in a body of water in which water temperature drops with increased depth faster than it does in other layers
pack ice a floating layer of sea ice that completely covers an area of the ocean surface	

1. Explain Why is ocean water denser than fresh water?

_____

_____

2. Summarize How does water temperature affect the ability of ocean water to dissolve gases?

_____

_____

3. Describe What is ocean water made up of?

_____

_____

4. Explain How does the density of ocean water control the movement of deep ocean currents?

_____

_____

5. Explain Why does ocean water appear to be blue?

_____

_____

_____

6. Analyze Processes Suppose that global temperatures increase. How could this change affect the ability of the ocean to absorb CO_2? Explain your answer.

_____

_____

_____

_____

CHAPTER 24 | Ocean Water

SECTION 2 | Life in the Oceans

KEY IDEAS

As you read this section, keep these questions in mind:

- How does marine life affect the chemistry of ocean water?
- Why are plankton called the *foundation of life in the ocean?*
- What are the major zones of life in the ocean?

How Does Marine Life Affect Ocean Chemistry?

Marine organisms are organisms that live in the ocean. Most marine organisms depend on two main factors to survive: sunlight and the nutrients in ocean water. Changes in these factors affect the survival of marine life.

Marine organisms help to balance the chemical composition of ocean water. They remove certain nutrients and gases from the ocean. They also return nutrients and gases to the ocean. For example, some marine organisms absorb carbon, hydrogen, oxygen, and sulfur. Marine organisms that use photosynthesis release oxygen into the water.

The chart below shows an example of how marine organisms recycle nutrients.

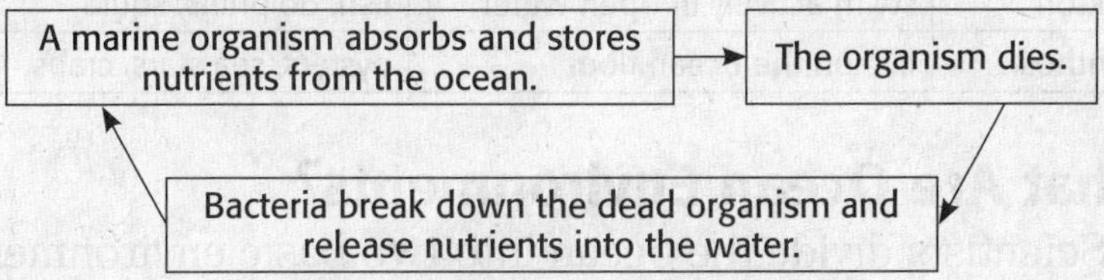

| A marine organism absorbs and stores nutrients from the ocean. | → | The organism dies. |

| Bacteria break down the dead organism and release nutrients into the water. |

UPWELLING

In general, marine organisms get nutrients near the surface of the ocean. When the organisms die, they sink to lower depths. These dead organisms decay and release nutrients back into the deep water.

Nutrients can return to the surface through a process called upwelling. **Upwelling** is the movement of deep, cold, nutrient-rich water to the surface. When wind blows along a coastline, surface water moves away from the shore. Then, more deep water rises to replace the surface water that moved offshore.

READING TOOLBOX

FoldNotes Make a key-term fold to learn the key terms in this chapter. Write each key term on the front of a tab. As you read this section, write the definition of each term under the correct tab.

LOOKING CLOSER

1. Explain How do bacteria help recycle nutrients?

_____

_____

_____

_____

Critical Thinking

2. Identify Relationships How can the movement of wind currents affect ocean chemistry?

_____

_____

_____

_____

SECTION 2 **Life in the Oceans** continued

Movement of surface water

Surface winds

Upwelling

Offshore movement of surface water causes upwelling.

LOOKING CLOSER
3. **Describe** In what direction is the surface water in this picture moving?

_____

_____

MARINE FOOD WEBS

Most marine organisms need sunlight and nutrients. For this reason, most marine organisms live in the upper 100 m of water. Organisms called plankton live in this sunlit zone. The term **plankton** refers to all the tiny organisms that float in the waters of lakes and oceans. ☑

Plankton form the base of ocean food webs. Small marine organisms eat plankton. Larger marine animals eat the small marine organisms. These larger animals fall into two groups: **nekton** and **benthos**. The table below describes nekton and benthos.

✓ READING CHECK
4. **Explain** Why do most marine organisms live near the surface of the water?

_____

_____

_____

Group	Characteristics	Examples
Nekton	swim actively in open water	fish, dolphins, squid
Benthos	live on the ocean floor	oysters, sea stars, crabs

LOOKING CLOSER
5. **Identify** Give two examples of nekton.

_____

_____

What Are Ocean Environments?

Scientists divide the ocean into two basic environments, or zones: the benthic zone and the pelagic zone. The **benthic zone** is the region near the bottom of the ocean. The **pelagic zone** is the upper region above the benthic zone. The amount of sunlight, the water temperature, and water pressure determine which organisms live in these zones.

BENTHIC ZONES

The benthic zone is divided into five smaller zones. The table on the next page describes the depths and characteristics of these zones.

SECTION 2 **Life in the Oceans** *continued*

Benthic Zones

Zone	Characteristics	Organisms
Intertidal zone	shifting tides, breaking waves; constantly changing water depth	seaweed, mussels
Sublittoral zone	has the most organisms of any benthic zone; always underwater; on the continental shelf	sea stars, sea lilies
Bathyal zone	begins at the continental slope; extends to a depth of 4,000 m; little or no sunlight; few photosynthetic organisms	octopuses, sea stars, brachiopods
Abyssal zone	depth of 4,000 m to 6,000 m; no sunlight	sponges, worms
Hadal zone	deeper than 6,000 m; unexplored by humans	unknown, but probably few living things

LOOKING CLOSER
6. Explain Why do few organisms that carry out photosynthesis live in the bathyal zone?

_____

_____

_____

_____

PELAGIC ZONES

The pelagic zone lies above the benthic zone. The pelagic zone is divided into two smaller zones: the neritic zone and the oceanic zone.

The *neritic zone* has plenty of sunlight, mild temperatures, and low water pressure. These are ideal conditions for marine life. Nekton are common in the neritic zone. These nekton include many fish and other types of seafood that humans eat. ☑

The *oceanic zone* stretches into the deep waters past the continental shelf. The oceanic zone is divided into four zones based on depth. The *epipelagic zone* is the upper area of the oceanic zone. It gets some sunlight and contains many marine organisms. The *mesopelagic*, *bathypelagic*, and *abyssopelagic zones* are the deeper areas of the oceanic zone. The amount of marine life in the pelagic zone decreases as depth increases.

☑ READING CHECK
7. Describe the neritic zone.

_____

_____

_____

_____

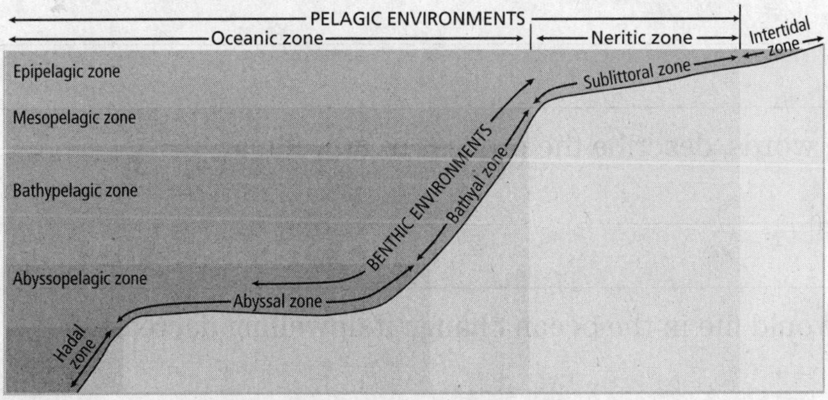

This diagram shows the locations of marine environments.

LOOKING CLOSER
8. Identify Which pelagic zone is the farthest from the ocean surface?

_____

_____

Section 2 Review

SECTION VOCABULARY

benthic zone the bottom region of oceans and bodies of fresh water	**pelagic zone** the region of an ocean or body of fresh water above the benthic zone
benthos organisms that live at the bottom of oceans or bodies of fresh water	**plankton** the mass of mostly microscopic organisms that float or drift freely in the waters of aquatic (freshwater and marine) environments
nekton all organisms that swim actively in open water, independent of currents	**upwelling** the movement of deep, cold, and nutrient-rich water to the surface

1. Organize Complete the concept map below using the terms *neritic zone, benthic zone, oceanic zone,* and *pelagic zone.*

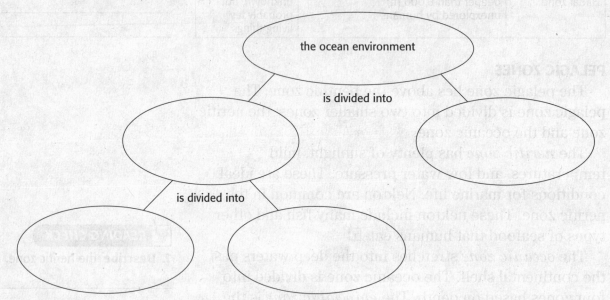

2. Explain How do marine organisms affect the chemistry of ocean water?

_____

_____

3. Explain What is the role of plankton in ocean food webs?

_____

_____

_____

4. Summarize In your own words, describe the process of upwelling.

_____

_____

_____

5. Make Predictions How would life in the ocean change if upwelling decreased?

_____

_____

_____

CHAPTER 24 Ocean Water

Ocean Resources

KEY IDEAS

As you read this section, keep these questions in mind:

- What are three important ocean resources?
- How does water pollution threaten marine organisms?

What Are Some Ocean Resources?

The ocean gives humans many natural resources. These resources include

- fresh water
- minerals
- food.

How Can the Ocean Provide Fresh Water?

Earth's growing population needs more and more fresh water. The ocean can help provide fresh water through desalination. **Desalination** is a process that removes salt from ocean water. Desalination can increase the freshwater supply, but it can be expensive.

There are different methods of desalination. One method is distillation. During *distillation*, ocean water is heated to remove the salts. Heat causes the liquid water to evaporate and leave the salts behind. The water condenses as pure fresh water. However, distillation uses a large amount of expensive heat energy. ☑

Another method of desalination is *freezing*. When water freezes, the first ice crystals that form do not contain salt. The ice can be removed and melted to get fresh water. This process uses much less energy than distillation does.

Reverse osmosis is a popular method of desalination. This process uses special membranes to remove salt. The membranes block salts and allow water to pass through.

What Minerals and Energy Resources Does the Ocean Provide?

Humans *extract*, or take out, many minerals and energy resources from the ocean. Some of these resources are easy to extract from the ocean. Others are difficult or expensive to extract.

READING TOOLBOX

Clarify Concepts Take turns reading this section aloud with a partner. Stop to discuss ideas that seem confusing.

READING CHECK

1. Explain Why is distillation so expensive?

_____

_____

PETROLEUM

The most valuable resource in the ocean is petroleum, or crude oil. Offshore petroleum deposits exist in the sea floor around the world. People drill oil wells to get the petroleum, as shown below. About 25% of the world's oil comes from offshore wells. People use this oil to make fuels such as gasoline.

This offshore oil rig is in the Gulf of Mexico.

LOOKING CLOSER

2. Explain How do people extract petroleum from the ocean?

_____

_____

_____

NODULES

Nodules are lumps of minerals found on the abyssal plain of the ocean. Nodules are a valuable source of manganese, iron, copper, nickel, cobalt, and phosphates. However, nodules are difficult and expensive to get because they are in very deep water. ☑

TRACE MINERALS

Many useful minerals are dissolved in ocean water. However, some of these minerals are found only in small, or trace, amounts. The extraction of these trace minerals is too expensive to be practical.

✓ **READING CHECK**

3. List Name three minerals found in nodules.

_____

_____

_____

How Does the Ocean Provide Food?

Food is a very important resource from the ocean. Seafood is a good source of protein. People get seafood through fishing and aquaculture.

FISHING

Talk About It

Discuss With a partner, talk about ways that the ocean supports human life. Support your ideas with examples from the text.

Fish are a source of food for people around the world. As a result, fishing has become an important industry. However, people sometimes remove too many fish from the ocean. Overfishing can cause fish populations to collapse. A collapsed fish population can damage the ecosystem and the fishing industry. Many countries have laws to prevent overfishing.

SECTION 3 **Ocean Resources** *continued*

This seaweed farm in Madagascar is a type of aquaculture.

AQUACULTURE

People can also get seafood by raising aquatic organisms. This method is called **aquaculture**. Places that use aquaculture are called *aquatic farms*. Aquatic farms can raise many animals, such as catfish, salmon, oysters, and shrimp. However, pollution can damage aquatic farms. Some aquatic farms may even cause pollution. ☑

An aquatic farm can produce more food than a farm on land. A farm on land can use only the top layers of soil. An aquatic farm can use water at different depths to produce food. In the future, aquatic farms may pump nutrient-rich deep water to the surface. The nutrients would help the organisms on the farm grow.

How Does Pollution Affect the Ocean?

People often dump wastes into the ocean. In the past, the ocean was able to absorb the wastes. However, the human population is producing more wastes and toxic substances. The ocean can no longer absorb the waste and renew itself.

Coastal areas and beaches are closest to the sources of pollution. As a result, these areas are in the most danger. Pollution destroys clam and oyster beds. Sea birds get caught in plastic products. Beaches close because of sewage and oil spills.

Pollution also affects other areas of the ocean. Substances like mercury, lead, and DDT pollute the ocean. These substances can make fish unsafe to eat.

Scientists and governments are working to reduce pollution. For example, laws now prohibit the use of DDT in the United States. These laws and others like them may help protect the oceans.

LOOKING CLOSER

4. Compare How is aquaculture different from fishing?

_____

_____

_____

_____

✔ *READING CHECK*

5. Identify What is one problem with aquaculture?

_____

_____

Critical Thinking

6. Predict Consequences How can pollution affect the fishing industry?

_____

_____

_____

_____

Section 3 Review

SECTION VOCABULARY

aquaculture the raising of aquatic plants and animals for human use or consumption	**desalination** the process of removing salt from ocean water

1. Organize Complete the spider map below to describe ocean resources. Use the terms *nodules, freezing, aquaculture, distillation, petroleum, reverse osmosis,* and *fishing* to complete the spider map.

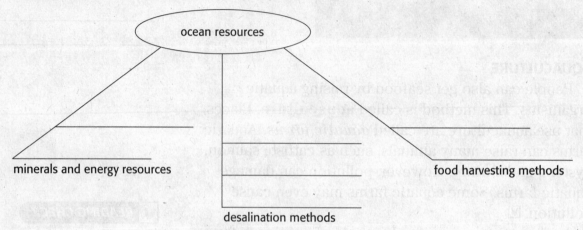

2. Describe In your own words, describe three methods of desalination.

_____

_____

_____

_____

3. Identify What is the most valuable resource that humans can get from the ocean?

_____

4. Define What is aquaculture, and why is it important?

_____

_____

5. Explain How does pollution threaten ocean environments?

_____

_____

6. Evaluate Methods Ocean water contains trace amounts of gold. Why isn't the ocean a key source of gold?

_____

_____

_____

CHAPTER 25 Movements of the Ocean

SECTION 1 Ocean Currents

As you read this section, keep these questions in mind:

• How do wind patterns, Earth's rotation, and continental barriers affect surface currents in the ocean?

• What determines the direction of a surface current?

• How do differences in the density of ocean water affect the flow of deep currents?

What Factors Affect Surface Currents?

The water in the ocean moves in currents. A **current** is a large stream of water that flows through the ocean. Scientists put ocean currents in two categories: surface currents and deep currents. **Surface currents** move near the surface of the ocean. The figure below shows Earth's major surface currents.

> **READING TOOLBOX**
>
> **Clarify Concepts** Take turns reading this section out loud with a partner. Stop to discuss ideas that seem confusing.

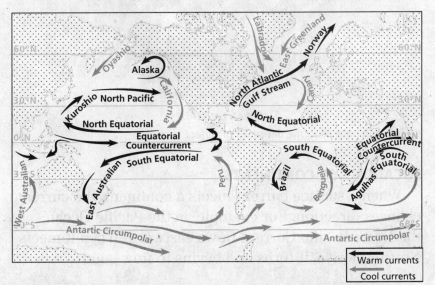

Warm currents
Cool currents

> # Talk About It
> **Discuss** Study this map with a partner. Together, identify some of the patterns you see in the movement of surface currents.

As you can see on the map above, some surface currents are warm, and others are cold. Warm surface currents are most common in areas near the equator. Cold surface currents generally form near the poles. ☑

If you study the map carefully, you will notice some patterns in how the surface currents move. Global winds, the locations of continents, and Earth's rotation all affect the directions of surface currents.

> **LOOKING CLOSER**
> **1. Identify** Do most of the currents in the Northern Hemisphere move clockwise or counterclockwise?
>
> _____
> _____

> ✓ **READING CHECK**
> **2. Describe** Where do most cold surface currents form?
>
> _____
> _____

SECTION 1 **Ocean Currents** *continued*

WIND

Wind causes all surface currents. Because wind is moving air, it has kinetic energy. As wind moves across the ocean's surface, its energy is transferred to the water. Therefore, the water at the surface begins to move. ☑

Remember that wind forms because of differences in air pressure. Air always moves from areas of high pressure to areas of low pressure. The moving air is wind.

Global wind belts have the strongest effect on surface currents. Recall that there are three main global wind belts: trade winds, westerlies, and polar easterlies. The map below shows where these wind belts occur.

LOOKING CLOSER

4. Compare What is the main difference between the trade winds in the Northern Hemisphere and the trade winds in the Southern Hemisphere?

_____

_____

_____

_____

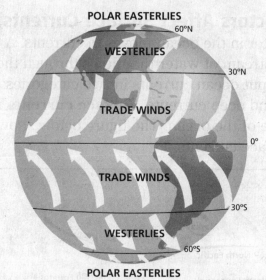

Global wind belts affect the directions of surface currents.

LOCATIONS OF CONTINENTS

When a surface current meets a continent, the current changes direction. For example, in the Pacific Ocean, the North Pacific Current flows eastward. When it meets North America, it turns and begins to flow south.

EARTH'S ROTATION

As Earth spins on its axis, ocean currents and wind belts curve. This curving is called the **Coriolis effect**. The Coriolis effect causes surface currents to move in huge circles. These circles of water are called **gyres**. In the Northern Hemisphere, the gyres flow clockwise. In the Southern Hemisphere, they flow counterclockwise. The Coriolis effect is the main factor that determines the direction in which a gyre flows. ☑

What Are the Major Surface Currents?

Scientists often divide surface currents into four groups: equatorial currents, Southern Hemisphere currents, North Atlantic currents, and North Pacific currents.

EQUATORIAL AND SOUTHERN HEMISPHERE CURRENTS

The equator passes through the Atlantic, Pacific, and Indian Oceans. Warm currents flow through each of these oceans near the equator. The North Equatorial Current and the South Equatorial Current both flow westward. Between them is the weaker *Equatorial Countercurrent*, which flows eastward. ☑

There are three main gyres in the Southern Hemisphere. These gyres are found in the Atlantic Ocean, the Pacific Ocean, and the Indian Ocean. Like the other gyres in the Southern Hemisphere, they flow counterclockwise.

The *Antarctic Circumpolar Current* is also found in the Southern Hemisphere. This current flows eastward. No continents strongly affect it. Therefore, it flows freely and completely circles Antarctica.

NORTH ATLANTIC CURRENTS

The North Atlantic Gyre is the main gyre in the North Atlantic Ocean. The figure below shows the four currents that make up the North Atlantic Gyre.

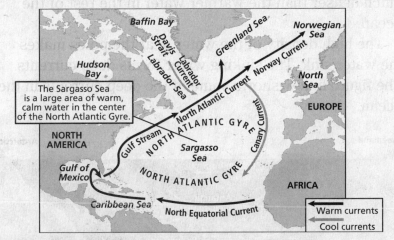

The North Atlantic Gyre is made up of the Gulf Stream, the North Atlantic Current, the Canary Current, and the North Equatorial Current.

The **Gulf Stream** is a warm surface current that flows northward along the east coast of North America. It affects the climate of much of eastern North America.

---

6. Identify Name three equatorial surface currents.

_____

_____

_____

Critical Thinking

7. Explain The water in the Sargasso Sea is very calm. It does not have many strong currents. What is the most likely reason for this?

_____

_____

_____

_____

_____

_____

NORTH PACIFIC CURRENTS

The pattern of currents in the North Pacific Ocean is similar to the pattern in the North Atlantic Ocean. A large gyre called the *North Pacific Gyre* is located in the North Pacific Ocean. The North Pacific Gyre is made of four currents: the Kuroshio Current, the North Pacific Current, the California Current, and the North Equatorial Current.

What Factors Affect Deep Currents?

Deep currents are cold, dense currents that flow far below the ocean's surface. Deep currents form when water near the poles sinks and flows beneath warmer, shallower water. The ocean water near the poles sinks because it is denser than the water in the rest of the ocean. Two main factors affect the density of the ocean water: salinity and temperature. ☑

Much of the water near the poles is frozen in icebergs and sea ice. Remember that when ocean water freezes, the ice that forms does not contain salt. The salt remains in the liquid water that is left behind when the ice forms. Therefore, the unfrozen water has a high salinity. The high salinity increases the water's density.

Ocean water near the poles is very cold. The molecules in cold water are closer together than the molecules in warm water. Therefore, the cold water near the poles is much denser than the warmer water in the rest of the ocean.

The high density of the water near the poles makes the water sink. The sinking water forms deep currents. The figure below shows some of the deep currents in the ocean.

✔ **READING CHECK**

8. Explain Why does the water near the poles sink?

_____

_____

_____

Critical Thinking

9. Apply Concepts Which current is probably denser—North Atlantic Deep Water or Antarctic Intermediate Water? Explain your answer.

_____

_____

_____

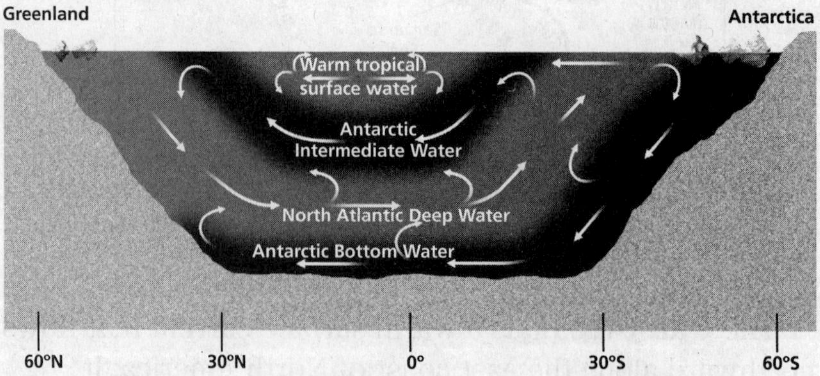

_____

Greenland   Antarctica

Warm tropical surface water
Antarctic Intermediate Water
North Atlantic Deep Water
Antarctic Bottom Water

60°N   30°N   0°   30°S   60°S

The two main deep currents are Antarctic Bottom Water and North Atlantic Deep Water.

SECTION 1   **Ocean Currents** *continued*

ANTARCTIC BOTTOM WATER

The water near Antarctica is very cold, and its salinity is high. Therefore, the water is very dense. In fact, the water near Antarctica is the densest in the world. This dense, cold water sinks to the ocean bottom and forms a deep current called the *Antarctic Bottom Water*. ☑

NORTH ATLANTIC DEEP WATER

The water in the North Atlantic Ocean, south of Greenland, is very cold. It also has a high salinity. This cold, salty water forms a deep current that moves along the east coast of the United States. It flows southward below the Gulf Stream.

Near the equator, this deep current divides. Part of it rises and begins to flow northward again. The other part continues to flow south toward Antarctica. This part of the North Atlantic Deep Water is less dense than the Antarctic Bottom Water. Therefore, it flows above the Antarctic Bottom Water. ☑

What Are Turbidity Currents?

A turbidity current is a strong current caused by an underwater landslide. Unlike surface and deep currents, turbidity currents last for only a short time. In addition, turbidity currents do not flow in specific, predictable directions, like surface and deep currents do. Instead, turbidity currents generally happen quickly and unpredictably. The flowchart below shows how a turbidity current forms.

✔ **READING CHECK**

10. Identify Where is the densest ocean water in the world?

_____

_____

✔ **READING CHECK**

11. Explain Why does the North Atlantic Deep Water flow above the Antarctic Bottom Water?

_____

_____

_____

_____

Large amounts of sediment build up on the continental shelf or continental slope.

↓

The sediment suddenly breaks off and slides downhill.

↓

The sediment mixes with the ocean water and makes it *turbid*, or cloudy. It is denser than the water around it.

↓

The turbid water flows quickly beneath the surrounding water in a turbidity current.

Section 1 Review

SECTION VOCABULARY

Coriolis effect the curving of the path of a moving object from an otherwise straight path due to Earth's rotation	**Gulf Stream** the swift, deep, and warm Atlantic current that flows along the eastern coast of the United States toward the northeast
current a horizontal movement of water in a well-defined pattern, such as a river or stream	**gyre** a huge circle of moving ocean water found above and below the equator
deep current a streamlike movement of ocean water far below the surface	**surface current** a horizontal movement of ocean water that is caused by wind and that occurs at or near the ocean's surface

1. **Compare** Describe the difference between how surface currents form and how deep currents form.

_____

_____

_____

2. **Describe** What happens when a surface current meets a continent?

_____

_____

3. **Explain** Describe two reasons why water near the poles is denser than water in the rest of the ocean.

_____

_____

_____

4. **Compare** What are two differences between turbidity currents and surface or deep currents?

_____

_____

_____

5. **Identify** What causes gyres to form?

_____

_____

_____

6. **Explain** Why is the Antarctic Circumpolar Current able to flow all the way around Antarctica without bending north or south?

_____

_____

_____

CHAPTER 25 Movements of the Ocean

SECTION 2 **Ocean Waves**

KEY IDEAS

As you read this section, keep these questions in mind:

• What factors affect the formation and size of waves?

• How do waves interact with the coastline?

• What causes destructive ocean waves?

How Do Waves Form?

A **wave** is a disturbance in a solid, liquid, or gas. Waves carry energy. Water waves, such as the waves in the ocean, form when wind blows over a body of water. When the wind blows over the water, some of the wind's energy is transferred to the water. The energy forms small waves called *ripples*. If the wind keeps blowing, more energy moves into the water, and the ripples become larger waves.

An ocean wave has a crest and a trough. The *crest* is the highest part of the wave. The *trough* is the low part between two crests. The table below summarizes some other characteristics of waves.

Characteristic	Description
Wave height	difference in height between the top of a crest and the bottom of a trough
Wavelength	distance between two crests or two troughs that are next to each other
Wave period	time it takes for two wave crests to pass a certain point
Wave speed	how quickly a wave moves, calculated by dividing the wavelength by the wave period

READING TOOLBOX

Predict Before reading this section, write each heading from the section on a piece of paper. Below each heading, write what you think you will learn.

Math *Skills*

1. Calculate The wavelength of a wave is 100 m. It takes 5 s for two crests to pass a certain point. What is the speed of the wave?

_____

Crest ⟷ Crest

Trough

LOOKING CLOSER

2. Describe Label the wavelength and the wave height on the diagram.

How Does the Water in a Wave Move?

The energy in a wave moves from water molecule to water molecule. However, each water molecule actually moves very little. The figure below shows that each water molecule moves in a circle when a wave passes.

When a wave passes, only the energy moves in the direction of the wave. The water molecules move in a circular motion.

LOOKING CLOSER

3. Describe Suppose you were in a boat in the middle of the ocean. What kind of motion would you most likely notice as waves passed by the boat?

_____

_____

_____

_____

Waves get their energy from wind that blows over the ocean's surface. Therefore, molecules on the surface of the ocean move in a larger circle than molecules deeper in the ocean. At the surface, the circles' diameters equal the height of the wave. Deeper in the water, the circles' diameters are smaller.

Critical Thinking

4. Apply Concepts Suppose a wave has a wavelength of about 10 m. How deep in the water would you have to go before the water would no longer be affected by the wave?

_____

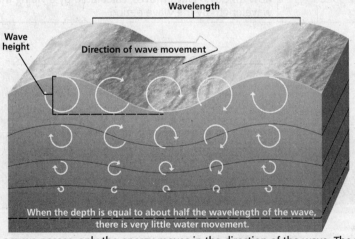

Wavelength

Wave height

Direction of wave movement

When the depth is equal to about half the wavelength of the wave, there is very little water movement.

When a wave passes, only the energy moves in the direction of the wave. The water molecules move in a circular motion.

What Factors Affect Wave Size?

Three factors affect the size of a wave:

- the speed of the wind
- the length of time the wind blows
- **fetch**, or the distance the wind can blow across open water. ☑

Very large waves form when strong steady winds blow for a long time over a long fetch. These winds are common during storms. Sometimes, however, strong winds blow only in short gusts. When that happens, waves with different heights form, and the water becomes choppy.

When the weather is calm, groups of small waves move across the ocean's surface. These waves are called *swells*. Swells that reach shore may have formed thousands of kilometers away from shore. ☑

How Do Waves Change When They Approach the Coastline?

As a wave approaches the coastline, its bottom touches the ocean floor. This makes the bottom of the wave slow down. However, the top of the wave continues to move quickly. The top of the wave gets farther and farther ahead of the bottom of the wave. Eventually, the top of the wave topples and forms a *breaker*.

As waves approach the coastline, breakers begin to form.

Breakers scrape sediment off the ocean floor and move it along the coastline. They also erode the coastline. If the slope of the ocean floor is steep, breakers topple, or fall over, with a lot of force. They cause a lot of erosion. If the slope is less steep, breakers topple more slowly. They cause less erosion.

READING CHECK

5. Define What is fetch?

_____

_____

_____

READING CHECK

6. Describe Under what conditions do swells form?

_____

_____

LOOKING CLOSER

7. Explain How do the wave's wavelength and wave height change as it approaches the shoreline?

_____

_____

_____

SECTION 2 Ocean Waves *continued*

REFRACTION

Most waves approach the shoreline at an angle. As they reach shallow waters, they begin to bend toward the coastline. This bending is called **refraction**.

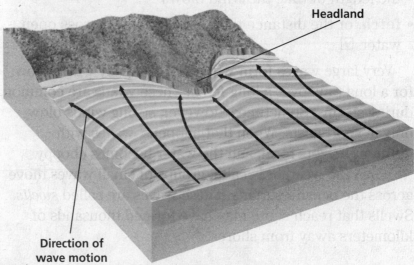

Headland

Direction of wave motion

The waves are bending as they approach the shoreline. This bending is called *refraction*.

LOOKING CLOSER
8. Describe According to this diagram, do waves bend toward headlands or away from headlands?
_____
_____

LONGSHORE CURRENTS

Longshore currents form where waves approach a beach at an angle. The water flows onto the beach at an angle, but it flows straight back into the ocean. The flowing water carries sand down the coastline. If there is a bay or inlet along the coastline, the waves refract. The longshore currents lose energy and deposit the sand along the coast. These sand deposits form *sandbars*, or ridges of sand.

UNDERTOWS AND RIP CURRENTS

After breakers crash on a beach, gravity pulls the water from the breakers back into the ocean. This water forms a current under the water called an *undertow*. Undertows are usually not very strong.

Unlike undertow, *rip currents* are very strong. Rip currents also form when water from breakers return to the ocean. However, the water in a rip current returns to the ocean through deep paths in underwater sandbars. Rip currents can carry a swimmer away from shore very quickly. Therefore, they are very dangerous.

Critical Thinking
9. Contrast What is one difference between rip currents and undertow?
_____
_____
_____

SECTION 2 **Ocean Waves** *continued*

What Are Tsunamis?

Tsunamis are giant ocean waves. Unlike other waves, they are not caused by wind. Earthquakes on the ocean floor cause most tsunamis. Other tsunamis are caused by volcanic eruptions or underwater landslides. Here are some other facts about tsunamis: ☑

- Tsunamis are commonly called *tidal waves*, even though they are not caused by tides.

- Tsunamis have long wavelengths—sometimes as long as 500 km.

- The wave height of a tsunami is usually less than 1 m, so ships cannot feel tsunamis.

- A tsunami may travel as fast as 890 km/h—as fast as a jet airplane.

Tsunamis can be very destructive. Tsunamis carry enormous amounts of energy and involve very large amounts of water. When the tsunami hits the shore, all of the energy is released at once. It can cause a great deal of destruction, as shown below.

In 2004, a tsunami destroyed many communities along the coast of Sri Lanka. The earthquake that caused the tsunami had a moment magnitude of 9.0.

As a tsunami approaches the shore, its speed decreases and its height increases. It may reach a height of 30 to 40 m. Eventually, the wave collapses, and huge amounts of water crash onto the shore.

✓ **READING CHECK**

10. Contrast How are tsunamis different from other waves?

_____

_____

_____

_____

LOOKING CLOSER
11. Identify What caused the tsunami that struck Sri Lanka in 2004?

_____

_____

Section 2 Review

SECTION VOCABULARY

fetch the distance that wind blows across an area of the sea to generate waves	**wave** a periodic disturbance in a solid, liquid, or gas as energy is transmitted through a medium
refraction the process by which ocean waves bend directly toward the coastline as they approach shallow water	**wave period** the time required for identical points on consecutive waves to pass a given point

1. Identify What three factors affect the size of a wave?

_____

_____

_____

2. Describe How do ocean waves form?

_____

_____

_____

3. Describe What happens to waves as they approach a coastline at an angle?

_____

_____

4. Apply Concepts The wave shown below has a period of 5 s. Label its crest and trough. Then, in the space below the picture, calculate the wave's speed.

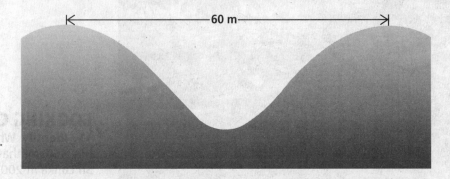

5. Define What is a tsunami?

_____

_____

_____

CHAPTER 25 Movements of the Ocean

SECTION 3 Tides

KEY IDEAS

As you read this section, keep these questions in mind:

- How does the gravitational pull of the moon cause tides?
- How are spring tides and neap tides similar and different?
- How do tidal oscillations affect tidal patterns?
- How does the coastline affect tidal currents?

What Causes Tides?

If you stand on a beach for a long time, you can see the water level slowly change. This change in the water level is called the **tide**. *High tide* is when the water level is at its highest. *Low tide* is when the water level is at its lowest.

Gravity causes most tides. As the moon revolves around Earth, the force of gravity between the moon and Earth pulls on the ocean water. The moon's gravitational force is strongest on the part of Earth that is closest to the moon. Therefore, the water on that side bulges outward, toward the moon. That side of Earth has a high tide.

At the same time, the ocean water on the far side of Earth is not pulled as much toward the moon. Therefore, it bulges away from the moon. It forms a high tide, too. ☑

As ocean water flows toward the area of high tides, the water level in other areas drops. Therefore, low tides form halfway between the two high tides, as shown below.

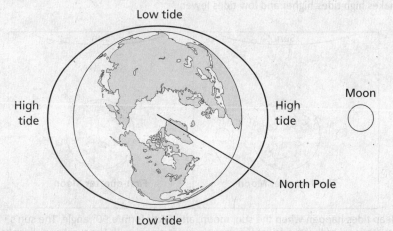

Because of Earth's rotation, most places on Earth have two high tides and two low tides every day.

READING TOOLBOX

Organize As you read this section, underline the main ideas and important terms. When you finish reading the section, create a concept map about tides using the ideas and terms you underlined.

✓ READING CHECK

1. Explain Why are there two tidal bulges?

_____

_____

_____

_____

_____

_____

Critical Thinking

2. Predict If the moon were on the opposite side of Earth, where would the tidal bulges be?

_____

_____

SECTION 3 **Tides** *continued*

How Does Earth's Rotation Affect Tides?

Earth rotates on its axis once every 24 h. All areas of the ocean pass under the moon every 24 h 50 min. Therefore, the times of high tide and low tide in an area are about 50 min later each day.

Because there are two tidal bulges, most places have two high tides and two low tides each day. A **tidal range** is the difference between the water level at high tide and at low tide. The tidal range is different in different places.

How Does the Sun Affect Tides?

The moon's gravitational pull is the main cause of tides. However, the sun's gravitational pull can also change the height of the tides.

The pictures below show the positions of the sun, Earth, and moon during spring tides and neap tides. *Spring tides* happen when the daily tidal range is larger than normal. *Neap tides* happen when the daily tidal range is lower than normal.

Math *Skills*

3. Calculate One day, the high tides on one coastline are at 9:56 A.M. and 10:24 P.M. About what time will the high tides be the next day?

_____

_____

Critical Thinking

4. Describe When do the lowest low tides occur?

_____

_____

_____

LOOKING CLOSER

5. Identify During which moon phases do spring tides happen?

_____

_____

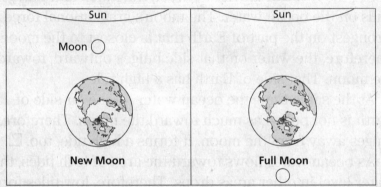

Spring tides happen when the sun, the moon, and Earth are aligned. The sun's gravitational pull and the moon's gravitational pull combine. This stronger pull makes high tides higher and low tides lower.

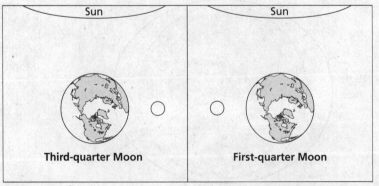

Neap tides happen when the sun, moon, and Earth form a 90° angle. The sun's gravitational pull acts against the moon's gravitational pull. The weaker pull makes high tides lower and low tides higher.

How Are Tides in Different Areas Different?

Tides are different in different parts of the ocean. The size, shape, depth, and location of a body of water affect the tides there. For example, the eastern coastline of North America has two high tides and two low tides every day. However, along the Gulf of Mexico, only one high tide and one low tide occur each day. ☑

Tidal oscillations also affect tidal patterns. **Tidal oscillations** are slow, rocking motions of ocean water. They happen as tidal bulges move through the oceans.

Tidal oscillations are not obvious in the open ocean or near straight coastlines. However, in some seas, tidal oscillations can reduce the effects of tidal bulges. As a result, these seas have very small tidal ranges. In other bodies of water, tidal oscillations can strengthen the effects of tidal bulges. As a result, these seas have very large tidal ranges.

The Bay of Fundy in Canada has a tidal range of 15 m. This large tidal range is caused by tidal oscillations.

What Are Tidal Currents?

While the tide is rising, ocean water moves onto the shore. When the tide falls, ocean water moves away from the shore. These movements are called **tidal currents**. When a tidal current flows toward the coast, it is called *flood tide*. When the tidal current flows back toward the ocean, it is called *ebb tide*. The time period between flood tide and ebb tide is called *slack water*.

When a river flows into the ocean, a tidal bore can sometimes form. A *tidal bore* is a surge of water that rushes upstream. Some tidal bores are large waves that move very quickly until they lose energy.

LOOKING CLOSER

7. Infer How would these pictures be different if tidal oscillations did not exist?

_____

_____

_____

_____

_____

_____

Section 3 Review

SECTION VOCABULARY

tidal current the movement of water toward and away from the coast as a result of the rise and fall of the tides	**tidal range** the difference in levels of ocean water at high tide and low tide
tidal oscillation the slow, rocking motion of ocean water that occurs as the tidal bulges move around the ocean basins	**tide** the periodic rise and fall of the water level in the oceans and other large bodies of water

1. Describe How can tidal oscillations affect tidal ranges?

_____

_____

_____

2. Explain How does the moon cause tidal bulges to form?

_____

_____

_____

3. Infer If you were in a boat on the open ocean, would you be able to see a tidal bore? Why or why not?

_____

_____

4. Compare Complete the Venn diagram below to compare spring tides and neap tides.

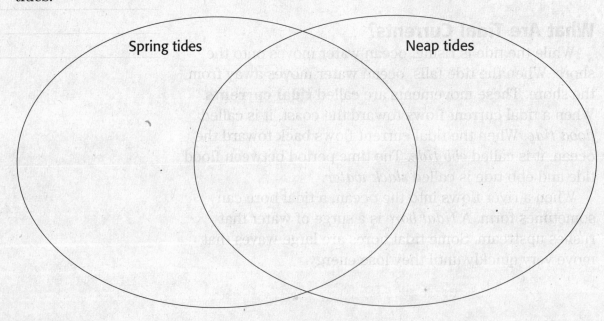

Spring tides   Neap tides

SECTION 1 | Viewing the Universe

KEY IDEAS

As you read this section, keep these questions in mind:

• In terms of age, size, and organization, what is the universe like?

• What are the visible and invisible parts of the electromagnetic spectrum?

• How are refracting telescopes and reflecting telescopes similar and different?

• How are optical telescopes different from telescopes for invisible electromagnetic radiation?

What Is Astronomy?

People studied the sky long before the telescope was invented. Farmers observed changes in daylight and star positions to track the seasons. Sailors observed stars to navigate in new places. Today, people study the sky to learn about the universe and how it changes. The scientific study of the universe is called **astronomy**. Scientists who study the universe are *astronomers*.

Astronomers study the universe for many reasons, including

• to discover new objects in space, such as planets, stars, black holes, and nebulas

• to find new energy sources by studying how stars shine

• to protect humans from possible dangers, such as a collision between asteroids and Earth ☑

Many government organizations, such as NASA, support research in astronomy. Private organizations also support this type of research.

What Are the Characteristics of the Universe?

One branch, or area, of astronomy is cosmology. *Cosmology* is the study of the origin, properties, processes, and evolution of the universe. Astronomers who study cosmology may use telescopes to observe distant objects. They may also use math and computer models to calculate time and distance in the universe.

READING TOOLBOX

Ask Questions As you read this section, underline ideas that seem confusing. Write any questions you have about the section in the margin or in your notebook. When you finish reading, discuss your questions with a partner. Together, try to find the answers to your questions.

✓ READING CHECK

1. Explain How could astronomy protect people from danger?

_____

_____

_____

THE AGE OF THE UNIVERSE

Astronomers think that the universe began about 13.7 billion years ago. At that time, all the matter in the universe began to expand outward from a single, tiny point. Scientists call this expansion the *big bang*. Since the big bang, the universe has expanded. In fact, the universe is expanding faster and faster.

THE ORGANIZATION OF THE UNIVERSE

The closest part of the universe to Earth is our solar system. The solar system includes the sun, Earth, and the other planets. It also includes smaller objects, such as dwarf planets, asteroids, and comets. ☑

Our solar system is part of a galaxy. A **galaxy** is a large collection of stars, dust, and gas held together by gravity. Our solar system is part of the *Milky Way galaxy*. The universe contains billions of other galaxies.

MEASURING DISTANCE IN THE UNIVERSE

The units of measurement used on Earth are too small to measure distances between objects in space. Astronomers use astronomical units to describe distances in the solar system. An **astronomical unit**, or AU, is the average distance between Earth and the sun. This distance is about 150 million km.

Astronomers also use the speed of light to describe distances in the universe. In one year, light travels 9.46×10^{12} km. This distance is called a *light-year*. Apart from the sun, the closest star to Earth is 4.22 light-years away. Therefore, light from this star takes 4.22 years to reach Earth.

✔ READING CHECK

2. Identify Name three objects that are found in our solar system.

_____

_____

_____

Math *Skills*

3. Calculate Venus is about 0.7 AU from the sun. About how many million kilometers is Venus from the sun?

_____

_____

Critical Thinking

4. Apply Concepts What are some objects that most likely exist in the Whirlpool galaxy?

_____

_____

The Whirlpool galaxy, M51, is 31 million light-years from the Milky Way.

SECTION 1 **Viewing the Universe** *continued*

How Do Astronomers Observe Space?

Light lets us observe the world around us. We can see objects in space because of light. Some objects in space, such as stars, produce light. Other objects, such as planets, reflect light from stars. Visible light is only one form of energy that comes from objects in space. Astronomers study different forms of energy to learn more about the universe.

THE ELECTROMAGNETIC SPECTRUM

Visible light is a form of energy. This energy is part of the electromagnetic spectrum. The **electromagnetic spectrum** is all the wavelengths of electromagnetic radiation. Light, radio waves, and X rays are examples of electromagnetic radiation. ☑

VISIBLE ELECTROMAGNETIC RADIATION

Electromagnetic radiation is made of waves that have fixed wavelengths. The human eye can see only wavelengths that are in the range of visible light.

White visible light is made of different colors of light. You can see these colors when white light refracts, or bends. Light refracts when it passes from one substance to another. For example, a rainbow appears because light passes from the air into raindrops and back out again.

During refraction, the different colors appear because each color of light has a different wavelength. The shortest wavelengths of visible light are blue and violet. The longest wavelengths are orange and red. Each wavelength refracts at a different angle. When white light moves from one substance into another, the different wavelengths bend by different amounts. The differences in bending make the colors spread apart, as shown below.

READING CHECK

5. Define What is the electromagnetic spectrum?

_____

_____

Talk About It

Model Make a model to show how white light refracts and splits into colored light. Share your model with a partner. Discuss the differences between your models.

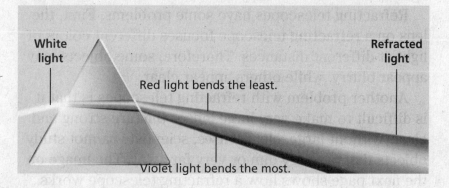

White light | Refracted light
Red light bends the least.
Violet light bends the most.

LOOKING CLOSER

6. Identify Label the part of the refracted light that has the longest wavelength.

INVISIBLE ELECTROMAGNETIC RADIATION

Humans cannot see electromagnetic radiation that has wavelengths outside the range of visible light. However, certain instruments can detect, or sense, these wavelengths. The table below shows examples of invisible wavelengths.

Wavelength	Examples (listed from shortest wavelength to longest)
Longer than red visible light	infrared waves microwaves radio waves
Shorter than blue visible light	gamma rays X rays ultraviolet rays

LOOKING CLOSER
7. Compare Which has a longer wavelength—gamma rays or X rays?

_____

How Do Telescopes Work?

Some things are too small or too far away for people to see with only their eyes. Scientists need special tools to see the details of distant objects in the sky. In 1609, the scientist Galileo used a special tool to look at the moon and stars.

Galileo's tool is called a telescope. A **telescope** is an instrument that collects electromagnetic radiation from the sky. The telescope focuses this radiation so that people can see distant objects more clearly. Early telescopes could collect only visible light. Telescopes that collect only visible light are called *optical telescopes*. There are two types of optical telescopes: refracting telescopes and reflecting telescopes. ☑

READING CHECK

8. Describe What is a telescope?

_____

_____

REFRACTING TELESCOPES

Refracting telescopes use a set of lenses to gather and focus light from distant objects. *Lenses* are clear objects that bend light in special ways. The bending of light by lenses is called *refraction*.

Refracting telescopes have some problems. First, the lens on a refracting telescope focuses different colors of light at different distances. Therefore, some objects may appear blurry, while others appear clear.

Another problem with refracting telescopes is that it is difficult to make very large lenses that are strong and clear. Without large, clear lenses, scientists cannot study objects that are very dim or very far away. The image on the next page shows how a refracting telescope works.

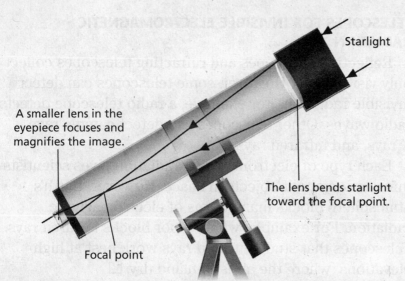

A refracting telescope uses lenses to produce images of distant objects.

A smaller lens in the eyepiece focuses and magnifies the image.

Starlight

The lens bends starlight toward the focal point.

Focal point

LOOKING CLOSER
9. Identify How does a refracting telescope collect and focus light?

_____

_____

REFLECTING TELESCOPES

Isaac Newton invented the reflecting telescope in the 1600s. A **reflecting telescope** uses a curved mirror to gather and focus light from distant objects. The figure below shows a reflecting telescope.

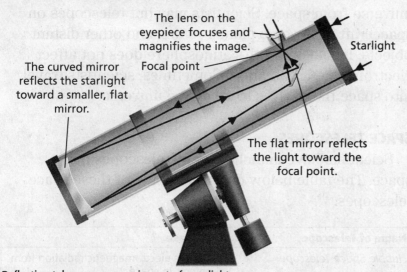

Reflecting telescopes use mirrors to focus light.

The lens on the eyepiece focuses and magnifies the image.

The curved mirror reflects the starlight toward a smaller, flat mirror.

Focal point

Starlight

The flat mirror reflects the light toward the focal point.

LOOKING CLOSER
10. Explain What is the function of the small, flat mirror?

_____

_____

_____

Reflecting telescopes solve some of the problems of refracting telescopes. For example, reflecting telescopes do not have the problem of color separation. Also, mirrors in reflecting telescopes can be very large and still produce a clear image. Therefore, reflecting telescopes can be larger and gather more light than a refracting telescope. The largest optical telescopes that astronomers use today are reflecting telescopes.

TELESCOPES FOR INVISIBLE ELECTROMAGNETIC RADIATION

Reflecting telescopes and refracting telescopes collect only visible light. However, some telescopes can detect invisible radiation. For example, a radio telescope detects radio waves. Other telescopes can detect gamma rays, X rays, and infrared rays.

Each type of electromagnetic radiation gives scientists information about objects in space. However, Earth's atmosphere blocks many forms of electromagnetic radiation. For example, water vapor blocks infrared rays. Telescopes that study infrared rays work best at high elevations, where the air is thin and dry. ☑

Particles in the atmosphere can also block short wavelengths, such as gamma rays and X rays. For this reason, the only way to study many forms of radiation is from space.

What Is Space-Based Astronomy?

In space-based astronomy, scientists observe the universe from space. Scientists may put telescopes on spacecraft to observe planets, stars, and other distant objects. In space, Earth's atmosphere does not affect electromagnetic radiation. Sometimes, scientists travel into space themselves to study the universe.

SPACE TELESCOPES

Scientists have launched many telescopes into space. The table below describes some of these space telescopes.

Name of Telescope	Purpose
Hubble Space Telescope	collects electromagnetic radiation from objects in space
Chandra X-ray Observatory	makes very clear images using X rays from objects in space
Swift	detects gamma rays and X rays from explosions and collisions of objects
Spitzer Space Telescope	detects infrared radiation
James Webb Space Telescope	will launch in 2013; will detect near and mid-range infrared radiation from objects in space

READING CHECK

11. Explain Why is it difficult to use many telescopes that detect invisible radiation on Earth's surface?

_____

_____

_____

LOOKING CLOSER

12. Identify What are two space telescopes that collect X rays?

_____

_____

SECTION 1 **Viewing the Universe** *continued*

OTHER SPACECRAFT

Scientists have used spacecraft to study other planets since the 1960s. The table below describes examples of past spacecraft and their discoveries.

Name of Spacecraft	Purpose
Voyager 1 and *Voyager 2*	collected images of Jupiter, Saturn, Uranus, and Neptune, and their moons
Galileo	collected information about Jupiter's atmosphere and storm systems
Huygens	studied the atmosphere and surface of Saturn's largest moon, Titan
Spirit and *Opportunity*	confirmed that water existed at one time on Mars
Phoenix	found ice on Mars

LOOKING CLOSER

13. Describe How did the *Galileo* spacecraft help astronomers learn about our solar system?

_____

_____

_____

HUMAN SPACE EXPLORATION

Some spacecraft carry only instruments and computers. These spacecraft are *robotic*. Robotic spacecraft can travel outside the solar system. Spacecraft that carry humans are called *crewed spacecraft*. Crewed spacecraft have never gone beyond Earth's moon.

The first humans went into space in the 1960s. Between 1969 and 1972, NASA landed 12 people on the moon. Now, crewed spacecraft only orbit Earth. During these flights, people fix satellites and perform experiments. People may also work on the International Space Station.

In the future, NASA wants to send people to explore Mars. However, this flight would be expensive, difficult, and dangerous. NASA is first planning to send astronauts back to the moon.

EFFECTS OF THE SPACE PROGRAM

Space programs have helped areas outside the field of astronomy. Satellites provide information about weather all over Earth. This information helps scientists predict future weather. Other satellites broadcast television signals from around the world. ☑

Space programs have also developed objects that are small and light for space travel. These developments have improved electronics, such as radios and televisions. In addition, medical instruments have improved because of space programs. For example, NASA's research on fluids has improved heart pumps.

READING CHECK

14. Identify Name one way satellites can be useful to people who are not astronomers.

_____

_____

_____

_____

Section 1 Review

SECTION VOCABULARY

astronomy the scientific study of the universe	**reflecting telescope** a telescope that uses a curved mirror to gather and focus light from distant objects
astronomical unit the average distance between Earth and the sun; approximately 150 million kilometers (symbol, AU)	**refracting telescope** a telescope that uses a set of lenses to gather and focus light from distant objects
electromagnetic spectrum all of the frequencies or wavelengths of electromagnetic radiation	
galaxy a collection of stars, dust, and gas bound together by gravity	**telescope** an instrument that collects electromagnetic radiation from the sky and concentrates it for better observation

1. Compare Complete the Venn diagram below to compare reflecting telescopes and refracting telescopes.

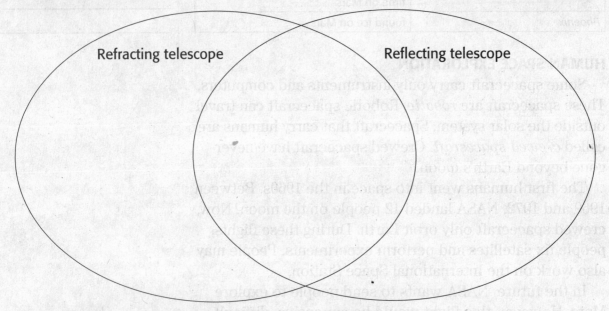

2. Apply Concepts List the following types of electromagnetic radiation in order from shortest wavelength to longest wavelength: red visible light, gamma rays, ultraviolet rays, radio waves.

_____

3. Describe How are stars, galaxies, and the universe related?

_____

_____

4. Compare What is one difference between optical telescopes and telescopes that collect invisible electromagnetic radiation?

_____

_____

_____

SECTION 2 Movements of Earth

KEY IDEAS

As you read this section, keep these questions in mind:

- What are two pieces of evidence for Earth's rotation?
- How does the change in apparent positions of constellations provide evidence of Earth's rotation and revolution around the sun?
- How do Earth's rotation and revolution provide a basis for measuring time?
- How do the tilt of Earth's axis and Earth's movement cause seasons?

What Is Rotation?

Earth is constantly moving. Earth's motions affect our daily lives. We use these motions to measure time. Earth's motions also cause seasons and changes in weather.

The spinning of Earth on its axis is called **rotation**. Each complete rotation takes one day. Earth's rotation causes day and night. As Earth spins, the sun appears to rise in the east in the morning. Then, the sun appears to cross the sky and set in the west. In fact, the sun does not move. Earth's rotation causes different parts of Earth to face the sun at different times.

- The part of Earth facing the sun has daylight.
- The part of Earth facing away from the sun has nighttime. ☑

THE FOUCAULT PENDULUM

In the 1800s, the scientist Jean-Bernard-Leon Foucault found evidence of Earth's rotation. First, he hung a wire from the ceiling. Then he attached a weight, called a *bob*, to the end of the wire. The wire and bob formed a pendulum, or a hanging mass that swings freely.

Throughout the day, the bob swung back and forth. The path of the pendulum seemed to change over time. However, the pendulum's path did not really change. Instead, the floor was moving. Foucault concluded that the floor moved because it was attached to the rotating Earth.

READING TOOLBOX

Predict and Summarize Before you read this section, review the headings and images. Use this information to predict what you will learn as you read the section. After you read the section, write a summary of the information in the section. With a partner, discuss whether your predictions match your summary.

☑ **READING CHECK**

1. Describe How does Earth's rotation cause day and night?

_____

_____

_____

_____

_____

Critical Thinking

2. Predict If Earth did not rotate, would the path of Foucault's pendulum seem to change over time?

_____

_____

SECTION 2 **Movements of Earth** *continued*

THE CORIOLIS EFFECT

The movement of ocean currents and wind belts also gives evidence of Earth's rotation. Ocean currents and wind belts do not move in a straight path. Earth's rotation causes them to curve as they move between the equator and the poles. This curving of ocean currents and wind belts is called the *Coriolis effect*. If Earth were not rotating, the Coriolis effect would not occur.

What Is Revolution?

As Earth spins on its axis, it also revolves around the sun. Earth travels around the sun at an average speed of 29.8 km/s. The motion of an object that travels around another object in space is called **revolution**. Each complete revolution of Earth around the sun takes one year. One year has about 365 ¼ days. ☑

EARTH'S ORBIT

An object follows a path as it revolves around another object in space. This path is called an *orbit*. Earth's orbit around the sun is not quite a circle. Earth's orbit is an *ellipse*, or oval. An ellipse has two points, or *foci* (singular, *focus*), that determine its shape. The planets in our solar system have orbits with one focus in the sun. No object is located at the other focus.

Because Earth's orbit is an ellipse, Earth is not always the same distance from the sun. The point in Earth's orbit where Earth is closest to the sun is **perihelion**. The point in Earth's orbit where Earth is farthest from the sun is **aphelion**.

✓ **READING CHECK**

3. Identify How long does Earth take to complete one rotation around the sun?

_____

_____

LOOKING CLOSER
4. Apply Concepts On the diagram, label Earth's aphelion and perihelion points.

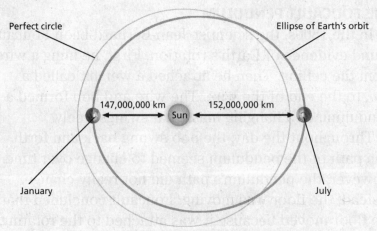

Earth is farthest from the sun in July and closest to the sun in January.

How Do Constellations Show Earth's Motion?

The motion of constellations gives evidence of Earth's rotation and revolution. A *constellation* is a group of stars that seem to form a pattern in the sky. Astronomers also use the word *constellation* to mean a section of the sky. Many of the names for constellations come from the ancient Greeks. For example, Taurus, the bull, and Orion, the hunter, are constellation names from Greek mythology.

EVIDENCE OF EARTH'S ROTATION

Like the sun, constellations seem to change position over time. During each night, they seem to move in a circle around a fixed point. Earth's rotation makes the constellations appear to move in this way. ☑

EVIDENCE OF EARTH'S REVOLUTION

Constellations also seem to change position because of Earth's revolution. Some constellations appear lower or higher in the sky in different months. This change in position is a result of Earth's revolution. As Earth revolves around the sun, the night side faces a different part of the universe. For this reason, different constellations are visible in different months and seasons.

How Do People Measure Time?

Earth's motion provides the basis for measuring time, such as days and years. The table below shows how these units of time are related to Earth's motion.

Unit of Time	Basis	Length
Day	one complete rotation of Earth on its axis	24 h
Year	one complete revolution of Earth around the sun	365 ¼ days

A month is based on the moon's motion around Earth. In fact, the word *month* comes from the word *moon*. In the past, a month was the period between two full moons, which is about 29.5 days. However, the number of full moons in a year is not a whole number. For this reason, a month is now defined to be about one-twelfth of a year. The months we use today are not related to the moon's phases.

READING CHECK

5. Explain Why do the constellations seem to move in a circle each night?

_____

_____

Critical Thinking

6. Describe Relationships Suppose Earth rotated more quickly on its axis than it does today. Would the faster rotation affect the length of the day or the year? Explain your answer.

_____

_____

_____

_____

_____

_____

FORMATION OF THE CALENDAR

A *calendar* is a system for describing long periods of time. Most modern calendars divide time into days, weeks, months, and years. Many ancient civilizations made calendars based on astronomical observations. For example, the ancient Egyptians used a calendar based on the movements of the sun through the sky.

Most calendar years have 365 whole days. However, Earth's revolution takes 365 ¼ days. To make up for the extra ¼ day, the calendar has an additional full day every four years. Any year that has an extra day is called a *leap year*. Leap years keep calendars on the same schedule as Earth's movements. ☑

Julius Caesar changed the calendar to include leap years more than 2,000 years ago. The next emperor made the extra day in a leap year come in February. He also made July and August long months with 31 days each.

Even with leap years, the calendar still did not match Earth's movements exactly. After hundreds of years, the calendar no longer matched the seasons. To solve this problem, Pope Gregory XIII changed the calendar in the 1500s. He decided that only century years divisible by 400 would have leap years. Century years are years that mark the beginning of a century, such as 1800 or 1900. The table below shows examples of century years.

READING CHECK

7. Describe What is a leap year?

_____

_____

Century Year	Divisible by 400?	Leap Year?
2000	yes	yes
2100	no	no
2200	no	no
2300	no	no

Math *Skills*

8. Calculate What is the next century year that will also be a leap year?

_____

TIME ZONES

We define noon as the time when the sun is highest in the sky. However, noon does not happen at the same moment everywhere around the world. For example, when it is noon in London, the sun may still be rising in New York City. Earth's rotation causes the sun to be above different places on Earth at different times.

Time zones help people account for differences in local times. Earth's surface has 24 standard time zones, one for each hour of the day. Each time zone is one hour earlier than the time zone to the east. In each zone, noon is the time when the sun is highest over that zone.

Talk About It

Describe Make a model of Earth and the sun to show why noon does not happen at all places at the same moment. Share your model with a partner. Together, compare your models to a map of time zones. Discuss how the map and the model are related.

SECTION 2 **Movements of Earth** *continued*

INTERNATIONAL DATE LINE AND DAYLIGHT SAVINGS TIME

There are 24 standard time zones and 24 h in a day. At some point on Earth, the date must change. The *International Date Line* marks this point. This line runs from north to south through the Pacific Ocean. When it is Friday west of the line, it is Thursday east of the line. The line does not cut through any countries. ☑

Earth's tilt causes changes in the amount of daylight on Earth. Daylight lasts longer in the summer months than in the winter months. During the summer, the sun rises earlier in the morning, when many people are sleeping.

The United States uses *daylight savings time* so that people can enjoy the extra sunlight. In this system, people set their clocks one hour ahead of standard time in March. This provides an extra hour of daylight in the evening. In November, people set their clocks back one hour to return to standard time.

Countries near the equator do not use daylight savings time. This is because the amount of daylight does not change much near the equator. In this region, daylight lasts about 12 h every day of the year. ☑

Why Does Earth Have Seasons?

Earth's axis is tilted by about 23.5°. As Earth revolves around the sun, Earth's axis always points toward the North Star. Thus, the North Pole is sometimes tilted toward the sun and is sometimes tilted away from the sun. This tilt affects the amount of daylight different parts of Earth have. The tilt also affects how the sun's rays hit Earth's surface.

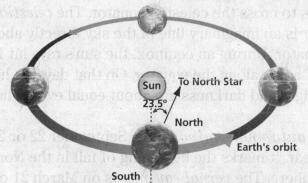

The part of Earth tilted toward the sun gets more direct sunlight and more hours of daylight.

> ☑ **READING CHECK**
>
> **9. Identify** What is the International Date Line?
>
> _____
>
> _____
>
> _____

> ☑ **READING CHECK**
>
> **10. Explain** Why do countries near the equator not use daylight savings time?
>
> _____
>
> _____
>
> _____
>
> _____
>
> _____
>
> _____
>
> _____

SECTION 2 **Movements of Earth** *continued*

SEASONAL WEATHER

Earth's tilt and revolution cause changes in temperature on Earth's surface. These changes in temperature cause the seasons.

For example, the North Pole tilts away from the sun for part of Earth's orbit. During this time, the sun's rays hit the Northern Hemisphere at a low angle. As a result, the solar energy is spread over a large area. This causes lower temperatures. Also, the Northern Hemisphere has fewer daylight hours during this time. Fewer daylight hours means less solar energy and lower temperatures. Lower temperatures cause the winter season. ☑

At the same time, the Southern Hemisphere tilts toward the sun. The sun's rays hit the Southern Hemisphere at a greater angle. As a result, the sun's rays concentrate in one area and cause higher temperatures. The Southern Hemisphere also has more daylight hours, which means higher temperatures. Thus, the Southern Hemisphere experiences summer. When the North Pole tilts toward the sun, the effects are opposite, as shown below.

✓ **READING CHECK**

11. Identify Give two reasons why temperatures are lower in the Northern Hemisphere during the winter.

_____

_____

_____

_____

_____

_____

Conditions When the North Pole Is Tilted Toward the Sun

	Northern Hemisphere	Southern Hemisphere
Daylight	long periods of daylight	short periods of daylight
Sun's rays	direct; greater angle	less direct; low angle
Temperature	high	low
Season	summer	winter

EQUINOX

The fall and spring seasons begin on days called equinoxes. The **equinox** is the moment when the sun appears to cross the celestial equator. The *celestial equator* is an imaginary line in the sky directly above the equator. During an equinox, the sun's rays hit Earth at a 90° angle along the equator. On that day, the hours of daylight and darkness are about equal everywhere on Earth.

The *autumnal equinox* is on September 22 or 23 of each year. It marks the beginning of fall in the Northern Hemisphere. The *vernal equinox* is on March 21 or 22 of each year. It marks the beginning of spring in the Northern Hemisphere.

Critical Thinking

12. Describe About how many hours of daylight do most areas on Earth receive during an equinox?

_____

SUMMER SOLSTICES

The seasons of summer and winter begin on days called solstices. On a **solstice**, the sun appears as far north or south of the equator as possible. As a result, the sun follows its highest or lowest path in the sky, as shown below.

June 21 - 22 — Summer solstice

Dec. 21 - 22 — Winter solstice

In the Northern Hemisphere, the sun appears to follow its highest path during the summer solstice.

LOOKING CLOSER
13. Identify On what date is the summer solstice in the Northern Hemisphere?

_____

In the Northern Hemisphere, the *summer solstice* is on June 21 or 22. On this day, the North Pole's tilt toward the sun is greatest. The sun's rays strike Earth at a 90° angle along the Tropic of Cancer.

The Northern Hemisphere has the most hours of daylight during the summer solstice. The farther north of the equator you are, the more daylight you have. Places north of the Arctic Circle have 24 h of daylight during the summer solstice. Places south of the Antarctic Circle have 24 h of darkness at that time.

WINTER SOLSTICES

On December 21 or 22, the North Pole is tilted farthest away from the sun. The sun's rays hit Earth at a 90° angle along the Tropic of Capricorn. This day is the *winter solstice*. It marks the beginning of winter in the Northern Hemisphere.

The Northern Hemisphere has the fewest daylight hours during the winter solstice. The sun follows its lowest path across the sky. Places north of the Arctic Circle have 24 h of darkness. Places south of the Antarctic Circle have 24 h of daylight at that time.

Critical Thinking
14. Apply Concepts On which day do areas in the Southern Hemisphere have the longest days—June 21 or December 21?

_____

_____

Section 2 Review

SECTION VOCABULARY

aphelion in the orbit of a planet or body in the solar system, the point that is farthest from the sun	**revolution** the motion of a body that travels around another body in space; one complete trip along an orbit
equinox the moment when the sun appears to cross the celestial equator	**rotation** the spin of a body on its axis
perihelion in the orbit of a planet or other body in the solar system, the point that is closest to the sun	**solstice** the point at which the sun is as far north or as far south of the equator as possible

1. Explain How do the motions of the constellations provide evidence that Earth both rotates on its axis and revolves around the sun?

_____

_____

_____

_____

2. Identify What are two pieces of evidence for Earth's rotation, aside from the motion of the constellations?

_____

_____

3. Describe How are Earth's motions related to how we measure time? Give two examples.

_____

_____

4. Explain What causes the seasons? Draw a diagram to help explain your answer.

_____

_____

CHAPTER 27 Planets of the Solar System

SECTION 1

Formation of the Solar System

KEY IDEAS

As you read this section, keep these questions in mind:

• What is the nebular hypothesis?

• How did the planets form?

• How did Earth's land, atmosphere, and oceans form?

How Did the Solar System Form?

The **solar system** consists of the sun, planets, dwarf planets, and other bodies. All of these bodies orbit the sun. **Planets** are the main bodies that orbit the sun.

Scientists have debated the origins of the solar system for a long time. Many scientists once thought that the sun formed first, and then threw off the materials that became the planets. In 1796, a mathematician named Pierre-Simon, marquis de Laplace, had another idea. His idea is now called the *nebular hypothesis*. Most scientists today think the nebular hypothesis is the best description of how the solar system formed.

Laplace's hypothesis states that the sun and the planets formed at about the same time. They formed out of a rotating cloud of gas and dust called a *nebula*. The nebula from which our sun and planets formed is called the **solar nebula**. About 5 billion years ago, the strength of gravity near the solar nebula increased. This probably occurred because of a nearby supernova or other forces. ☑

Energy from collisions and pressure from gravity made the center of the solar nebula hotter and denser. When the temperature at the nebula center became high enough, hydrogen fusion began. The star that we call the sun formed. About 99% of all the matter that was in the solar nebula now makes up the sun.

The force of gravity pulls together the particles of gas and dust in a nebula.

READING TOOLBOX

Ask Questions Scan the section, looking at headings, vocabulary, and pictures. Write three questions that you have about the section. As you read, look for the answers to your questions and write them in your notebook.

✓ READING CHECK

1. Describe What was the solar nebula?

_____

_____

_____

_____

LOOKING CLOSER

2. Describe What role did gravity play in the formation of the solar system?

_____

_____

_____

SECTION 1 **Formation of the Solar System** *continued*

How Did the Planets Form?

While the sun was forming at the center of the solar nebula, planets were forming in the outer parts of the nebula. During the early stages of planet formation, only small bodies called **planetesimals** existed. Some planetesimals joined together, forming larger bodies called *protoplanets*. ☑

The gravitational pull of the protoplanets attracted other planetesimals. These planetesimals collided with the protoplanets, and the masses combined. Eventually, the protoplanets became very large and formed the planets and moons.

3. Describe Relationships What is the relationship between protoplanets and planetesimals?

_____

_____

_____

Talk About It

Share Create a book, poster, or brochure to help others understand the nebular hypothesis. Work with a partner to correct any errors in your product. Present your final product to a small group.

LOOKING CLOSER
4. Describe How do planetesimals grow bigger?

_____

_____

_____

The Nebular Hypothesis for the Formation of the Solar System

Gravity causes the young nebula to collapse.

Planetesimals grow. As they become larger, their gravitational pull increases. The largest planetesimals pull in more gas and dust.

As the nebula rotates, it flattens into a disk. The nebula becomes warmer at its center.

Most of the gas in the nebula moves toward the center. The gases are pressed together and they begin to react with one another. The reactions release huge amounts of energy. The star (sun) forms.

Planetesimals form in the disk.

Small planetesimals collide with larger ones, forming planets.

SECTION 1 **Formation of the Solar System** *continued*

FORMATION OF THE INNER PLANETS

The features of a newly formed planet depended on the distance between the protoplanet and the sun. The protoplanets that became Mercury, Venus, Earth, and Mars were close to the sun. These planets are small, so they did not have enough gravitational pull to hold onto some of their gases. Other lighter elements may have been blown or boiled away by the sun.

As the denser material sank to the planet centers, layers formed. Today the inner planets have solid surfaces. They are smaller, denser, and rockier than the outer planets.

FORMATION OF THE OUTER PLANETS

Four other protoplanets became Jupiter, Saturn, Uranus, and Neptune. These planets formed in the cold, outer regions of the nebula. They did not lose their lighter elements, such as helium and hydrogen. They also kept ices, such as water, methane, and ammonia ice.

At first, thick ice layers surrounded small cores of heavy elements. Intense heat and pressure in the interiors made the ices melt and form layers of liquid and gas. Today, the outer planets are called *gas giants* because they are large and are made up mostly of gases. Uranus and Neptune are also sometimes called *ice giants*. Gas giants have low density, and are larger than the inner planets. ☑

Pluto was once known as the ninth planet, but scientists now classify Pluto as a dwarf planet. Like a planet, a *dwarf planet* is a spherical body. Unlike a planet, a dwarf planet has not cleared other objects from the path of its orbit.

How Did Solid Earth Form?

When Earth first formed, it was very hot. Three sources of energy contributed to the high temperatures:

• Energy was produced when the planetesimals that formed the planets collided with each other.

• The increasing weight of the outer layers compressed the inner layers, which generated energy.

• Radioactive materials were very abundant when Earth formed. These materials give off radiation, which warms the rock around them.

Critical Thinking

5. Infer If the protoplanets that became Mercury, Venus, Earth, and Mars had been much larger, would they have lost as much of their gases? Explain your answer.

_____

_____

_____

_____

READING CHECK

6. Explain Why are the outer planets called *gas giants?*

_____

_____

_____

EARTH'S LAYERS

Earth's center is a dense *core* composed of heavy elements. A thick layer of rock called the *mantle* surrounds the core. The outer layer is a thin *crust* of rock. These layers formed through a process called *differentiation*. During differentiation, dense materials sink and less dense materials rise, forming layers. ☑

Eventually, Earth's surface cooled enough for solid rock to form. Earth's surface continued to change as a result of heat in Earth's interior. The surface also changed because of impacts and through interactions with the newly forming atmosphere.

How Did Earth's Atmosphere Form?

Like solid Earth, Earth's atmosphere formed through the process of differentiation. Earth's early atmosphere was made up mostly of hydrogen and helium. The sun heated the gases, allowing them to escape Earth's gravity. The solar wind probably blew away the gases.

OUTGASSING

As Earth's surface continued to form, volcanic eruptions occurred much more frequently than they do today. The eruptions released large amounts of gases, such as water vapor, carbon dioxide, nitrogen, methane, sulfur dioxide, and ammonia. This process, known as *outgassing*, formed a new atmosphere.

Solar radiation caused the ammonia and some of the water vapor in the atmosphere to break down. Some of the oxygen released during the breakdown formed *ozone*. The ozone collected high in Earth's atmosphere and blocked some ultraviolet radiation, which is harmful to living things.

Earth's early atmosphere formed as volcanic eruptions released different gases into the air.

✓ **READING CHECK**

7. Describe What happened during differentiation?

_____

_____

_____

_____

_____

Critical Thinking

8. Infer Scientists think Earth's core is made up mainly of iron. Earth's mantle contains rocks rich in magnesium. What can you infer about the relative densities of iron and magnesium?

_____

_____

LOOKING CLOSER

9. Identify What was the main source of the gases in Earth's early atmosphere?

_____

_____

EARTH'S PRESENT ATMOSPHERE

Organisms that could survive in Earth's early atmosphere developed. Some of these organisms, such as cyanobacteria and green plants, used carbon dioxide for photosynthesis. This process released oxygen. Over time, the amount of oxygen in the atmosphere increased. About 2 billion years ago, the percentage of oxygen in the atmosphere increased rapidly. It has not changed very much since then.

As Earth's surface changed, the gases in the atmosphere changed as well.

Critical Thinking

10. Compare Describe two differences between Earth's early atmosphere and Earth's atmosphere today.

_____

_____

_____

_____

How Did Earth's Oceans Form?

Some scientists think part of Earth's water came from space. Icy bodies, such as comets, collided with Earth. Water from these bodies became part of Earth's atmosphere. As Earth cooled, water vapor condensed to form rain. The rain collected on Earth's surface to form the first oceans. ☑

The first oceans were probably made of fresh water. Over millions of years, rainwater fell to Earth. The water dissolved many solids and carried them to the oceans. As water evaporated from the oceans, some chemicals combined to form salts. This process made the oceans more and more salty.

LOOKING CLOSER

11. Describe Where do some scientists think some of Earth's water came from?

_____

_____

EFFECTS OF THE OCEAN ON THE ATMOSPHERE

Carbon dioxide from the atmosphere dissolves in the oceans. When carbon dioxide levels in the atmosphere decrease, more heat can escape into space. Over Earth's history, the concentration of carbon dioxide in the atmosphere has increased and decreased periodically. As a result, Earth has had climates that were warmer and cooler than today's climate.

Section 1 Review

SECTION VOCABULARY

planet a celestial body that orbits the sun, is round because of its own gravity, and has cleared the neighborhood around its orbital path	**solar nebula** a rotating cloud of gas and dust from which the sun and planets formed; *also* any nebula from which stars and exoplanets may form
planetesimal a small body from which a planet originated in the early stages of development in the solar system	**solar system** the sun and all of the planets and other bodies that travel around it

1. Identify Relationships What is the relationship between the solar nebula and the solar system?

_____

_____

_____

2. Describe How did Earth's layers develop?

_____

_____

_____

3. Describe How did the process of outgassing help shape Earth's atmosphere?

_____

_____

_____

4. Explain How do scientists think Earth's oceans formed?

_____

_____

_____

5. Analyze Information In this section, you have learned about the formation of Earth's land, atmosphere, and oceans. Which components of Earth's current composition make it capable of supporting life?

_____

_____

_____

_____

SECTION 2 Models of the Solar System

KEY IDEAS

As you read this section, keep these questions in mind:

• How do the two models of the universe that were developed by Ptolemy and Copernicus compare?

• What are Kepler's three laws of planetary motion?

• How did Newton explain Kepler's laws of motion?

What Were Some Early Models of the Solar System?

More than 2,000 years ago, the philosopher Aristotle suggested a model of the solar system. Aristotle's model was *geocentric*, or Earth-centered. In this model, the sun, stars, and planets revolved around Earth. Aristotle's model did not explain certain events, however. For example, it did not explain why planets sometimes seem to move backward relative to the stars. ☑

In 150 CE, an astronomer named Claudius Ptolemy suggested changes to Aristotle's model. Ptolemy thought that planets moved in small circles called *epicycles* while they also revolved in larger circles around Earth. Epicycles seemed to explain *retrograde motion*, or why planets sometimes seem to move backward.

In 1543 CE, an astronomer named Nicolaus Copernicus proposed a *heliocentric* model of the solar system. In this model, the planets revolve around the sun, not around Earth. Fast-moving planets pass slow-moving planets. As a result, planets that move more slowly than Earth appear to move backward.

Ptolemy's model is geocentric, or Earth-centered. Copernicus's model is heliocentric, or sun-centered.

READING TOOLBOX

Summarize As you read, underline key information in each subsection. Once you are finished, summarize each subsection in your notebook. Pay special attention to Kepler's three laws of planetary motion.

✓ READING CHECK

1. Describe What is the defining feature of a geocentric model of the solar system?

_____

_____

LOOKING CLOSER

2. Synthesize Text and Graphics Based on the information in the text, label the diagrams to identify each one as "Ptolemy's model" or "Copernicus's model."

SECTION 2 **Models of the Solar System** *continued*

What Are Kepler's Laws of Planetary Motion?

In the late 1500s, an astronomer named Tycho Brahe observed the positions of the planets and made detailed notes. After Tycho died, Johannes Kepler studied Tycho's notes. From these notes, Kepler developed three laws that explain planetary motion. Kepler's laws are so accurate that scientists today still use them.

LAW OF ELLIPSES

Kepler's *law of ellipses* states that each planet orbits the sun along a path called an *ellipse*, or oval. Some ellipses are more elongated than others. Some are almost perfect circles. The shape of a particular ellipse is determined by two points, or *foci*, within the ellipse. A perfect circle has only one focus at its center. ☑

Ellipse

Two foci

READING CHECK

3. Describe What is the shape of a planet's orbit?

_____

_____

Critical Thinking

4. Apply Concepts The eccentricity of Earth's orbit is 0.0167. Mercury's orbit has an eccentricity of 0.2056. A perfect circle has an eccentricity of zero. Compare the shapes of Earth's orbit and Mercury's orbit.

_____

_____

_____

Elliptical orbits can vary in shape. Scientists describe the elongation of a planet's orbit by a number value called **eccentricity**. The greater an orbit's eccentricity is, the more oval shaped the orbit is.

LAW OF EQUAL AREAS

Kepler's *law of equal areas* describes the speed of objects at different points in their orbits. Imagine a line that connects the center of the sun to the center of an object orbiting the sun. When the object is near the sun, the line is short and the object moves quickly. When the object is farther from the sun, the line is long and the object moves slowly. Therefore, objects orbiting the sun cover equal areas in equal amounts of time.

LOOKING CLOSER

5. Explain Why does Haley's comet move faster when it is nearer to the sun?

_____

_____

_____

_____

2,313 days

2,313 days

Sun

Halley's comet

According to Kepler's second law, an object moves faster when it is close to the sun than when it is far away.

LAW OF PERIODS

The time it takes for a planet or other body to complete one orbit is called the **orbital period**. Kepler's *law of periods* describes how the distance from a planet to the sun is related to orbital period. The equation below represents the law of periods.

$$K \times a^3 = p^2$$

In the equation above, a is the average distance of a planet from the sun and p is the planet's orbital period. K is a constant. When scientists measure distance in astronomical units (AU) and measure the period in Earth years, $K = 1$.

Scientists can measure orbital periods by observing the planets. They can then use Kepler's law of periods to figure out how far a planet is from the sun.

6. Apply Ideas Jupiter's orbital period is about 12 Earth years. According to the law of periods, about how far is Jupiter from the sun? Assume that $K = 1$.

_____

_____

_____

How Did Newton Explain Kepler's Laws?

Isaac Newton asked why planets move in the ways Kepler observed. Newton's explanation describes the motion of objects on Earth and the motion of objects in space. He hypothesized that a moving body tends to remain in motion. It will not change in speed or direction until an outside force acts on it. This resistance to change is called **inertia**.

NEWTON'S MODEL OF ORBITS

Because of inertia, a planet should move in a straight line. However, a planet does not follow a straight path. Therefore, an outside force must cause its path to curve. Newton called this force *gravity*. He realized that gravity exists between any two objects in the universe. An object such as a planet stays in orbit around the sun because of the sun's gravitational pull. Together, the motions caused by inertia and gravity produce a stable orbit. ☑

The farther a planet is from the sun, the weaker the sun's gravitational pull on the planet is. Thus, the sun does not pull as strongly on the outer planets as it pulls on the inner planets. As a result, the outer planets have larger orbits and longer revolution periods than the inner planets.

READING CHECK

7. Explain According to Newton, why are orbits curved?

_____

_____

_____

_____

_____

Section 2 Review

SECTION VOCABULARY

eccentricity the degree of elongation of an elliptical orbit (symbol, *e*) **inertia** the tendency of an object to resist a change in motion unless an outside force acts on the object	**orbital period** the time required for a body to complete a single orbit

1. Explain Because of inertia, a planet should keep moving forward in a straight line. Why, then, are planetary orbits curved?

_____

_____

2. Compare Complete the Venn diagram below to compare and contrast Ptolemy's and Copernicus's models of the solar system.

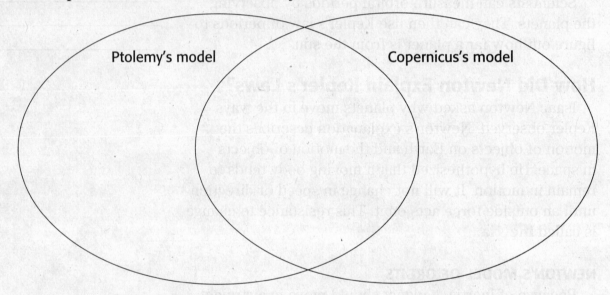

Ptolemy's model   Copernicus's model

3. Analyze How did Kepler's law of ellipses challenge the accepted model of planetary orbits?

_____

_____

_____

4. Apply Concepts Earth is closest to the sun in January and farthest from the sun in July. At which times of year is Earth moving fastest along its orbit? Explain your answer using one of Kepler's laws of planetary motion.

_____

_____

_____

_____

CHAPTER 27 Planets of the Solar System

SECTION 3 The Inner Planets

As you read this section, keep these questions in mind:

• What are the basic characteristics of the inner planets?

• What are some similarities and differences between the inner planets?

• What planetary features allow Earth to sustain life?

What Are the Inner Planets?

The *inner planets* are the planets closest to the sun. These planets are Mercury, Venus, Earth, and Mars. They are also called **terrestrial planets**, because they are all rocky, like Earth. In Latin, *terra* means "earth." The terrestrial planets are made up mostly of solid rock, and they have metallic cores. Their surfaces have bowl-shaped depressions called *impact craters*. These craters formed when other objects in space collided with the planets. ☑

What Are the Characteristics of Mercury?

Mercury is the planet closest to the sun. It circles the sun every 88 Earth days, and it rotates on its axis once every 59 Earth days. Its surface has many craters, and it has cliffs that are hundreds of kilometers long. These cliffs may be wrinkles that developed in the crust when the molten core cooled and shrank.

Mercury has almost no atmosphere. The lack of an atmosphere and a slow rotation cause temperatures on Mercury to vary widely. During the day, the temperature may reach as high as 427 °C. At night, the temperature may drop to –173 °C.

READING TOOLBOX

Organize As you read this section, use a four-corner fold to compare the inner planets. Label the outer flaps with the planet names. Describe each planet underneath the correct flap.

✓ READING CHECK

1. Explain What are two characteristics the terrestrial planets have in common?

_____

_____

_____

_____

Mercury

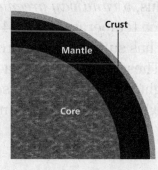

Crust
Mantle
Core

Characteristics of Mercury

Diameter	4,880 km, or 38% of Earth's diameter
Density	5.4 g/cm³, or 98% of Earth's density
Surface gravity	38% of Earth's surface gravity

What Are the Characteristics of Venus?

Venus is the second planet from the sun. It has an orbital period of 225 Earth days. In some ways, Venus is much like Earth. The two planets have similar size, mass, and density. However, Venus rotates very slowly, only once every 243 Earth days. Venus and Earth also differ in other ways.

Critical Thinking

2. Identify How long does it take for Venus to revolve around the sun?

_____

_____

Venus

LOOKING CLOSER

3. Compare Which planet is smallest—Mercury, Venus, or Earth?

_____

_____

Characteristics of Venus

Diameter	12,100 km, or 95% of Earth's diameter
Density	5.2 g/cm³, or 95% of Earth's density
Surface gravity	91% of Earth's surface gravity

VENUS'S ATMOSPHERE

Venus and Earth have very different atmospheres. The atmospheric pressure of Venus is 90 times the pressure on Earth. Venus's atmosphere is composed of about 96% carbon dioxide. High carbon dioxide levels and the planet's nearness to the sun make temperatures on Venus very high. ☑

The large amount of carbon dioxide prevents most of the radiation that enters Venus's atmosphere from escaping. The heat remains trapped at Venus's surface, raising temperatures. This process is called a *greenhouse effect*. On Venus, a *runaway greenhouse effect* raises the average surface temperature to 464 °C.

Venus also has sulfur dioxide droplets in its upper atmosphere. These droplets form a cloud layer that reflects sunlight. The reflection is so strong that Venus is one of the brightest objects in the night sky.

READING CHECK

4. Identify Which two features are responsible for high temperatures on Venus?

_____

_____

_____

_____

| SECTION 3 | The Inner Planets *continued* |

SURFACE FEATURES OF VENUS

Scientists have used probes and satellites to study Venus. Data show that Venus has a rocky landscape. The surface is made of basalt and granite. Scientists also discovered landforms such as mountains, volcanoes, lava plains, and sand dunes.

The surface of Venus has some craters. All the craters are about the same age, and they are relatively young. This evidence makes scientists think that volcanic activity changes Venus's surface. Energy inside the planet heats the interior over time. Volcanoes erupt and cover the surface of the planet with lava. The lava buries older craters. Scientists think that this kind of event probably won't happen again for another 100 million years. ☑

What Are the Characteristics of Earth?

Earth is the third planet from the sun. Its orbital period is 365.25 days. Earth completes one rotation on its axis about every 24 hours.

Earth has had a very active geologic history. Over the last 250 million years, Earth's continents separated from a single landmass and moved to their present positions. Weathering and erosion have changed (and continue to change) the surface of Earth.

Surface temperatures on Earth range from –90 °C to 60 °C. Earth's average temperature is 15 °C. Earth's unique atmosphere and distance from the sun allow water to exist in a liquid state here. Mercury and Venus are so close to the sun that any liquid water would boil. The other planets are so far from the sun that any water would freeze. Earth is the only planet scientists know of that has oceans of liquid water.

READING CHECK

5. Describe What evidence do scientists have that volcanic activity completely changes the surface of Venus?

_____

_____

_____

_____

_____

Earth

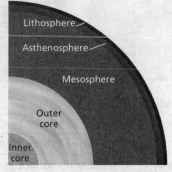

Lithosphere
Asthenosphere
Mesosphere
Outer core
Inner core

Characteristics of Earth

Diameter	12,756 km
Density	5.515 g/cm³
Surface gravity	9.8 m/s²

SECTION 3 **The Inner Planets** *continued*

Critical Thinking

6. Apply Concepts What would have happened if Earth's oceans did not absorb carbon dioxide in the atmosphere?

_____
_____
_____
_____
_____
_____

LIFE ON EARTH

Earth is the only known planet that has the proper combination of water, temperature, and oxygen to support life. Scientists think that as oceans formed on Earth, carbon dioxide from the atmosphere dissolved in the oceans. This process kept carbon dioxide from building up in the atmosphere. With less carbon dioxide in the atmosphere, less heat was trapped at Earth's surface.

As a result, Earth maintained the moderate temperatures living things need to survive. Plants and cyanobacteria added oxygen to the atmosphere. As oxygen levels increased, living things that breathe oxygen began to develop.

What Are the Characteristics of Mars?

Mars is the fourth planet from the sun. It has an average distance of about 228 million kilometers from the sun. Its orbital period is 687 Earth days, and it rotates on its axis every 24 h 37 min. Mars's axis tilts at almost the same angle that Earth's axis does. Thus, Mars's seasons are similar to those on Earth. ☑

Massive volcanoes on the surface of Mars are evidence that the planet was once geologically active. A system of deep canyons also covers part of the surface. Scientists think that the canyons are cracks that formed in the crust as the planet cooled. Water may have then further eroded the cracks.

☑ **READING CHECK**

7. Explain Why do Mars and Earth have similar seasons?

_____
_____
_____
_____
_____

Critical Thinking

8. Apply Prior Knowledge On which planet would you weigh more—Earth or Mars? Explain your answer.

_____
_____
_____
_____

Mars

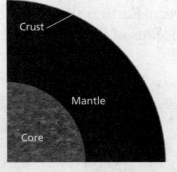

Crust

Mantle

Core

Characteristics of Mars

Diameter	6,800 km, or 53% of Earth's diameter
Density	3.9 g/cm³, or 71% of Earth's density
Surface gravity	38% of Earth's surface gravity

SECTION 3 **The Inner Planets** *continued*

MARTIAN VOLCANOES

Tharsis Montes is one of several volcanic regions on Mars. Volcanoes in this region are 100 times as large as Earth's largest volcano. The biggest volcano on Mars is Olympus Mons. It is about three times as tall as Mount Everest. Its base is about the size of Nebraska.

Scientists think that Olympus Mons has grown so large because Mars has no moving tectonic plates. As a result, the mountain may have built up around a steady magma source for millions of years.

Scientists are not yet sure whether Martian volcanoes are still active. However, they have observed certain events that produced seismic waves. These events are called *marsquakes*.

WATER ON MARS

The pressure and temperature on Mars are too low for water to exist as a liquid on the planet's surface. However, several NASA missions have found evidence that liquid water did exist on the surface in the past. Many surface features look like water eroded them. Other features might be evidence of flood plains produced by massive volumes of water.

The surface temperatures on Mars can range from 20 °C to –130 °C, depending on location and season. Although most of the water on Mars is trapped in polar icecaps, frozen water also exists below the surface. If liquid water exists below Mars's surface, the odds of finding life on the planet would increase. However, scientists have not yet found evidence for life on Mars. ☑

READING CHECK

9. Explain Why do scientists look at Mars for signs of life?

_____

_____

_____

_____

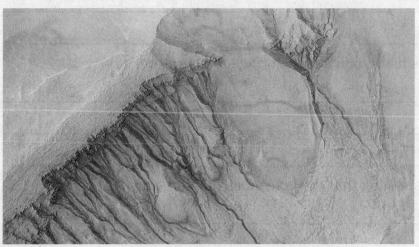

Scientists think liquid water possibly formed these gullies on Mars.

Section 3 Review

SECTION VOCABULARY

terrestrial planet one of the highly dense planets nearest to the sun; Mercury, Venus, Mars, and Earth	

1. Identify Relationships What is the relationship between the terms *inner planet* and *terrestrial planet*?

_____

_____

2. Summarize Use the graphic organizer below to describe the characteristics of the inner planets.

	Orbital Period	Rotation Period	Temperature Range	Size Ranking (1 is largest, 4 is smallest)
Mercury	88 Earth days	59 Earth days	−173 °C to 427 °C	
Venus			up to 464 °C	
Earth				1
Mars				

3. Identify What characteristics of Earth make it possible for life to exist here?

_____

_____

4. Describe Why does Mercury have such a large daily temperature range?

_____

_____

5. Explain Why does Venus have such a high surface temperature?

_____

_____

_____

6. Explain Why do scientists think that the volcanoes on Mars may still be active?

_____

_____

_____

CHAPTER 27 Planets of the Solar System
SECTION 4 The Outer Planets

As you read this section, keep these questions in mind:

- How do the outer planets differ from the terrestrial planets?
- How do the characteristics of the outer planets compare to one another?
- Why is Pluto considered a dwarf planet?

What Are the Outer Planets?

The four planets farthest from the sun—Jupiter, Saturn, Uranus, and Neptune—are called the *outer planets*. Scientists once considered Pluto an outer planet, too, but they now classify it as a *dwarf planet*.

The outer planets are also called **gas giants** because they are large planets made mostly of gases. A ring of debris called the *asteroid belt* separates the inner planets from the outer planets.

How Do the Gas Giants Differ from the Terrestrial Planets?

The gas giants are larger and more massive than the terrestrial planets. However, the gas giants are much less dense. Each gas giant has an atmosphere made mostly of hydrogen and helium. These gases create a thick cloud layer, so scientists can observe only the topmost part of the atmosphere. However, scientists think that each gas giant probably has a core of rock and metal. All four gas giants have ring systems made of dust and icy debris. ☑

FoldNotes As you read this section, use a four-corner fold to compare the outer planets. Label the outer flaps with the planet names. Describe each planet under the correct flap.

READING CHECK

1. Explain Why aren't scientists certain about the compositions of the gas giants' cores?

_____
_____
_____
_____

The four gas giants are all much larger than Earth, but they are far less dense.

What Are the Characteristics of Jupiter?

Jupiter is the fifth planet from the sun. It is by far the largest planet in the solar system. Its mass is more than 300 times that of Earth. Jupiter's orbital period is almost 12 Earth years. It rotates on its axis once every 9 h 50 min, which is faster than any other planet. The temperature of Jupiter's outer layers is −160 °C.

JUPITER'S ATMOSPHERE

Hydrogen and helium make up 92% of Jupiter, so its composition is similar to the sun. However, when Jupiter formed, it did not have enough mass for nuclear fusion to begin. Thus, Jupiter never became a star. ☑

Jupiter has a set of light and dark bands on its surface. Orange, gray, blue, and white bands spread out parallel to the equator. The colors are evidence that Jupiter's atmosphere has organic molecules mixed with ammonia, methane, and water vapor. Jupiter's rapid rotation causes the gases to swirl around the planet and form the bands.

An important feature of Jupiter is its *Great Red Spot.* This spot is a giant rotating storm that has been raging for several hundred years. Scientists can also see other spots, so they think storms are very common on Jupiter. However, only a few of the largest storms last for a long time.

Winds on Jupiter reach up to 540 km/h. Winds are caused by regions of different temperatures. However, scientists think that Jupiter's internal heat affects the planet's weather more than heat from the sun does.

Jupiter

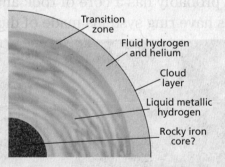

- Transition zone
- Fluid hydrogen and helium
- Cloud layer
- Liquid metallic hydrogen
- Rocky iron core?

Characteristics of Jupiter

Diameter	143,000 km, or 11 times Earth's diameter
Density	1.33 g/cm³, or 24% of Earth's density
Surface gravity	2.54 times Earth's surface gravity

READING CHECK

2. Describe Why didn't Jupiter become a star?

_____

_____

_____

Critical Thinking

3. Apply Prior Knowledge On which planet would you weigh more—Earth or Jupiter? Explain your answer.

_____

_____

_____

SECTION 4 **The Outer Planets** *continued*

JUPITER'S INTERIOR

Jupiter's large mass causes the temperature and pressure in the planet's interior to be very high. The high pressure and temperature have changed Jupiter's interior into a sea of liquid, metallic hydrogen. Scientists think that Jupiter has a solid, rocky, iron core.

What Are the Characteristics of Saturn?

Saturn is the sixth planet from the sun. It has an orbital period of 29.5 Earth years, and it rotates on its axis every 10 h 30 min. Saturn is very far from the sun, so it is extremely cold. It has an average cloud-top temperature of −176 °C. Like Jupiter, Saturn is made almost entirely out of hydrogen and helium. It also likely has a rocky, iron core. However, Saturn is less dense than Jupiter. ☑

Saturn

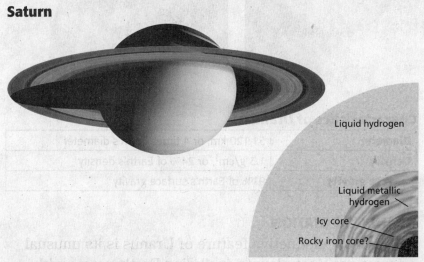

Liquid hydrogen

Liquid metallic hydrogen

Icy core

Rocky iron core?

Characteristics of Saturn

Diameter	120,500 km, or 9.4 times Earth's diameter
Density	0.70 g/cm³, or 13% of Earth's density
Surface gravity	1.07 times Earth's surface gravity

SATURN'S BANDS AND RINGS

Saturn is best known for its rings, which are twice the planet's diameter. The other gas giants also have rings, but Saturn's rings are the most extensive. The rings are made of billions of dust and ice particles.

Like Jupiter, Saturn has bands of colored clouds that run parallel to its equator. These bands are caused by Saturn's rapid rotation. This rotation, combined with Saturn's low density, causes Saturn to bulge at its equator and flatten at its poles.

READING CHECK

4. Compare Name two characteristics that Jupiter and Saturn have in common.

_____

_____

_____

_____

LOOKING CLOSER

5. Apply Prior Knowledge On the diagram, circle Saturn's region of greatest density. Draw an X on the region with the smallest density.

SECTION 4 **The Outer Planets** *continued*

What Are the Characteristics of Uranus?

Critical Thinking

6. Compare On which planet are days longer—Earth or Uranus?

_____

_____

Uranus is the seventh planet from the sun. It is the third-largest planet in the solar system, after Jupiter and Saturn. Uranus is almost 3 billion kilometers from the sun. Its orbital period is almost 84 Earth years, and it rotates on its axis once every 17 h.

Uranus

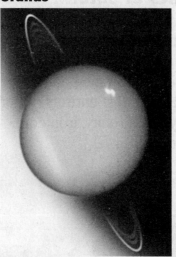
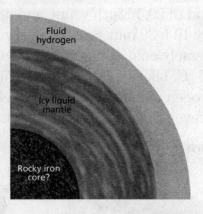

Fluid hydrogen

Icy liquid mantle

Rocky iron core?

Characteristics of Uranus

Diameter	51,120 km, or 4 times Earth's diameter
Density	1.3 g/cm^3, or 24% of Earth's density
Surface gravity	91% of Earth's surface gravity

URANUS'S ROTATION

The most distinctive feature of Uranus is its unusual orientation. Most planets, including Earth, rotate with their axes perpendicular to their orbital planes. However, Uranus's axis is almost parallel to the plane of its orbit. ☑

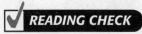

READING CHECK

7. Describe What is unusual about Uranus's rotation?

_____

_____

_____

URANUS'S ATMOPSHERE

Like the other gas giants, Uranus has an atmosphere that contains mainly hydrogen and helium. Its blue-green color is evidence that the atmosphere also contains large amounts of methane.

The average cloud-top temperature of Uranus is about −214 °C. However, astronomers think that the planet's temperature could be much higher below the clouds. There may be a mixture of liquid water and methane beneath the atmosphere. Scientists also think that Uranus has a core of rock and melted elements.

What Are the Characteristics of Neptune?

Neptune is the eighth planet from the sun. It is similar to Uranus in size and mass. Neptune's orbital period is nearly 164 Earth years. The planet rotates on its axis about every 16 h.

Scientists predicted Neptune's existence before they actually discovered it. Astronomers observed that Uranus's actual orbit was different from its calculated orbit. They thought that the gravity of an unknown planet was responsible for the difference. ☑

In the 1800s, two scientists independently calculated the position of the unknown planet. An astronomer named Johann Galle then discovered the bluish-green planet in the predicted location.

8. Explain How did astronomers predict the existence of Neptune before it was actually discovered?

_____

_____

_____

Neptune

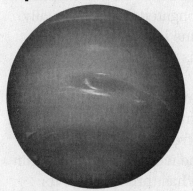
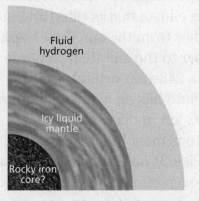

Fluid hydrogen

Icy liquid mantle

Rocky iron core?

Characteristics of Neptune

Diameter	49, 530 km, or 3.9 times Earth's diameter
Density	1.6 g/cm³, or 30% of Earth's density
Surface gravity	1.2 times Earth's surface gravity

Critical Thinking

9. Compare Which two gas giants are most similar in terms of density?

_____

_____

NEPTUNE'S ATMOSPHERE

Neptune's atmosphere is made up mostly of hydrogen, helium, and methane. Its average cloud-top temperature is about –225 °C. Neptune's upper atmosphere contains some white clouds of frozen methane. These clouds appear as continually changing bands between the equator and poles of Neptune.

Neptune has an active weather system. Winds can reach more than 1,000 km/h. At one time, a storm the size of Earth appeared and disappeared on Neptune's surface. It was known as the *Great Dark Spot*.

SECTION 4 **The Outer Planets** *continued*

What Objects Lie Beyond Neptune?

In recent years, scientists have discovered hundreds of objects in our solar system beyond Neptune's orbit. These objects are called *trans-Neptunian objects* (TNOs). ☑

PLUTO

Pluto was discovered in 1930. Until 2006, it was known as the ninth planet. Now, scientists classify Pluto as a dwarf planet. A *dwarf planet* is an object that

- orbits the sun
- is round because of its own gravity
- has not cleared the region around its orbit
- is not a satellite of another planet

The shape of Pluto's orbit is unusual. Its orbital path is an ellipse that is tilted and elongated. Pluto is usually farther from the sun than Neptune is. However, it is closer to the sun than Neptune is for about 20 years out of its 248-year orbital period.

Pluto has an average temperature of −235 °C. It is only 2,302 km in diameter, which is smaller than Earth's moon. Pluto is most likely made up of frozen methane, rock, and ice. It has extensive methane icecaps and a very thin nitrogen atmosphere. Pluto also has three moons. Its largest moon, Charon, is more than half Pluto's size.

This illustration shows several of the largest trans-Neptunian objects, or TNOs.

As you can see in the figure above, Pluto is not the only TNO. Some TNOs are similar to Pluto in shape and size. For example, Eris and Makemake are other TNO dwarf planets, or *plutoids*. However, most TNOs are just small chunks of ice. TNOs exist in a region beyond Neptune's orbit called the **Kuiper Belt**.

☑ **READING CHECK**

10. Define What is a trans-Neptunian object (TNO)?

_____

_____

_____

Talk About It

The decision to change Pluto's status from a planet to a dwarf planet was a hotly debated topic. Do you think scientists should have changed Pluto's classification? Why or why not? Discuss your ideas with a partner.

LOOKING CLOSER

11. Identify What is the largest known trans-Neptunian object?

_____

_____

EXOPLANETS

Until the 1990s, all the planets that astronomers had discovered were in our own solar system. More recently, astronomers have discovered hundreds of planetlike objects orbiting distant stars. These objects are called *exoplanets*, because they are outside of our solar system. The root *exo-* means "outside." ☑

Most known exoplanets orbit stars that are similar to Earth's sun. As a result, some scientists wonder if life could exist in another solar system.

READING CHECK

12. Define What is an exoplanet?

_____

_____

_____

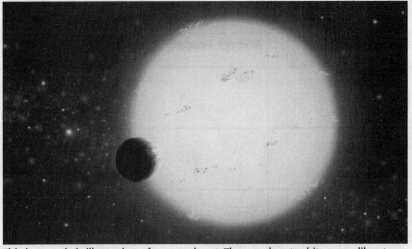

This is an artist's illustration of an exoplanet. The exoplanet orbits a sun-like star 150 light-years away.

Critical Thinking

13. Apply Concepts How long does it take light from the star shown in the drawing to reach Earth? Explain your answer.

_____

_____

_____

_____

_____

Scientists have only recently been able to observe exoplanets directly. Most are too small and too far away for astronomers to observe with telescopes or satellites. Scientists detect most exoplanets by observing how their gravity affects the stars they orbit.

When scientists study some distant stars, they notice that the light coming from the stars shifts in wavelength. The stars' movement slightly toward, then away from, Earth explains this shift. Scientists know that the gravity of a planet can affect a star's movement. Therefore, by studying the movement of the star, they can detect exoplanets.

Most identified exoplanets are larger than Uranus. However, astronomers are gradually discovering exoplanets that are closer to Earth in size. One might even be the right temperature to support life. Scientists hope to use information about exoplanets to learn more about how solar systems form.

Section 4 Review

SECTION VOCABULARY

gas giant a planet that has a deep, massive atmosphere, such as Jupiter, Saturn, Uranus, or Neptune	**Kuiper Belt** a region of the solar system that starts just beyond the orbit of Neptune and that contains dwarf planets and other small bodies made mostly of ice

1. Describe What are the relative positions of the gas giants and the Kuiper Belt?

_____

_____

2. Summarize Complete the table below to describe the characteristics of the outer planets.

	Orbital Period	Rotation Period	Average Temperature	Components of Atmosphere
Jupiter	12 Earth years	9 h 50 min	−160 °C	mostly hydrogen and helium
Saturn				
Uranus				
Neptune				

3. Compare How do the general characteristics of the gas giants differ from those of the terrestrial planets?

_____

_____

4. Compare Identify two similarities between Uranus and Neptune. Then, identify one difference. Choose characteristics that are not identified in the table above.

_____

_____

5. Describe How do astronomers detect most exoplanets?

_____

_____

CHAPTER 28 Minor Bodies of the Solar System

SECTION 1 Earth's Moon

As you read this section, keep these questions in mind:

• What are four kinds of lunar surface features?

• What are the three layers of the moon?

• How did the moon form?

What Is a Satellite?

Normally, we think of Earth's moon as the only moon. In fact, Earth's moon is one of many in our solar system. A **moon** is a natural object, or body, that orbits a larger object. Moons are a type of satellite. A **satellite** is any natural or artificial object that orbits another object. Humans have sent many artificial satellites into orbit around Earth. These satellites include weather satellites and space telescopes such as the *Hubble Space Telescope*.

EARTH'S NATURAL SATELLITE

The moon is the only body in the solar system other than Earth that humans have walked on. The United States sent six spacecraft to the moon as part of the Apollo space program. The moon has much less mass than Earth has. Thus, the gravity at the moon's surface is much weaker than gravity at Earth's surface. Because the moon's gravity is so low, astronauts found that bouncing on the moon was actually easier than walking.

The gravity at the moon's surface is not even strong enough to hold gases near the surface. Without gases near its surface, the moon has little atmosphere. Because the moon has no gases to absorb and transport thermal energy, temperatures are less stable than those on Earth. Surface temperatures on the moon vary from 134 °C during the day to −170 °C at night. ☑

Astronauts move more easily on the moon by bouncing or by riding in vehicles such as this Lunar Roving Vehicle.

READING TOOLBOX

Summarize After you read this section, create a concept map to describe the moon's characteristics. Use vocabulary words and other key terms from the section.

Math *Skills*

1. Calculate Gravity on the moon's surface is 1/6 the gravity on Earth's surface. What would a person who weighs 690 N on Earth weigh on the moon?

_____

✓ READING CHECK

2. Explain Why are temperatures on the moon less stable than those on Earth?

_____

_____

_____

_____

SECTION 1 **Earth's Moon** *continued*

What Are the Features of the Moon's Surface?

Luna is the Latin word for "moon." Any feature of the moon is referred to as *lunar*. The moon's surface has many landforms, or *lunar features*. Some of these features are highlands, maria, craters, rilles, and ridges.

HIGHLANDS AND MARIA

Most people can see light and dark patches on the moon. The light areas are rough highlands. The rocks in these areas are called *anorthosites*. The dark areas are smooth, flatter regions, or plains. The rock in these areas is dark, solid, basaltic lava. Each dark region is a **mare** (plural, *maria*). *Mare* means "sea" in Latin. Galileo gave this name to the dark regions because he thought they looked like Earth's seas. The maria do not contain water. ☑

CRATERS, RILLES, AND RIDGES

The surface of the moon is covered with many craters. A **crater** is a bowl-shaped low area, or depression. In some places, long channels run through maria. These channels are called *rilles*. Some rilles are as long as 240 km. The moon's surface also has ridges. *Ridges* are long, narrow areas of rock that rise out of the moon's surface and cross the maria.

Lunar Features

Feature	Description
Highlands	rough, light-colored areas made of anorthosite
Maria	
Craters	
Rilles	long channels that run through maria
Ridges	

REGOLITH

Because the moon has no atmosphere to protect it, many meteorites have hit its surface. Over billions of years, meteorites crushed much of the rock on the moon's surface into dust and small rock pieces. Layers of this dust and rock, called *regolith*, cover almost the entire lunar surface. The depth of the regolith layer varies from 1 m to 6 m. ☑

Talk About It

Compare With a partner, talk about how the lunar maria are different from Earth's seas. Do you think Galileo would have named them *maria* if he knew what today's scientists know?

✔ **READING CHECK**

3. Describe In your own words, describe the maria.

_____

_____

_____

LOOKING CLOSER

4. Describe Complete the table to describe the moon's features.

✔ **READING CHECK**

5. Identify What caused the formation of regolith?

_____

_____

_____

SECTION 1 **Earth's Moon** *continued*

LUNAR ROCKS

Lunar rocks are similar to Earth rocks. Lunar rocks and Earth rocks contain many of the same elements, but the rocks have different amounts of each element.

Lunar rocks are igneous rocks. Like rocks in Earth's crust, lunar surface rocks are made up mainly of silicon and oxygen. Highland rocks are rich in calcium and aluminum. Rocks from the maria are basalts, and they contain large amounts of titanium, magnesium, and iron.

One type of rock found in both the maria and the highlands is *breccia*. Lunar breccias contain pieces of other rocks that have been fused together. These breccias formed when meteorites struck the moon. ☑

What Is the Structure of the Moon's Interior?

Recall that scientists used data from seismic waves as an indirect method for studying Earth's interior. Scientists also used indirect methods to determine the moon's interior structure. Apollo astronauts placed seismographs on the moon. These seismographs have recorded moonquakes, which are similar to earthquakes. From waves made by moonquakes, scientists have learned that the moon's interior has three layers, as shown below.

Like Earth, the moon has three compositional layers: crust, mantle, and core.

6. Explain How did breccias form on the moon?

_____

_____

_____

LOOKING CLOSER

7. List What are the three compositional layers of the moon?

_____

_____

_____

THE MOON'S CRUST

One side of the moon always faces Earth. That side of the moon is called the *near side*. The side of the moon that faces away from Earth is called the *far side*. The far side of the moon has mountains and only a few small maria.

On the near side, the crust is about 60 km thick. However, on the far side, the crust is up to 100 km thick. Scientists think the difference in thickness was caused by the pull of Earth's gravity on the moon as it formed.

Critical Thinking

8. Connect to Prior Knowledge How does the structure of the moon's core differ from the structure of Earth's core?

_____

_____

_____

_____

_____

THE MOON'S MANTLE AND CORE

The moon's mantle is beneath its crust. Scientists think the mantle rock is rich in silica, magnesium, and iron. The mantle makes up the largest part of the moon's volume.

Scientists think the moon has a small iron core. Evidence suggests that the core is neither completely solid nor completely liquid.

How Did Earth's Moon Form?

Apollo astronauts brought moon rocks back to Earth. Scientists studied these rocks to learn about the moon's history, including how the moon formed. Based on evidence, most scientists think Earth's moon formed in three stages. The figure below describes the first stage, called the *giant impact hypothesis*.

**The Giant Impact Hypothesis:
the First Stage of Moon Formation**

Scientists think that an object about the size of Mars crashed into, or collided with, Earth. The collision sent part of Earth's mantle into space.

The pull of Earth's gravity caused debris from the collision to revolve around Earth.

The debris eventually collected and formed Earth's moon.

LOOKING CLOSER

9. Identify What was the source of rock that formed the moon?

_____

FORMATION OF LAYERS

During the second stage of the moon's formation, the moon's layers developed. Right after the moon formed, its surface was covered by *molten*, or melted, rock. Over time, the densest materials moved toward the moon's center. These dense materials formed the core. The least dense materials formed the outer layer, the crust. The rest of the materials settled between the core and outer layer to form the moon's mantle.

METEORITE IMPACTS

During the third stage of the moon's formation, the moon's outer layer cooled to form the solid crust. During this period of cooling, debris left over from the formation of the solar system hit the surface. The impacts produced craters and regolith.

About 3 billion years ago, the number of small objects in the solar system decreased. Thus, there were fewer objects to hit the moon's surface. Scientists think the moon today looks almost exactly as it did 3 billion years ago. ☑

How Did the Maria Form?

Impacts on the moon's surface formed deep basins in the crust. Lava flowed out of the moon's interior through cracks called *fissures*. The lava filled the basins and formed the maria. Scientists think rilles are lava channels left over from the formation of the maria. The presence of maria suggests that eruptions of lava through fissures were once common. However, scientists have found no evidence of large active volcanoes on the moon.

 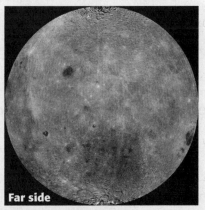

The near side of the moon has fewer visible craters than the far side has. Scientists think lava flows covered many impact sites on the near side with maria.

Scientists do not know how magma formed in the moon's interior. A lot of energy would be needed to produce magma. Some scientists think this energy may have come from meteorites hitting the moon's surface. Others think energy came from radioactive decay inside the moon. Scientists agree that lava flows stopped about 3.1 billion years ago when the moon's interior cooled completely.

Critical Thinking

10. Identify Main Ideas What were the three stages of moon formation?

_____

_____

_____

✓ READING CHECK

11. Explain Why are most of the craters on the moon's surface more than 3 billion years old?

_____

_____

_____

LOOKING CLOSER

12. Explain Why are there fewer visible craters on the near side of the moon?

_____

_____

_____

Section 1 Review

SECTION VOCABULARY

crater a bowl-shaped depression that forms on the surface of an object when a falling body strikes the object's surface or when an explosion occurs **mare** a large, dark area of basalt on the moon (plural, *maria*)	**moon** a celestial body that revolves around a body that is greater in mass; a natural satellite **satellite** a natural or artificial body that revolves around a celestial body that is greater in mass

1. Describe How did the lunar maria form?

_____

_____

2. Compare Describe two differences between the near side of the moon and the far side of the moon.

_____

_____

3. Infer Suppose the number of small objects in the solar system had not decreased about 3 billion years ago. How might the moon's surface look different today? Explain your answer.

_____

_____

_____

_____

4. Describe Identify two features of the moon and describe how each formed.

_____

_____

_____

_____

5. Apply Concepts The composition of the moon and the composition of Earth's mantle are similar. How does this information provide evidence for the giant impact hypothesis?

_____

_____

_____

_____

SECTION 2 **Movements of the Moon**

As you read this section, keep these questions in mind:

• What is the shape of the moon's orbit around Earth?

• Why do eclipses happen?

• How does the moon appear in each of its phases?

• How do movements of the moon affect tides on Earth?

What Is the Earth-Moon System?

To people on Earth, the moon appears to orbit Earth. However, if you could observe Earth and the moon from space, you would see that Earth and the moon revolve around each other. Together they form a single system that moves around the sun.

The mass of the moon is only about 1/80 the mass of Earth. Thus, the balance point within the Earth-moon system is not halfway between the two bodies. The balance point, or *barycenter*, is actually located within Earth. The barycenter follows a smooth orbit around the sun. The barycenter is not a real place. It is an imaginary point. ☑

THE MOON'S ELLIPTICAL ORBIT

The path of the moon's orbit is an ellipse. The ellipse is about 5% more elongated than a circle. Therefore, the distance between Earth and its moon varies over time. When the moon is farthest from Earth, the moon is at **apogee**. When the moon is closest to Earth, the moon is at **perigee**.

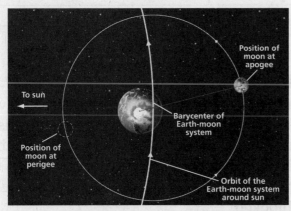

To sun

Position of moon at apogee

Barycenter of Earth-moon system

Position of moon at perigee

Orbit of the Earth-moon system around sun

Because the moon's orbit is elliptical, the moon is not always the same distance from Earth.

Identify Cause and Effect
As you read this section, underline examples of cause and effect. Discuss each example with a partner to make sure you understand the cause and the effect.

1. Explain Why is the barycenter of the Earth-moon system located inside Earth?

_____

_____

Talk About It

Relate Concepts Remember that Earth is at aphelion when it is farthest from the sun, and it is at perihelion when it is closest to the sun. With a partner, talk about how the terms *aphelion*, *apogee*, *perihelion*, and *perigee* are similar in structure and in meaning. Together, think of a way to remember the meaning of each term.

APPEARANCE OF THE MOON IN THE SKY

If you watched the moon every night, you would see the moon rises and sets 50 minutes later each night. It appears to rise and set later because of Earth's rotation and the moon's revolution. While Earth completes one rotation each day, the moon also moves in its orbit around Earth. It takes 1/29 of Earth's rotation, or 50 minutes, for the horizon to catch up to the moon.

While the moon revolves around Earth and the sun, it also rotates on its axis. The moon completes a rotation only once during one revolution around Earth. The moon revolves around Earth once every 27.3 days. Because the moon's rotation and revolution take about the same time, observers on Earth always see the same side of the moon. People can observe the other side of the moon only by looking at images taken by spacecraft. ☑

The sun always lights up half the moon. As the moon orbits Earth, the part of the moon's surface that is lighted, or *illuminated*, by sunlight changes. Sometimes the side of the moon facing Earth is fully illuminated. At other times, however, the side of the moon we see from Earth is dark. The position of the moon in its orbit determines how much of its lighted half we can see.

What Is an Eclipse?

Bodies that orbit the sun, including Earth and the moon, cast long shadows into space. When one body passes into the shadow of another body, an **eclipse** occurs. ☑

Types of Eclipses

Type of Eclipse	Description
Solar	The moon's shadow falls on Earth.
Lunar	Earth's shadow falls on the moon.

What Happens During a Solar Eclipse?

The shadows that Earth and the moon cast have two parts: the umbra and the penumbra. The *umbra* is the inner, cone-shaped part of the shadow. In the umbra, sunlight is completely blocked. The *penumbra* is the outer part of the shadow. In the penumbra, sunlight is partially blocked.

☑ **READING CHECK**

2. Explain Why can't people take photos of the whole moon from Earth?

_____

_____

_____

_____

_____

☑ **READING CHECK**

3. Define What is an eclipse?

_____

_____

_____

_____

_____

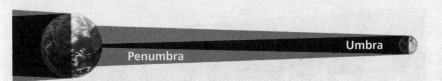

During a solar eclipse, the moon passes between Earth and the sun.

4. Interpret Diagrams Draw arrows on the diagram to show the directions the sun's rays are coming from.

When the moon is directly between the sun and Earth, the moon's shadow falls on Earth, causing a **solar eclipse**. During a *total solar eclipse*, the moon completely blocks the sun's light from the parts of Earth in the umbra. Observers in the penumbra see a *partial solar eclipse*.

The umbra of the moon is small. Thus, a total eclipse covers only a small part of Earth. A total eclipse is visible in an area of only a few hundred square kilometers. A total solar eclipse also lasts for a short time. It lasts for no more than seven minutes at any one location.

A total eclipse will not be visible in the United States until 2017. However, there is a total eclipse somewhere on Earth about every 18 months.

ANNULAR ECLIPSES

If the moon is at or near apogee when it moves between Earth and the sun, the moon's umbra does not reach Earth. When the umbra does not reach Earth, a ring-shaped eclipse occurs. This type of eclipse is called an *annular eclipse. Annulus* is the Latin word for "ring." During an annular eclipse, the moon does not block the sun completely. Instead, a thin ring of sunlight is visible around the edge of the moon. ☑

What Happens During a Lunar Eclipse?

Two things have to happen for a lunar eclipse to occur:

• Earth must be between the moon and the sun.

• Earth's shadow must cross the lighted part of the moon.

A total lunar eclipse happens only when the entire moon passes into Earth's umbra. The figure on the next page shows a diagram of a total lunar eclipse.

✓ READING CHECK

5. Compare What is one difference between a total solar eclipse and an annular eclipse?

_____

_____

_____

_____

_____

_____

_____

SECTION 2 **Movements of the Moon** *continued*

During a lunar eclipse, Earth's shadow falls on the moon.

LOOKING CLOSER

6. Infer On the diagram, circle the part of Earth that a total lunar eclipse would be visible from.

When only part of the moon passes into Earth's umbra, a *partial lunar eclipse* occurs. When the entire moon passes through Earth's penumbra, a *penumbral eclipse* occurs. A penumbral eclipse is barely noticeable.

A lunar eclipse lasts for several hours. Although the moon is in Earth's shadow during a lunar eclipse, the eclipsed moon appears reddish. The red color results because some sunlight bends around Earth through our atmosphere. The light that reaches the moon is mainly red light. ☑

Why Don't Eclipses Happen More Often?

As many as seven eclipses may happen during one year. Four of the eclipses may be lunar eclipses, and three may be solar eclipses, or vice versa. However, total eclipses of the sun and moon do not happen often.

Solar and lunar eclipses do not happen during every lunar orbit. This is because the orbits of Earth and the moon are not in the same plane. The moon crosses the plane of Earth's orbit only twice during each revolution around Earth. A solar eclipse will occur only if this crossing happens when the moon is between Earth and the sun. A lunar eclipse will occur only when Earth is between the moon and the sun during that crossing.

Why Does the Moon Appear Lighted?

Although the moon seems very bright on certain nights, the moon does not produce its own light. The moon reflects light from the sun. Because the moon is a sphere, sunlight always lights half of it. As the moon revolves around Earth, we can see different amounts of the lighted side.

☑ **READING CHECK**

7. Explain Why does the moon often look reddish during a total lunar eclipse?

_____

_____

_____

Critical Thinking

8. Apply Concepts If the moon's orbit and Earth's orbit were in the same plane, how many times during each revolution of the moon would solar eclipses happen?

_____

What Are the Phases of the Moon?

Recall that one side of the moon, called the near side, always faces Earth. As the moon revolves around Earth, different amounts of the near side of the moon are lighted.

Because different parts of the near side are lighted, the moon appears to have different shapes on different nights. The different shapes are called **phases** of the moon. The figure below shows the moon phases. It also shows the positions of Earth and the moon during each phase. ☑

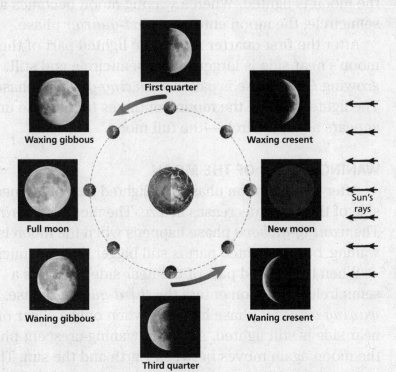

The positions of the moon, sun, and Earth determine which phase the moon is in. The photographs show how the moon looks from Earth at each phase.

When the moon is directly between the sun and Earth, the sun's rays strike only the far side of the moon. As a result, the entire near side of the moon is dark. During the *new moon*, the near side is completely dark. During this phase, the moon is between Earth and the sun. At *full moon*, Earth is between the sun and the moon. During this phase, the sun illuminates the entire near side of the moon.

Throughout the moon's orbit, however, different amounts of the near side are illuminated. As the lighted parts of the moon's near side change, people say the moon is waxing or waning.

READING CHECK

9. Explain Why does the moon go through phases?

_____

_____

_____

LOOKING CLOSER

10. Describe What are the relative positions of the sun, Earth, and moon during a new moon?

_____

_____

_____

WAXING PHASES OF THE MOON

As the moon moves around Earth after its new moon phase, part of the near side becomes illuminated. When the size of the lighted part of the moon is increasing, the moon is *waxing*. A *waxing-crescent* phase happens when a sliver of the moon's near side is illuminated. ☑

When the moon has moved through one-quarter of its orbit after the new moon phase, the moon looks like a half circle, or semicircle. Half of the near side of the moon is lighted. When a waxing moon becomes a semicircle, the moon enters its *first-quarter* phase.

After the first-quarter moon, the lighted part of the moon's near side is larger than a semicircle and still growing. This phase is called a *waxing-gibbous* phase. The lighted part of the moon continues to increase until it appears as a full circle—the full moon.

WANING PHASES OF THE MOON

After the full moon phase, the lighted part of the near side of the moon decreases in size. The moon is *waning*. The *waning-gibbous* phase happens when the moon is waning, but the lighted part is still bigger than a semicircle.

When the lighted part of the near side becomes a semicircle, the moon enters the *third-quarter* phase. A *waning-crescent* phase happens when only a sliver of the near side is still lighted. After the waning-crescent phase, the moon again moves between Earth and the sun. The moon once again appears as the new moon, and the cycle of moon phases begins again.

During the crescent moon phases, only part of the moon shines brightly. However, the rest of the moon's near side is not completely dark, as shown below.

During the crescent moon phases, sunlight that reflects off Earth (earthshine) can light the dark part of the moon. The darker part of the moon in this photo is lit by earthshine.

Talk About It

Infer Make a prediction about what the words *waxing* and *waning* probably mean. Write a sentence using each term. Your sentences should not be about moon phases. Share your sentences with a partner. Together, use the Internet or a dictionary to figure out whether your predicted meanings are correct.

LOOKING CLOSER

12. Identify On the picture, label the part of the moon that is lit by the sun and the part of the moon that is lit by earthshine.

SECTION 2 **Movements of the Moon** *continued*

TIME FROM NEW MOON TO NEW MOON

The moon revolves around Earth in 27.3 days. However, the moon takes longer than that to go through a complete cycle of phases. The period from one new moon to the next new moon is 29.5 days. The difference of 2.2 days is a result of the orbit of the Earth-moon system around the sun.

As the moon orbits Earth, both bodies move slightly farther along their orbit around the sun. Therefore, the moon must go a bit farther to be directly between Earth and the sun. The moon takes about 2.2 days to travel this extra distance. When the moon is directly between Earth and the sun, the moon is in the new-moon phase.

How Do Movements of the Moon Affect Tides?

Recall that tides are a periodic rise and fall of the water level in the ocean and other large water bodies. Tidal bulges form due to the moon's gravitational pull on ocean water. The moon's gravitational pull decreases with distance. Thus, the moon pulls more strongly on the ocean on Earth's near side. The moon pulls less strongly on the ocean on Earth's far side. Because Earth rotates, the tides in a given area change during a day.

The sun also affects tides. The effect of the sun's gravitational pull is smaller, however, because the sun is farther away. Twice each month, when the sun, moon, and Earth are almost in line, the gravitational pull combines. The combined gravitational pull produces especially high tides.

Math *Skills*

13. Calculate A typical year is 365 days long. About how many new moons are there in a typical year?

_____

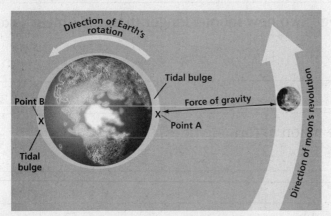

The moon's pull on Earth is greatest at point A, on Earth's near side. The moon's pull on Earth is weakest at point B, on Earth's far side.

LOOKING CLOSER

14. Identify Are point A and point B experiencing high tide or low tide?

_____

Section 2 Review

SECTION VOCABULARY

apogee in the orbit of a satellite, the point that is farthest from Earth	**phase** the change in the illuminated areas of one celestial body as seen from another celestial body; phases of the moon are caused by the changing positions of Earth, the sun, and the moon
eclipse an event in which the shadow of one celestial body falls on another	
lunar eclipse the passing of the moon through Earth's shadow at full moon	**solar eclipse** the passing of the moon between Earth and the sun; during a solar eclipse, the shadow of the moon falls on Earth
perigee in the orbit of a satellite, the point that is closest to Earth	

1. Compare Describe three differences between total lunar eclipses and total solar eclipses.

_____

_____

_____

_____

2. Explain Why is the moon not always the same distance from Earth?

_____

_____

3. Apply Concepts You observe the moon one night and notice that only a sliver is illuminated. Two nights later, a larger portion of the moon is illuminated. What phase was the moon in on the first night?

_____

_____

4. Relate Ideas During which moon phase do all solar eclipses happen? Explain your answer.

_____

_____

_____

5. Explain Why is the time between two new moons longer than the time it takes the moon to orbit Earth once?

_____

_____

_____

6. Identify What is the role of the moon in forming tides?

_____

_____

_____

CHAPTER 28 | Minor Bodies of the Solar System
SECTION
3 **Satellites of Other Planets**

KEY IDEAS

As you read this section, keep these questions in mind:

- How are the two moons of Mars similar, and how are they different?
- How did scientists discover volcanoes on Io?
- What is one special characteristic of each of the Galilean moons?
- How do the rings of Saturn differ from the rings of the other outer planets?

What Are the Characteristics of Mars's Moons?

Mars has two tiny moons named Phobos and Deimos. They revolve around Mars relatively quickly. Unlike most other moons, Phobos and Deimos are not spherical. Instead, they are chunks of rock with irregular shapes. Scientists think these moons are actually asteroids that were captured by Mars's gravitational pull. At its longest, Phobos is about 27 km across. Deimos is about 15 km across.

Both Phobos and Deimos are dark, like the maria on the surface of Earth's moon. Phobos and Deimos both have many craters. These craters indicate that many asteroids and comets have hit the moons. Scientists think the large number of craters means the moons are quite old. ☑

What Are the Characteristics of Jupiter's Moons?

In 1610, Galileo Galilei discovered four moons orbiting Jupiter. Since then, scientists have discovered that Jupiter has many more than 60 moons. Most of Jupiter's moons are relatively small. The largest of the moons are those that Galileo discovered. These four moons are called the **Galilean moons**. They are

- Io
- Europa
- Ganymede
- Callisto ☑

READING TOOLBOX

Summarize Before you read this section, create a two-column table with six rows. In the first column, list the names of the six main objects described in this section (Mars, Jupiter, Saturn, Uranus, Neptune, and Pluto). In the second column, describe the moons and other characteristics of each object.

✓ READING CHECK

1. Explain Why do scientists think Phobos and Deimos are very old?

_____

_____

_____

✓ READING CHECK

2. Identify What are the four Galilean moons?

_____

_____

_____

_____

SECTION 3 **Satellites of Other Planets** *continued*

IO

Io orbits closest to Jupiter. It is the first body other than Earth on which scientists saw evidence of active volcanoes. An engineer discovered the volcanoes while studying images of Io that were taken by the *Voyager* spacecraft. Volcanoes on Io eject thousands of metric tons of material each second. The lava that erupts on Io is even hotter than lava on Earth. ☑

Parts of Io's surface are yellow-red. This color is evidence that volcanic material on Io is mostly sulfur and sulfur dioxide. Data collected by the *Galileo* spacecraft show that Io has a giant iron core and may have its own magnetic field.

☑ **READING CHECK**

3. Describe How was Io's volcanism discovered?

_____

_____

_____

_____

Io is one of the most volcanically active bodies in our solar system.

EUROPA

Europa is the second closest Galilean moon to Jupiter. Europa is about the same size as Earth's moon. Astronomers think Europa has a rocky core that is covered with ice up to 100 km deep. Spacecraft have made observations of Europa. From the observations, scientists have concluded that liquid water may exist under the ice. If liquid water exists, it is possible that life might also exist on Europa.

Critical Thinking

4. Compare Describe two differences between Io and Europa.

_____

_____

_____

_____

_____

GANYMEDE

Ganymede is the third Galilean moon from Jupiter. It is also the largest moon in the solar system. However, the mass of Ganymede is relatively small because the moon is made up mainly of ice mixed with rock. Images of Ganymede show that it has dark, crater-filled areas. It also has light areas that scientists think are long ridges and valleys. Ganymede is the only moon in our solar system that has its own magnetic field.

CALLISTO

Of the Galilean moons, Callisto is the farthest from Jupiter. Callisto is similar to Ganymede in size, density, and composition. However, the surface of Callisto is much rougher than the surface of Ganymede. Its surface has a very large number of craters.

Callisto has more craters per square kilometer than most other moons in the solar system.

LOOKING CLOSER
5. Infer How did Callisto's craters form?

_____

_____

_____

What Are the Characteristics of Saturn's Moons?

Saturn has dozens of moons. Many of them are small, icy bodies that have many craters. However, five of Saturn's moons are quite large. Saturn's largest moon, Titan, has a diameter of 5,000 km.

TITAN

Unlike other moons in our solar system, Titan has a thick atmosphere. Its atmosphere contains so many hydrocarbons that smog hides most of Titan's surface. ☑

In 2005, the *Huygens* probe gathered data about Titan's atmosphere. Scientists are using the data to find clues about how Titan and its atmosphere formed. The probe sent back images of Titan's surface as well. The images show signs of a flowing liquid, which scientists think is liquid methane.

READING CHECK

6. Identify What is the main difference between Titan and other moons in our solar system?

_____

_____

SATURN'S OTHER MOONS

Saturn's icy moons resemble Jupiter's icy Galilean moons. Enceladus has erupting geysers, so scientists think this moon may have underground water near the surface. The presence of water could mean Enceladus might have conditions needed for life. Saturn's other smaller moons have irregular shapes.

LOOKING CLOSER
7. Identify Name three of Saturn's moons other than Enceladus and Titan.

_____

_____

_____

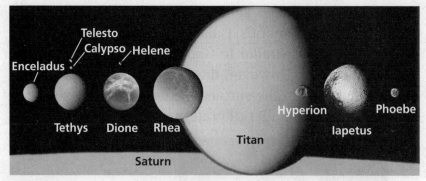

This image shows some of Saturn's largest moons. Distances are not to scale.

What Are the Characteristics of the Moons of Uranus and Neptune?

By the mid-1800s, scientists had discovered Uranus's four largest moons: Oberon, Titania, Umbriel, and Ariel. A fifth moon, Miranda, was discovered in 1948. Scientists have recently discovered many smaller moons using spacecraft and observatories such as the *Hubble Space Telescope.* Scientists now know that Uranus has at least 24 small moons. ☑

Neptune has at least 13 moons. Triton, which is a large icy moon, is unusual. It revolves around Neptune in a backward, or *retrograde*, orbit. Some scientists think Triton formed somewhere else in the solar system and was captured later by Neptune's gravity. Triton's diameter is 2,705 km, and its atmosphere is thin.

What Are the Characteristics of Pluto's Moons?

Scientists no longer consider Pluto a planet. However, Pluto has at least three moons. Pluto's largest moon, Charon, is almost half the size of Pluto. Because Charon and Pluto are so close in mass, both bodies orbit a common balance point called a *barycenter* that is located between both bodies.

Charon orbits Pluto in 6.4 days, which is the same length of time as one day on Pluto. Thus, Charon stays in the same place in Pluto's sky. In the same way that one side of Earth's moon always faces Earth, one side of Pluto always faces Charon.

Pluto's other two moons, Nix and Hydra, are much smaller. Nix and Hydra also orbit the barycenter between Pluto and Charon.

READING CHECK
8. Explain How did scientists discover most of Uranus's smaller moons?

_____

_____

Talk About It
Model With a partner, create a model to represent the motions of Pluto and Charon. Together, talk about how to use your model to figure out whether you could see Charon from all points on Pluto's surface, or whether Charon would be visible only from certain places.

SECTION 3 **Satellites of Other Planets** *continued*

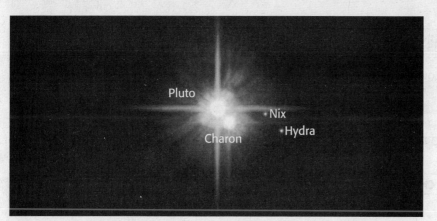

Scientists discovered Nix and Hydra in 2005 using the *Hubble Space Telescope*.

Critical Thinking

9. Infer Why do you think scientists had to use very strong telescopes to discover Nix and Hydra?

_____

_____

What Are the Characteristics of the Rings of the Gas Giants?

Each of Saturn's rings is divided into hundreds of smaller rings, or ringlets. The ringlets are made up of billions of pieces of rock and ice. The pieces range in size from particles the size of dust to chunks as big as a house. Each piece follows its own orbit around Saturn. ☑

Scientists once thought that the material in Saturn's rings was as old as Saturn itself. Evidence now shows that the rings are much younger. Scientists think the particles came from a large cometlike body that entered Saturn's orbit and broke apart.

The other gas giants also have rings. These rings are relatively narrow, and thus harder to detect. For instance, Saturn's rings were discovered more than 300 years ago, but Jupiter's ring was not discovered until 1979. The table below describes the rings of the gas giants.

✓ READING CHECK

10. Identify What are Saturn's rings made of?

_____

_____

Characteristics of the Rings of Gas Giants

Planet	Description of Rings
Saturn	• hundreds of small ringlets forming larger rings • very thin ring system
Jupiter	• single thin ring • made up of particles that may have come from Io or another one of Jupiter's moons
Uranus	• 12 thin rings
Neptune	• a relatively small number of rings • clumpy rather than thin and uniform

LOOKING CLOSER

11. Compare How are Neptune's rings different from the rings of the other gas giants?

_____

_____

_____

Section 3 Review

SECTION VOCABULARY

Galilean moon any one of the four largest satellites of Jupiter—Io, Europa, Ganymede, and Callisto—that were discovered by Galileo in 1610	

1. Describe Complete the table below to describe the special characteristics of the Galilean moons.

Moon	Special Characteristics
Io	
	covered with a thick layer of ice; may have liquid water under the ice
	largest moon in the solar system; has its own magnetic field
Callisto	

2. Compare How are Io's volcanoes different from volcanoes on Earth?

_____

_____

3. Describe Give one similarity and one difference between Phobos and Deimos.

_____

_____

4. Compare What is the main difference between Saturn's rings and the rings of other planets?

_____

_____

5. Identify How is Triton different from most other planets in the solar system?

_____

_____

6. Describe How do scientists think Saturn's rings formed?

_____

_____

7. Infer Scientists did not discover Jupiter's ring until 1979. What is the most likely reason it took scientists so long to discover Jupiter's ring?

_____

_____

Asteroids, Comets, and Meteoroids

KEY IDEAS

As you read this section, keep these questions in mind:

- What are the physical characteristics of asteroids and comets?
- Where is the Kuiper Belt located?
- How do meteoroids, meteorites, and meteors differ?
- What is the relationship between the Oort cloud and comets?

What Are Asteroids?

Asteroids are chunks of rock that orbit the sun. Astronomers have discovered more than 300,000 asteroids, and they think that millions may exist. Like the orbits of planets, the orbits of asteroids are ellipses.

Asteroids vary greatly in size. Asteroid Ida is 56 km long. Asteroid Dactyl is 1.5 km across.

LOCATION OF ASTEROIDS

Most asteroids are located in a region between the orbits of Mars and Jupiter. This region is called the *asteroid belt*. Some asteroids, however, orbit the sun more closely. The closest asteroids to the sun are located inside the orbit of Mars. The *Trojan asteroids* are groups of asteroids found near Jupiter.

READING TOOLBOX

Compare After you read this section, create a three-way Venn diagram to compare asteroids, comets, and meteoroids. Some of the overlapping spaces in the diagram may be left blank.

LOOKING CLOSER
1. Identify On the picture, label which asteroid is Ida and which is Dactyl.

READING CHECK
2. Describe Where are most asteroids located?

_____

_____

_____

SECTION 4 **Asteroids, Comets, and Meteoroids** *continued*

COMPOSITION OF ASTEROIDS

The composition of an asteroid is similar to the composition of the inner planets. Scientists group asteroids into three main categories based on their main component. The table below describes these categories.

LOOKING CLOSER

3. Compare How is the appearance of a carbon asteroid different from the appearance of an iron and nickel asteroid?

_____

_____

_____

_____

_____

The Main Categories of Asteroids

Category (main component)	Description
Carbon	• the most common type of asteroid • generally dark colored
Silicate minerals	• look like Earth rocks
Iron and nickel	• the rarest type of asteroid • look shiny and metallic

NEAR-EARTH ASTEROIDS

More than 1,000 asteroids have orbits that sometimes bring the asteroids very close to Earth's orbit. Thus, scientists call them *near-Earth asteroids*.

Near-Earth asteroids make up only a very small percentage of the total number of asteroids. However, these asteroids could cause a great deal of damage if they struck Earth. Asteroid detection programs track asteroids whose orbits may bring them close to Earth. By monitoring these asteroids, scientists hope to predict and possibly avoid future collisions.

Critical Thinking

4. Connect Ideas When an asteroid collides with Earth, it produces effects similar to those of a large volcanic eruption. What is one way an asteroid impact might harm life on Earth?

_____

_____

_____

_____

_____

Barringer Meteorite Crater in Arizona formed when a small asteroid with a diameter of only 50 m struck Earth. This impact happened 49,000 years ago. Asteroid impacts have produced dozens of craters on Earth. However, most craters have eroded, or sediments have covered them. Therefore, they are hard to see.

Barringer Meteorite Crater, which is also called Meteor Crater, is the result of an asteroid impact.

SECTION 4 **Asteroids, Comets, and Meteoroids** *continued*

What Are Comets?

A comet is a small body of ice, rock, and dust that follows a highly elliptical orbit around the sun. One of the most famous comets is Halley's Comet, which passes by Earth every 76 years. It last passed Earth in 1986. Another comet, Hale-Bopp, is visible from Earth every 5 to 10 years.

COMPOSITION OF COMETS

A comet has several parts: a core (nucleus), a coma, and two tails. The *core* of a comet is made up of rock, metals, and ice. Comet cores are typically between 1 km and 100 km in diameter. The *coma* is a cloud of gas and dust that surrounds the core. A comet looks bright because the coma reflects sunlight. Together, the core and coma form the *head* of the comet.

Solar energy causes ice in a comet to change to a gas. Solar winds push the gas off behind the comet, forming the gas tail, or *ion tail*. Thus, the ion tail of a comet points away from the sun. A comet's second tail, the *dust tail*, is made up of dust. The dust tail curves backward along the comet's orbit.

The upper tail on this comet is the ion tail. The lower tail is the dust tail.

THE KUIPER BELT

The **Kuiper Belt** is a region beyond Neptune's orbit. It forms a ring of dwarf planets and small icy bodies. The dwarf planets Pluto and Eris are located in the Kuiper Belt.

Talk About It

Connecting Ideas You have probably heard the word *nucleus* used in different contexts. With a partner, identify several uses of this term and talk about what these uses have in common. If you are unfamiliar with other uses of *nucleus*, look up the word in a dictionary. You could also use the glossaries of life science and physical science textbooks.

LOOKING CLOSER

5. Apply Concepts On the diagram, draw an arrow to show the direction in which the sun lies.

THE OORT CLOUD

Astronomers think most comets come from the Oort cloud. The **Oort cloud** is a cloud of dust and ice that lies far beyond Neptune's orbit. It surrounds the solar system and contains the nuclei of billions of comets. Scientists think that the matter in the Oort cloud is left over from the formation of the solar system. Studying this matter helps scientist understand the history of the solar system. ☑

Bodies within the Oort cloud may take a few million years to complete one circular orbit. Comets follow elliptical paths that take them closer to the sun. Those that take more than 200 years to complete one orbit are called *long-period comets*. Comets that complete one orbit in less than 200 years are called *short-period comets*. Recently, scientists discovered that most short-period comets actually come from the Kuiper Belt.

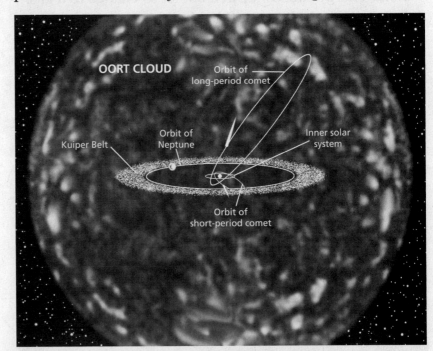

Most comets come from the Oort cloud. The Oort cloud is located far beyond Neptune's orbit, in the outer parts of the solar system.

✔ **READING CHECK**

6. Identify What is the Oort cloud?

_____

_____

_____

LOOKING CLOSER

7. Identify On the diagram, circle the region that scientists think most short-period comets come from.

What Are Meteoroids?

Small bits of rock and metal called **meteoroids** also move through the solar system. Most meteoroids have a diameter less than 1 mm. Scientists think that most meteoroids are pieces of matter that broke off comets. Some comets may be pieces of asteroids.

SECTION 4 **Asteroids, Comets, and Meteoroids** *continued*

METEORS

Sometimes, meteoroids enter Earth's atmosphere. In Earth's atmosphere, friction between the meteoroid and the air heats the meteoroid. As a result, the meteoroid burns up. As the meteoroid burns, it produces a bright light called a **meteor**. Some people call meteors *shooting stars*. When many meteoroids enter Earth's atmosphere in a short time, a *meteor shower* occurs. ☑

METEORITES

Most meteoroids that enter Earth's atmosphere burn up, but some larger meteoroids do not burn up completely. These meteoroids fall to Earth's surface. A meteoroid that hits Earth's surface is called a *meteorite*. Most meteorites are small. However, some meteorites strike Earth with the force of a large bomb. These impacts leave large craters.

Scientists group meteorites into three categories. The table below describes these categories.

The Main Categories of Meteorites

Category	Description
Stony	• similar in composition to rocks on Earth • most common type of meteorite
Iron	• have a metallic appearance
Stony-iron	• contain both iron and stone • rarest type of meteorite

Some stony meteorites contain carbon compounds.

Iron meteorites look very different from most Earth rocks.

Many stony-iron meteorites contain pieces of stone surrounded by iron.

✔ **READING CHECK**

8. Describe How does a meteor form?

_____

_____

_____

_____

_____

_____

_____

LOOKING CLOSER

9. Explain Iron meteorites are the easiest kind of meteorite to identify. What is the most likely reason for this?

_____

_____

_____

Section 4 Review

SECTION VOCABULARY

asteroid a small, rocky object that orbits the sun; most asteroids are located in a band between the orbits of Mars and Jupiter	**meteor** a bright streak of light that results when a meteoroid burns up in Earth's atmosphere
comet a small body of rock, ice, and cosmic dust that follows an elliptical orbit around the sun and that gives off gas and dust in the form of a tail as it passes close to the sun	**meteoroid** a relatively small, rocky body that travels through space
Kuiper Belt a region of the solar system that starts just beyond the orbit of Neptune and that contains dwarf planets and other small bodies made mostly of ice	**Oort cloud** a spherical region that surrounds the solar system, that extends from the Kuiper Belt to almost halfway to the nearest star, and that contains billions of comets

1. Compare Describe two differences between asteroids and comets.

_____

_____

_____

2. Infer Could the ion tail of a comet ever point in the opposite direction from the dust tail? Explain your answer.

_____

_____

_____

3. Describe List the following parts of the solar system from closest to the sun to farthest from the sun: Kuiper Belt, asteroid belt, Neptune, Oort cloud.

_____

4. Apply Concepts Suppose astronomers discovered a comet that takes about 875 years to orbit the sun. Is the comet a short-period comet or a long-period comet? Where did it probably come from?

_____

_____

5. Identify Errors Your friend tells you that he found a meteor in his backyard. What is wrong with your friend's statement?

_____

_____

Structure of the Sun

KEY IDEAS

As you read this section, keep these questions in mind:

- How do the sun's radiative and convective zones compare?
- What are the three layers of the sun's atmosphere?
- How does the sun convert matter to energy in its core?

What Are the Sun's Layers?

Scientists cannot see inside the sun. They use models to figure out what the sun's interior is like. They also study the sun's surface to learn more about the inside of the sun. The sun has four main layers:

- the core
- the radiative zone
- the convective zone
- the atmosphere ☑

THE CORE

The *core* is the sun's center. Like the rest of the sun, the core is made up of ionized gas. Because the sun's mass is so large, the gas in the core is under a great deal of pressure. In fact, the pressure is so great that the core is as dense as iron.

THE RADIATIVE ZONE

The energy produced in the core moves through two other zones until it reaches the sun's atmosphere. In the **radiative zone**, energy moves in the form of electromagnetic waves, or radiation.

THE CONVECTIVE ZONE

The next layer is the convective zone. In the **convective zone**, energy moves by convection. *Convection* is the transfer of energy by moving matter. In the convective zone, hot gases transfer energy to the sun's surface. As the gases approach the sun's surface, they become cooler and denser. The cooler, denser gases sink back to the bottom of the convective zone, and the cycle begins again.

READING TOOLBOX

Organize On a separate piece of paper, create a graphic organizer describing the layers of the sun.

☑ READING CHECK

1. Identify What are the four main layers of the sun?

_____

_____

_____

Critical Thinking

2. Infer Where is the temperature probably higher—at the bottom of the convective zone or at the top?

_____

Layers of the
sun's atmosphere

Layers of the
sun's interior

Corona
>1,000,000 °C

Convective Zone
2,000,000 °C

Chromosphere
6,000 °C
to 50,000 °C

Radiative Zone
2,000,000 °C to
7,000,000 °C

Photosphere
6,000 °C

Core
15,000,000 °C

Sunspot
3,800 °C

Reactions in the sun's core produce energy. This energy moves toward the outer parts of the sun through radiation and convection.

What Are the Layers of the Sun's Atmosphere?

Although the sun itself is made up of gases, scientists consider the uppermost gases as the atmosphere. The sun's atmosphere surrounds the convective zone. The sun's atmosphere has three layers: the photosphere, the chromosphere, and the corona. ☑

THE PHOTOSPHERE

The **photosphere** is the layer closest to the convective zone. It is made up of gases that have risen from the convective zone. The photosphere gives off most of its energy in the form of visible light. The visible light we see from Earth comes from the photosphere. The other layers of the sun's atmosphere are transparent. Thus, scientists sometimes refer to the photosphere as the sun's "surface."

LOOKING CLOSER

3. Compare What is the hottest layer of the sun?

_____

_____

_____

☑ **READING CHECK**

4. Describe What are the three layers of the sun's atmosphere?

_____

_____

_____

LOOKING CLOSER

5. Define What are sunspots?

_____

_____

The dark spots in the figure are called *sunspots*. Sunspots are cooler regions in the sun's photosphere.

THE CHROMOSPHERE

The **chromosphere** is the thin layer above the photosphere. It is made up of gases that glow with a reddish light. These gases move outward from the photosphere.

THE CORONA

The **corona** is the outermost layer of the sun's atmosphere. The corona is not very dense, but its magnetic field can stop most subatomic particles from escaping into space. However, some particles do escape into space. Some of these particles are electrons, and others are electrically charged particles called *ions*.

The charged particles from the corona make up the *solar wind*, which flows from the sun. We cannot usually see the chromosphere or the corona from Earth. However, during a solar eclipse, these layers become visible.

Normally, we cannot see the sun's corona. During a solar eclipse, however, the moon blocks the photosphere and the corona becomes visible.

Where Does the Sun's Energy Come From?

The sun produces energy through a process called nuclear fusion. During **nuclear fusion**, the nuclei of small atoms fuse, or combine, to form larger nuclei. Nuclear fusion releases huge amounts of energy.

On Earth, atoms are made of a nucleus surrounded by electrons. The nucleus and electrons stay together. However, the high temperature and pressure in the sun's core cause the electrons to separate from the nucleus. The nuclei in the sun tend to push away from each other. However, the high temperature and pressure force the nuclei close enough to fuse together. ☑

The most common form of nuclear fusion in the sun is the fusion of hydrogen into helium. This kind of nuclear fusion has three main steps.

Talk About It
Use Word Roots Use a dictionary or the Internet to learn the meaning of the prefix *chromo-*. With a partner, talk about why the reddish layer of the sun is called the *chromosphere*.

LOOKING CLOSER
6. Explain Why is the corona visible during a total solar eclipse?

_____

_____

 **READING CHECK**

7. Describe What causes electrons to separate from nuclei inside the sun?

_____

_____

SECTION 1 **Structure of the Sun** *continued*

HOW NUCLEAR FUSION HAPPENS

In the first step of nuclear fusion, two hydrogen nuclei collide and fuse to form a larger nucleus. Each hydrogen nucleus contains only one proton, which has a positive charge. When the two nuclei fuse, one of the protons emits a particle called a *positron*. When the proton emits a positron, the proton changes into a neutron. Therefore, at the end of step 1, the nucleus has one proton and one neutron. ☑

During the second step of nuclear fusion, another proton fuses with the new nucleus. The nucleus now contains two protons and one neutron. It is a nucleus of the element helium.

During the final step of nuclear fusion, two nuclei from step 2 fuse together. As this fusion happens, two protons are released. The remaining two protons and two neutrons are fused together. The protons and neutrons form a new nucleus of a different form of the element helium.

☑ **READING CHECK**

8. Explain What happens when two protons fuse?

_____

_____

_____

LOOKING CLOSER

9. Identify All together, how many protons have to fuse together to form one $_4$He nucleus? Explain your answer.

_____

_____

_____

_____

_____

_____

Steps in Nuclear Fusion

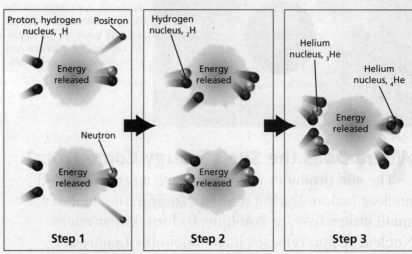

Step 1 — Proton, hydrogen nucleus, $_1$H; Positron; Energy released; Neutron; Energy released

Step 2 — Hydrogen nucleus, $_2$H; Energy released; Energy released

Step 3 — Helium nucleus, $_3$He; Helium nucleus, $_4$He; Energy released

THE SUN'S ENERGY

One of the final products of this type of nuclear fusion is a helium nucleus. The helium nucleus has about 0.7% less mass than the hydrogen nuclei that formed it. The lost mass has been converted into energy during the fusion process. This energy causes the sun to shine and to have a high temperature.

SECTION 1 **Structure of the Sun** *continued*

How Can Matter Change into Energy?

In 1905, Albert Einstein suggested that a small amount of matter can become a large amount of energy. This suggestion was part of Einstein's theory of relativity. His theory of relativity includes the equation $E = mc^2$. Scientists can use this equation to calculate how much energy a certain amount of matter can become. In this equation,

- E represents energy

- m represents mass

- c represents the speed of light (about 300,000 km/s) ☑

You can see that c^2 is a very large number. Therefore, even a tiny amount of mass can become a very large amount of energy.

Scientists have used Einstein's equation to explain how the sun produces so much energy. Each second, the sun uses nuclear fusion to change about 4 million tons of mass into energy.

What Is the Sun Made Of?

Scientists use a *spectrograph* to break up a star's light into a spectrum of colors. They can use this spectrum to figure out what elements the star is made of. Dark lines in the spectrum form when elements in the star's outer layers absorb certain wavelengths of light. Each element produces a unique pattern because of the wavelengths it absorbs. Astronomers use this information to infer which elements are part of a star.

In this way, scientists have discovered that about 75% of the sun's mass is hydrogen. About 24% of the sun's mass is helium. However, the sun's spectrum shows that the sun contains small amounts of almost all chemical elements.

READING CHECK

10. Restate In words, state the relationship between matter and energy that Einstein's equation describes.

_____

_____

_____

LOOKING CLOSER

11. Explain Why are there more lines in the sun's spectrum than in the hydrogen spectrum?

_____

_____

_____

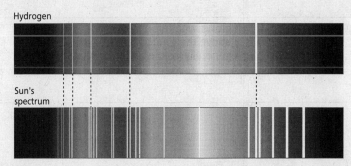

The first spectrum shows which wavelengths of light are absorbed by hydrogen. The second spectrum shows which wavelengths of light are absorbed by the sun.

Section 1 Review

SECTION VOCABULARY

chromosphere the thin layer of the sun that is just above the photosphere and that glows a reddish color during eclipses	**nuclear fusion** the process by which nuclei of small atoms combine to form a new, more massive nucleus; the process releases energy
convective zone the region of the sun's interior that is between the radiative zone and the photosphere and in which energy is carried upward by convection	**photosphere** the visible surface of the sun **radiative zone** the zone of the sun's interior that is between the core and the convective zone and in which energy moves by radiation
corona the outermost layer of the sun's atmosphere	

1. Explain Why does nuclear fusion happen only in the sun's core?

_____

_____

2. Infer Will the amount of hydrogen in the sun increase or decrease over the next million years? Explain your answer.

_____

_____

3. Compare What is the main difference between the radiative zone and the convective zone?

_____

_____

4. Describe Complete the table below to describe the layers of the sun's atmosphere.

Layer	Average Temperature	Other Characteristics
	6,000 °C	
Chromosphere		• glows with a reddish color • above the photosphere • generally visible only during solar eclipses

CHAPTER 29 **The Sun**
SECTION
2 **Solar Activity**

> **KEY IDEAS**
>
> **As you read this section, keep these questions in mind:**
>
> • How are sunspots related to powerful magnetic fields on the sun?
>
> • What are the differences between prominences, solar flares, and coronal mass ejections?
>
> • How can the solar wind cause auroras on Earth?

Why Do the Sun's Gases Move?

The gases in the sun are constantly moving. Energy from the core pushes the gases outward. The force of gravity pulls them inward.

The sun's rotation also causes the gases to move. Because the sun is a sphere, each point on the sun rotates at a different speed. For example, places close to the sun's equator rotate once every 25.3 Earth days. Places near the poles take 33 Earth days to rotate once. On average, the sun rotates once every 27 days.

What Are Sunspots?

The movement of gases forms magnetic fields in the sun. These fields slow down convection in parts of the convective zone. That means that less energy is transferred from the core to those parts of the photosphere. Therefore, those areas are cooler than other areas of the photosphere. These cooler areas are called **sunspots**. Sunspots appear darker than the photosphere around them. The rest of the photosphere has a grainy appearance, called *granulation*.

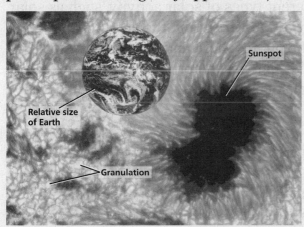

The diameter of this sunspot is larger than Earth's diameter. The area around the sunspot shows granulation.

> **READING TOOLBOX**
>
> **Ask Questions** As you read this section, write down any questions you have. Discuss your questions in a small group. Together, try to figure out the answers to your questions.

LOOKING CLOSER

1. Synthesize Text and Graphics How is the area of the convective zone beneath the sunspot different from the area beneath the granulation?

_____
_____
_____
_____
_____
_____
_____

SECTION 2 Solar Activity continued

Critical Thinking

2. Infer What might scientists have observed about sunspots that led them to conclude that the sun rotates?

_____

_____

_____

_____

LOOKING CLOSER

3. Estimate When will the next high point in the sunspot cycle probably occur?

_____

_____

THE SUNSPOT CYCLE

Astronomers have studied sunspots for hundreds of years. In fact, they discovered that the sun rotates by watching how sunspots move. Later, they discovered that the number and location of sunspots change in a cycle that lasts about 11 years.

At the beginning of a sunspot cycle, the number of sunspots is very small. Slowly, more sunspots appear, especially in the area about halfway between the equator and the poles. The number of sunspots increases every year, until there are more than 100 sunspots. Then, sunspots at higher latitudes slowly begin to disappear, and new ones appear near the equator. Slowly, the number of sunspots decreases, and the cycle begins again.

Sunspots Recorded

The sunspot cycle lasts an average of 11 years.

What Are Solar Eruptions?

The sun's magnetic fields can affect the *solar activity cycle*, too. This cycle describes the increases and decreases in different types of solar activity, such as solar eruptions. During a *solar eruption*, the sun lifts a lot of material above the photosphere and emits tiny particles. Prominences, solar flares, and coronal mass ejections are three examples of solar eruptions. ☑

PROMINENCES

Prominences are huge clouds of glowing gas that form arches above the sun's surface. The shape of the sun's magnetic field makes prominences form huge arches. The prominences bend to follow the sun's magnetic field.

✓ **READING CHECK**

4. Define What is a solar eruption?

_____

_____

_____

_____

SOLAR FLARES

Solar flares are the most violent of all solar eruptions. A **solar flare** is a sudden eruption of electrons, protons, or other electrically charged particles. Scientists do not know what causes solar flares. However, they do know that solar flares release the energy that is stored in a sunspot's magnetic field. Solar flares rarely last longer than one hour. During a peak in the sunspot cycle, 5 to 10 solar flares may happen every day. ☑

Coronal loops like this one sometimes form during solar flares. A coronal loop can stretch more than 500,000 km above the sun's surface.

✔ **READING CHECK**

5. Describe What is a solar flare?

_____

_____

_____

CORONAL MASS EJECTIONS

Sometimes, the sun can throw off parts of the corona. This is called a **coronal mass ejection**. Particles from a coronal mass ejection fly into space and can hit Earth's magnetosphere. Earth's *magnetosphere* is the area around Earth that contains a magnetic field. A coronal mass ejection can disturb Earth's magnetic field. This disturbance is called a *geomagnetic storm.* ☑

Geomagnetic storms can interfere with radio communications on Earth. They can also damage satellites or cause blackouts. A few small geomagnetic storms happen each month. Severe geomagnetic storms happen, on average, less than once a year.

✔ **READING CHECK**

6. Explain How does a geomagnetic storm form?

_____

_____

_____

_____

_____

What Are Auroras?

When the solar wind interacts with Earth's magnetosphere, auroras can form. **Auroras** are bands of colored light in the sky. The particles in the solar wind are attracted to Earth's magnetic poles. When the particles interact with the magnetosphere, they give off light. Most auroras form near the north or south magnetic poles. Auroras can also be called *aurora borealis* (northern lights) or *aurora australis* (southern lights).

Section 2 Review

SECTION VOCABULARY

aurora colored light produced by charged particles from the solar wind and from the magnetosphere that react with and excite the oxygen and nitrogen of Earth's upper atmosphere; usually seen in the sky near Earth's magnetic poles	**prominence** a loop of relatively cool, incandescent gas that extends above the photosphere and above the sun's edge as seen from Earth
coronal mass ejection coronal gas that is thrown into space from the sun	**solar flare** an explosive release of energy that comes from the sun and that is associated with magnetic disturbances on the sun's surface
	sunspot a dark area of the photosphere of the sun that is cooler than the surrounding areas and that has a strong magnetic field

1. Explain Why are sunspots cooler than the other areas of the photosphere?

_____

_____

_____

_____

2. Compare Describe one difference between prominences and solar flares.

_____

_____

_____

3. Explain Why are most auroras seen near the magnetic poles?

_____

_____

_____

4. Describe How are sunspots related to solar flares?

_____

_____

_____

5. Describe Relationships Describe two examples of how solar activity can affect people on Earth.

_____

_____

_____

CHAPTER 30 Stars, Galaxies, and the Universe

SECTION 1

Characteristics of Stars

KEY IDEAS

As you read this section, keep these questions in mind:

- How do astronomers determine the composition and temperature of a star?
- Why do stars appear to move in the sky?
- How do astronomers describe the distances to stars?
- What is the difference between absolute magnitude and apparent magnitude?

What Is a Star?

A **star** is a ball of very hot gases that emits, or gives off, light. This light comes from nuclear fusion within the star. *Nuclear fusion* happens when small atomic nuclei combine to form larger atomic nuclei.

Most stars in the night sky appear to be tiny dots of white light. In fact, stars vary in color. For example, the star Antares shines with a slightly reddish color. Our own star, the sun, is a yellow star.

How Do Astronomers Learn About Stars?

Astronomers learn about stars by studying the light that stars emit. Astronomers study starlight with spectrographs. *Spectrographs* are tools that separate light into different colors, or wavelengths. Light that passes through a spectrograph produces a range of colors and lines called a *spectrum*.

A star's spectrum shows the star's composition and temperature. The flowchart below describes how a spectrum indicates a star's composition.

Elements in a star's outer layers absorb different colors of light emitted by the star. Therefore, the star produces a spectrum that does not contain all the colors of light.

↓

Astronomers study a star's spectrum to find out which colors of light the star's outer layers absorbed.

↓

The colors missing from the star's spectrum tell the astronomers what elements are in the star.

READING TOOLBOX

Outline Before you read this section, create an outline using the headings. As you read, fill in the outline with details from the section.

READING CHECK

1. Identify What is a spectrograph?

_____

_____

_____

LOOKING CLOSER

2. Describe How do scientists use a star's spectrum to determine the star's composition?

_____

_____

_____

Critical Thinking

3. Apply Prior Knowledge
A star is made mainly of hydrogen and helium. Name one difference between a star's composition and Earth's composition.

_____

_____

LOOKING CLOSER

4. Identify Name three stars that are hotter than our sun.

_____

_____

_____

5. Explain How can a star that has more mass than our sun be smaller than our sun?

_____

_____

_____

THE COMPOSITION OF STARS

Each chemical element absorbs and emits certain wavelengths of light. The colors and lines in the spectrum of a star show which elements make up the star.

Spectrum analysis shows that stars do not contain any elements that are not found on Earth. The most common element in stars is hydrogen. Helium is the second most common element in stars. Stars have small amounts of other elements, such as carbon, oxygen, and nitrogen.

THE TEMPERATURES OF STARS

The color of a star indicates the star's temperature. Most star temperatures range from 2,800 °C to 24,000 °C. Blue stars are the hottest. Their average surface temperature is 35,000 °C. Red stars are the coolest. Their average surface temperature is 3,000 °C. Yellow stars have surface temperatures of about 5,500 °C. The table below shows the relationship between star color and temperature.

Color	Surface Temperature (°C)	Examples
Blue	above 30,000	10 Lacertae
Blue-white	10,000–30,000	Rigel, Spica
White	7,500–10,000	Vega, Sirius
Yellow-white	6,000–7,500	Canopus, Procyon
Yellow	5,000–6,000	our sun, Capella
Orange	3,500–5,000	Arcturus, Aldebaran
Red	below 3,500	Betelgeuse, Antares

THE SIZES AND MASSES OF STARS

Stars vary in size. The smallest stars are slightly bigger than Jupiter. These stars are about one-seventh the size of our sun. Most of the stars you see in the sky are about the size of our sun. The sun is a medium-sized star. It has a diameter of about 1,390,000 km. Some giant stars have diameters that are 1,000 times the sun's diameter.

Stars also vary in mass. Many stars have about the same mass as the sun. However, some stars have higher or lower masses than the sun. Very dense stars may have more mass than the sun and still be smaller than the sun. Less dense stars may be larger than the sun but have less mass than the sun. ☑

How Do Stars Move in the Sky?

Two kinds of motion are associated with stars:

• apparent motion across the night sky

• actual motion through space

The apparent motion of stars is easy to see. Astronomers must use telescopes and spacecraft to study the actual motion of stars.

APPARENT MOTION OF STARS

From Earth, stars appear to move across the night sky. This *apparent motion* of stars results from the movement of Earth. As Earth rotates, stars seem to move in a circle around a central star. This central star is called Polaris, or the North Star. Polaris does not seem to move much because it is directly over the North Pole. ☑

Earth's revolution around the sun also causes apparent motion. As Earth orbits the sun, different stars become visible during different seasons. The visible stars seem to move slightly to the west each night. After many months, some stars disappear below the western horizon.

CIRCUMPOLAR STARS

Some stars are always visible in the night sky. These stars never pass below the horizon. These stars are called *circumpolar stars*. The stars of the Little Dipper are circumpolar for most people in the Northern Hemisphere.

At the North Pole, all visible stars are circumpolar. As you move away from the North Pole toward the equator, you can see fewer circumpolar stars.

Stars appear as curved trails in this long-exposure photograph. These trails result from Earth's rotation.

> **☑ READING CHECK**
>
> **6. Explain** What causes the apparent motion of stars?

> **LOOKING CLOSER**
>
> **7. Identify** Circle the North Star on the picture.

Talk About It

Discuss In most cases, when a star seems to move across the sky, its motion is apparent motion. However, some stars move across the sky because of actual motion. With a partner, talk about how you can tell whether a star's motions across the sky are apparent motions or actual motions.

LOOKING CLOSER

8. Apply Concepts Suppose distant galaxies had blue-shifted spectra instead of red-shifted spectra. What could astronomers conclude about the motions of these galaxies?

_____

_____

_____

_____

ACTUAL MOTION OF STARS

Most stars have several types of *actual motion*. First, they move through the universe. This motion is not related to Earth's rotation or revolution. Second, they may revolve around another star. Third, they either move away from or toward our solar system.

Astronomers study a star's spectrum to learn about the star's motion toward or away from Earth. As a star moves, its spectrum seems to shift, or change. This shift in the spectrum is called the **Doppler effect**. The Doppler effect happens when an observer and a light source move toward or away from each other.

For example, light from stars moving toward Earth shifts toward blue. This shift is called *blue shift*. The wavelengths of light appear to be shorter as the star moves toward Earth. Light from stars moving away from Earth shifts toward red. This shift is called *red shift*. The wavelengths of light appear to be longer.

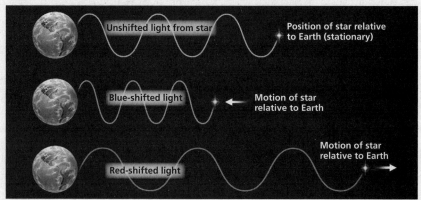

Distant galaxies have red-shifted spectra. This red shift shows that the galaxies are moving away from Earth.

How Do Astronomers Describe Distances?

Objects in space are very far apart. For this reason, astronomers describe distances in space using light-years. A **light-year** is the distance that light travels in one year. Light travels about 9.46 trillion km in one year. ☑

Light from stars takes time to reach Earth. As a result, we see light that left stars sometime in the past. For instance, light from the sun takes about 8 minutes to reach Earth. The light leaves the sun 8 minutes before we see it.

Polaris is about 430 light-years from Earth. Therefore, when you look at Polaris, you see the star the way it was 430 years ago.

✓ **READING CHECK**

9. Identify How many kilometers are in one light-year?

_____

SECTION 1 **Characteristics of Stars** *continued*

PARALLAX

Scientists can use parallax to determine the distance to stars that are relatively close to Earth. **Parallax** is the apparent shift in a star's position when it is viewed from different places. Observers can study stars from different places as Earth orbits the sun. As Earth orbits, a nearby star will appear to move compared to stars that are farther from Earth. The closer the star is to Earth, the larger the shift will be.

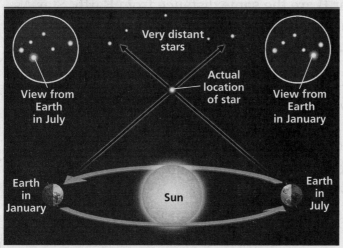

Astronomers can also measure parallax from spacecraft. They have measured the distance to about a million stars within 1,000 light-years of Earth.

How Do Astronomers Describe Brightness?

About 6,000 stars are visible from Earth without a telescope. With a telescope, about 3 billion stars are visible. Billions more stars are visible from telescopes that orbit the Earth, such as the *Hubble Space Telescope*. The visibility of a star depends on its brightness and distance from Earth. Astronomers use two scales to describe the brightness of a star.

The brightness of a star as seen from Earth is called the star's **apparent magnitude**. The apparent magnitude of a star depends on how much light the star emits. It also depends on how far the star is from Earth. The brighter the star appears from Earth, the lower the number of its apparent magnitude. ☑

Astronomers also measure the true brightness, or absolute magnitude, of stars. The **absolute magnitude** is how bright a star would appear if all stars were the same distance from Earth. The brighter a star is, the lower the number of its absolute magnitude.

✓ **READING CHECK**

11. Identify What two factors does apparent magnitude depend on?

_____

_____

_____

Section 1 Review

SECTION VOCABULARY

absolute magnitude the brightness that a star would have at a distance of 32.6 light-years from Earth	**light-year** the distance that light travels in one year
apparent magnitude the brightness of a star as seen from the Earth	**parallax** an apparent shift in the position of an object when viewed from different locations
Doppler effect an observed change in the frequency of a wave when the source or observer is moving	**star** a large celestial body that is composed of gas and that emits light

1. **Apply Concepts** Star A and star B are the same distance from Earth. Star A's apparent magnitude is 10. Star B's apparent magnitude is 15. Which star has the larger absolute magnitude? Explain your answer.

_____

_____

_____

2. **Describe** How do scientists determine the temperature of a star? Give one example to support your answer.

_____

_____

_____

3. **Explain** Why do stars appear in different parts of the sky during different months?

_____

_____

4. **Define** What is a circumpolar star? How could you tell by observation whether a star is a circumpolar star?

_____

_____

_____

5. **Describe** The closest star to Earth, apart from the sun, is Proxima Centauri. Proxima Centauri is about 4.2 light-years from Earth. How long does it take light from our sun to reach Proxima Centauri? About how many kilometers is Proxima Centauri from Earth?

_____

_____

CHAPTER 30 Stars, Galaxies, and the Universe
SECTION 2 Stellar Evolution

KEY IDEAS

As you read this section, keep these questions in mind:
- How does a protostar become a star?
- How does a main-sequence star generate energy?
- How does a star evolve after its main-sequence stage?

How Do Scientists Study and Classify Stars?

A typical star exists for billions of years. For this reason, astronomers cannot observe one star for its entire lifetime. Instead, astronomers study stars in different stages of development. Astronomers use this information to learn how stars change over time.

CLASSIFYING STARS

To classify stars, scientists measure temperature and luminosity. *Luminosity* is the total amount of energy that a star gives off each second. Scientists have found a relationship between temperature and luminosity. The graph that shows this relationship is the *Hertzsprung-Russell diagram*, or *H-R diagram*. ☑

Astronomers plot the highest temperatures on the left. They plot the highest luminosities at the top. The temperature and luminosity of most stars fall in a diagonal band on the graph. This band is called the **main sequence**. Stars in this band are called *main-sequence stars* or *dwarfs*. The sun is a main-sequence star.

Diagram After you read this section, create flowcharts describing the life cycles of sun-like stars and massive stars.

✓ READING CHECK

1. Define What is luminosity?

_____

_____

_____

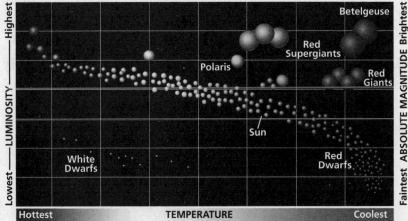

The Hertzsprung-Russell Diagram

Cool, dim, red stars are in the lower right. Hot, bright, blue stars are in the upper left.

LOOKING CLOSER
2. Identify On the diagram, circle the main sequence.

How Do Stars Form?

A star begins in a nebula. A **nebula** is a cloud of gas and dust. Most nebulas contain 70% hydrogen, 28% helium, and 2% heavier elements. An outside force, such as the explosion of a nearby star, may cause the nebula to start to collapse. The nebula may also start to collapse without a known force. ☑

Nebulas follow Newton's *law of universal gravitation*. This law states that all objects in the universe attract each other. This force of attraction increases as the mass of an object increases. The force also increases when objects get closer together.

Therefore, the attraction between the particles in a nebula increases as gravity pulls them closer together. The increased force of attraction pulls in more nearby particles. The mass continues to increase. As more particles come together, dense regions of matter build up in the nebula.

Critical Thinking

4. Apply Concepts Jupiter's mass is very large. What is the most likely reason that we do not generally feel the effects of Jupiter's gravity on Earth?

_____

_____

_____

_____

PROTOSTARS

Over time, nebulas may form protostars. This process has many stages, as described below.

1. Gravity causes dense regions in the nebula to contract. As a result, any spin in the region increases.

2. The shrinking, spinning region flattens into a disk called a *protostar*. Matter collects in the center of the protostar.

3. As more matter enters the protostar, gravitational energy changes to heat. This heat energy increases the temperature of the protostar.

4. The protostar continues to contract and increase in temperature for millions of years.

5. Over time, the gas in the protostar becomes extremely hot. As a result, electrons in the gas separate from their parent atoms.

6. The nuclei and free electrons move independently. The gas becomes a *plasma*. Plasma is a hot gas that is made up of electrically charged particles. It has an equal number of positive ions and electrons. ☑

THE BIRTH OF A STAR

Temperature continues to increase in a protostar to about 10,000,000 °C. At this temperature, *nuclear fusion* begins. High temperature and pressure cause small atomic nuclei to combine into larger nuclei. Nuclear fusion releases large amounts of energy. The start of fusion marks the birth of a star. Nuclear fusion can continue for billions of years. ☑

A BALANCING ACT

Fusion happens faster as gravity increases the pressure on the matter in the star. At the same time, the energy from fusion heats the gas in the star. The energy and hot gas push outward and resist the inward pull of gravity. These forces balance each other, as shown below. This balance makes the star stable in size.

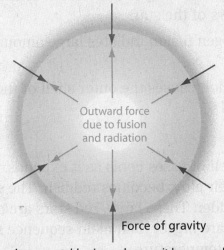

Outward force due to fusion and radiation

Force of gravity

A main sequence star keeps a stable size as long as it has enough hydrogen for fusion.

What Is the Main-Sequence Stage?

The longest stage in the life of a star is the main-sequence stage. During this stage, nuclear fusion continues in the core of the star. Hydrogen fuses into helium and produces energy. ☑

A star with the same mass as the sun stays on the main sequence for about 10 billion years. Stars with more mass fuse hydrogen more quickly. They may stay on the main sequence for only 10 million years. However, less massive stars can stay on the main sequence for hundreds of billions of years.

✓ READING CHECK

6. Identify What process begins when a star is born?

_____

_____

LOOKING CLOSER

7. Predict What would happen to the star if it could not produce enough energy to balance the force of gravity?

_____

_____

✓ READING CHECK

8. Identify How does a main-sequence star produce energy?

_____

_____

THE SUN AND THE MAIN SEQUENCE

Our sun has fused about 5% of its hydrogen over a period of 5 billion years. After another 5 billion years, the rate of fusion in the core will decrease. The sun's temperature and luminosity will change. At that time, the sun will leave the main sequence. ☑

How Do Stars Leave the Main Sequence?

Eventually, stars leave the main sequence. This process starts when about 20% of the hydrogen atoms in a star's core have fused into helium atoms. This process has several stages:

1. Gravity causes the core of the star to contract.

2. The contraction heats the core. The helium core transfers energy to a shell of hydrogen around the core.

3. The energy causes hydrogen fusion to continue in the outer layers of the star.

4. The hydrogen fusion radiates large amounts of energy outward.

5. The radiation causes the outer shell of the star to expand. ☑

GIANT STARS

A star's shell of gases cools as it expands. As the gases get cooler, their glow becomes reddish. The star becomes larger and redder. These large, red stars are called **giants**. They are bigger than main-sequence stars of the same surface temperature.

Giant stars have large surface areas. For this reason, they are very bright. Giants can be more than 10 times larger than the sun. Over time, stars with the same mass as the sun will become giants. As these stars become larger and cooler, they move off the main sequence. ☑

SUPERGIANTS

Massive stars become larger than giants as they leave the main sequence. These very luminous stars are called *supergiants*. Supergiants can be more than 100 times larger than the sun. The supergiant Betelgeuse is 1,000 times larger than the sun. Supergiants are easy to find in the night sky because they are so bright. However, their surfaces are cool compared to the surfaces of other stars.

What Are the Final Stages of a Sun-like Star?

The final stages in a star's life cycle depend on the size of the star. Stars about the size of the sun follow a similar cycle. Fusion in the core stops when helium atoms have fused into carbon and oxygen. The supply of energy from fusion drops, and the star enters its final stages. ☑

READING CHECK

12. Identify When does fusion in the core of a sun-like star stop?

_____

_____

_____

Final Stages of Sun-like Stars

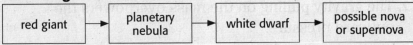

red giant → planetary nebula → white dwarf → possible nova or supernova

PLANETARY NEBULAS

In its final stages, a star's outer gases drift away. The remaining core heats these gases. The gases appear as a *planetary nebula*. A planetary nebula is a cloud of gas that forms around a dying star. These clouds may form different shapes around the star, such as a sphere or ring.

WHITE DWARFS

Over time, the gases in a planetary nebula drift away. Gravity pulls the remaining matter in the star inward. The matter moves inward until it cannot contract any more. A hot, dense core of matter called a **white dwarf** remains. White dwarfs shine for billions of years before they cool completely. ☑

White dwarfs are hot but dim. As white dwarfs cool, they lose brightness. This is the final stage in the life cycle of many stars.

READING CHECK

13. Identify What is a white dwarf?

_____

_____

_____

_____

NOVAS

Some white dwarf stars are part of binary star systems. A binary star system involves two stars. For example, a white dwarf may revolve around a red giant. The gravity of the white dwarf may pull gases from the red giant. These gases collect on the surface of the white dwarf and build up pressure. This pressure may cause large explosions, which release energy and matter into space. This release of energy is called a **nova**.

A nova may cause a star to become much brighter than it normally is. However, the nova starts to fade after a few days. Novas do not usually destroy the binary star system. Thus, a white dwarf may become a nova many times.

SUPERNOVAS

A white dwarf in a binary system may also become a supernova. A *supernova* is a star that explodes and blows itself apart. The steps below describe how a supernova forms.

1. A white dwarf collects mass on its surface from a nearby red giant.

2. The gravity pulling on the mass overpowers the outward pressure.

3. The star collapses. It becomes so dense that the outer layers explode outward.

Supernovas are much more violent than novas. The explosion of a supernova destroys the white dwarf star. It may also destroy much of the red giant.

What Are the Final Stages of Massive Stars?

Some stars have masses more than 8 times the mass of the sun. The final stages of these massive stars are different from the final stages of less-massive stars.

Final Stages of Massive Stars

red supergiant → supernova → neutron star *or* black hole

SUPERNOVAS IN MASSIVE STARS

Only a small percentage of white dwarfs become supernovas. However, massive stars become supernovas as part of their life cycle. After the supergiant stage, these stars contract very quickly.

The collapse of a massive star creates very high pressures and temperatures. Nuclear fusion begins again. This time, carbon atoms fuse into heavier elements, such as oxygen, magnesium, or silicon.

Fusion continues until the core is made of iron. Iron has a very stable nuclear structure. Therefore, fusion of iron takes energy from the star instead of releasing energy. The star loses its supply of fuel, and the core begins to collapse. The collapse releases energy. This energy moves to the outer layers of the star. The outer layers explode outward with great force in a supernova. ☑

Critical Thinking

14. Compare Name one difference between a nova and a supernova.

_____

_____

_____

_____

_____

_____

READING CHECK

15. Identify What is the last element that forms by nuclear fusion in massive ___?

NEUTRON STARS

Massive stars do not become white dwarfs. After a supernova, the core may become a small, dense ball of neutrons called a **neutron star**. Neutron stars spin very quickly.

PULSARS

Some neutron stars emit a beam of radio waves. These neutron stars are called **pulsars**. A pulsar rotates, or spins. As it spins, its beam sweeps across space. Scientists can detect the beam every time it sweeps past Earth. The star rotates between each pulse they detect.

Newly formed pulsars often have the remains of a supernova around them, as shown below. However, most known pulsars are very old. The supernova remains have gone away. Only the spinning star is left.

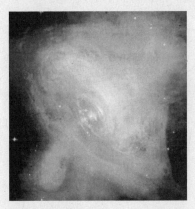

The remains of a supernova explosion still surround this pulsar.

Talk About It

Model Work with a partner to create a model that shows why scientists on Earth detect regular pulses of radio waves from a pulsar. Share your model with the class.

LOOKING CLOSER

16. Identify Did the object in the picture form from a sun-like star or a massive star? How do you know?

_____

_____

_____

_____

BLACK HOLES

After a supernova, some massive stars leave a core that is more than 3 times the sun's mass. In this case, the star may contract more because of gravity. This force crushes the dense core and leaves a **black hole**. The gravitational pull of a black hole is very strong. Not even light can escape it.

Black holes are hard to find because they do not emit light. However, black holes have effects on nearby stars. The black hole pulls matter from the star. The matter swirls around the black hole before being absorbed. The matter becomes very hot and releases X rays.

Astronomers can detect these X rays. Then, astronomers try to find the object affecting the star. The star's motion may show that a massive, invisible object is nearby. Astronomers conclude that the object is a black hole.

Section 2 Review

SECTION VOCABULARY

black hole an object so massive and dense that even light cannot escape its gravity	**neutron star** a star that has collapsed under gravity to the point that the electrons and protons have smashed together to form neutrons
giant a very large and bright star whose hot core has used most of its hydrogen	
main sequence the location on the H-R diagram where most stars lie; it has a diagonal pattern from the lower right to the upper left	**nova** a star that suddenly becomes brighter
	pulsar a rapidly spinning neutron star that emits pulses of radio and optical energy
nebula a large cloud of gas and dust in interstellar space; a region in space where stars are born	**white dwarf** a small, hot, dim star that is the leftover center of an old sunlike star

1. Explain How can scientists detect a black hole if it does not emit light?

_____

_____

2. Compare Complete the Venn diagram below to compare sun-like stars and massive stars.

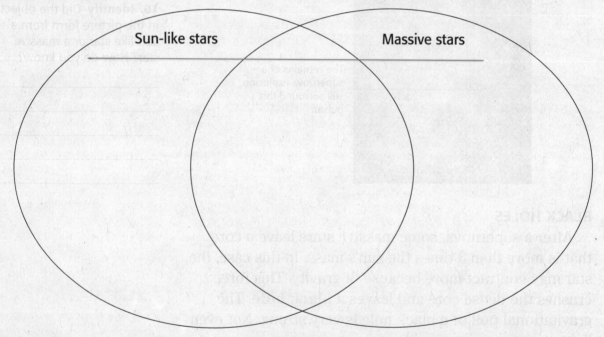

Sun-like stars   Massive stars

3. Identify What is the main force that causes a protostar to become a star?

_____

4. Explain Over time, how does the amount of hydrogen in a star change? Explain your answer.

_____

_____

CHAPTER 30 | **Stars, Galaxies, and the Universe**
SECTION
3 | **Star Groups**

As you read this section, keep these questions in mind:
- What are the characteristics of a constellation?
- What are the three main types of galaxies?
- How is a galaxy with a quasar in it different from a typical galaxy?

What Are Constellations?

You can see many individual stars on a clear night. These visible stars are only some of the stars in the universe. Most of the stars we see are within 100 light-years of Earth.

Astronomers organize individual stars into patterns. These patterns of stars and the space around them are called **constellations**. The stars in a constellation appear to be close together. However, these stars are not all the same distance from Earth. In fact, they may be very distant from each other. ☑

Stars appear to stay fixed in their patterns. The positions of the stars in relation to each other do not seem to change over weeks and months. This is because we view the stars from a great distance.

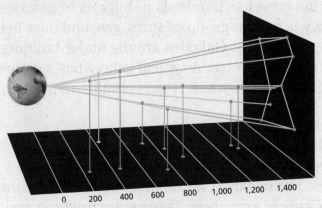

Distance (light-years)
The stars in the constellation Orion are different distances from Earth.

DIVIDING UP THE SKY

In 1930, astronomers around the world agreed on a standard set of 88 constellations. These constellations divide the sky into regions. You can use a map of the constellations to find a specific star.

READING TOOLBOX

Summarize As you read this section, make two-column notes to summarize the information. In the first column, write the main ideas of the section. In the second column, write details related to those main ideas.

☑ **READING CHECK**

1. Define What is a constellation?

_____

_____

_____

Critical Thinking

2. Apply Concepts About how many years does it take light from Earth to reach the most distant stars in Orion?

_____

What Are Multiple-Star Systems?

Stars are not always isolated, or alone. Two or more stars may form multiple-star systems. More than half of all sun-like stars are part of multiple-star systems.

Binary stars are pairs of stars that revolve around each other. Gravity holds the pairs of stars together. A binary star has a center of mass, or *barycenter*. The stars orbit around the barycenter. When the two stars have similar masses, the barycenter is somewhere between the stars. If one star is more massive, the barycenter is closer to the more massive star.

Multiple-star systems can have more than two stars. For instance, two stars may revolve quickly around a common barycenter. A third star may revolve around the same barycenter slowly, farther away from the two stars.

What Is a Star Cluster?

Sometimes, nebulas collapse to form groups of stars called clusters. Clusters can have hundreds or thousands of stars. The table below describes two types of clusters.

Type of Cluster	Shape	Number of Stars
Globular cluster	sphere	up to 1,000,000 stars
Open cluster	loosely shaped	a few hundred stars

What Is a Galaxy?

The universe has hundreds of billions of galaxies. A **galaxy** is a large group of stars, gas, and dust held together by gravity. Galaxies are the major building blocks of the universe. A typical galaxy has a diameter of about 100,000 light-years. It may contain more than 200 billion stars. ☑

DISTANCES TO GALAXIES

Astronomers can use stars to find distances to galaxies. For instance, astronomers can study giant stars called *Cepheid variables*. These stars brighten and fade in a regular cycle. Most Cepheid variables have cycles that range from 1 to 100 days. The longer the cycle, the brighter the star's absolute magnitude is.

Astronomers can compare a Cepheid variable's absolute magnitude and apparent magnitude to find the distance to the star. This distance tells astronomers the distance to the galaxy where the star is.

Talk About It
Learn Word Roots Use the Internet or a dictionary to learn the meaning of the prefix *bi-*. With a partner, discuss why a pair of stars that revolve around each other is called a *binary star system*.

LOOKING CLOSER
3. Identify Which type of cluster contains the most stars?

_____

_____

✔ **READING CHECK**
4. Define What is a galaxy?

_____

_____

_____

_____

SECTION 3 **Star Groups** continued

TYPES OF GALAXIES

Astronomers classify galaxies by shape. The most common type of galaxy is a *spiral galaxy*. Some spiral galaxies have a straight bar of stars through the center. These galaxies are called *barred spiral galaxies*. The other two types of galaxies are *elliptical galaxies* and *irregular galaxies*. Irregular galaxies make up a small percentage of the total known galaxies. The table below describes the three types of galaxies.

Type of Galaxy	Shape	Description
Spiral galaxy	flat arms that spiral around a center of bright stars	billions of young stars, gas, and dust
Elliptical galaxy	a sphere or oval with a bright center	a few young stars; not much gas and dust
Irregular galaxy	no particular shape	low total mass; large amounts of gas and dust

LOOKING CLOSER
5. Identify Which type of galaxy contains more young stars—a spiral galaxy or an elliptical galaxy?

_____

_____

THE MILKY WAY

Sometimes, a cloudlike band is visible across the night sky. This band is called the Milky Way. We see this band of stars when we look through our own galaxy.

The *Milky Way galaxy* is a spiral galaxy. The sun is one of billions of stars in this galaxy. Each star orbits around the center of the galaxy. The sun takes about 225 million years to complete one orbit around the galaxy's center.

About 30 other galaxies are within 5 million light-years of the Milky Way. These galaxies and the Milky Way galaxy make up the *Local Group*. ☑

What Are Quasars?

The word **quasar** is a shortened term for *quasi-stellar radio source*. Through a telescope, a quasar looks like a small, faint star. However, quasars are not related to stars. They are related to galaxies.

Quasars appear in some very distant galaxies. Galaxies with quasars in them have very bright centers. Some quasars emit a stream of gas. The large amount of energy a quasar emits may be produced by a giant black hole. The mass of this black hole may be billions of times the mass of our sun.

READING CHECK
6. Describe What is the Local Group?

_____

_____

_____

_____

Section 3 Review

SECTION VOCABULARY

constellation one of 88 regions into which the sky has been divided in order to describe the locations of celestial objects; a group of stars organized in a recognizable pattern	**galaxy** a collection of stars, dust, and gas bound together by gravity **quasar** quasi-stellar radio source; a very luminous object that produces energy at a high rate

1. Infer How can a constellation map help you find a specific star?

_____

_____

2. Describe How can astronomers use Cepheid variables to figure out how far away a galaxy is?

_____

_____

_____

_____

_____

_____

3. Identify What are the three main types of galaxies?

_____

_____

4. Compare How is a galaxy with a quasar in it different from other galaxies?

_____

_____

_____

5. Explain Why do the stars in a constellation not seem to change position over time?

_____

_____

6. Apply Concepts Suppose the barycenter in a particular binary star system is much closer to one star than to the other. What can you conclude about the relative masses of the stars in the binary star system?

_____

_____

CHAPTER 30 Stars, Galaxies, and the Universe
SECTION 4 The Big Bang Theory

KEY IDEAS

As you read this section, keep these questions in mind:

• How did Hubble's discoveries lead to an understanding that the universe is expanding?

• What is the big bang theory?

• What evidence supports the big bang theory?

What Is Cosmology?

The study of the origin, structure, and future of the universe is called **cosmology**. Scientists who study cosmology are *cosmologists*. Cosmologists study the universe as a whole. Astronomers study the parts of the universe, such as planets, stars, and galaxies.

Cosmologists have theories about how the universe began and how it is changing. They test these theories against new observations. Many of these theories began with observations made less than 100 years ago.

How Do We Know That Galaxies Move?

Scientists use light to study the movement of objects in space. As an object moves, its light seems to shift on the spectrum toward red or blue, as shown below.

• blue shift = object moving toward Earth

• red shift = object moving away from Earth ☑

In the early 1900s, the astronomer Edwin Hubble studied spectra from galaxies. His research uncovered new information about the universe.

MEASURING RED SHIFTS

In the 1920s, Hubble found that the spectra of distant galaxies are all red-shifted. Hubble used this red shift to determine how fast the galaxies are moving away from Earth. Hubble found that the most distant galaxies show the greatest red shift. Thus, these distant galaxies are moving away from Earth the fastest. ☑

Modern telescopes with cameras can take images of spectra. These spectra all confirm Hubble's original observations.

READING TOOLBOX

Summarize As you read this section, underline sentences that give evidence to support the big bang theory. After you read the section, use the underlined ideas to write a summary of the evidence for the big bang.

✓ READING CHECK

1. Describe If an object's spectrum is blue-shifted, what can you conclude about the object's motion?

_____

_____

_____

✓ READING CHECK

2. Identify What did Hubble discover in the 1920s?

_____

_____

_____

THE EXPANDING UNIVERSE

Imagine a raisin cake rising in an oven. If you could sit on one raisin, you would see the other raisins moving away from you. Raisins that are farther away would move away faster. This is because more cake is between you and these distant raisins, and the whole cake is expanding. The situation is similar with galaxies and the universe, as shown below.

Critical Thinking

3. Apply Analogies Why are distant galaxies moving away from our galaxy more quickly than nearby galaxies are?

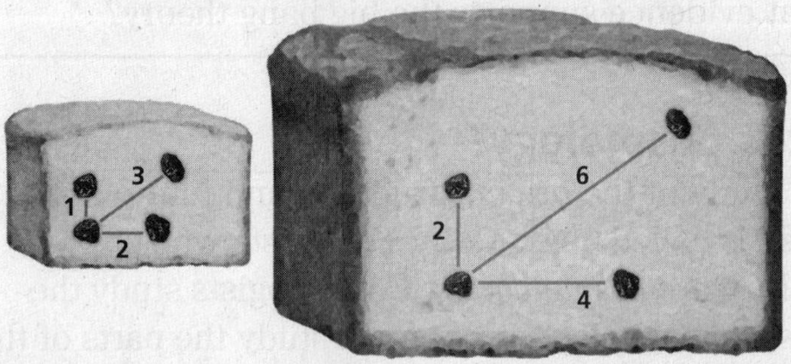

_____

_____

_____

_____

Just like these raisins, distant galaxies move away from the observer faster.

What Is the Big Bang Theory?

Cosmologists have offered different theories to explain why the universe is expanding. The current and most accepted theory is the **big bang theory**. This theory states that all matter and energy in the universe was once compressed into a very small space. About 14 billion years ago, a sudden event called the *big bang* happened. The big bang sent all of the matter and energy outward in all directions.

As a result, the universe expanded. Some of the matter came together in clumps, which evolved into galaxies. Today, the universe is still expanding. The galaxies continue to move apart from each other. This expansion explains the red shift of distant galaxies. ☑

COSMIC BACKGROUND RADIATION

A discovery made in the 1960s supports the big bang theory. In 1965, scientists detected **cosmic background radiation**, or low levels of energy, from all directions in space. Astronomers think that this background radiation formed just after the big bang.

The universe has cooled since the big bang. The energy of background radiation has a temperature of about –270 °C. This temperature is only 3 °C above absolute zero, which is the lowest temperature possible.

✔ **READING CHECK**

4. Describe How does the red shift of distant galaxies support the big bang theory?

_____

_____

_____

_____

_____

_____

SECTION 4 **The Big Bang Theory** continued

RIPPLES IN SPACE

Satellite maps of cosmic background radiation show "ripples" in temperature. These ripples show that cosmic background radiation is uneven in some places. This is because matter was not spread evenly in the early universe. The ripples show the early stages of the universe's first galaxies. ☑

What Materials Make Up the Universe?

Astronomers are continuing to research ripples in cosmic background radiation. They are also studying distances to supernovas in ancient galaxies. This research has helped astronomers learn more about the structure of the universe. Astronomers now think that the universe is made of more mass and energy than they can detect.

DARK MATTER

The ripples in cosmic background radiation show that the universe may contain different types of matter. Regular, visible matter makes up only 4% of the universe. Another 23% of the universe is made of *dark matter*. Dark matter does not emit or reflect light, but scientists can detect its gravity. ☑

DARK ENERGY

Research also shows that most of the universe is made of an unknown material called *dark energy*. Dark energy acts as a force against gravity. Scientists think that some form of dark energy is pushing galaxies apart. Dark energy is causing the universe to expand faster and faster.

Composition of the Universe

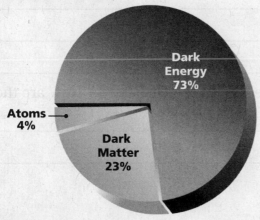

✓ READING CHECK

5. Explain Why is the cosmic background radiation uneven in some places?

_____

_____

_____

✓ READING CHECK

6. Explain How do scientists detect dark matter?

_____

_____

Section 4 Review

SECTION VOCABULARY

big bang theory the theory that all matter and energy in the universe was compressed into an extremely small volume that 13 to 15 billion years ago exploded and began expanding in all directions	**cosmic background radiation** radiation uniformly detected from every direction in space; considered a remnant of the big bang **cosmology** the study of the origin, properties, processes, and evolution of the universe

1. Compare How is cosmology different from astronomy?

_____

_____

2. Explain Describe Edwin Hubble's observations, and explain how they show that the universe is expanding.

_____

_____

_____

_____

_____

3. Summarize In your own words, describe the big bang theory for the origin of the universe.

_____

_____

_____

_____

4. Explain How does the big bang theory explain the existence of cosmic background radiation?

_____

_____

_____

_____

_____

5. Compare How is dark matter different from regular matter? How are they similar?

_____

_____

_____

Photo Credits

3, Dr. Howard B. Bluestein; 7, NASA; 8, Kuni/AP/Wide World Photos; 9, (all) Sam Dudgeon/HRW; 17, Andy Christiansen/HRW; 18, Andy Christiansen/HRW; 19, Darrell Gulin/CORBIS; 27, Raymond Gehman/CORBIS; 33, Christopher Cormack/CORBIS; 36, Ohio Department of Transportation; 37, (t) Rand McNally; (b) Bill Frymire/Masterfile; 42, National Conservation Resource Service; 43, Courtesy U.S. Geological Survey; 61, (l) Colin Keates/Dorling Kindersley, Courtesy of the Natural History Museum, London; (r) Jose Manuel Sanchez Calvate/CORBIS; 64, Tom Pantages Photography; 83, Bernhard Edmaier/Photo Researchers, Inc.; 86, Galen Rowell/CORBIS; 101, Stefan Schott/Panoramic Images; 108, Getty Images/MedioImages; 110, (l) Christian Haas; (r) Bernhard Edmaier/Photo Researchers, Inc.; 113, Alan Smith/Getty Images/Stone; 114, Bruce Molnia/Terra Photo Graphics; 120, (mummy) Patrick Landmann/Getty Images; (amber) Layne Kennedy/CORBIS; (tar) Nick Ut/AP/Wide World Photos; (mammoth) Bettmann/CORBIS; (log) Bernhard Edmaier/Photo Researchers, Inc.; 121, (leaf) Layne Kennedy/CORBIS; (mold) G. R. Roberts/Natural Sciences Image Library (NSIL) of New Zealand; (coprolite) Sinclair Stammers/SPL/Photo Researchers, Inc.; (gastrolith) Francios Gohier/Photo Researchers, Inc.; 127, Reuters New Media Inc./CORBIS; 128, John Reader/SPL/Photo Researchers, Inc.; 129, (t) Kaj R. Svensson/Photo Researchers, Inc.; (b) James L. Amos/CORBIS; 130, Kaj R. Svensson/SPL/Photo Researchers, Inc.; 133, (t) Sue Ogrocki/Reuters; (b) James L. Amos/CORBIS; 134, Doug Henderson; 136, (t) Bettmann/CORBIS; (b) Stuart Westmorland/CORBIS; 137, Wardene Weiser/Bruce Coleman, Inc.; 155, Y. Arthus-B./Peter Arnold, Inc.; 164, Tom Brownold Photography; 172, Russ Bishop; 173, Alan Schein Photography/CORBIS; 182, Paula Bronstein/Getty Images; 193, (b) Bill Ross/CORBIS; 199, Roger Ressmeyer/CORBIS; 203, Layne Kennedy/CORBIS; 205, Adam Hart-Davis/SPL/Photo Researchers, Inc.; 217, (l) Jim Richardson/CORBIS; (r) Photo by Tim McCabe, USDA NRCS; 218, Keren Su/CORBIS; 219, Yuri Cortez/AFP/Getty Images; 220, CORBIS; 221, (t) Galen Rowell/CORBIS; (c) Steve Terrill/CORBIS; (b) Robert Frerck/Odyssey/Chicago; 223, Annie Reynolds/PhotoLink/Getty Images; 231, Jim Wark/Airphoto; 244, Adam Woolfitt/CORBIS; 245, Bettmann/CORBIS; 247, Kevin R. Morris/CORBIS; 257, Scott T. Smith/CORBIS; 267, Walter H. Hodge/Peter Arnold, Inc.; 275, Aerial by Caudell; 297, Paul Zahl/National Geographic Image Collection; 299, Breck Kent/Animals Animals/Earth Scenes; 303, Gary Braasch/CORBIS; 304, Royalty Free/CORBIS; 307, Gary W. Carter/CORBIS; 309, Gene Rhoden/Weatherpix; 323, NASA; 343, Yann Arthus-Bertrand/CORBIS; 345, Wendy Stone/CORBIS; 348, Ocean Drilling Program - Texas A&M University; 349, (b) David Shale/naturepl.com; 355, Ocean Drilling Program - Texas A&M University; 356, Tom McHugh/Photo Researchers, Inc.; 357, (l) Jim Zuckerman/CORBIS; (r) Andrew Syred/SPL/Photo Researchers, Inc.; 362, NODC/National Oceanic & Atmospheric Administration; 363, Tom Stewart/CORBIS; 372, Bohemian Nomad Picturemakers/CORBIS; 373, Chris Hellier/CORBIS; 385, John Stanmeyer/VII/AP/Wide World Photos; 389, (l) Paul A. Souders/CORBIS; (r) Buddy Mays/CORBIS; 392, Jean-Charles Cuillandre/Canada-france-Hawaii Telescope/SPL/Photo Researchers, Inc.; 417, 418, (l) NASA/SPL/Photo Researchers, Inc.; 419, (l) NASA; 420, (l) NASA/ESA/STScI/SPL/Photo Researchers, Inc.; 421, NASA; 423, Kevin Kelley/Getty Images; 424, (l) NASA/SPL/Photo Researchers, Inc.; 425, (l) NASA/JPL/Space Science Institute; 426, (l) NASA. ESA, and M. Showalter (SETI Institute); 427, (l) NASA; 428, Wikipedia based on a NASA image; 429, Lynette R. Cook; 431, NASA; 435, (all) USGS; 441, (all) John Bova/Photo Researchers, Inc.; 441, NASA; 442, John Sanford/Photo Researchers, Inc.; 446, Galileo Project/JPL/NASA; 447, 448, NASA; 449, NASA, ESA, H. Weaver (JHU/APL), A. Stern (SwRI), and the HST Pluto Companion Search Team; 451, NASA; 452, Getty Images/PhotoDisc; 453, Wally Pacholka/AstroPics.com; 455, (t) Tom McHugh/Photo Researchers, Inc.; (c) Breck P. Kent/Animals Animals/Earth Scenes; (b) Ken Nichols/Institute of Meteorites; 458, NOAO/AURA/NSF; 459, Fred Espenak; 462, (inset) Getty Images/Photodisc; (bkgd) The Institute for Solar Physics, The Royal Swedish Academy of Sciences; 464, M. Aschwanden et al. (LMSAL), TRACE, NASA; 469, Grant Faint/Getty Images; 479, NASA.